THE CAMBRIDGE COMPANION TO MACHIAVELLI

Niccolò Machiavelli (1469–1527) is the most famous and controversial figure in the history of political thought and one of the iconic names of the Renaissance. *The Cambridge Companion to Machiavelli* brings together sixteen original essays by leading experts, covering his life, his career in Florentine government, his reaction to the dramatic changes that affected Florence and Italy in his lifetime, and the most prominent themes of his thought, including the founding, evolution, and corruption of republics and principalities, class conflict, liberty, arms, religion, ethics, rhetoric, gender, and the Renaissance dialogue with antiquity. In his own time Machiavelli was recognized as an original thinker who provocatively challenged conventional wisdom. With penetrating analyses of *The Prince*, *Discourses on Livy*, *Art of War*, *Florentine Histories*, and his plays and poetry, this book offers a vivid portrait of this extraordinary thinker as well as assessments of his place in Western thought since the Renaissance.

JOHN M. NAJEMY is Professor of History at Cornell University. His previous work includes *Corporatism and Consensus in Florentine Electoral Politics, 1280–1400* (1982), *Between Friends: Discourses of Power and Desire in the Machiavelli–Vettori Letters of 1513–1515* (1993), *A History of Florence, 1200–1575* (2006) and essays on Machiavelli and Renaissance political thought.

A complete list of books in the series is at the back of this book

THE CAMBRIDGE
COMPANION TO
MACHIAVELLI

EDITED BY
JOHN M. NAJEMY

CAMBRIDGE
UNIVERSITY PRESS

CAMBRIDGE UNIVERSITY PRESS

Cambridge, New York, Melbourne, Madrid, Cape Town, Singapore,
São Paulo, Delhi, Dubai, Tokyo

Cambridge University Press
The Edinburgh Building, Cambridge CB2 8RU, UK

Published in the United States of America by Cambridge University Press, New York

www.cambridge.org
Information on this title: www.cambridge.org/9780521678469

First published 2010

Printed in the United Kingdom at the University Press, Cambridge

A catalogue record for this publication is available from the British Library

Library of Congress Cataloguing-in-Publication data
The Cambridge companion to Machiavelli / edited by John M. Najemy.
p.   cm. – (Cambridge companions to literature) ISBN 978-0-521-86125-0 (hardback)
1. Machiavelli, Niccolò, 1469–1527 – Criticism and interpretation.   2. Machiavelli, Niccolò,
1469–1527 – Political and social views.   I. Najemy, John M., 1943–   II. Title.   III. Series.
JC143.M14C36   2010
320.1092–dc22
2009050510

ISBN 978-0-521-86125-0 Hardback
ISBN 978-0-521-67846-9 Paperback

CONTENTS

CONTENTS

CONTRIBUTORS

ALBERT RUSSELL ASCOLI is Terrill Distinguished Professor of Italian Studies at the University of California, Berkeley. He is the author of *Ariosto's Bitter Harmony: Crisis and Evasion in the Italian Renaissance* (1987) and of *Dante and the Making of a Modern Author* (Cambridge 2008); with Victoria Kahn he edited *Machiavelli and the Discourse of Literature* (1993).

JAMES B. ATKINSON has taught at Rutgers University, Earlham College, and Dartmouth College. His translations of Machiavelli include *The Prince*, a fully annotated critical edition and translation (1976, reprinted 2008); *The Complete Comedies*, a bilingual edition with David Sices (1985, reprinted 2007); *Machiavelli and His Friends: Their Personal Correspondence*, with David Sices (1996); and *The Sweetness of Power: Machiavelli's Discourses on Livy and Guicciardini's Considerations*, an edited translation with David Sices (2002). He is currently translating selected essays of Michel de Montaigne and Étienne de La Boétie.

JÉRÉMIE BARTHAS has his PhD from the European University Institute (Florence) in History and Civilization and was a fellow of Villa I Tatti, the Harvard University Center for Italian Renaissance Studies in Florence, in 2007–8. He edited and contributed an essay to *Della tirannia; Machiavelli con Bartolo* (Olschki, 2007) and recently published "Machiavelli e i 'libertini' fiorentini (1522–1531). Una pagina dimenticata nella storia del libertinismo, col *Sermone sopra l'elezione del gonfaloniere* del libertino Pierfilippo Pandolfini (1528)," *Rivista storica italiana* (2008). His book on Machiavelli, *L'argent n'est pas le nerf de la guerre. Dette publique et peuple en armes: essai sur le discours machiavélien* is forthcoming from the École Française de Rome.

ROBERT BLACK is Research Professor of Renaissance History at the University of Leeds. His books include *Benedetto Accolti and the Florentine Renaissance* (Cambridge, 1985); *Humanism and Education in Medieval and Renaissance Italy* (Cambridge, 2001); and *Education and Society in Florentine Tuscany*, vol. 1 (2007). He is currently writing *Machiavelli and Renaissance Florence*, a survey of Machiavelli's writings in their historical context, as well as completing the second volume of *Education and Society in Florentine Tuscany*.

ALISON BROWN is Emerita Professor of Italian Renaissance History at Royal Holloway, University of London. Her books on Florentine politics and political thought include *Bartolomeo Scala, 1430–1497, Chancellor of Florence: The Humanist as Bureaucrat* (1979); *The Medici in Florence: The Exercise and Language of Power* (1992); *The Renaissance* (1999); and *The Return of Lucretius to Renaissance Florence* (2010). A volume of essays, *Medicean and Savonarolan Florence: Politics and Ideas in the Late Quattrocento* is forthcoming.

HUMFREY BUTTERS is Reader in History at University of Warwick and was a fellow of Villa I Tatti, the Harvard University Center for Italian Renaissance Studies in Florence, in 1971–2 and 1979–80. He is the author of *Governors and Government in Early Sixteenth-Century Florence* (1985) and editor of two of the volumes of the letters of Lorenzo de' Medici, *Lettere*, vol. VIII (1484–5) (2001), and *Lettere*, vol. IX (1485–6) (2002). His current project is on "Public Law and the State in Italy, 1100–1300."

ANNA MARIA CABRINI is professore associato of Italian literature in the Department of Modern Philology at the Università degli studi in Milan. Her books on Machiavelli include *Per una valutazione delle "Istorie fiorentine" del Machiavelli. Note sulle fonti del secondo libro* (1985); and *Interpretazione e stile in Machiavelli. Il terzo libro delle "Istorie"* (1990). She has also written on other aspects of Renaissance historiography and humanism, including a study of Leonardo Bruni: "Le 'Historiae' del Bruni: risultati e ipotesi di una ricerca sulle fonti," in the volume *Leonardo Bruni cancelliere della repubblica di Firenze* (1990), pp. 247–319, and essays on Machiavelli, the Florentine chronicle tradition, Alberti, Guicciardini, Ariosto, and Renaissance theater.

ANGELA MATILDE CAPODIVACCA is Assistant Professor of Italian Language and Literature at Yale. She received her PhD in Italian Studies at the University of California, Berkeley with a dissertation on the relationship between curiosity and the imagination in early modern Italy.

VIRGINIA COX has taught at Edinburgh, London, and Cambridge and is currently Professor of Italian at New York University. Her publications include *The Renaissance Dialogue: Literary Dialogue in its Social and Political Contexts, Castiglione to Galileo* (Cambridge, 1992); *The Rhetoric of Cicero in its Medieval and Early Renaissance Commentary Tradition*, co-edited with John O. Ward (2006); and *Women's Writing in Italy, 1400–1650* (2008). She has also edited and translated two volumes for the series "The Other Voice in Early Modern Europe," Moderata Fonte, *The Worth of Women*, and Maddalena Campiglia, *Flori: A Pastoral Drama*, co-edited with Lisa Sampson.

MIKAEL HÖRNQVIST is Senior Lecturer in the Department of the History of Science and Ideas at Uppsala University (Sweden). He has held fellowships at Villa I Tatti, the Harvard University Center for Italian Renaissance Studies in Florence; the Stanford Humanities Center; and the National Humanities Center. He is the author of *Machiavelli and Empire* (Cambridge, 2004) and of several major articles on Machiavelli and Renaissance political thought, including "The Two Myths of Civic Humanism," in *Renaissance Civic Humanism: Reappraisals and Reflections* (Cambridge, 2000). His current project deals with the concepts of prudence, justice and equality in Machiavelli, Tocqueville, Nietzsche, and Foucault.

VICTORIA KAHN is Professor of English and Comparative Literature at the University of California at Berkeley. She is co-editor with Albert Ascoli of *Machiavelli and the Discourse of Literature* (1993) and the author of *Rhetoric, Prudence, and Skepticism in the Renaissance* (1985); *Machiavellian Rhetoric: From the Counter-Reformation to Milton* (1994); and *Wayward Contracts: The Crisis of Political Obligation in England, 1640–1674* (2004). She has also co-edited *Politics and the Passions, 1500–1850* (1996).

RONALD L. MARTINEZ is Professor of Italian Studies at Brown University. He has published, in collaboration with Robert M. Durling, *Time and the Crystal: Studies in Dante's 'Rime petrose'* (1990), and two volumes of a translation and commentary on Dante's *Divine Comedy* (*Inferno*, 1996; *Purgatorio*, 2003; *Paradiso* is forthcoming). He has also published over thirty essays on medieval and early modern Italian literature and culture, including articles on Guido Cavalcanti, Dante, Petrarch, Boccaccio, Machiavelli, and Ariosto. He is currently writing a book-length study on Dante's adaptation of medieval liturgical materials to the *Comedy*.

JOHN M. NAJEMY is Professor of History at Cornell University. He is the author of *Corporatism and Consensus in Florentine Electoral Politics, 1280–1400* (1982) and *A History of Florence, 1200–1575* (2006). His work on Machiavelli includes *Between Friends: Discourses of Power and Desire in the Machiavelli–Vettori Letters of 1513–1515* (1993) and many essays, among them "'Occupare la tirannide': Machiavelli, the Militia, and Guicciardini's Accusation of Tyranny," in *Della tirannia: Machiavelli con Bartolo*, ed. Jérémie Barthas (2007). His next project is an intellectual biography of Machiavelli.

ROSLYN PESMAN is Professor Emeritus at the University of Sydney where she was previously Challis Professor of History and Pro-Vice-Chancellor for the College of Humanities and Social Sciences. A fellow of the Australian Academy of the Humanities, her recent publications include: *Pier Soderini and the Ruling Class in Renaissance Florence* (2002); *From Paesani to Global Italians: Veneto Migrants in Australia*, with L. Baldassar (2005); and an edited volume with B. Kent and C. Troup, *Australians in Italy: Contemporary Lives and Impressions* (2008). She is currently working on transnational and gender issues in the Risorgimento through a study of the foreign women who became disciples of Mazzini.

J. G. A. POCOCK is Harry C. Black Professor of History Emeritus at the Johns Hopkins University. His major work on Machiavelli is *The Machiavellian Moment: Florentine Political Thought and the Atlantic Republican Tradition* (1975; reissued with an afterword, 2003). He has also edited the writings of James Harrington (Cambridge, 1977) and published a series of volumes, *Barbarism and Religion* (Cambridge, 1999–2005; other volumes in preparation), relating to Gibbon's *Decline and Fall of the Roman Empire*.

WAYNE A. REBHORN is the Celanese Centennial Professor of English at the University of Texas at Austin. He has written extensively on Renaissance literature, on authors from Boccaccio to More, Shakespeare, and Milton. Among his recent books are *The Emperor of Men's Minds: Literature and the Renaissance Discourse of Rhetoric* (1995); *Renaissance Debates on Rhetoric* (1999); and a critical edition, with Frank Whigham, of George Puttenham's *Art of English Poesy* (2007). He has also published a new translation of Machiavelli's *The Prince and Other Writings* (2003). His *Foxes and Lions: Machiavelli's Confidence Men* (1988) won the Howard R. Marraro Prize of the Modern Language Association of America. Currently, he is working on a new translation of Boccaccio's *Decameron*.

BARBARA SPACKMAN is Professor of Italian Studies and Comparative Literature at the University of California, Berkeley, where she holds the Giovanni and Ruth Elizabeth Cecchetti Chair in Italian Literature. She is the author of *Decadent Genealogies: The Rhetoric of Sickness from Baudelaire to D'Annunzio* (1989) and *Fascist Virilities: Rhetoric, Ideology, and Social Fantasy in Italy* (1996). Her current work is a study of Italian Orientalism, entitled *Detourism: Traveling Fictions from Italy to Islam*.

ACKNOWLEDGMENTS

As always, my deepest thanks go to my wife, Amy Bloch, who gave me wise and patient counsel concerning every problem, large and small, and valuable criticism of my contributions to the volume. My loving appreciation of her indispensable support knows no bounds. I am grateful as well to Jérémie Barthas, who agreed to join the project at a late stage and also provided thoughtful advice concerning the chronology, and to Angela Turnbull for careful and generously attentive copyediting that improved the manuscript in many ways.

JN
Florence

CHRONOLOGY

<table>
<tr><td>1434</td><td>Cosimo de' Medici assumes power in Florence.</td></tr>
<tr><td>1464</td><td>Cosimo dies and is succeeded by his son Piero.</td></tr>
<tr><td>1466</td><td>Piero de' Medici is unsuccessfully challenged by former Medici allies.</td></tr>
<tr><td>1469</td><td>May 3: Niccolò Machiavelli is born in Florence; December: Piero de' Medici dies; his son Lorenzo assumes leadership of the regime.</td></tr>
<tr><td>1476</td><td>The Tuscan translation by Donato Acciaiuoli of Leonardo Bruni's History of the Florentine People is published in Venice; it will be published in Florence in 1492.</td></tr>
<tr><td>1478</td><td>April: Pazzi conspiracy against the Medici; Lorenzo's brother, Giuliano, is assassinated; savage reprisals carried out by Lorenzo.</td></tr>
<tr><td>1483</td><td>Francesco Guicciardini is born.</td></tr>
<tr><td>1492</td><td>April: Lorenzo de' Medici dies; his son Piero assumes leadership of the regime; August: Rodrigo Borgia, father of Cesare, is elected Pope Alexander VI.</td></tr>
<tr><td>1494</td><td>September: French invasion of Italy under Charles VIII; the French allow Pisa to declare its independence from Florence; November: the Medici are expelled from Florence; December: Girolamo Savonarola influences the resolution of the political crisis in Florence; the Great Council is instituted.</td></tr>
<tr><td>1495</td><td>July: Battle of Fornovo between France and a league of Italian states; October: the French leave Italy.</td></tr>
<tr><td>1497</td><td>Possibly in this year, Machiavelli copies the De rerum natura of Lucretius.</td></tr>
<tr><td>1498</td><td>January or February: Savonarola publishes the Treatise on the Constitution and Government of the City of Florence; March:</td></tr>
</table>

Machiavelli analyzes two of Savonarola's last sermons in a letter to the Florentine ambassador in Rome; May: Savonarola is accused of heresy and executed; June: Machiavelli is elected head of the second chancery and soon thereafter secretary to the Dieci (Ten), the magistracy that supervised foreign and dominion policy.

1499   March: Machiavelli is sent as envoy to the lord of Piombino; June: Machiavelli writes the "Discourse on Pisa"; July: his legation to Caterina Sforza Riario, countess of Forlì and Imola; October: second French invasion of Italy, under Louis XII; the French occupy the Duchy of Milan and Cesare Borgia begins his conquest of the petty principalities of the Romagna.

1500   Louis XII sends troops to assist Florence in its war to regain Pisa; the attack fails and the troops are withdrawn; July (to January 1501): Machiavelli's first legation to the French court; November: agreement between France and Spain to divide Naples.

1501   April: Machiavelli writes the "Discourse on peace between the emperor and the king [of France]"; May: Cesare Borgia invades Florentine territory, but soon departs; July: Machiavelli sent to Pistoia (under Florentine rule) to quell factional conflicts; in the fall Machiavelli marries Marietta Corsini.

1502   February: another mission to Pistoia; March: Machiavelli writes the memorandum "On the affairs of Pistoia"; May: legation to Giovanni Bentivoglio, lord of Bologna; June: rebellion of Arezzo and the Valdichiana against Florentine rule fomented by Cesare Borgia's lieutenants, followed by Machiavelli's first legation (with Francesco Soderini) to Cesare Borgia; August: Machiavelli is sent to Arezzo after its recovery; September: Piero Soderini is elected lifetime Standardbearer of Justice in Florence and assumes office in November; October–January 1503: Machiavelli's second legation to Borgia; December: Machiavelli is present as Cesare Borgia traps and kills the former lieutenants who conspired against him.

1503   March: Machiavelli may have drafted the "Words to be spoken on the law for raising money [for defense]"; April: legation to Siena; August: Pope Alexander dies; after the brief pontificate of Pius III, Giuliano della Rovere is elected Pope Julius II in November; October: Machiavelli's first legation to the papal court to observe the conclave; December: Spain defeats France in southern Italy and takes control of the Kingdom of Naples; Piero de' Medici dies in exile; Machiavelli present in Rome, observes Cesare Borgia's sudden collapse at the hands of Pope Julius.

1504   January–March: Machiavelli's second legation to the French court; April: second legation to Piombino; November: Machiavelli dedicates the first *Decennale* to Alamanno Salviati.

1505   April and June: legations to Perugia and Mantua to negotiate mercenary contracts with Giampaolo Baglioni and Francesco Gonzaga; July: legation to Siena; Florence's war to recapture Pisa again goes badly; Machiavelli's urgent proposal for the institution of a homegrown militia becomes politically controversial.

1506   Early in the year, the first *Decennale* is published, but without the dedication to Alamanno Salviati; Soderini allows Machiavelli to begin recruiting and training troops for the militia; September(?): Machiavelli writes the "Discourse on the organization of the Florentine state for arms," also known as "La cagione dell'Ordinanza," on the militia; August–October: second legation to the papal court, during which he witnesses Julius's audacious seizure of Perugia and writes the "Ghiribizzi" to Giovanbattista Soderini; November: Julius retakes Bologna; December: Machiavelli writes the law instituting the militia and its civilian board of overseers, the Nine.

1507   January: Machiavelli becomes chancellor of the Nine; Soderini's intention to send Machiavelli to the Emperor Maximilian is blocked by *ottimati* who oppose his foreign policy; Francesco Vettori is chosen instead, although Machiavelli joins him at the imperial court at the end of the year.

1508   January–June: Machiavelli and Vettori serve on their joint mission to the imperial court; June: Machiavelli writes the "Report on German affairs"; spends much of the rest of the year in the field supervising the campaign against Pisa; December: Julius forms the League of Cambrai against Venice.

1509   May: Venetian armies are routed by the League of Cambrai; June: Pisa surrenders to Florence, with Machiavelli among the Florentine signatories; he supervises the occupation; receives congratulations from his friends for the success of his militia in the recovery of Pisa; November–December: Machiavelli is sent to Mantua and Verona to attend to matters relating to the Emperor Maximilian's descent into Italy.

1510   Julius turns against France to expel the "barbarians" from Italy; June–September: Machiavelli's third mission to the French court.

1511   September–October 1511: Machiavelli's fourth legation to the French court; writes the "Portrait of French affairs" either in this year or in 1510; October: Julius forms the Holy League (papacy, Spain, and Venice) against France.

1512   April: France defeats the league at the battle of Ravenna; May–June: the Swiss attack the French, who withdraw from Italy; August: the league sends into Tuscany a Spanish army to punish Florence; the Spaniards sack Prato and Piero Soderini is forced from office; September: Cardinal Giovanni de' Medici and his brother Giuliano return to Florence; November: Machiavelli writes the "Memoir to the Mediceans" but is quickly dismissed from his posts and confined to the Florentine dominion for one year.

1513   February: Machiavelli is arrested, incarcerated, and tortured for suspected complicity in the Boscoli–Capponi plot against the Medici; Pope Julius dies; March: Giovanni de' Medici is elected Pope Leo X; Machiavelli is released from prison and goes to live at the family's country home in Sant'Andrea in Percussina, south of Florence; the correspondence with Francesco Vettori begins; August: Lorenzo de' Medici the younger, Leo's nephew, assumes control of the regime in Florence; Machiavelli writes most or all of *The Prince* in the second half of the year.

1514   Likely date of composition of Machiavelli's second *Decennale*.

1515   January: Louis XII dies and is succeeded by Francis I; September: Francis invades Italy, defeats the Swiss at Marignano, and occupies Milan; possibly in this year or the next, Machiavelli joins the largely republican literary and historical discussions in the gardens of the Rucellai family and begins writing the *Discourses on Livy*.

1516   January: King Ferdinand of Spain dies; March: Giuliano de' Medici dies; Pope Leo orchestrates the conquest of Urbino by his nephew Lorenzo, who becomes duke of Urbino; Machiavelli dedicates *The Prince* to Lorenzo; Ludovico Ariosto publishes the first edition of the *Orlando furioso*.

1517   Likely date of composition of Machiavelli's *Asino*; *Discourses on Livy* probably complete by this year.

1518   Machiavelli writes *Mandragola*, possibly also in this year the *Favola*, called *Belfagor*.

1519   Lorenzo de' Medici dies; Cardinal Giulio de' Medici assumes control of Florence; possibly in this year Machiavelli finishes writing the *Art of War*; June: Charles, king of Spain since 1516, is elected Holy Roman Emperor.

1520   August: Machiavelli writes the *Life of Castruccio Castracani of Lucca*; November: he receives the commission, approved by Cardinal Giulio, to write the *Florentine Histories*; December: he writes the *Discourse on Florentine Affairs after the Death of the Younger Lorenzo de' Medici*.

1521   May: Machiavelli is sent as observer to the chapter general of the Franciscans in Carpi and begins his correspondence with Francesco Guicciardini, papal governor of Modena since 1516; Guicciardini begins writing the *Dialogue on the Government of Florence* (completed in 1524); August: Machiavelli's *Art of War* is printed in Florence by Giunta; war renews between Spain and France for control of Milan; November: imperial forces occupy Milan; December: Leo X dies.

1522   January: Adrian of Utrecht is elected Pope Adrian VI; May: an anti-Medici conspiracy led by Zanobi Buondelmonti and involving several members of the Rucellai circle (but not Machiavelli) is revealed; all talk of reform ends; Piero Soderini dies in Rome.

1523   Agostino Nifo plagiarizes much of *The Prince* in his *De regnandi peritia*; November: Giulio de' Medici is elected Pope Clement VII.

1524   October: the French retake Milan; Machiavelli continues writing the *Florentine Histories*.

1525   January: Machiavelli's play *Clizia* is performed; February: Emperor Charles V's armies inflict a massive defeat on the French at Pavia, taking King Francis prisoner and reoccupying Milan; May: Machiavelli presents the *Florentine Histories* to Pope Clement in Rome; June: Machiavelli proposes to Clement the organization of a militia for the defense of the Romagna; Clement sends him to hear the views of Guicciardini (now papal president of the Romagna) on its feasibility; Guicciardini dissuades the pope from the idea.

1526   Antonio Brucioli publishes the first edition of his *Dialogi*, representing Machiavelli as a central participant in the discussions of the Orti Oricellari some years earlier; March: King Francis is released by Charles V; May: the League of Cognac (France, papacy, Venice, and, unofficially, Florence) is formed against Charles; Machiavelli is appointed to a magistracy instituted to strengthen Florence's walls and fortifications; June: Guicciardini is named lieutenant-general of the papal armies of the League of Cognac; July–October: Machiavelli is at the camp of the league to coordinate Florence's defenses with Guicciardini.

1527   February–April: Machiavelli is again sent to the camp of the league; April: an imperial army invades Tuscany and threatens Florence; Guicciardini rushes forces of the league to Florence's defense; a revolt against the Medici regime begins; May: the imperial army sacks Rome, making Clement a prisoner; in Florence the Medici are expelled and the republic, including the Great Council, is restored; June 21: Machiavelli dies.

1528   A revived and expanded militia is instituted by the Florentine Republic; Baldassare Castiglione publishes *The Book of the Courtier*.

1529   June: in the Treaty of Barcelona, Charles agrees to restore the Medici in Florence; October: the ten-month siege of Florence by imperial forces begins; Machiavelli's *Art of War* is published again.

1530   August: Florence surrenders to the imperial forces; the emperor begins the process, completed two years later, of terminating the Florentine Republic and instituting a formal principate under the Medici.

1531   First printing of Machiavelli's *Discourses on Livy*.

1532   First printing of the *Florentine Histories* and *The Prince*.

1559   Machiavelli's works are placed on the Papal Index of Prohibited Books.

JOHN M. NAJEMY

Introduction

Against the current: Machiavelli's "contraria professione"

Machiavelli introduces himself nowhere better than in his correspondence, particularly with challenging interlocutors like Francesco Guicciardini, his younger contemporary who, when they exchanged a memorable set of letters in 1521, had already risen to political prominence and written a lively history of Florence as well as several memoranda on Florentine government. Their friendship was made possible by a shift in Machiavelli's political fortunes. After eight years in which the Medici had shunned Machiavelli following the 1512 coup d'état that restored them to power in Florence, their antagonism finally softened. Friends intervened to win the assent of Pope Leo X (Giovanni de' Medici) for a Roman performance of Machiavelli's play, *Mandragola*, and smoothed the way for Cardinal Giulio de' Medici's approval of Machiavelli's commission from the university (the Studio) to write a history of Florence. In May 1521, the Florentine government, again with Cardinal Giulio in the background, sent Machiavelli, who had once negotiated with kings, emperors, and popes, as its representative to the chapter general of the Franciscans in Carpi, near Modena, with instructions to promote a plan for the separate administration of Franciscan convents in Florentine territory. When the consuls of Florence's guild of manufacturers of woolen cloth learned of Machiavelli's assignment, they gave him the additional task of finding a Lenten preacher for the cathedral, whose administration was the guild's responsibility. Machiavelli, formerly an influential chancery official, adviser, military organizer, and diplomatic envoy for the republican government displaced by the Medici, was now on a mission of almost comical modesty. Guicciardini, by contrast, had accepted the reimposition of Medici rule in Florence in 1512 (as did many members of his elite class of *ottimati*), subsequently entered papal service under the Medici pope, and in 1516 became governor of Modena and Reggio in the papal state.

Traveling north in May 1521, Machiavelli probably stopped in Modena to spend a few days with the governor before moving on to Carpi, where, on the 17th, he received from Guicciardini a short, jocular letter.[1] Although this seems to have been the first letter sent by either to the other, its familiar tone and acerbic humor suggest a background of friendly but forthright conversations during their meeting in Modena. The letter elicited a similarly open and candid response from Machiavelli, and the exchange that followed over the next three days reveals, behind the humor, an awkward tension between these two most celebrated political thinkers of the Florentine Renaissance, so close in their origins and culture, yet so distant in their political experiences, loyalties, and inner convictions. Affably mocking Machiavelli, Guicciardini ironically praised the "good judgment" of those who had entrusted the selection of a Lenten preacher to one who, according to common repute, had never thought much about salvation. He was nonetheless certain that Machiavelli would carry out his commission according to the expectations the consuls had of him and as was required by his honor, which "would be dimmed if at this age you became concerned about your soul, for, since you have always lived with different beliefs [*contraria professione*], it would be attributed to senility rather than goodness." Machiavelli's skepticism concerning religion was no secret, but it is still startling to see Guicciardini openly underscore Machiavelli's "contraria professione" and apparent lack of belief in the soul.

In his reply, penned the same day, Machiavelli retorted that he would of course select a preacher "to his own specifications," the implication being that he might not meet the expectations of the "reverend consuls." In insisting that he would choose a preacher as *he* wanted him to be, "because in this matter I want to be as obstinate as I am in my other opinions," Machiavelli was defending his "contraria professione" – his different ideas, and not only on salvation. He also affirmed that the steadfastness with which he maintained such views was the foundation of the loyal service he had always given his republic, for never, he avers, had he "failed his republic" whenever he "was able to help her, if not with deeds, with words, if not with words, with gestures." Nor would he fail her now, knowing full well that his ideas were often at odds with those of most Florentines: "True it is – and I know it – that I am at variance [*contrario*] with the views of my fellow citizens, as I am in many other things." Machiavelli thus turns his "contraria professione" and allegedly insufficient concern for his own soul, for which Guicciardini had amusingly scolded him, into a more general sense of distance, in religion as "in many other things," from the conventional views of most Florentines, among them, implicitly, Guicciardini himself. The consuls of the wool guild had indeed asked the right man to find them their preacher, Machiavelli asserts, because his "contraria professione" allowed him to understand that, whereas they wanted a preacher to show them the way to Heaven, it was better to give them one who would teach them the way to the Devil, because "the true way to get to Paradise is to learn the way to Hell in order to escape it." Guicciardini had chided him for lack of faith, but Machiavelli turned the accusation on its head, claiming, with a hint of indignation, that he knew better than those who hide behind the "cloak of religion" the difference between "good men" and "bad men," and even how to get to Paradise.

In the same letter Machiavelli also recounts the trick he was playing on the friars. Pretending that the letters he received from Guicciardini were filled with "inside information" about world events, he let them think that he was (as indeed he had once been) a major player on the political stage. Guicciardini agreed to go along with the joke, sending a messenger "as quickly as possible" to make them believe "that you are a great dignitary." Machiavelli reported that everyone was taken in by the prank and that the friars assumed he was receiving bulletins of the highest importance. Even Sigismondo Santi, his host in Carpi and chancellor of that city's lord, was so impressed that he "drooled" over the letters. In mock self-deprecation, Machiavelli signed this letter "Niccolò Machiavelli, ambassador of the Florentine Republic to the Friars Minor," intimating that, although he never achieved the rank of ambassador ("orator") in his chancery days, he had now finally gained the elusive honor in this inglorious mission. Guicciardini replied with a gratuitously unkind amplification of the meaning of that signature: "When I saw your title of 'ambassador' of the Republic to the friars and thought of how many kings, dukes, and princes you once negotiated with, I was reminded of Lysander," the Spartan general who, as Guicciardini recalled from Plutarch, fell into disgrace "after many victories and triumphs" and was relegated to the demeaning task of serving food "to the same soldiers he had once so gloriously commanded." No one needed to remind Machiavelli of how far he had fallen, and, although he could laugh over it himself, it was the kind of laughter that masked, or exposed, sorrow.

Prompted by this unhappy comparison between the demoted "ambassador" and the unfortunate Lysander, Guicciardini further suggests, somewhat maliciously, that Machiavelli's mission to the Franciscans might serve him well in writing the history of Florence, whose commission he had just received. He then parodies Machiavelli's well-known view that, because human nature and the basic structures of things remain constant, events can usefully be compared with their analogous counterparts in earlier ages: "so you see that, with only the appearances of individuals and the surface aspects of things changing, all the same events repeat, and we never see any occurrence that has not been seen before." In the preface to book 1 of his *Discourses on Livy*, Machiavelli had presented a similar theory of history that serves as the foundation, or enabling fiction, of the work's many comparisons between antiquity and modernity and of the possibility of imitating the ancients. It was not an approach that Guicciardini found congenial, preferring as he did to emphasize the uniqueness of each historical moment and its complex circumstances. "Only prudent observers," Guicciardini says with irony, can see through the "changes in the names and outward features of things" to perceive their underlying sameness: "therefore history is good and useful because it sets before you and makes you recognize and see anew that which you have never known or seen" in your own experience. For this reason "those who gave you the task of writing a work of history are much to be commended, and you should be urged to carry out this assigned duty diligently. I believe this legation will not be entirely useless to you in this regard," he continues, because, even spending a few days among the friars, "you will have savored the entire Republic of the Wooden Clogs," as he derisively refers to the Franciscans, "and you will make use of this model for some purpose, by comparing it to, or assessing it in terms of, one of those forms of yours." Guicciardini was challenging – in playful, friendly, teasing, but still confrontational terms – Machiavelli's basic presuppositions about the study of politics and history: that comparisons across the ages to antiquity are indeed relevant and that one must understand the "forms" – the theoretical structures of governments and states – in order to grasp the particulars.

Machiavelli kept his reply and defense brief, in the last letter of this exchange, holding his ground and maintaining the validity of both his method and his experience:

> As for writing history and the Republic of the Wooden Clogs, I don't believe that coming here has cost me anything, because I've learned about many of the [Franciscans'] constitutions and institutions [*constitutioni et ordini*], which have much of value, so that I believe I can indeed make use of them for some purpose, especially in comparisons. Should I have to write about silence, I'll be able to say that they're more silent than friars eating. And I'll be able to refer to many other things that this humble experience has taught me.

A poor thing perhaps, this "esperienza" of the gullible friars, but Machiavelli in effect tells Guicciardini that he will not on that account abandon his convictions about the utility of "comparisons," any more than he was about to relinquish, or apologize for, his "contraria professione."

The exchange with Guicciardini illuminates central aspects of Machiavelli's intellectual personality: his pleasure in the punch and counterpunch of intellectual combat; his willingness to dispute accepted wisdom; his insistence that only by thinking apart from the crowd – even the sharp crowd of the Florentines, Guicciardini included – is it possible to see through appearances and the fog of conventional piety; and his readiness to make use of "experience," even seemingly insignificant experiences, to illuminate the theoretical constructs that constitute what in *The Prince* he had called "verità effettuale," the kind of truth that can have an effect in the world. Given his humanist formation and the extent to which antiquity was his constant point of reference, Machiavelli is inconceivable without the culture of the Renaissance of the preceding two centuries; yet he, more than anyone, subjected that culture's orthodoxies and habits of thought to analytical, skeptical scrutiny. He is both the epitome of the Renaissance and its moment of unsparing self-reflection: shaped by its reverence for the ancients and desire to emulate the Romans, by its assumptions concerning the beneficent power of language, and by the civic culture of city-republics – yet all the while standing back and taking critical distance. As the speaker in the prologue of *Mandragola* says about its author, "If anyone supposes that by finding fault he can get the author by the hair and scare him or make him draw back a bit, I give any such man warning and tell him that the author, too, knows how to find fault, and that it was his earliest art; and in no part of the world where *sì* is heard [where Italian is spoken] does he stand in awe of anybody, even though he plays the servant to such as can wear a better cloak than he can."[2]

Machiavelli's universality

Machiavelli is now everywhere: routinely invoked by political commentators and talking heads; appropriated, adapted, and distorted by authors of manuals for success in politics, business, and war; denounced by self-appointed defenders of political virtue for having unleashed the dark forces of the modern world; and admired for having exposed such naiveté in a world in which, allegedly, only toughness works. He is studied, analyzed, and debated by scholars from a greater variety of academic disciplines and intellectual directions (literature, history, philosophy, government, political science, theater studies, religion, military science, and even art history) and assigned as required reading (albeit usually only *The Prince*) in more university courses and departments than any other writer. "Machiavellian" has taken on a life of its own as a universally recognized proper adjective and become common currency, particularly in English, used (and abused) in everyday speech far beyond academic and intellectual circles, in senses unconnected with the historical Machiavelli. In television debates and newspaper opinion columns on political and social issues, whereas "Marxist" and "Freudian" have by now acquired a musty whiff of quaintness and most other historical names mean little to the general reading or listening public, no one, regrettably, thinks it necessary to ask what a speaker means in characterizing some person or idea as "Machiavellian" or whether the characterization is justified.

Books proclaiming the applicability of purportedly "Machiavellian" principles to modern life pay an odd kind of homage to him. Machiavelli's relevance to business is claimed in an astonishing number of books, including (and this is merely a sample of what Amazon.com gave me when I searched the keywords "Machiavelli" and "business"): Antony Jay, *Management and Machiavelli: A Prescription for Success in Your Business* (Prentice Hall, 1996); Alistair McAlpine, *The New Machiavelli: The Art of Politics in Business* (Wiley, 1999); Ian DeMack, *The Modern Machiavelli: The Seven Principles of Power in Business* (Allen & Unwin, 2002); Stanley Bing, *What Would Machiavelli Do? The Ends Justify the Meanness* [sic] (HarperCollins, 2002); Gerald R. Griffin, *Machiavelli on Management: Playing and Winning the Corporate Power Game* (Praeger, 1991); Phil Harris et al. (eds.), *Machiavelli, Marketing, and Management* (Routledge, 2000); and (sadly and perhaps inevitably) *The Mafia Manager: A Guide to the Corporate Machiavelli*, whose author hides as V (St. Martin's Griffin, 1997).

Machiavelli's applicability to modern politics is asserted by, among others, Michael Ledeen in *Machiavelli on Modern Leadership: Why Machiavelli's Iron Rules Are as Timely and Important Today as Five Centuries Ago* (Truman Talley Books, 1999); by Carnes Lord in *The Modern Prince: What Leaders Need to Know Now* (Yale, 2003), written in the "now" of the aftermath of 9/11, published as the United States and Britain were launching their invasion of Iraq, and organized, like Machiavelli's *Prince*, in twenty-six chapters addressed to "leaders who rule the people in a manner not altogether different from the princes and potentates of times past" (p. xi); and by Leslie Gelb, whose *Power Rules: How Common Sense Can Rescue American Foreign Policy* (Harper, 2009) draws on Machiavelli's alleged lessons and directly addresses the American president as *The Prince* addressed Lorenzo de' Medici. Not all efforts to relate Machiavelli to modern problems assume that the only relevant lessons are about power and empire (as Machiavelli's misleading modern reputation might cause one to imagine). In the mid-1990s, historians Susan Dunn and James MacGregor Burns, who have written about early Americans who knew Machiavelli well, condensed their reflections on Machiavelli in an essay entitled, "The Lion, the Fox, and the President: What Advice Might Niccolò Machiavelli give Bill Clinton?" Pondering the vicissitudes of his modern reputation, they concluded that "Machiavelli's true vision of life" was not unlike that of "our Founding Fathers: life, liberty, and the pursuit of happiness," and that, although "sometimes a strong and duplicitous prince would have to rule, [Machiavelli] never wavered in his belief that a republic, based on civic virtue, was the superior form of government."[3] In 2008 *The New Yorker* published an essay by Claudia Roth Pierpont on Machiavelli's life and thought that begins with his experience of torture and concludes with ruminations on the question of torture in our time in the light of what Machiavelli does and does not say about ends and means.[4] John Bernard has recently offered an enthusiastic defense of Machiavelli for the vital lessons he offers in civic virtue and the ethics of democratic politics.[5] Feminists too have found inspiration in Machiavelli: in *The Princessa: Machiavelli for Women* (Doubleday, 1997), Harriet Rubin outlines eighteen strategies for women to overcome "power anorexia." There is even a "Machiavellian" guide for children: Claudia Hart's *A Child's Machiavelli: A Primer on Power* (Studio, 1998). Whatever their differences (and these books and essays range from the silly to the thoughtful), such appropriations of Machiavelli share the assumption that he taught timeless lessons.

Frequently accompanying the notion that Machiavelli still speaks to us is the conviction, shared by many commentators, critics, and scholars, that he marked, and may even have been the chief protagonist of, an epochal turning point in the history of the West, the emergence of modernity, or indeed in the evolution of human consciousness – but without any consensus as to whether this was a good or a very bad thing. Early in the last decade of the twentieth century, the conservative political commentator George Will nominated five "finalists" for the honor of "person of the millennium." His selections were governed by the premise that the "two great, and related, developments of this millennium are the nation-state and political freedom, which involves limiting the state." Will's five contenders were Machiavelli, Martin Luther, George Washington, Thomas Jefferson, and Abraham Lincoln (and not surprisingly, given the lopsided American representation, Jefferson took home the trophy). Will explained Machiavelli's inclusion on the grounds that he "disturbed the Western mind as an early, vivid example of modern masterless man, obedient to no god and only to the rules he wrote." Despite this implicitly negative judgment of Machiavelli's contribution to modernity, Will underscored its importance in claiming that Machiavelli and Luther were "hammer[s] that helped shatter suffocating systems of thought and governance."

To appropriate Machiavelli as a guide to modern life and politics and to attribute to him such transformative significance presume a familiarity with his writings, which is nonetheless often accompanied by indifference to close analysis and context. Indeed, such philological and historical grounding is sometimes seen as an obstacle to a deeper understanding of his importance.

We are sometimes told what he meant, or what his works mean or should mean to us, by readers who know him only slightly and have read him hurriedly, in English (or other) translations, without much awareness of the historical circumstances in which he wrote. Perhaps the only true parallels in the Western tradition to this curious combination of willful distance from Machiavelli's language and context and profound certitude concerning the "truths" he gives us are Marx and the Bible. Machiavelli has been assigned, we might say, the status of a prophet whose revelations concerning what is constant in human nature and politics are still and always valid (quite apart from whether or not we welcome or like them), because they are believed to have foretold our condition.

As with all prophets, or those deemed prophets, Machiavelli's message has been furiously fought over, and the truths he allegedly gave us have been defined in chaotically different ways. He is often characterized in contradictory terms: for example, idealist/cynic; republican/monarchist; coolly analytical/passionately patriotic. Among the revelations attributed to him are the autonomy and amorality of politics; the indispensable role of force and fraud in the conquest and preservation of power; reason of state, or the state as its own moral system; arms as the essence of princely power; the people in arms as the essential ingredient of a state's survival; the rational, scientific nature of politics; the irrational power of fortune and human inability to comprehend or control it; the capacity (or incapacity) of free will to adapt to circumstances and change outcomes; the crucial role of charisma, intimidation, and spectacular theatricality in successful leadership; religion as the essence of a people and critical to a strong state; religion as an instrument to be manipulated by leaders or elites; human nature as fundamentally evil; the superiority of republics over monarchies; the superiority of princely freedom of action over the slow deliberateness of republics; liberty as the good state's chief goal; empire and expansion as the state's highest goal. Some of these are obviously (and here deliberately juxtaposed as) mutually exclusive. All have their believers and devoted defenders, even among scholarly specialists. What they have in common is making Machiavelli a harbinger of modernity and a "prophet" vindicated.

Machiavelli is indeed a writer of enduring fascination. Five centuries of readers have found him captivating, albeit for wildly different reasons, negative and positive. While explanations of his appeal are as varied and nearly as numerous as his interpreters and have shifted with evolving constellations of thought over these centuries, one can reasonably surmise that the overriding reason is that Machiavelli provocatively addressed, with his characteristic freedom from the chains of convention and tradition, fundamental issues of his and all political cultures. He refused, moreover, to resolve such questions with straightforward dogmatic pronouncements or doctrinal declarations, preferring instead a discursive, dialectical style of analysis that enters into the terms of debates (in some cases already centuries old), ponders contrasts, measures the different sides and aspects of controversies, subverts received solutions, and proposes new and unsettling perspectives. Depending on how far one wishes to subdivide these issues and consider their constituent parts separately, the list could be very long. For purposes of overview and introduction, however, five recurring questions can be highlighted.

Perhaps the most pervasive of these issues is Machiavelli's meditation on the role of the past in understanding the human condition. Two centuries of humanism's attempts to recover antiquity had profoundly instilled the idea that proper apprehension of the world and effective action in it, both theoretical wisdom and practical knowledge, began with the study of ancient history and literature. From this perspective, the trajectory of history led from the perfection of antiquity to long centuries in which that perfection was dispersed and fragmented, and then to the heroic, if still precarious, attempt to revive and rescue it. This vision of history no longer appeals to us, because we know more about the legacy of the Middle Ages to modernity than the Renaissance did and no longer so fulsomely idealize antiquity (not the Romans, in any case). Yet only by appreciating how axiomatic this assumption was for the Renaissance can we approach its sense of the relevance of the past. From Petrarch in the fourteenth century to the spread of the humanist movement in the fifteenth, the Romans were the paragons of political excellence and their historians and poets the unrivalled exemplars of eloquence and sources of political and ethical wisdom. To assimilate and emulate the ancient Romans, who had inhabited the same cities and walked the same streets as did Renaissance Italians, became the essence of education and culture, in language, literature, historiography, art, moral philosophy, and political theory.

Machiavelli's education was deeply immersed in these assumptions, which he shared to a significant extent. He pondered the power of historical myths and the exemplarity of legendary founders of states and religions; he felt the forceful attraction of cyclical theories of history and the need for societies to renew contact with their life-giving origins and first principles. But he also raised questions about historical memory, about how quickly it can be lost or overwhelmed and how far it is dictated by history's winners. Although he frequently urged imitation of the Romans, in the *Art of War* Machiavelli simultaneously acknowledged the desirability of such imitation and recognized its impossibility in the utterly changed circumstances of the modern world. At the beginning of the dialogue, set in the Rucellai family gardens (where Machiavelli participated in actual discussions of politics and history with friends and young disciples sometime between 1515 and 1519), the host, Cosimo Rucellai, notices that their guest, the mercenary captain Fabrizio Colonna, does not recognize some of the garden's more unusual trees. Cosimo explains that certain trees planted by his grandfather Bernardo were "more popular in antiquity than they are today," to which Fabrizio replies that he wishes that Bernardo and others who planned gardens on ancient models had preferred to imitate the Romans in "arduous and difficult" rather than "delicate and soft" matters like gardens. Defending his grandfather, Cosimo asserts that no one more than Bernardo detested the "soft life" or was a greater lover of the "rugged life" that Fabrizio praises. But Bernardo knew that neither he nor his sons could actually live such a life, because he "had been born in such a time of corruption that anyone who departed from common customs would have been ridiculed and considered crazy." Cosimo's defense of Bernardo anticipates Fabrizio's defense of himself (in book 1) for never having put into practice the ancient principles of warfare that he nonetheless insists are far superior to modern methods. This is one of several places where Machiavelli admits that imitating the ancients is an ideal destined never to be realized. The purpose of trying, as he suggests in chapter 6 of *The Prince*, is that aiming high, as archers do, hoping to reach not the heights but distant targets, at least comes closer to the goal. One should still strive to imitate the greatest examples, even if one never attains their greatness. Machiavelli's meditations on antiquity as a lost, elusive, but deeply appealing object of desire permeate his writings. The awesome magnitude of both the achievements and utter ruin of the Romans made them the indispensable point of reference for Machiavelli's inquiry into political greatness and decline: impossible not to seek to emulate, equally impossible to replicate. And his reflections on history, historians, collective memory, and the power of historical myths have made *him* an indispensable point of reference for anyone searching for meaning in the relationship of past and present.

The most contentious of the foundational issues treated by Machiavelli is the relationship of morality and politics. Rejecting what he considered the naive and simplistic view that good government is necessarily virtuous government, he argued that princes and republics may not survive if they unthinkingly follow the strictures of traditional morality expected of individuals. States have an overriding responsibility to survive and defend their populations, obligations that often require disregarding conventional moral codes. But this only scratches the surface of Machiavelli's approach to ethics and politics. Although he never quite wrote what is often attributed to him – that the ends justify the means – he did worry a great deal about ends and means: about whether a meaningful correlation between them is possible or even discernible, about whether and when crisis conditions require setting moral imperatives aside, and about whether states have ethical standards of their own, not necessarily less stringent or less moral than those incumbent on individuals. He wrestles with dilemmas of morality in his plays, *Mandragola* and *Clizia*, and in the poems on "Fortune," "Ambition," and "Ingratitude." In *The Prince* he overturns traditional morality, albeit within an ethical framework much indebted to ancient rhetorical theory. In *Discourses* 1.9 he allows that the supreme task of founding a state might entail situations in which deeds "accuse" while their effects "excuse." He also asks, in *Discourses* 1.17–18, whether a prince should be given freedom from moral constraints in seeking to rescue a moribund state from an otherwise fatal incapacity to heal itself. Yet the hypothesis of transgressive redemption crumbles when Machiavelli confronts the immutability of moral personality in acknowledging that no good man will ever be willing to use the violent means needed to take power, even for the good end of reforming a state, while no bad man is willing to turn to such good purpose the violent means he willingly employs to gain power. Machiavelli's views on political ethics are complex and should not be reduced to caricature.

Particularly thorny for Machiavelli was the philosophical conundrum of agency and contingency, or, as he liked to put it, the struggle between *virtù* and *fortuna*. The unpredictability of events, the irrationality of history, and people's inability to deviate from their inborn natures and inclinations (all of which flow into what he meant by fortune) caused him to wonder where and how agency, or free will, could determine or influence the outcome of events (which is at least one important sense of Machiavellian *virtù*). He sometimes succumbed to a form of fatalism that denied human ability to adapt to changing times and circumstances. *The Prince* was a valiant but desperate attempt to define the requirements of autonomy and *virtù*, but the solution offered in chapter 25 falls victim, despite his stated intention, to such fatalism. If, in theory, random variation and unpredictability can be tamed either by prudence or by impetuosity, in practice both methods are rendered inefficacious by the prison of unchanging individual natures that occludes the required flexibility. In his poetry and letters Machiavelli recast the problem by relocating the "variation" of fortune in both nature and human nature, and thus no longer only in external randomness, a redirection that opened the possibility that self-awareness can mitigate at least the worst effects of fortune. Machiavelli also rethought the question of free will in the light of what he read in Lucretius's *De rerum natura*, a text he knew well. His reading of the poets crucially influenced his reflections on this theoretical dilemma that never ceased to trouble him.

A fourth issue with which Machiavelli endlessly grappled is liberty: the conditions under which it can be established, recovered if lost, and protected from tyranny and license. He inherited, but also challenged, the well-established discourses of liberty and tyranny of ancient historians and Renaissance humanists, dissenting in particular from the assumption that liberty required the suppression of conflicts of interest and class, and arguing, in *Discourses* 1.4, that Rome's liberty actually depended on the sometimes noisy and disruptive conflicts between the senatorial aristocracy and the plebs. In the *Florentine Histories* he rejected the civic humanist tributes to Florentine liberty, insisting that Florence regularly fell prey to factional discord and never created the balance of class interests needed to preserve liberty. Addressing the question of whether liberty is more effectively protected by elites or by the people, he contested the paternalistic and patriarchal assumption that liberty requires aristocratic guardians. His understanding of liberty as a function of class relations likewise entailed reformulating the notion of tyranny, which he believed resulted from the efforts of one class (usually the nobility) to protect itself from its rivals. Liberty, for Machiavelli, is ultimately a function of the laws and public institutions he called *ordini*: constitutional procedures capable of diverting political ambition away from private, factional interests toward the public good. The gravest danger to liberty and *ordini* is the power of ambitious and wealthy citizens with the resources to build factions that bypass, disrupt, and undermine laws, courts, and public restraints on their ambition. Subversion of the *ordini* is what Machiavelli called "corruption," and in the *Discourses* and *Florentine Histories* he condemned the corrupting patronage politics that had engulfed Florence since the beginning of the fifteenth century under both the Medici and the oligarchy that preceded them. Machiavelli was the first to situate liberty's fate squarely in the crucible of class dialectics. Since then, the problem has resurfaced repeatedly, and explosively, and with frequent recognition that the centuries-long debate over the role of social conflicts in republics began with Machiavelli.

A fifth foundational problem addressed by Machiavelli is that of religion and the state. His devastating critique of both Christianity and the Church are among the most notorious aspects of his thought. He contrasted ancient religion's decisive contribution to the strength and stability of the Roman state and to the loyalty of its citizen-soldiers with what he saw as Christianity's debilitating effect on modern states, especially Italy. He also raised more theoretical questions about religion itself – whether it should be seen as the foundation of a people's culture or as an instrument invented and manipulated by clever leaders to control the people, albeit sometimes (as in Rome) to useful ends. The paradox may go back to his observation of the

Dominican friar Girolamo Savonarola, who launched reforms of Florentine culture and mores in the 1490s and also inspired a political party that used religious fervor for political ends. Living between the "Savonarolan moment" and the early rumblings of reform emanating from Germany, Machiavelli witnessed dramatic changes in European religious consciousness. It was not so much the theological aspects of religious ferment that interested him, but rather the ways in which religion affected politics, the state, the political morality of citizens and soldiers, and one's obligations to fellow citizens and country. His critique of both Christianity and the Church in the *Discourses* is unsparing, but he nonetheless believed that no society can cohere and function without religious discipline that makes people afraid to disobey the laws – another question much debated ever since, and perhaps never more than at the beginning of the twenty-first century.

Machiavelli's engagement with these issues – the meaning of the past, politics and morality, agency and contingency, liberty and class conflict, and religion and the state – have made his pages perennially fresh, sometimes troubling, but always stimulating. Like all thinkers, he belonged to his time; but like very few he is timeless and universal.

NOTES

1. These letters are in Niccolò Machiavelli, *Tutte le opere*, ed. Mario Martelli (Florence: Sansoni, 1971), pp. 1202–7; also in *Opere di Niccolò Machiavelli*, vol. 3, *Lettere*, ed. Franco Gaeta (Turin: UTET, 1984), pp. 518–29; and translations in *Machiavelli and His Friends: Their Personal Correspondence*, ed. and trans. James B. Atkinson and David Sices (DeKalb, Ill.: Northern Illinois University Press, 1996), pp. 335–42.
2. Trans. Allan Gilbert in *Machiavelli: The Chief Works and Others*, 3 vols. (Durham, N.C.: Duke University Press, 1958; reprinted 1989), 2:778.
3. Susan Dunn and James MacGregor Burns, *Harvard Magazine* 96 (January–February 1995): 41–4.
4. Claudia Roth Pierpont, "The Florentine: The Man Who Taught Rulers How to Rule," *The New Yorker* 84 (September 15, 2008): 87–92.
5. John Bernard, *Why Machiavelli Matters: A Guide to Citizenship in a Democracy* (Westport, Conn.: Praeger, 2009).

I

JAMES B. ATKINSON

Niccolò Machiavelli: a portrait

Machiavelli's grandson Giuliano de' Ricci, who devoted much of his life to gathering, preserving, and copying his grandfather's papers, tells a perhaps apocryphal story that reveals how Machiavelli's contemporaries understood his personality and unconventional attitudes. In 1504, four years after Machiavelli's father died, a friar at the Franciscan church of Santa Croce, where the family chapel was located, informed Machiavelli that some bodies of persons not from the family had been illegally buried there and that he ought to have them removed. But Machiavelli told the friar, "Well, let them be, for my father was a great lover of conversation, and the more there are to keep him company, the better pleased he will be."[1]

The kernel of truth in this story lies in Machiavelli's gratitude to his father for passing on an enjoyment of conversation and initiating him into the world of writers, and also in Machiavelli's penchant for viewing things with a slant frequently at odds with propriety. Indeed, the pragmatism and sly, ironic wit that characterize his response to the friar appear repeatedly in his writings. The anecdote underscores the significance that "conversation" had for a man who delighted in talking to and questioning people and books and enjoyed an easy familiarity with them. His love of friendship, dialogue (even imagined ones), and irony, frequently leavened with a mischievous and mocking wit, never left him (not even, as another legend has it, on his deathbed). In letters to him, chancery colleagues and other friends affectionately acknowledged his roguish, scoffing irreverence. But "conversation" was also his favorite metaphor for the serious pursuits of intellectual life. In the most famous passage of his December 1513 letter to Francesco Vettori, Machiavelli described his study of ancient texts as conversation:

> I chat with passersby, I ask news of their regions, I learn about various matters, I observe mankind … When evening comes, I return home and enter my study; on the threshold I take off my workday clothes, covered with mud and dirt,

and put on the garments of court and palace. Fitted out appropriately, I step inside the venerable courts of the ancients, where, solicitously received by them, I nourish myself on that food that *alone* is mine and for which I was born; where I am unashamed to converse [*parlare*] with them and to question them about their motives for their actions, and they, out of their human kindness, answer me. And for four hours at a time I feel no boredom, I forget all my troubles, I do not dread poverty, and I am not terrified by death. I absorb myself into them completely.[2]

His ability to "absorb" himself "completely" into his interlocutors is intrinsic to his virtuosity as a writer and originality as a political theorist.

Youth (1469–1489) and "lost" years (1489–1498)

Niccolò Machiavelli was born on May 3, 1469, into an old Florentine family with a distinguished record of political participation but without the wealth and political status of the elite families (*ottimati*). "I was born in poverty and at an early age learned how to scrimp rather than to thrive."[3] His father, Bernardo, was a doctor of law who, although chronically short of income, nonetheless provided his son with a solid humanist education. According to the snapshots of family life in Bernardo's diary, Niccolò was learning Latin at age seven, studying arithmetic at eleven, and translating vernacular texts into Latin at twelve.[4] Bernardo was also a friend of the humanist chancellor Bartolomeo Scala, who gave Bernardo's name to a speaker in his dialogue *On Laws and Legal Judgments* and referred to him as "amicus et familiaris meus."[5] That Machiavelli grew up in a household that valued learning is also apparent from the contents of Bernardo's library, which, given that book printing began only in the 1460s and many books were still expensive manuscripts, was an admirable collection. Among the books Bernardo owned or borrowed that would later influence his son were Livy's *History of Rome* and Cicero's *On Moral Duties*, *Philippics*, and *On the Orator*. Years later, Machiavelli implicitly acknowledged the importance of his father's library. In *The Prince*'s dedicatory letter, he wrote that "I have found nothing among my resources that I cherish or value as much as my knowledge of the deeds of great men, learned from a wide experience of recent events and a constant reading of classical authors." In the *Discourses* (3.46) he opined that what "a young boy" takes in "at an early age" has a profound influence "because he must needs be impressed by it, and then afterward throughout all periods of his life he regulates his way of doing things from that."

Among the ancient authors Machiavelli studied were Greeks that, because he never learned that language, he read in Latin translations, including Aristotle, Plato, Plutarch, Polybius, and Thucydides, and Romans whose works he read in Latin, including the moral philosophers Cicero and Seneca, the historians Caesar, Livy, Tacitus, and Sallust, the poets Ovid and Virgil, and the playwrights Plautus and Terence. One Roman poet he never mentions by name but who had a profound influence on him is Lucretius, whose sober, philosophical book-length poem *De rerum natura* permeates Machiavelli's outlook on religion and a host of other topics. Machiavelli acquired his familiarity with Lucretius the hard way, copying the entire poem by hand from a humanist manuscript edition.[6] He wrote some poetry, and one early poem, addressed to Lorenzo de' Medici's son Giuliano with an allusive pun on his name, "Se avessi l'arco e le ale, giovanetto giulìo" ("If, cheerful young man, you had a bow and wings"),[7] suggests some connection to the Medici, possibly as a result of Bernardo's friendship with Scala. But we know little else about Machiavelli's early adulthood between 1489 and 1498, when he was elected as head of Florence's second chancery, which administered the city's relations with its subject territories.

That other pillar of Machiavelli's "knowledge of the deeds of great men" was his experience of the dramatic events of Florentine and Italian history. Late fifteenth-century Florence was a thriving commercial and cultural center under the political sway of the Medici. Lorenzo de' Medici began his unofficial rule the year Machiavelli was born, but his first decade in power was punctuated by threats to his supremacy, chiefly the 1478 Pazzi conspiracy and subsequent war launched by the Pazzi's co-conspirators, Pope Sixtus IV and King Ferrante of Naples – events to which Machiavelli later devoted many pages of both the *Discourses* and the *Florentine Histories*. Lorenzo survived these challenges and tightened his control over the republic, but two years after his death Charles VIII of France invaded Italy in 1494 and swept through the peninsula so easily that Machiavelli later wrote in *The Prince* (chapter 12) that he "was allowed to conquer Italy with chalk." Internal and external threats against the Medici converged when Lorenzo's son Piero surrendered Florentine territory and fortresses to the French, angering the Florentines and undermining the regime. A revolt removed the Medici from power and sent them into exile in November 1494. Into the ensuing political vacuum came the powerful voice of the Dominican friar Girolamo Savonarola, who excoriated both the Florentines and a hedonistic Church for moral degeneracy, welcomed Charles VIII as a purifying "sword of God," and helped persuade the Florentines that moral reform would begin with the establishment of a republican government built around the Great Council whose creation he urged and inspired.

Savonarola's denunciation of Florentine sins and secularism ignited fierce controversy that led to his downfall. In March 1498, as Savonarola desperately fended off his enemies, Machiavelli, his curiosity obviously piqued, attended two of the friar's last sermons. In a letter to the Florentine ambassador in Rome, he described the embattled preacher's skillful tactical adjustments in addressing his followers, concluding that he "acts in accordance with the times and colors his lies accordingly."[8] Behind this harsh judgment and his cold skepticism toward Savonarola's dire prophecies, Machiavelli may have felt admiration, or at least respect, for the friar's adaptability and support of republican government. Savonarola's enemies in Florence and elsewhere, including Pope Alexander VI, who accused him of heresy and being a false prophet, had him arrested, tried, and then executed on May 23, 1498.

Less than a month later, on June 19, Machiavelli was elected second chancellor and soon thereafter secretary to the foreign policy magistracy of the Ten. Although his entrance into government may have been facilitated by association with Savonarola's adversaries, Machiavelli remained deeply ambivalent about him. In the first *Decennale*, a poem recounting the turbulent decade of Italian history that opened in 1494, he lamented the profound political divisions caused by Savonarola. Yet he referred to him as "that great Savonarola, whose words, inspired by divine *virtù*, kept you [Florentines] enmeshed. But because many feared to see their city gradually collapse under his prophetic teaching, no place to bring you together again could be found unless his divine light grew dark or a more intense fire quenched it."[9] Calling him an "unarmed prophet" in chapter 6 of *The Prince*, Machiavelli faulted Savonarola for lacking the means to keep power but implicitly put him in the company of great lawgivers like Moses. In *Discourses* 1.11 he wrote that Savonarola "convinced" the Florentines "that he spoke with God" (as Moses had similarly persuaded the Hebrews) and that "countless people believed him without ever having seen anything unusual to make them believe him, because his life, learning, and the subject that he chose were enough to make them lend him credence ... I do not wish to judge whether or not it was true, because one must speak of so great a man with reverence."

Molded by this "experience of recent events" and a humanist education centered on "a constant reading of classical authors," Machiavelli entered the chancery already in possession of that combination of "resources" of which he boasted in *The Prince*. He was perhaps referring to the influence of these formative years when he wrote, in an April 1513 letter to Vettori, that "Fortune has seen to it that since I do not know how to talk about either the silk or the wool trade, or profits or losses, I have to talk about politics [*lo stato*]. I need either to take a vow of silence or to discuss this."[10]

In 1496 Machiavelli's mother, Bartolomea Nelli, died, and in 1500 his father died. In 1501 Niccolò married Marietta Corsini. The couple had several children who died young or in infancy and one daughter, Bartolomea (the mother of Giuliano de' Ricci), and four sons who reached adulthood: Bernardo, Ludovico, Piero, and Guido, the youngest and perhaps his father's favorite. Machiavelli's many diplomatic missions kept him frequently away from home, and Marietta chafed at his absences. In November 1503, after their first son was born, she wrote him in Rome: "I would be flourishing more if you were here . . . The baby is well, he looks like you: he is white as snow, but his head looks like black velvet, and he is hairy like you. Since he looks like you, he seems beautiful to me . . . Remember to come back home."[11]

Government career (1498–1512)

The paucity of documentation before 1498 gives way to a wealth of information from Machiavelli's years in government, especially his private correspondence and the dispatches he sent to the Ten and to the republic's chief executive magistracy, the Signoria, from his legations (diplomatic missions). These fourteen years were the valuable seed time for the judgments that season his later political and historical writing. A good point of departure is his letter of October 1499 to "a chancellery secretary in Lucca" in which Machiavelli delineates his conception of a secretary's job – to be his government's "interpreter," its *lingua*, literally its "language," "tongue," or "mouthpiece" – and reveals how he saw himself and his work:

> Among the many considerations that show what a man is, none is more important than seeing either how easily he swallows what he is told or how carefully he invents what he wants to convince others of, so that every time he swallows what he ought not or invents badly what he wants to convince people of, he can be termed both thoughtless and reckless.[12]

An efficient secretary must render the thoughts of his interlocutors accurately and strive to uncover the mind behind their words. He wanted the Ten, for example, to understand the difficulty he experienced in deciphering the secretive Cesare Borgia in their thorny exchanges in late 1502. As he told them, Cesare "makes all his own decisions, and whoever doesn't want to write mere speculations [*ghiribizzi*] and far-fetched ideas must check the facts, and checking them requires time."[13] As the Ten's "interpreter" in Borgia's camp, Machiavelli would not "swallow what he is told" or "invent badly what he wants to convince people of." Earlier he had reported that, although Borgia "would seem to want a treaty between you and him to be drawn up quickly, nevertheless, in spite of the fact that I pressed him closely in order to get some particulars out of him, I was always outflanked and never could get out of him more than I have written."[14] A constant concern for correct interpretation of political situations and figures characterized Machiavelli's work as an envoy; the skillful, effective use of language that he acquired in this work later shaped his habits of thought and expression.

Machiavelli's responsibilities as second chancellor involved the administration of Florence's dominion in Tuscany, but he soon became the Ten's favorite envoy to foreign governments and princes. He was never a full-fledged ambassador, a post reserved for members of elite families; his tasks were the less glamorous but perhaps more crucial ones of gathering information, uncovering secrets, and interpreting intentions. There were also some memorable encounters. In 1500, the Signoria ordered Machiavelli to France, where he met Georges d'Amboise, cardinal of Rouen and King Louis XII's finance minister. In *The Prince* (chapter 3) Machiavelli recalled rebuffing the cardinal's arrogant assertion that the "Italians had no understanding of warfare" with the retort that "the French had no understanding of statecraft; for, if they had, they would not have let the Church gain such strength."

In 1502 a major constitutional reform resulted in the election of Piero Soderini as lifetime Standardbearer of the republic in an effort to assure greater continuity of policy and stronger leadership. Soderini admired Machiavelli's talents and astute judgments and increased his influence in government, particularly in allowing him in 1505–6 to implement the project for a homegrown militia that Machiavelli had long believed necessary because of the unreliability of mercenaries. He persuaded Soderini to permit him to raise a militia from the dominion territories, to be administered under a new magistracy, the Nine, whose secretary he became in January 1507. Machiavelli was as proud of these troops as was a contemporary who wrote that they were "the finest thing that had ever been arranged for Florence."[15]

External events dominated Machiavelli's experience of politics and nourished his growing theoretical interests. In September 1506, he watched Julius II, attended by only 150 bodyguards, boldly march into Perugia to bring that city back under papal rule. In a famous letter to Giovanbattista Soderini (Piero's nephew) known as the "Ghiribizzi" ("Speculations"), he pondered the apparent illogic of the pope's success and wondered how it was possible to establish a meaningful correlation between means and ends, tactics and results: "The reason why different actions are sometimes equally useful and sometimes equally detrimental I do not know – yet I should very much like to."[16] He theorized that, because individuals are fixed in their ways and unable to adapt as circumstances around them change, success is purely a matter of chance: if one's built-in "way of doing things" is what the times require, success will follow; if not, not. The question would continue to haunt him, especially in *The Prince*'s penultimate chapter on "The power of Fortune in human affairs and how she can be countered," where he came to a similar conclusion (again using the example of Pope Julius). In his 1517 poem *L'Asino* he still believed in the essential immobility of each human temperament: "the mind of man, steadily intent on pursuing what is natural to it, does not yield to any plea contrary either to habit or nature."[17]

In 1507 Soderini wanted to send Machiavelli to negotiate with Emperor Maximilian, but powerful *ottimati*, who perceived Machiavelli as Soderini's "lackey" who would loyally support the pro-French policy they were trying to undermine, blocked the appointment and replaced him with Francesco Vettori. Machiavelli was humiliated and furious. His friend Filippo Casavecchia consoled Machiavelli in his bitterness over what he regarded as Soderini's betrayal: "Do you not know that there have been very, very few friendships that in the passage of time do not become their opposite?"[18] Soderini later had Machiavelli join the mission with Vettori, but the episode made starkly clear that Machiavelli had enemies among the *ottimati*. Another reason for their hostility toward him was the militia, which they feared might become an instrument of personal power in Soderini's hands, but which Machiavelli continued to build for the war to regain Pisa. In June 1509, after fifteen years of resistance, Florentine forces finally forced the port city to submit. In this high point of Machiavelli's career, his chancery colleague Agostino Vespucci exulted: "If I did not think it would make you too proud, I should dare say that you with your battalions" have "restored" the Florentine state.[19] Casavecchia lauded "the outstanding acquisition of that notable city" and declared that "truly it can be said that your person was the cause of it to a very great extent." Mindful of Machiavelli's adversaries, however, he added a word of caution: "Niccolò, this is a time when if ever one was wise it should be now. I do not believe your ideas will ever be accessible to fools, and there are not enough wise men to go around ... Every day I discover you to be a greater prophet than the Hebrews or any other nation ever had." He urged him to "come and stay here with me ... I am saving you a ditch full of trout and a wine like you have never drunk."[20] In 1509 Machiavelli's friend and chancery colleague Biagio Buonaccorsi warned him of efforts to remove him from his posts. Matters were so precarious that Buonaccorsi even encoded parts of this letter: "Believe me, Niccolò, I am not telling you half of the things that are going around," and then in code: <You have so few people here that want to help you>."[21]

The many letters Machiavelli exchanged with Buonaccorsi, Vespucci, and others in the chancery enable us to feel the close-knit friendship among them. They shared gossip, off-color jokes, good-natured banter, and allusions to Machiavelli's peccadilloes and political vulnerability. The intersection of Machiavelli's public duties and intellectual interests occasionally emerges. Buonaccorsi responded to a request Machiavelli sent from Borgia's camp in Imola in 1502: "We have tried to locate some *Lives* of Plutarch, and there are none for sale in Florence. Be patient, because we have to write to Venice; to tell you the truth, you can go to the devil for asking for so many things."[22] Evidently, Machiavelli was already determined to ferret out clues from ancient examples in interpreting the actions of his contemporaries.

Machiavelli's political work and literary vocation continued to overlap in these years. Some of the memoranda he drafted after returning from diplomatic missions are cast as literary narratives that interpret and even dramatize, rather than merely report, the facts. A notable example is the "Description of the method used by Duke Valentino [Cesare Borgia] in killing Vitellozzo Vitelli, Oliverotto da Fermo, and others" (1503). Politics and literature also converge in his early poetry, including the first *Decennale* of 1504 and its sequel, the second *Decennale*, which stops in 1509 but opens with another lament for Italy's fate ("I shall venture to sing amid so many tears, although I have become almost lost in grief").[23] Usually dated to these years as well are his poetic meditations on the forces he saw governing men and events, the tercets on "Ingratitude," "Fortune," "Ambition," and "Opportunity."

The republic's days were numbered once Pope Julius organized the Holy League against France in 1511, with a battle cry to free Italy from the "barbarians." Soderini remained loyal to France, and when the league's forces drove the French from Italy in the summer of 1512, the angry pope let the Spaniards invade Florentine territory in support of a Medici restoration. After they sacked the nearby city of Prato, futilely defended by Machiavelli's militia, Soderini was forced into exile. On September 1, Giuliano de' Medici entered Florence in triumph and a pro-Medici party took over. In November Machiavelli was relieved of his duties, confined to Florentine territory for a year, and barred from the government palace. Mortified at his militia's drubbing and what he termed its "cowardice,"[24] he scrawled (ironically in the margins of a copy of his 1506 "Discourse on the organization of the Florentine state for arms" ["La cagione dell'Ordinanza"]) the rueful words *post res perditas* ("after all was lost").

Contemplative years (1513–1520)

The mutual reinforcement of Machiavelli's outer and inner lives during his active years dissolved with the fall of the republic. Forced away from the political ferment in Florence, he led an outwardly dreary life on his farm near San Casciano, ten miles south of the city. But his intellectual life, animated by the correspondence with Francesco Vettori, among his closest friends since their joint service on the mission to Maximilian in 1507–8, became richer and more exciting.

First Machiavelli had to confront accusations, never proven and certainly false, of complicity in an anti-Medici conspiracy early in 1513. Someone foolishly listed Machiavelli's name among potential sympathizers, and he was arrested, imprisoned with a "pair of shackles" on his legs, and tortured with the *strappado* – hoisted with a rope, his arms tied behind his back, and then dropped just short of the floor with excruciating dislocation of the shoulders. He was held for twenty-two days in (as he put it with bitter irony in one of the "prison sonnets" he addressed to Giuliano de' Medici) the stench of his "refined lodging" among "lice" large enough to seem "like butterflies."[25] He was released in March as part of a general amnesty when Cardinal Giovanni de' Medici was elected pope as Leo X.

Freedom was cold comfort for his physical and psychological pain. Depressed at being disparaged and treated as a criminal, he wrote to his nephew, Giovanni Vernacci, that

> I have had so much trouble ... it is a miracle that I am alive, because my post was taken from me and I was about to lose my life, which God and my innocence have preserved for me. I have had to endure all sorts of other evils, both prison and other kinds. But, by the grace of God, I am well and I manage to live as I can – and so I shall strive to do, until the heavens show themselves to be more kind.[26]

He frequently showed his frustrations to Vernacci, revealing his pain more openly to him than he could to Vettori, with whom he often camouflaged his feelings in literary quotations. In one letter to Vettori he expressed his despair by rewriting lines from Petrarch and substituting "give vent to" in place of Petrarch's "hide": "Therefore, if at times I laugh or sing, I do so because I have no other way than this to give vent to [*sfogare*] my bitter tears."[27]

Within a week of his liberation, the correspondence with Vettori began. Machiavelli hoped that Vettori, now Florentine ambassador to the papal court, might come to his aid; if so, "I shall do honor to you." Machiavelli expressed a wish for employment by the Medici, not because he was a sycophant, but because, as he said in the December 1513 letter to Vettori and in the dedicatory letter to *The Prince*, he could offer experience and competence. But Vettori could offer little tangible help and lamented that he did "not know how to be bold enough to be of use to myself and to others."[28] What he did do, however, proved to be more valuable, for with his letters he drew Machiavelli into dialogue about politics, probing him with questions about current events and encouraging him to gather and refine his thoughts and write about them. In letters of the spring and summer of 1513, Machiavelli began to conceptualize the issues at the core of *The Prince*, which he wrote between August and December.

Two central themes of *The Prince* emerged from the correspondence. First is the desperate concern over Italy's suffering and the yearning for a redeemer. Machiavelli began to theorize the possibility of a leader of "immense *virtù*" capable of infusing "spirit and order" into the downtrodden Italian people.[29] In chapter 12 of *The Prince* his grief explodes into an anguished lament for an Italy bereft of *virtù* and "overrun by Charles, plundered by Louis, violated by Ferdinand, and reviled by the Swiss." In the last chapter, the "Exhortation to seize Italy and free her from the barbarians," Machiavelli magnifies the redeemer-prince, who first appears in letters to Vettori:

> In order that after so long a time Italy may behold her redeemer, this opportunity must not be allowed to slip by. I cannot express with what love that redeemer would be received in all these regions that have suffered from these inundations of foreign invaders: with what thirst for vengeance, what determined loyalty, what devotion, what tears ... What Italian would withhold homage from him? This barbarous tyranny stinks in the nostrils of everyone.

Behind *The Prince*'s apparently dispassionate advice about securing power lie fervor, impatient wrath, and emotional intensity over Italy's humiliations.

The second theme that carries over from the letters is Machiavelli's unflinching insistence that history and politics are after all intelligible. Rejecting Vettori's sense of the limits of reasoned discourse and the inevitable recourse to "imagination" or interpretation,[30] Machiavelli affirms an ability to penetrate the words and actions of princes and, as he then says in *Prince* 15, to go behind the surface meaning of things to the "verità effettuale": "I depart from the precepts given by others. But the intention of my writing is to be of use to whoever understands it; thus it has seemed to me more profitable to go straight to the actual truth of matters rather than to a conception about it." Whom did Machiavelli have in mind in referring to "whoever understands it"? Was he implying that, while the Medici might learn rules for maintaining power, these lessons would not be lost on supporters of republics anywhere? Lorenzo, to whom *The Prince* was dedicated in 1516 (although originally "addressed" to Giuliano), showed no interest in the work, which failed to rescue Machiavelli from oblivion.

The correspondence with Vettori reveals other facets of Machiavelli's temperament also reflected in his later works. In humorous exchanges they parried thoughts about love and the nature of desire. Vettori's description of a dinner party drew Machiavelli into an imaginative recreation of it that invites the reader to see it as a play or short story.[31] Reflecting in early 1515 on the "variety" of their letters, Machiavelli justified their frequent changes of subject matter and tone with the idea that in this "variety" they were imitating nature: while some of their letters might suggest that they were "serious men completely directed toward weighty matters," other letters could give the impression "that we – still the very same selves – were petty, fickle, lascivious, and directed toward chimerical matters [cose vane]. If to some this behavior seems contemptible, to me it seems laudable because we are imitating nature, which is changeable; whoever imitates nature cannot be censured."[32] Much as he did with the ancients, in the correspondence with Vettori Machiavelli similarly "transfers himself" inside a "variety" of characters, real and imaginary. Nowhere did he do so more inventively than in *Mandragola* (c. 1518), his richly anticlerical, politicized domestic comedy of seduction whose mordant wit, sometimes ruefully turned on himself (as in act 2, scene 3: "anybody who doesn't have connections [stato] in this town won't find even a dog to bark at him"), makes it one of the most brilliant comedies of the Renaissance.

In these same years Machiavelli wrote his *Discourses on Livy* and *Art of War*, the latter the only one of his major political works printed in his lifetime (in 1521). Both were inspired by conversations in which he participated in the gardens of the Rucellai family, the Orti Oricellari, where humanists and historians hosted by Cosimo Rucellai (one of the two dedicatees of the *Discourses* and a speaker in the *Art of War*) discussed politics and history. Indeed, the Rucellai gardens are the setting for the dialogues in the *Art of War*, which suggests how grateful Machiavelli was for these stimulating conversations after the years of enforced isolation. The preface to book 2 of the *Discourses* conveys Machiavelli's changing self-image: once an adviser to princes, he now sees himself as a teacher to the young. In asserting the political superiority of antiquity when "*virtù* flourished," Machiavelli says he will "be courageous and say openly what I understand about those times and our own [when vice "flourishes"] ... so that the minds of the young who read my writings can avoid the latter and prepare to imitate the former, whenever Fortune gives them the opportunity to do so." He acknowledges, perhaps with a hint of melancholy, that this would be the work of future generations: "For it is the duty of a good man to teach others the good that you have been unable to bring about because of the hostility of the times and of Fortune, so that once many are aware of it, some of them – more beloved of Heaven – may be able to bring it about." Even as the Medici tightened their grip on power, he desperately hoped for a revival of the republican values of ancient Rome.

Treated unkindly by "the hostility of the times and of Fortune," Machiavelli was still on the outside looking in and occasionally reacted with anxious dejection. In the allegorical poem he called *L'Asino* (1517) the woman who consoles the narrator/actor for the ingratitude with which his "great toil" has been rewarded tells him that, "because tears were always unbecoming in a man, one must turn a face with dry eyes to the blows of fortune."[33] In another poem, modeled on conventional Petrarchan emotions, despair adds poignancy: "I hope, and hope aggravates my suffering: I weep and weeping nourishes the weary heart; I laugh and my laughter remains external; I burn and my burning remains within … everything imparts new suffering."[34] That such discontent was palpable, not trite, is supported by what he wrote to Vernacci in 1518: "Fate has done the worst she can to me … I am reduced to a condition where I can do little good for myself and less for others."[35] In the proem to the *Art of War* he identified himself as "Niccolò Machiavelli, Florentine citizen and secretary," thus reminding readers of the pride he took in both his Florentine citizenship and his years of government service.

Rehabilitation (1520–1527)

Despite the partial rehabilitation of his last years, Machiavelli's doldrums were always close to the surface. In 1525 he signed a letter to Francesco Guicciardini "Niccolò Machiavelli, Historian, Comic Author, and Tragic Author."[36] He was indeed a writer of history and plays, but in calling himself a "tragic author" he implied that Italy's tragic fate was the implicit subject of all his historical and political writing.

Friends from the Orti Oricellari mediated the reconciliation with the Medici in 1520 that opened the way for Cardinal Giulio de' Medici (Leo's cousin, who was himself elected pope as Clement VII in 1523) to approve Machiavelli's commission from the Florentine Studio to write a history of Florence. It was an ironic challenge for a zealous partisan of Soderini's republic to be yoked to the Medici and to write a history of Florence in which it would have been imprudent to be too openly critical of the family's role. Machiavelli confided to Donato Giannotti, a friend from the Orti Oricellari who would hold Machiavelli's old post of secretary to the Ten under the last republic of 1527–30, that he "could not write" about the period of Medici dominance "as I would if I were free from all worries." He said he would describe the events but not the "causes" and "methods" of the Medici ascendancy; and what he was unwilling to say as coming from himself he would put into the mouths of their adversaries.[37] Was he also referring to this dilemma when he told Guicciardini in 1521, in mocking self-deprecation, that "for some time now I have never said what I believe or never believed what I said"?[38] But his commitment to telling difficult truths never wavered. In 1524 he told Guicciardini that he wished he could have him by his side "so that I might show you where I am [in the history], because, since I am about to come to certain details, I would need to learn from you whether or not I am being too offensive in my exaggerating or understating of the facts ... I shall try to do my best to arrange it so that – still telling the truth – no one will have anything to complain about."[39] As far as we know, Clement VII, to whom Machiavelli dedicated and presented the history in 1525, did not complain.

The correspondence with Guicciardini is vital to understanding Machiavelli's last years. Although Guicciardini came from a family of wealth and status and linked his destiny to the Medici, their letters reveal mutual admiration, respect, and friendship in an interchange rife with irony, chiefly in aid of their anticlericalism. In May 1521, when Guicciardini was governor of Modena, Machiavelli was appointed Florentine envoy to the Franciscan chapter general in Carpi, with an additional commission from Florence's wool guild to find a preacher for the following year's Lenten season. Guicciardini warned him "to take care of" this business "as swiftly as possible, because in staying there long you run" the risk "that those holy friars might pass some of their hypocrisy on to you." Guicciardini sardonically approved the "good judgment" of the "reverend consuls of the wool guild" in having "entrusted you with the duty of selecting a preacher, not otherwise than if the task had been given to [the notorious homosexual] Pachierotto ... to find a beautiful and graceful wife for a friend." Guicciardini's next comment tells us much about how contemporaries saw Machiavelli: "I believe you will serve [the consuls] according to the expectations they have of you and as is required by your honor, which would be stained if at this age you started to think about your soul, because, since you have always lived in a contrary belief, it would be attributed rather to senility than to goodness."[40]

Responding to Guicciardini's letter, which he said he received while "sitting on the toilet ... mulling over the absurdities of this world," Machiavelli enlisted Guicciardini's help in perpetrating a practical joke on the friars. He asked him to send messengers more frequently with letters that Machiavelli would pretend were full of big news about the emperor, the king of France, and the Swiss, and which would cause his reputation to "rise among those friars ... once they saw the dispatches arriving thick and fast." Machiavelli loved making fools of the naive friars. Rising to Guicciardini's remark about the danger of starting "to think about your soul" so late in life, Machiavelli shows again his characteristic blend of comic unconventionality and serious purpose: "In truth, I know that I am at variance with the ideas of [Florence's] citizens ... They would like a preacher who would teach them the way to Paradise, and I should like to find one who would teach them the way to go to the Devil ... For I believe that the following would be the true way to go to Paradise: learn the way to Hell in order to steer clear of it." Machiavelli concluded these thoughts with an assertion that his detractors should not forget: "Since I am aware how much belief there is in an evil man who hides under the cloak of religion, I can readily conjure up how much belief there would be in a good man who walks in truth, and not in pretense, tramping through the muddy footprints of Saint Francis."[41]

In 1525 Machiavelli and Guicciardini discussed a possible Florentine performance of *Mandragola*, and Machiavelli explicated for Guicciardini some of the play's proverbial witticisms.[42] Guicciardini (and others) commented on Machiavelli's affair with Barbera Salutati,[43] who sang the songs preceding the acts of *Mandragola* and who may have inspired Machiavelli's *Clizia*, the comedy about the elderly Nicomaco (an obvious play on Machiavelli's name) foolishly enamored of a young woman.

Machiavelli's last two years were dominated by the storm that was about to break over Italy, now the battleground of the rivalry between Charles V, king of Spain and Holy Roman Emperor, and Francis I of France. In 1526, as Florence shored up its defenses, the Medici regime finally asked Machiavelli for advice on the militia and fortifications and made him secretary of a new magistracy he himself recommended, the Overseers of the Walls. But it was not an auspicious moment to return to government work. Clement's vacillations so enraged the emperor that the latter let an ill-paid and uncontrolled imperial army descend into Tuscany in early 1527. In February, Machiavelli was sent to Guicciardini, now lieutenant-general of the papal armies in the north, to urge him to come to his city's defense, and in April Florence narrowly averted being sacked when Guicciardini led papal–French forces to the rescue. Machiavelli wrote to Vettori: "I love Messer Francesco Guicciardini, I love my native city more than ..." – and here there is an erasure in his grandson's copybook of the letters. It is speculated that Machiavelli may have written "more than my own soul."[44] Florence escaped, but the hungry army proceeded to Rome and inflicted the devastating sack of May 1527 that resulted in Clement's imprisonment, an anti-Medici revolt in Florence, and the creation of a new republic.

A tormented Italy is the backdrop for the tender, solicitous letter from "a good man who walks in truth, and not in pretense" that Machiavelli wrote to his son Guido in April 1527. Fatherly advice pours out: "You must study ... take pains to learn letters and music, for you are aware how much distinction is given me for what little ability I possess ... Study, do well, and learn, because everyone will help you if you help yourself." To impress upon his son the values of freedom and compassion, Machiavelli moves on to a topic dear to Guido's heart – his young mule, which "has gone mad." Machiavelli advises that "it must be treated just the reverse of the way crazy people are, for they are tied up, and I want you to let it loose ... Take off its bridle and halter and let it go wherever it likes to regain its own way of life and work off its craziness. The village is big, and the beast is small; it can do no one any harm." Machiavelli was fond of animal metaphors, and we may surmise that these lines were also about his desire to regain his "own way of life" in freedom. Machiavelli also asked Guido to "greet Madonna Marietta for me ... I have never longed so much to return to Florence as I do now ... Simply tell her that, whatever she hears, she should be of good cheer, since I shall be there before any danger comes. Kiss Baccina, Piero, and Totto ... Live in happiness and spend as little as you can ... Christ watch over you all."[45]

Back in Florence, Machiavelli died on June 22, 1527, "from pains in the belly" caused by an attack of peritonitis. According to a letter (of doubtful authenticity) of his son Piero, Machiavelli "allowed Brother Matteo ... to hear the confession of his sins."[46] A story has it that he told those "who kept him company until his death" about a dream in which he chooses to remain in Hell and discuss politics with Plato, Plutarch, Tacitus and other ancients, rather than go to Heaven and associate with the blessed souls of Paradise.[47] With a dream of an afterlife devoted to conversation, we end where we began. The deathbed story may also be apocryphal, but it is true to the sly, ironic wit of a man who was frequently "at variance with the ideas" of his contemporaries.

NOTES

1. Roberto Ridolfi, *Vita di Niccolò Machiavelli*, 7th edition (Florence: Sansoni, 1978), p. 56; *The Life of Niccolò Machiavelli*, 2nd edition, trans. Cecil Grayson (London: Routledge & Kegan Paul, 1963), p. 35.
2. *Machiavelli and His Friends: Their Personal Correspondence*, trans. James B. Atkinson and David Sices (De Kalb, Ill.: Northern Illinois University Press, 1996), p. 264.
3. To Francesco Vettori, March 18, 1513; *Correspondence*, p. 222.
4. Bernardo Machiavelli, *Libro di Ricordi*, ed. Cesare Olschki (Florence: Le Monnier, 1954), pp. 31, 103, 138.

5. Trans. David Marsh, in *Cambridge Translations of Renaissance Philosophical Texts*, vol. 2, *Political Philosophy*, ed. Jill Kraye (Cambridge University Press, 1997), pp. 173–99 (174).

6. Ridolfi, *Vita*, p. 426.

7. Niccolò Machiavelli, *Opere*, ed. Mario Martelli (Florence: Sansoni, 1971), p. 994.

8. To Ricciardo Becchi, March 9, 1498; *Correspondence*, pp. 8–10 (quotation at p. 10).

9. *Opere*, pp. 942–3, vv. 155–65.

10. *Correspondence*, p. 225.

11. *Correspondence*, p. 93.

12. *Correspondence*, p. 22.

13. *Opere*, p. 443.

14. *Opere*, p. 404.

15. Luca Landucci, *A Florentine Diary from 1450 to 1516*, trans. Alice de Rosen Jervis (London: Dent; New York: Dutton, 1927), p. 218.

16. *Correspondence*, p. 135.

17. *Opere*, p. 956, vv. 88–90.

18. *Correspondence*, pp. 157–8 (July 30, 1507).

19. *Correspondence*, pp. 180–1 (June 8, 1509).

20. *Correspondence*, pp. 181–2 (June 17, 1509).

21. *Correspondence*, p. 193 (December 28, 1509).

22. *Correspondence*, p. 55 (October 21, 1502).

23. *Opere*, p. 950, vv. 7–9.

24. Letter "to a Noblewoman," sometime after September 16, 1512; *Correspondence*, p. 216.

25. *Opere*, p. 1003.

26. *Correspondence*, p. 239 (June 26, 1513).

27. *Correspondence*, p. 228 (April 16, 1513).

28. *Correspondence*, p. 223 (March 30, 1513).

29. *Correspondence*, p. 259 (August 26, 1513).

30. *Correspondence*, pp. 241–2 (July 12, 1513).

31. *Correspondence*, pp. 274–8 (Vettori to Machiavelli, January 18, 1514; Machiavelli to Vettori, February 4, 1514).

32. *Correspondence*, p. 312 (January 31, 1515).

33. *L'Asino* 3, vv. 85–7; *Opere*, p. 961.

34. "Strambotto I," vv. 1–4, 6; *Opere*, p. 997.

35. *Correspondence*, p. 319 (January 25, 1518).

36. *Correspondence*, p. 371 (after October 21, 1525).

37. Ridolfi, *Vita*, p. 310; *Life*, pp. 198–9.

38. *Correspondence*, p. 337 (May 17, 1521).

39. *Correspondence*, p. 351 (August 30, 1524).

40. *Correspondence*, p. 335 (May 17, 1521).

41. *Correspondence*, pp. 336–7 (May 17, 1521).

42. *Correspondence*, pp. 367–8 (October 16–20, 1525).

43. *Correspondence*, pp. 360–1, 377, 384–5, 393.

44. *Correspondence*, pp. 416, 562 (April 16, 1527).

45. *Correspondence*, pp. 413–14 (April 2, 1527).

46. *Correspondence*, p. 425.

47. Ridolfi, *Vita*, pp. 391–2; *Life*, pp. 249–50.

FURTHER READING

Atkinson, Catherine. *Debts, Dowries, Donkeys: The Diary of Niccolò Machiavelli's Father, Messer Bernardo, in Quattrocento Florence*. Frankfurt, Peter Lang, 2002.

Bertelli, Sergio and Gaeta, Franco. "Noterelle machiavelliane: un codice di Lucrezio e di Terenzio," *Rivista storica italiana* 73 (1961): 544–57.

Black, Robert. "Machiavelli, Servant of the Florentine Republic," in *Machiavelli and Republicanism*, ed. Gisela Bock, Quentin Skinner, and Maurizio Viroli. Cambridge University Press, 1990, pp. 71–99.

"New Light on Machiavelli's Education," in *Niccolò Machiavelli politico storico letterato*, ed. Jean-Jacques Marchand. Rome, Salerno Editrice, 1996, pp. 391–8.

Frazier, Alison K. "Machiavelli, Trauma, and the Scandal of *The Prince*: An Essay in Speculative History," in *History in the Comic Mode: Medieval Communities and the Matter of Person*, ed. R. Fulton and B. W. Holsinger. New York, Columbia University Press, 2007, pp. 192–202.

Martelli, Mario. "Preistoria (medicea) di Machiavelli," *Studi di filologia italiana* (1971): 377–405.

Najemy, John M. *Between Friends: Discourses of Power and Desire in the Machiavelli–Vettori Letters of 1513–1515*. Princeton University Press, 1993.

"The Controversy surrounding Machiavelli's Service to the Republic," in *Machiavelli and Republicanism*, ed. Gisela Bock *et al.*, pp. 101–17.

Viroli, Maurizio. *Niccolò's Smile: A Biography of Machiavelli*, trans. Antony Shugaar. New York, Farrar, Straus & Giroux, 2000.

2

ROBERT BLACK

Machiavelli in the chancery

From June 19, 1498, to November 7, 1512, Niccolò Machiavelli served as a high-ranking official in the chancery of the Florentine republic. His election as second chancellor, aged twenty-nine, without previous notarial, secretarial, or administrative experience, was doubtless a political success. The faction supporting the firebrand preacher and fundamentalist religious reformer Girolamo Savonarola had reached the height of its power under Florence's new popular constitution at the end of 1497. Although by the beginning of 1498 its control was already teetering, it still managed to assert its influence in elections to the chancery in February, when Machiavelli lost, possibly because he was known to be critical of Savonarola in private, although he was not associated with any anti-Savonarolan faction.[1] But the friar's party suffered a precipitate fall from power in April when its political leader, Francesco Valori, was murdered; at the end of May, Savonarola himself was tried and executed, and many of his supporters, including chancery staff, were removed from office. This gave Machiavelli his chance.

Another circumstance favored Machiavelli after Savonarola's fall. Traditionally, the chancery was meant to be nonpolitical; unlike political magistrates who held power for short periods in order to limit, at least in theory, factional or personal influence over government, chancery officials served long periods, often for life. But during the ascendancy of Lorenzo de' Medici (1469–92) and his son Piero (1492–94), and in the Savonarolan period (1494–98) as well, chancery officials became embroiled in partisan politics. With Savonarola gone, a reaction ensued and chancery staff were again expected to be nonpolitical: Piero Parenti, the most important Florentine chronicler of these years, remarked that "the officials elected should be beholden to the people and the whole city, not just a few citizens."[2] Although critical of Savonarola, Machiavelli had no overt involvement in factional politics. Indeed, his father, Bernardo, may have deliberately kept a low political profile in order to distance himself from the memory of a family member, Girolamo Machiavelli, who had been arrested, tortured, and driven from Florence in 1458 for opposing the Medici. Niccolò's lack of factional affiliation may therefore explain why, on June 19, 1498, he defeated two prominent anti-Savonarolans and one leading Savonarolan for the post of second chancellor.

The chancery administered the republic's external relations according to decisions made by the city's chief magistracy, the Signoria, and by the Dieci di Balìa (Ten of War), who were appointed during wartime to oversee military operations. Presiding over the chancery staff were the first chancellor, who in theory administered relations with foreign states, and the second chancellor, who supervised relations with Florence's subject territories. In practice, however, there was considerable overlap in the responsibilities of the first and second chancellors. A month after his election as second chancellor, Machiavelli was given the additional duty of serving the Ten as their secretary. His third major chancery post was the appointment, in January 1507, as chancellor to the newly instituted Nine Officials of the Florentine Militia, the indigenous infantry force whose creation he himself had urged on the government.

As with other chancery officials, Machiavelli's principal formal duty was the preparation of written documents, consisting mainly of letters on behalf of the Signoria or Ten to foreign individuals and states, to Florentine diplomats and private citizens abroad, to Florentine officials serving in the subject territories or to citizens resident there, to military captains in the service of the Florentine government, to Florentine military commissioners supervising the military captains, and to Florentine subjects and subject cities. Machiavelli also shared in the general administrative work of the chancery, for example, preparing lists of citizens for elections or nominations and minuting the meetings of consultative assemblies.

Machiavelli's duties went beyond these administrative tasks. Because the militia was chiefly his idea, he drafted the legislation by which it was instituted and, as chancellor to the Nine, worked as their general administrator, supervising the recruitment, training and deployment of troops. As secretary to the Ten, he became directly involved in Florentine diplomacy and military affairs and was employed as a negotiator, military supervisor, and diplomatic envoy with the title of *mandatario* (mandatory). In the latter capacity, although he sometimes accompanied formal ambassadors (a rank he never enjoyed because it was reserved to Florence's social elite, the *ottimati*) serving as their secretary, reporter, and assistant, he was also often sent on his own. In either case, he had major responsibilities as negotiator, bearer of secret communications to foreign lords, and intelligence gatherer. He undertook missions within the Florentine dominions and elsewhere in Italy, including the papal court, as well as to France and Germany, sending back to the Ten and the Signoria a stream of dispatches in which he reported information, conversations, and messages from rulers and influential foreigners. In all, he carried out more than forty such legations and commissions, more than twenty of major significance and a few lasting as long as six months. Modern editions of Machiavelli's instructions from, and dispatches to, the magistracies that assigned him these missions fill many volumes.[3]

Machiavelli's first important mission occurred in March 1499, when he was sent to negotiate the pay of Iacopo d'Appiano, lord of Piombino, one of Florence's mercenary captains. In July he was sent to Caterina Sforza, ruler of Imola and Forlì, to negotiate the continued service of her son Ottaviano Riario as a mercenary. In 1500 Florence secured the services of a French captain, Charles de Beaumont, to lead the assault on the rebel city of Pisa, and in early summer Machiavelli was sent as secretary to the two Florentine civilian commissioners who oversaw the campaign. He was subsequently dispatched, together with a commissioner, to answer French charges that the Pisan assault had failed owing to Florence's inadequate provisioning of the French troops. Machiavelli's first major diplomatic mission was to the French court, from July 1500 to January 1501, with the task of placating the French king Louis XII after the Pisan fiasco. Here Machiavelli met and had long discussions with leading players in French politics, most notably the king's first minister, the cardinal of Rouen, Georges d'Amboise (as Machiavelli would recall in chapter 3 of *The Prince*).

Later in 1501 Machiavelli was sent three times to attempt to pacify the subject city of Pistoia, which was riddled with factional conflict and thus tempting prey for enemy meddling. In 1502 came a second major diplomatic commission: to the son of Pope Alexander VI, Cesare Borgia, who was carving out a state for himself from territories nominally subject to the papacy in the Romagna. That summer, Cesare's lieutenants fomented rebellion in Florence's subject town of Arezzo, and Cesare requested a Florentine embassy to discuss the crisis. Florence sent Francesco Soderini, brother of Piero (not yet *gonfaloniere* [Standardbearer]), and Machiavelli. This was followed by a delicate and difficult mission to Cesare Borgia, from October 1502 to February 1503. Following the collapse of the Aretine rebellion, Cesare's lieutenants had conspired to strip him of power in the Romagna, and Borgia again requested a Florentine embassy. This time the Florentine government, eager to know more of his aims and strength but not to agree to his demand that Florence appoint him its military captain, sent only Machiavelli, who as a mandatory could negotiate, listen, and collect and report information, but not sign treaties. Machiavelli was on hand to witness the infamous murder of Ramiro de Lorqua, Borgia's chief agent in the pacification of the Romagna, whose mutilated body was displayed in the main piazza of Cesena on December 26, 1502 (an event dramatically described in *Prince* 7), and then the crushing of the conspirators, lured to their deaths at Senigallia on January 1, 1503 (also recalled in *Prince* 7). Shortly after this unforgettable legation, Machiavelli was sent to Pandolfo Petrucci, the Sienese despot and erstwhile ally of the conspirators, removed from power after Borgia's triumph over the conspiracy, but restored by Florence and King Louis in April 1503.

Machiavelli also witnessed Borgia's sudden and dramatic fall from power not long afterwards. In August 1503 both Cesare and Alexander fell ill; Cesare survived, but the pope, aged seventy-two, succumbed. The new pope, Pius III, died just two months later, and a crucial election loomed. Borgia, now restored to health and in Rome, still posed a threat to Florence, which sent Machiavelli to observe the papal conclave. Cardinal Giuliano della Rovere, supported by Borgia, who had considerable power within the College of Cardinals, was elected as Julius II on November 1, 1503. This was Borgia's greatest mistake, for Della Rovere had been forced into exile years before by Alexander and was determined to destroy Cesare. During tortuous negotiations regarding the restoration of Romagnol possessions to the papacy, Borgia was suddenly imprisoned by Julius. In his dispatches Machiavelli described in detail Borgia's staggering reversal of fortune and his betrayal by the wily pope.

Immediately after Machiavelli's return home, Florence was thrown into consternation by the defeat of its French allies by Spain at the battle of Garigliano on December 29. With the French now expelled from the south, Florence felt vulnerable to a Spanish march on Milan, and Machiavelli was dispatched to the French court to sound out Louis's resolve. The danger soon evaporated when a Franco–Spanish truce was signed on February 11, 1504. Florentine attention now turned again to the recapture of Pisa, and Machiavelli was sent a second time to Iacopo d'Appiano at Piombino in April 1504 to secure his support. Piero Soderini, head of the Florentine government since November 1502, was backing a scheme to divert the Arno River and deprive Pisa of access to the sea, and Machiavelli was sent to help execute what turned out to be a spectacular fiasco in the summer of 1504.

Pisa and military affairs continued to preoccupy the Florentines throughout 1505. Several families of Italian mercenaries, including the Vitelli of Città di Castello, who bore a special grudge against Florence for executing the condottiere (mercenary captain) Paolo Vitelli as a traitor in 1499, were in league against the Florentines, who also feared the defection of their military captain, Giampaolo Baglioni of Perugia. Machiavelli was sent to

Baglioni in April 1505 and concluded (correctly) that he was far from trustworthy. The following month he was dispatched to secure the services of an alternative captain, Francesco Gonzaga, marquis of Mantua, but the negotiations fell through. Soon afterwards Pandolfo Petrucci, frequently an enemy of Florence, began making unexpected noises about providing help for the recapture of Pisa; in July Machiavelli was sent to Siena to investigate, but the inscrutable Petrucci left him no wiser. That same summer the Florentines recommenced the assault on Pisa, and Machiavelli was again sent to the field of operations. Although Pisa's walls were breached, the campaign failed because the forces in Florence's employ refused to make a second assault.

Early in his chancery career, Machiavelli had been critical of Florence's reliance on mercenaries, and repeated military setbacks at Pisa fueled his disquiet. From at least 1503, he had been promoting the idea of a native militia, to be recruited from the subject territories, securing first the support of Cardinal Francesco Soderini and then that of his brother Piero. He worked out the structure of the new force in 1506, wrote the law instituting the militia in December, and supervised the recruitment, provisioning, and mustering of troops. In August 1506 Machiavelli was entrusted with a second mission to the papal court. Pope Julius led a small contingent to take Perugia and Bologna, cities nominally subject to the papacy but long ruled by independent lords. He requested help from mercenaries in Florence's employ, and Machiavelli was sent to negotiate. He was thus on the scene to witness the pope's incredible bravado in impetuously entering Perugia, at considerable risk to his life, and obtaining the submission of its ruler, Giampaolo Baglioni. Machiavelli followed Julius north into the Romagna but returned home just before the pope triumphantly entered Bologna, swept aside legalities and existing treaties, expelled the Bentivoglio lords, and reformed the city's government according to his demands.

In 1507 a new player entered the Italian theater, the German emperor Maximilian I, who had long pondered a march to Rome to receive the imperial crown from the pope and now revived plans for an Italian expedition. Julius dispatched a legation to Germany, and Florence sent Machiavelli to Siena to intercept the papal legate and sound out the pope's attitude towards Maximilian's possible descent into Italy. In these uncertain circumstances, Florence needed a representative at the imperial court. Soderini wanted to send Machiavelli, but the Standardbearer's opponents blocked the appointment and arranged to have the young *ottimate*, Francesco Vettori, sent instead. The legation to Germany became a heated partisan issue. Soderini supported the French alliance, but his *ottimati* enemies wanted a formal agreement with Maximilian and the appointment of fully accredited ambassadors, which would have undermined both Florence's alliance with France and Soderini himself. Soderini acquiesced in Vettori's appointment, but as mandatory, not ambassador, and at the end of 1507 Soderini succeeded in having Machiavelli sent as a second mandatory with supplementary instructions. Machiavelli's collaboration with Vettori at the imperial court was one of his longest missions, from December 1507 to June 1508, allowing him to observe the ineffectual Maximilian (whose incompetence he recalls in *Prince* 23) and also to acquire firsthand knowledge of Germany and Switzerland to complement the acquaintance with France already gained during his legation there in 1500.

The fall of Pisa in May 1509 was largely the result of the preoccupation of the major powers with the war of the League of Cambrai against Venice, depriving the Pisans of the foreign aid that had hitherto been their lifeline. Florentine military operations were nonetheless still needed, and from February to June Machiavelli was completely engrossed at the scene of the conflict, dealing with all aspects of the enterprise and supervising his militia's battalions. In March, he made brief trips to the nearby independent cities of Lucca and Piombino to sound out possible peace negotiations. After Pisa's surrender on 4 June, his friend and colleague Filippo Casavecchia wrote to Machiavelli: "I wish you a thousand benefits from the outstanding acquisition of that noble city, for truly it can be said that your person was cause of it to a very great extent."[4] This must have seemed to him, as it did to his friends, the high-water mark of his chancery career.

Late 1509 saw Machiavelli once more in a theater of military action, this time in northern Italy, as Venice began to recapture subject cities lost in the disastrous defeat inflicted by the League of Cambrai in May. Maximilian's arrival in Italy required Florence to pay him the funds promised (through Vettori and Machiavelli) the year before, and Machiavelli was dispatched to Mantua to make a partial payment and report on the war. He stayed for the rest of the year in the Veneto, where he had the opportunity to ponder Venice's recent military fiasco, Maximilian's failings as a military leader, and the structural flaws of the Holy Roman Empire.

The final years of Machiavelli's government service were shaped by Pope Julius's diplomatic revolution. The humiliation of Venice had removed a major threat to papal consolidation of the Romagna, but Julius was aggrieved by France's acquisition of former Venetian territories. The occasion for the pope's diplomatic realignment was a dispute over Ferrara, nominally subject to papal rule but at the moment a French dependency; Julius's ultimate aim was to expel the "barbarians" (i.e., the French) from Italy. For Machiavelli, this meant another French legation from June to October 1510. He found

Louis adamantly antipapal and insistent upon organizing a general council of the church in Pisa (now Florentine territory) to depose Julius, a venue that would compromise and possibly rupture Florentine–papal relations. Florence was becoming increasingly aware of its vulnerable position, tied to an alliance with France in the teeth of an impending anti-French league led by Julius. Therefore, on his return from France, Machiavelli set about raising a cavalry militia to complement the infantry force already in place. In early 1511 he inspected fortresses in Florentine territory and was sent again to Siena to renew the truce with Pandolfo Petrucci.

Machiavelli's last major diplomatic mission was again to the French court in September–October 1511. On the way he intercepted the pro-French cardinals in transit to the antipapal council and attempted to dissuade them from proceeding to Pisa. In Milan he pleaded with the French viceroy to change the council's location and then went to the court at Blois, where the king personally minimized the risk to Florence not only of the council but of war itself.[5] Even before Machiavelli returned home in November, Julius had promulgated the Holy League (the papacy, Spain, and Venice, with the Swiss in the background) against France in October. Although the French defeated the forces of the league at Ravenna on April 11, 1512, they were forced by Swiss attacks on French positions in Lombardy to withdraw from Italy that summer. Julius and the league, determined to punish Florence for not joining the war against France, sent a Spanish army into Tuscany to remove Soderini and restore the Medici. On August 29 the Spaniards inflicted a horrific sack on Prato; two days later Soderini went into exile. Giuliano de' Medici and his brother Cardinal Giovanni entered the city and on September 16 engineered a coup d'état supported by the Spanish army. Within weeks the new Medici regime dismantled the republican constitution and the militia, and on November 7 Machiavelli was dismissed from the chancery.

Machiavelli's mature writings, laden as they are with anecdotes, narratives, descriptions, and portraits of personalities taken directly from his diplomatic and military experience, testify to the profound impression that his chancery career made on his political thought and literary endeavors. Characteristic themes of his later analyses of politics and history are frequently first encountered in his voluminous official papers and correspondence. The secretary who advised his government in October 1502 to exaggerate the numbers of its troops to Cesare Borgia[6] later argued in *The Prince* that politics exists outside the ordinary rules of morality and that a liberal use of deception and bad faith can be justified, when needed, in a wicked political world. In November 1503 he wryly observed that Cesare Borgia, "believing the word of others to be more reliable than his own has been," allowed himself to be deceived by Julius II.[7] Of Julius he said in 1503, "we see that this pope is already paying his debts very honorably, and that he cancels them with the cotton of the inkstand."[8]

Machiavelli's comments on Cesare Borgia were not, of course, always negative. In *Prince* 26 he was evidently referring to Borgia in lamenting the lost opportunities in a man, unnamed, "in whom some spark seemed to show that he was ordained by God to redeem" Italy, but who was "rejected by fortune" at the height of his potential. As early as 1502 he had told his government that "anybody who examines the qualities of one side and the other recognizes this Lord as a man courageous, fortunate, and full of hope, favored by a pope and by a king."[9] After his first encounter with him he wrote:

> This lord is very proud [*splendido*] and fine [*magnifico*], and as a soldier is so enterprising [*animoso*] that nothing is so great that it does not seem small to him, and for the sake of glory and acquiring lands he does not rest, and acknowledges no fatigue or danger. He arrives at one place before he is known to have left the other; he endears himself to his soldiers; he has got hold of the best men in Italy, and these factors, together with continual good fortune, make him victorious and dangerous.[10]

On January 8, 1503, after Borgia defeated his former lieutenants' conspiracy, Machiavelli declared that he "exhibits a fortune unheard of, a courage and a confidence more than human that he can attain all his desires."[11]

Borgia provided the occasion for reflection on other themes that found a central place in Machiavelli's thought. The problems facing "new princes" and the necessity of force, so prominent in *The Prince*, received early expression when Machiavelli asserted, in a November 1502 dispatch, that "one should discuss [Borgia] as a new potentate in Italy, with whom it is more proper to make a league or an alliance than an agreement as general ... alliances between rulers are maintained with arms, and those alone are what keep them in force."[12] Elemental emotions were central to Machiavelli's view of human nature: hatred, as he wrote in *Prince* 19, had to be avoided at all costs, and he could not believe that Borgia would ever forget or forgive the betrayal of his rebellious lieutenants, despite their feigned reconciliation.[13] The fickle lady Fortune was a constant problem in Machiavelli's analysis of politics; in 1503, discussing Borgia's sudden fall, he wrote: "these blows from Fortune have stunned him, and since he is unaccustomed to receive them, his mind is confused."[14] In his dispatches Machiavelli denounced mercenaries and emphasized the need for states to have their own armies, just as he would in *The Prince*. In November 1502, he wrote that Borgia had learned that the way to keep his possessions was "to continue to be armed with his own arms";[15] he then offered his government the benefit of the same wisdom: "he who is armed well, and with his own arms, gets the same effects wherever he turns."[16]

By their very nature, however, Machiavelli's dispatches offered limited scope for prolonged reflection: intensely involved as he was in the nitty-gritty of diplomatic negotiations and military maneuvers, he had little time to indulge in lengthy theoretical or historical digressions, nor did his political superiors expect such lessons from him. He nonetheless managed to produce occasional memoranda to his government on political and military topics and reports following the conclusion of legations. These writings are often considered to offer the fullest picture of Machiavelli's early emergence as a political thinker and analyst, but the relation of at least some of them to the development of his thought is far from clear. A few are little more than casual, disorganized jottings; others were reworked over a considerable period of time, making it difficult to tie them to specific historical situations. Many are undated and have generated controversy with regard to chronology. Especially problematic are four texts: the "Description of the method used by Duke Valentino [Cesare Borgia] in killing Vitellozzo Vitelli, Oliverotto da Fermo, [and others]," "Words to be spoken on the law for raising money," "On the method of dealing with the rebels of the Valdichiana," and the "Portrait of German affairs,"[17] ostensibly among the most interesting and reflective, but which some believe were written years after his chancery career ended as drafts for inclusion in historical writings never realized. Telling here is their literary, rhetorical, generic style, more consistent with classicizing history than with the down-to-earth discourse of diplomatic dispatches or speeches made in Florentine assemblies; all four, moreover, have notable anachronisms, inconsistent with contemporaneous dating.

Other writings, which date securely from the chancery years, are less literary and reflect the intense but pragmatic character of Machiavelli's dispatches. Themes from his later works appear intermittently, but fleetingly, and are rarely developed at length. In the "Discourse on Pisa" (June 1499),[18] he argues that the rebellion can be overcome not by goodwill ("amore") but by force alone. In "The reason for the militia, from where it should be recruited, and what needs to be done," also known as the "Discourse on the organization of the Florentine state for arms" (September 1506), justifications for the militia are hurried over in a few sentences, forming a generic prologue to the real topic of the memorandum: the practicalities of why the militia should be recruited from the *contado* (countryside) and how to organize it. A passing allusion to the political uses of religion, later of great interest to Machiavelli, remains undeveloped: the constables need to "instill something of religion" into the troops "in order to enhance their obedience."[19] Similarly practical were his drafts of legislation concerning the militia: brief generic justificatory prologues, typical of Florentine legislation, followed by extensive administrative detail. Occasional significant passages appear in these military writings; for example, in the "Discourse on the mounted militia" (October/November 1510), responding to fears that a mounted militia from the countryside might not obey its commanders from the city, Machiavelli asserts that justice can make armies obedient and that those who worry about every potential problem will never undertake anything.[20]

More rewarding are Machiavelli's early writings on foreign powers: the "Discourse on peace between the emperor and the king [of France]," the "Report on German affairs," and the "Portrait of French affairs." Their purpose was to assess the power of transalpine nations and gauge their potential effectiveness in the Italian theater. These are the texts that exhibit the most direct continuity between Machiavelli's diplomatic experience and the first writings following his dismissal: the correspondence with Francesco Vettori in 1513 and *The Prince*, which are similarly preoccupied with the potentialities of foreign powers in Italy. The "Discourse on peace" (early 1501) is ostensibly the report of a comparison between Germany and France made by an anonymous French courtier. Some have hypothesized that the courtier was Florimond Robertet, Louis XII's secretary,[21] but it seems more likely that this is a fictitious dialogue, especially because the topics treated – centralization/decentralization of power, fiscal efficiency, military structure and effectiveness, and the economic advantages of native troops – are all central themes of Machiavelli's subsequent writings on France and Germany.

The "Report on German affairs" (not to be confused with the "Portrait of German affairs") was written in June 1508 after Machiavelli's return from the legation to Maximilian. Here Machiavelli went beyond conventional reporting to deal with Maximilian's fatal character flaws and weakness as a leader, the intractable disunity of the empire, and Germany's primitive and uncorrupted way of life.[22] The "Portrait of French affairs" similarly has the overall character of a report compiled following a diplomatic mission[23] and probably emerged from Machiavelli's last legation to France, in September–October 1511. Here he analyzes the power of the monarchy, France's military strength, natural resources, administrative and military organization, and the royal court; more peripheral is the discussion of the French character and way of life. In broadening the scope of political analysis to geography, economics, institutions, and military organization, this is the most wide-ranging treatment of a foreign state from Machiavelli's period in government, and it foreshadows the breadth of treatment that France would receive in *The Prince* and the *Discourses*. A few of Machiavelli's chancery memoranda thus show movement toward the reflective thinker of the mature works.

Machiavelli's private correspondence before 1513 is more limited: many more letters to him than from him survive, and his letters deal mainly with personal or specific political issues. There is one striking exception: his letter of September 1506[24] to Giovanbattista Soderini, nephew of Piero. It is the only letter to which a title ("Ghiribizzi": musings, fancies, caprices) has been given, and its remarkable contents justify this unique status. Machiavelli wrote it after witnessing Julius's risky but successful march into Perugia and was inspired to reflect on why different policies sometimes achieve the same result, on why the impetuous Julius was successful contrary to all rational expectations, on the possibilities and limits of human agency in affecting outcomes, and on the power of fortune as the consequence of the immutability of individual character in the face of changing times and circumstances. In the letter's comparison of the different methods of Hannibal and Scipio, we have Machiavelli's first reference to Roman history as an essential guide to understanding contemporary politics (if the "Valdichiana" memorandum, which contains a memorable passage about the Roman consul Camillus and translates a passage from Livy, is considered a later work). Julius's audacious seizure of Perugia stimulated Machiavelli to compose his first piece of profound theoretical reflection and remained vivid in his memory (he returned to the incident in *Discourses* 1.27). The mature political thinker emerges in the "Ghiribizzi."

Machiavelli wrote several substantial verse compositions in the all too infrequent moments of leisure in the chancery years. Indeed, he lamented that he had only fifteen days in 1504 to compose the 550 verses of the earliest of these poems, the first *Decennale* (*Decade*, or history of ten years).[25] (Sometime after 1512, Machiavelli began a second *Decennale* on the years 1504–14, but which he brought only to 1509.)[26] Encouraged by, and first dedicated to, Alamanno Salviati, the first *Decennale* recounts in *terza rima* (the interlacing rhyme scheme Dante used in the *Comedy*) the major events of Italian history since 1494. In 1506 Machiavelli's chancery colleague Agostino Vespucci had it published, and it was well received. Machiavelli sent a copy to Florence's captain general, Ercole Bentivoglio, who warmly praised the poem's "elegance" and concision. A pirated edition, whose sale Machiavelli's publisher managed to block, further suggests its popularity;[27] indeed, one or two other editions, corrected and approved by Machiavelli, followed shortly.

By contrast with the later *Discourses*, where Machiavelli argues that dissension and conflict could be signs of political vitality, in the *Decennale* he saw discord as a cause of Italy's and Florence's ills (vv. 16, 70, 155, 286–7). Conventional moral sentiments, quite unlike his later separation of politics and morality, are also in evidence: Florence was favored by right (v. 133); and Cesare Borgia met the fate merited by rebels against Christ (v. 513). This condemnation of Borgia was later reversed in *Prince* 7, where Cesare is proposed as the model new prince.[28] The portrait of Savonarola is more subtle and ironic than in the 1498 letter in which Machiavelli had openly referred to his "lies." Although the portrait in the *Decennale* is ostensibly positive – "I speak of that great Savonarola, who, inspired with heavenly vigor [*virtù divina*], kept you closely bound with his words" (vv. 154–9) – the friar is nonetheless seen as a source of discord and ruin. Florence had to choose between "increasing his divine light" or "extinguishing" it "with a greater fire" – a gruesome allusion to Savonarola's execution that suggests the firebrand got the fire he deserved. Here the positive aspects of Savonarola's political use of religion, evident in the *Discourses* (1.11), have not yet emerged. Nor has the later critique of Piero Soderini, seen in the *Discourses* as a weak and naively innocent leader (3.3 and 3.30),[29] but in the *Decennale* as (in a pun on his name) the "solid rock [*soda petra*]" of "your peace" (vv. 377–8) who deserved unquestioning allegiance (vv. 379–81), and as the state's "skillful steersman" (v. 547). The poem praises Florence's established leadership, not only Soderini but also the other Florentine political grandee explicitly alluded to: Alamanno Salviati, whom Machiavelli lauds (as Francesco Guicciardini also does in chapter 22 of his *Florentine Histories*) for rescuing the Florentine state from disaster in 1502 (vv. 357–72). In light of the growing rift between Salviati and Soderini in 1504, the first *Decennale* can be seen as a plea to Salviati (and other potential malcontents) to preserve the unity of the regime. The poem is intimately tied to the immediate political context: relief at Florence's liberation from the Medici, Savonarola, and the Borgias; and hope for the future with Soderini and the embryonic militia project: "the path would be easy and short if you reopened the temple of Mars" (v. 550).[30]

More indicative of the genesis of Machiavelli's mature political thought are his poems on fortune, ingratitude, and ambition.[31] The tercets on "Fortune" probably originated in proximity to the "Ghiribizzi" of September 1506: they share the same dedicatee and several common themes. The view that audacity and youth can overcome fortune, hinted at in the "Ghiribizzi," is further developed in "Fortune" with language strikingly similar to chapter 25 of *The Prince*. Just as the latter says that Fortune, being a woman and thus a friend of the young, can be controlled only by beating and pushing her around ("urtarla"), the poem similarly declares (vv. 75, 163–5) that "Audacity and Youth make highest showing" and that "we well realize how much he pleases Fortune and how acceptable he is who pushes her [*l'urta*], who shoves her, who jostles her." A key argument of the "Ghiribizzi" that Machiavelli will likewise elaborate in *Prince* 25 and also in *Discourses* 3.9 – that adaptability to the times and circumstances, the essential ingredient of success, is rendered impossible by the immutability of each man's nature and consequent inability to change his way of doing things – is already powerfully articulated in "Fortune":

> That man most luckily forms his plan, among all the persons in Fortune's palace, who chooses a wheel befitting her wish, since the inclinations that make you act, so far as they conform with her doings, are the causes of your good and your ill ... And since you cannot change your character nor give up the disposition that Heaven endows you with, in the midst of your journey she abandons you. Therefore, if this he understood and fixed in his mind, a man who could leap from wheel to wheel would always be happy and fortunate, but because to attain this is denied by the occult force that rules us, our condition changes with her course. (vv. 100–5, 112–20)

The tercets on "Ingratitude" seem to have been written after the failed attempt to send Machiavelli as mandatory to the imperial court in 1507. His frustration is vented in the poem's embittered outburst against the ingratitude shown by popular governments to their servants:

> [Ingratitude] triumphs in the heart of every ruler, but takes more delight in the heart of the populace when it is master ... because in the eyes of the crowd towns that are captured, blood that is shed and honored wounds are wiped from the record by the slightest censure for a tiny fault. (vv. 61–3, 145–7)

Ingratitude was a theme of the moment in 1506–7, when Ferdinand of Spain suddenly dismissed his victorious general and viceroy of Naples, Gonzalo de Córdoba. The episode, which Machiavelli would reprise with the same arguments in *Discourses* 1.29, is highlighted in "Ingratitude":

> The Apulian lands Gonsalvo has left forsaken and he lives under his king's suspicion as recompense for overthrowing the Gauls [the French]. Seek through all the world's wide spaces; you will find few grateful princes, if you read what is written of them; and you will see shifters of governments and givers of kingdoms with death or exile always repaid, because when you cause a government to shift, the prince you have made then fears your taking what you have bestowed and does not keep faith or compact with you, because more powerful is his dread of you than the obligation incurred, and for just so long this terror lasts as he requires to see your family destroyed, and the sepulchre of you and yours. (vv. 163–80)

Particularly arresting are the tercets on "Ambition," dedicated to Luigi Guicciardini and probably written in 1509. Here Machiavelli rehearses several important themes of his later political thought. The "effectual truth" of the political world that he seeks in *Prince* 15 is anticipated in his admonition to Guicciardini: "it does not seem to me that you take the world as it really is" (v. 3). The poem expresses the same conviction in the fundamental permanence of nature and history that the preface to book 1 of the *Discourses* will affirm: "and so always the world has been, modern and ancient" (vv.71–2). The insistence in *Prince* 17–18 on evil human nature receives these formulations in "Ambition":

> Meditate a little deeper on mortal craving; because from the sun of Scythia to that of Egypt, from Gibraltar to the opposite shore, we see the sprouting of this transgression. What province or what city escapes it? What village, what hovel? Everywhere Ambition and Avarice penetrate. (vv. 6–12)

> Oh human spirit insatiable, arrogant, crafty, and shifting, and above all else malignant, iniquitous, violent, and savage, because through your longing so ambitious, the first violent death was seen in the world, and the first grass red with blood! Since this evil seed is now mature, since evil's cause is multiplied, there is no reason for men to repent of doing evil. (vv. 55–63)

"Ambition" likewise anticipates the vital role of upbringing, or discipline (*educazione*), in the formation of national character and in political and military success, ideas Machiavelli will elaborate in *Discourses* 2.2 as the underlying cause of ancient military glory and modern weakness:

> Discipline can make up where Nature is lacking. This in times gone by made Italy flourish, and for conquering the world from end to end, stern discipline gave her daring.[32] (vv. 113–17)

Just before his removal from office, Machiavelli wrote a memorandum entirely different from all the other texts of his chancellorship. Datable between November 1 and 7, 1512, the "Memoir to the Mediceans" ("Ricordo ai palleschi") is the only piece of political writing by Machiavelli from the chancery years that addresses Florence's internal politics rather than foreign and military affairs.[33] In it he urges the restored Medici to place their trust not in the upper classes but in the people. This sudden shift of interest and focus bears witness to Machiavelli's desperation to impress Florence's new rulers. Yet, though fully aware that his close association with Piero Soderini and the fallen popular republic put him in extreme jeopardy, even at this proverbial eleventh hour Machiavelli did not tell the Medici what they wanted to hear: the "people" and their popular republic were anathema to Florence's new masters, who proceeded to dismantle all of its institutions, including the militia. The idea that a ruler should base his power on the people rather than the nobles became an important theme of *The Prince* as well. The "Memoir to the Mediceans" foreshadows the dilemma Machiavelli faced after his dismissal: although he needed the favor of the Medici if he were to regain any political role, his political inclinations were out of step with the regime they established in 1512.

NOTES

1. See his letter to Ricciardo Becchi, March 9, 1498: Niccolò Machiavelli, *Tutte le opere* (cited as *Opere*), ed. Mario Martelli (Florence: Sansoni, 1971), pp. 1010–12; James B. Atkinson and David Sices, ed. and trans., *Machiavelli and His Friends: Their Personal Correspondence* (Dekalb, Ill.: Northern Illinois University Press, 1996), pp. 10–12.
2. Piero Parenti, *Storia fiorentina*, ed. Andrea Matucci, vol. 2 (Florence: Olschki, 2005), p. 139.
3. *Legazioni, commissarie, scritti di governo* (cited as *Scritti di governo*), ed. Fredi Chiappelli and Jean-Jacques Marchand, 4 vols. (Bari: Laterza, 1971–85), up to 1505; *Legazioni, commissarie, scritti di governo*, general eds. Jean-Jacques Marchand and Denis Fachard (section 5 of the *Edizione nazionale delle opere di Niccolò Machiavelli*), 5 of projected 7 volumes published (Rome: Salerno Editrice, 2002–); Niccolò Machiavelli, *Legazioni e commissarie*, ed. Sergio Bertelli, 3 vols. (Milan: Feltrinelli, 1964). The 1502–3 legation to Borgia and the first (1503) and second (1506) legations to the papal court are in *Opere*, pp. 399–612. See also note 5 below.
4. *Opere*, p. 1108; *Correspondence*, p. 182.
5. *Le legazioni e commissarie di Niccolò Machiavelli*, vol. 4 (and vol. 6 of the *Opere di Niccolò Machiavelli*), ed. Luigi Passerini and Gaetano Milanesi (Florence and Rome, 1877), p. 166.
6. *Opere*, p. 415; *Scritti di governo*, 2:221. Allan Gilbert translated selections from the legations to Borgia in late 1502 and to the papal court in 1503 in *Machiavelli: The Chief Works and Others*, 3 vols. (Durham, N.C.: Duke University Press, 1958). This passage is in 1:127.
7. *Opere*, p. 508; *Scritti di governo*, 3:108; *Works*, 1:144.
8. *Opere*, p. 548; *Scritti di governo*, 3:194; *Works*, 1:157.
9. *Opere*, p. 427; *Scritti di governo*, 2:247; *Works*, 1:128.
10. *Scritti di governo*, 2:125; trans. John R. Hale, *Machiavelli and Renaissance Italy* (New York: Macmillan, 1960), p. 62.
11. *Opere*, p. 487; *Scritti di governo*, 2:383; *Works*, 1:142.
12. *Opere*, p. 441; *Scritti di governo*, 2:277; *Works*, 1:132.
13. *Opere*, p. 428; *Scritti di governo*, 2:247–8; *Works*, 1:128.
14. *Opere*, p. 523; *Scritti di governo*, 3:142; *Works*, 1:150.
15. *Opere*, p. 444; *Scritti di governo*, 2:286; *Works*, 1:133–4.
16. *Opere*, p. 456; *Scritti di governo*, 2:314; *Works*, 1:137.
17. They are published in several places: in the *Edizione nazionale delle opere di Niccolò Machiavelli. Sezione 1. Opere politiche*, vol. 3, *L'arte della guerra. Scritti*

politici minori, ed. Jean-Jacques Marchand, Denis Fachard and Giorgio Masi (Rome: Salerno Editrice, 2001), pp. 446–52, 460–5, 570–8, 597–606; in Jean-Jacques Marchand, *Niccolò Machiavelli. I primi scritti politici (1499–1512): nascita di un pensiero e di uno stile* (Padua: Antenore, 1975), pp. 420–6, 412–16, 427–31, 525–32; in *Opere*, pp. 8–16, 68–71; and in Sergio Bertelli, ed., *Arte della guerra e scritti politici minori* (Milan: Feltrinelli, 1961), pp. 41–8, 57–62, 71–5, 209–15. The first, second, and a fragment of the third are translated in *Works*, 1:163–9, 3:1439–43; 1:161–2.

18. *Opere*, p. 3; *Primi scritti*, pp. 403–4; *Edizione nazionale*, 1.3:422–4.
19. *Primi scritti*, pp. 432–7; *Opere*, pp. 37–40 (39); *Edizione nazionale*, 1.3:467–9.
20. *Primi scritti*, p. 487; *Edizione nazionale*, 1.3:521.
21. *Primi scritti*, pp. 405–8; *Edizione nazionale* 1.3:428 (text on pp. 429–34).
22. *Primi scritti*, pp. 462–81; *Opere*, pp. 63–8; *Edizione nazionale*, 1.3:496–508.
23. *Primi scritti*, pp. 507–24; *Opere*, pp. 55–63; *Edizione nazionale*, 1.3:546–66.
24. *Opere*, pp. 1082–3; *Correspondence*, pp. 134–6.
25. *Opere*, pp. 940–50; *Works*, 3:1444–57.
26. *Opere*, pp. 950–54; *Works*, 3:1457–62.
27. *Opere*, pp. 1072–75; *Correspondence*, pp. 118–19, 121–3.
28. See also Machiavelli's letter to Francesco Vettori, January 31, 1515: "Duke Valentino, whose deeds I should imitate on all occasions were I a new prince"; *Opere*, p. 1191; *Correspondence*, p. 313.
29. See also the epigram on Soderini, written after his death in 1522: "That night when Piero Soderini died, his spirit went up to the mouth of Hell. Pluto roared: 'Why to Hell? Silly spirit, go up into Limbo with all the rest of the babies'"; *Works*, p. 1463.
30. On the first *Decennale*, see Andrea Matucci, "Sul *Decennale* 1 di Niccolò Machiavelli," *Filologia e critica* 3 (1978): 297–327; Giorgio Inglese, "Contributo al testo critico dei 'Decennali' di Niccolò Machiavelli," *Annali dell'Istituto Italiano per gli Studi Storici* 8 (1983–4): 115–70; Anna Maria Cabrini, "Intorno al primo *Decennale*," *Rinascimento*, ser. 2, 33 (1993): 69–89; Emanuela Scarpa, "L'autografo del primo 'Decennale' di Niccolò Machiavelli," *Studi di filologia italiana* 51 (1993): 149–80.
31. *Opere*, pp. 976–87; *Works*, 2:735–49.
32. On these early poems, see the introduction to Niccolò Machiavelli, *I capitoli*, ed. Giorgio Inglese (Rome: Bulzoni, 1981); Andrea Matucci, "Le terze rime di Machiavelli," *Atti e memorie dell'Accademia Toscana di Scienze e Lettere La Colombaria* 47, n.s. 32 (1982): 91–182; and Carlo Dionisotti, "I capitoli di Machiavelli," in Dionisotti, *Machiavellerie* (Turin: Einaudi, 1980), pp. 61–99.
33. *Opere*, pp. 16–17; *Primi scritti*, pp. 533–5; *Edizione nazionale*, 1.3:582–4.

FURTHER READING

Bausi, Francesco. *Machiavelli*. Rome, Salerno Editrice, 2005.
Black, Robert. *Benedetto Accolti and the Florentine Renaissance*. Cambridge University Press, 1985.
  "Florentine Political Traditions and Machiavelli's Election to the Chancery," *Italian Studies* 40 (1985): 1–16.

"Machiavelli, Servant of the Florentine Republic," in *Machiavelli and Republicanism*, ed. Gisela Bock, Quentin Skinner, and Maurizio Viroli. Cambridge University Press, 1990, pp. 71–99.

Brown, Alison. *Bartolomeo Scala, 1430–1497, Chancellor of Florence: The Humanist as Bureaucrat*. Princeton University Press, 1979.

Devonshire Jones, Rosemary. "Some Observations on the Relations between Francesco Vettori and Niccolò Machiavelli during the Embassy to Maximilian I," *Italian Studies* 23 (1968): 93–113.

Guidi, Andrea. *Un Segretario militante: politica, diplomazia e armi nel Cancelliere Machiavelli*. Bologna, Il Mulino, 2009.

Marchand, Jean-Jacques, ed. *Machiavelli senza i Medici (1498–1512). Scrittura del potere/potere della scrittura*. Rome, Salerno Editrice, 2006.

Najemy, John M. "The Controversy surrounding Machiavelli's Service to the Republic," in *Machiavelli and Republicanism*, pp. 101–17.

Richardson, Brian. "Per la datazione del *Tradimento del duca Valentino* del Machiavelli," *La bibliofilia* 81 (1979): 75–85.

Rubinstein, Nicolai. "The Beginnings of Niccolò Machiavelli's Career in the Florentine Chancery," *Italian Studies* 11 (1956): 72–91.

"Machiavelli and the World of Florentine Politics," in *Studies on Machiavelli*, ed. Myron Gilmore. Florence, Sansoni, 1972, pp. 5–28.

3

ROSLYN PESMAN

Machiavelli, Piero Soderini, and the republic of 1494–1512

In the dedications to both *The Prince* and the *Discourses*, Machiavelli asserted that he had acquired his understanding of politics through lengthy experience of the contemporary world and continual reading of ancient texts. His fourteen-year career in the Florentine chancery placed him at the hub of government and politics and afforded him manifold opportunities, whether at his desk in Florence or as an emissary abroad, to observe and experience at close hand the problems of Florentine politics and territorial administration and European diplomacy and statecraft, problems on which he meditated and began to write during his career in government. Machiavelli's participation in the political world came to an abrupt end in 1512, when a successful coup against Piero Soderini, the elected permanent head of Florentine government, caused the collapse of the republic, the restoration of a generally unpopular Medici regime, and Machiavelli's dismissal from his posts and banishment from political action. The coup and his fate gave Machiavelli the time to write more discursively about his understanding of political affairs from a perspective sharpened by the failure of the regime and personal loss. Among the issues that preoccupied Machiavelli in the major works of his enforced retirement were military strength and force, political stability, and leadership, or rather their reverse: the military weakness, instability, inadequate justice, factionalism, and absence of leadership that dogged the Florentine Republic for much of his time in the chancery.

In November 1494, Piero de' Medici's mishandling of the arrival in Tuscany of Charles VIII and the French army created the space for the expression of aspirations for a share in government long held in check by the ever-narrowing Medici regime, and for ambitions, rivalries, and frustrations within the Medici party to come to the surface. The immediate power vacuum also allowed free range to the prophetic preaching of the Dominican friar Girolamo Savonarola, who exhorted the Florentines to create God's kingdom on earth and to institute a broadly based republican government as the first step toward that goal. The outcome of the revolt against the Medici was the popular government (*governo popolare*) centered on the Great Council, which became both the final legislature and the candidature and electorate for filling the short-term offices that were the norm in Florence. Membership in the Council was permanent and virtually hereditary, since it depended on the political eligibility of a citizen's forebears in the fifteenth century. But, as some recent studies have pointed out, this continuity should not obscure the revolutionary changes that came with the establishment of the Council,[1] which conferred an equal voice in legislation, including laws on taxation and eligibility for offices (both the governing magistracies and the salaried positions in the administration), on some three and a half thousand citizens divided by wealth, social standing, age, political experience, abilities, and ambitions.

With the introduction of the *governo popolare*, the control and astute apportionment of offices practiced by the Medici were replaced by an open and intense competition for place and power. Contemporary witnesses represented these struggles as the confrontation of two social groups: the rank and file of the political class known as the *popolo, moltitudine,* or *universale*; and the men of wealth, high family status, and extensive connections who were accustomed to occupying the seats of authority and were variously termed the *primi cittadini, ottimati, uomini da bene,* or *grandi*. Those modern historians whose working model presents Florentine politics as operating through bonds of family, friendship, marriage, and neighborhood have viewed this competition as taking place among fluctuating alliances that crossed social lines and were held together by ties of patronage and clientage, mutual interest, and religious alignments. Strongest in the early years were the *frateschi*, the followers of the friar (*frate*) Savonarola and his religious-political vision, who came from all classes and included many citizens from elite families. But the social division between *ottimati* and *popolo* and the political force represented by the aspirations of the latter should not be underestimated.

What the constitutional reforms of 1494 did not provide was a permanent institutional place for the elite, a counterpart to the Medicean Council of Seventy. A smaller council, the Eighty, was established in 1494 as an institution of review and advice, but it was nothing like the Seventy since its membership changed every six months and its powers were limited. Over the next eighteen years, the chief goal of many (though not all) of Florence's *ottimati* was to transfer much of the power of the Great Council to a smaller oligarchic council, a goal they failed to achieve not only because of opposition from the Council's rank and file but also because the *ottimati* themselves were divided by rivalries and differing views concerning the size, membership and powers of the projected aristocratic council. Champions of aristocratic government insisted that short-term executive offices and the absence of a smaller council with permanent or long-term membership made it difficult to achieve continuity and stability in government policy, and they could thus claim that what they wanted was also better government. Machiavelli was later to identify the failure to provide a permanent and powerful institutional place for the ambitious elite as a fatal weakness of the republican regime.

From its inception, the new regime was threatened by internal dissension, external pressures, and unrest in the dominion. A crisis point was reached in the years 1500–2 with repeated failures to recapture Pisa (which had taken advantage of the French invasion in 1494 to regain its independence), the threatening presence of Cesare Borgia on the state's borders, inability to control civil war in Pistoia, and, in the summer of 1502, rebellion in Arezzo and the Valdichiana. Government was virtually paralyzed by the failure to secure the passage of financial bills in the Great Council in an environment of general complaint about corruption in the administration of finance and justice and suspicions within the *popolo* that *ottimati* were plotting to overthrow the regime. In the first *Decennale* (1504), Machiavelli portrayed these years as a sad story of Florentine defeats, retreats, appeasement, and humiliations, disasters he angrily attributed to military weakness, "confusion" and "disunion," and a government that "did not know how to make decisions" and conducted affairs "haphazardly."[2]

Florence's parlous situation in the summer of 1502 made constitutional reform a live issue. A number of reform projects were discussed in the consultative meetings (*pratiche*) of the Signoria, focusing on the introduction of a new and smaller council of *ottimati*. In the event, the proposal that was unexpectedly successful in the Great Council was not for such a council, but for lifetime tenure for the Standardbearer (*gonfaloniere*) of Justice, the titular head of state and presiding officer of the Signoria. This was a solution to the problem of continuity and direction in government that in no way reduced the powers of the Great Council and was therefore acceptable to its rank and file membership. The prominence of leading Savonarolans among the reform's sponsors suggests that it may have had its origins in *frateschi* circles, and there is some evidence that Savonarola himself had advocated a *gonfaloniere* for life.[3] To assuage fears of tyranny and forestall its imposition, procedures for dismissal in the event the *gonfaloniere* exceeded his powers were included in the law establishing the office.

In September 1502, the Great Council elected as the republic's first *gonfaloniere a vita* Piero Soderini, a member of a powerful elite family, whose father, Tommaso, had been a leading figure in the Medici regime. Although he had considerable experience in government and diplomacy, Piero's religious and political alignments were not clear. Unlike his older brother,

Paolantonio, who was a prominent *fratesco*, Piero was not identified with the Savonarolans and was not their candidate. He may have kept his distance from the friar as part of a family strategy to ensure political survival in all circumstances, a common practice in the faction-ridden Florentine political world. He was known as a man of deep personal piety and upright life, and his policy of broad consultation during an earlier two-month term as Standardbearer of Justice gave him a reputation for loyalty to the *governo popolare* that was no doubt crucial to his election. According to Francesco Guicciardini, moderate *ottimati* like Alamanno Salviati (to whom Guicciardini was politically close, having married Salviati's daughter) backed Soderini's candidacy believing he would sponsor the reforms they wanted, in particular the smaller aristocratic council.[4] When it became clear that he had no intention of doing so, *ottimati* hostility to the *gonfaloniere* became a prime fact of political life until 1512.

From his first days, Soderini's chief goals and commitments were clear and did not waver: financial and judicial reform; a system of taxation acceptable to the Great Council and capable of generating sufficient revenue; and the recapture of Pisa. In foreign policy, Soderini believed that Florence's security was best protected by unswerving loyalty to France. In 1506–7 *ottimati* hostile to Soderini tried to undermine him by advocating a turn away from France and accommodation with the Emperor Maximilian. Soderini's refusal to countenance such a policy shift appeared vindicated when Maximilian's descent into Italy was stopped by Venice in February 1508. Until 1511–12 Soderini's pro-French stance served the republic well. Successes were few in the early years but increased over time, particularly with the victory over Pisa in 1509, achieved in part by the militia force promoted and organized by Machiavelli. In permitting the creation of the militia, Soderini took a small but significant step toward reducing Florence's dependence on mercenaries. One area in which little improvement occurred, despite major reforms, was the criminal justice system. Among the justifications for lifetime tenure in the office of the *gonfaloniere* was that, since its holder would not return to private life and would thus not have to fear retaliation, the weight of his authority in judicial proceedings would encourage the courts to apply penalties as prescribed by the laws.[5] So he was given the constitutional prerogative to intervene and vote in all criminal cases. But Soderini did not avail himself of this right and was blamed when certain *ottimati* continued to influence judicial decisions and manipulate the courts.

By the end of his first year in office, it was obvious that Soderini would not sponsor the institution of a smaller council or otherwise privilege consultation with the *ottimati* in governing. By law, the Signoria was required to summon the Eighty at least once a week. Soderini not only held these mandatory consultations but also sought on many occasions to explain and justify government policy and obtain wide consensus for decisions in meetings of the Eighty expanded to include additional invited citizens. When the councils refused to approve tax bills, Soderini demanded that they present their own solutions and protested their evasion of responsibility in referring issues back to the Signoria. In the dramatic circumstances of a plot against his life in 1510, he reminded the members of the Great Council that they were "the lords and protectors of the government" and that if they did not take responsibility they would lose it.[6]

Opposition to Soderini's leadership from the ranks of the *ottimati* was intense from the outset. Even if not all *ottimati* were hostile and the opposition was more divided and flexible than Guicciardini implies, the *gonfaloniere* had powerful critics and dangerous enemies. It had its sources in varying degrees of dissatisfaction with the *governo popolare* and anger over Soderini's failure to introduce a more oligarchic element into government, and also in policy differences, personal enmities, and the frustration of *ottimati* envious of his status and power. Moderate *ottimati* such as the Salviati cousins and Giovanbattista Ridolfi acted as a kind of "constitutional" opposition, criticizing Soderini when they held office or spoke in the large consultative forums over which he presided or in the smaller gatherings summoned by the Ten of War, the office responsible for foreign policy. Soderini's critics did not oppose him on everything, and alignments and opinions often changed. While it seemed unlikely (at least until the 1510 attempt on his life) that they would act illegally or violently to remove him, most *ottimati* had little interest in supporting him or keeping him in office and did not conceal their hope that his departure by one means or another might provide the long-sought opportunity to eliminate the Great Council and institute an oligarchy.

Particularly dangerous to Soderini were the Mediceans. Although few citizens wanted the return of the Medici, the family was always a resource for internal and external enemies of the popular government. Some of the more hostile *ottimati*, including Bernardo Rucellai (who had married a sister of the elder Lorenzo de' Medici) and others who believed they could gain advantage from the Medici, turned to the obliging and influential Cardinal Giovanni de' Medici in Rome. Also gravitating to the Medici were the raucous, fast-living younger *ottimati*, who were held responsible for much of the trouble in the city and were accustomed to living not according "to a civic order but as they saw fit and as their whims dictated."[7] Although penalties for consorting with the Medici had been laid down in 1497 after an attempted coup by the exiled Piero and his friends within the city, Soderini was reluctant to take punitive action against citizens in contact with the rebel family, in part because the Medici still had ties to many *ottimati* families. The impunity with which some opponents of the popular government cultivated these ties must have encouraged others to follow suit, if only as insurance in the event of a Medici restoration.

Machiavelli later wrote in the *Discourses* (1.52) that Soderini acquired much of his reputation by favoring the "universale," the rank and file of the Great Council. Guicciardini's way of putting it was that Soderini governed with "men of lesser brain and quality" and ignored the advice of his fellow *ottimati* in order to enhance his authority.[8] This is no doubt partly true, as there is a whiff of demagogy in accounts of Soderini's speeches to the councils. Cultivation of the *popolo* was one way to increase personal power in Florence, and it has even been argued that Soderini was attempting to establish personal lordship.[9] In the considerable debate over Soderini's ambitions, much depends on what is meant by personal lordship. He certainly exploited all the authority of his position to tackle the problems of the republic and deployed a variety of means, including the skillful outmaneuvering of opposition and manipulation of emotion in the councils, to secure the implementation of measures he favored. He also engaged in a degree of personal diplomacy in efforts to regain Pisa and hold Florence to the French alliance. But another of the justifications for the establishment of his office was precisely the need for a guiding hand and greater continuity in the conduct of foreign affairs.

Soderini was determined to exercise and defend his office, but it has yet to be shown that he overreached its powers or attempted to manipulate electoral procedures. When, as happened often, he encountered opposition to his proposals in the councils, he accepted that there was little he could do if they were rejected. Machiavelli later argued (again in *Discourses* 1.52) that Soderini refused to conciliate his enemies with favors and did not build a retinue of supporters in the manner of the Medici, because this would have meant destroying the liberty over which he had been set as guardian. This was a mistake, Machiavelli says, and it caused Soderini's downfall, but it was an error for which he deserves to be excused because he could not have honorably adopted such methods. Other contemporaries also described Soderini as cautious and circumspect, and he appears to have been acutely aware of the delicacy of his position, the limits of his authority, and the dangers to himself and his office of any attempt to exceed his legal powers. In 1510, he presented a defense of his government to the Great Council, justifying his decision not to intervene in judicial proceedings with the argument that it would have brought down on himself the hatred of all citizens and rendered his office untenable; once a *gonfaloniere a vita* "has the blood of citizens on his hands," he argued, the way was open to tyranny.[10] Rather than seeking personal lordship, Soderini used his power, no doubt on occasion with high-handed tactics, to preserve the *governo popolare* that had conferred on him the honor of permanent headship.

The Great Council had been central to Savonarola's political vision, and Soderini was in many ways Savonarola's political heir, especially as the *frateschi*, who remained a powerful presence in Florentine politics, were among his staunchest supporters. Not all *ottimati* associated with Savonarola supported Soderini, but the latter's most committed allies came from their ranks. Crucial reforms undertaken by Soderini, such as the introduction of the militia and the new court of appeal, the Quarantia, had Savonarolan associations, as did other laws including sumptuary regulations of the dress of young men and women, limitations on dowries, and tougher penalties for gambling, swearing, and sodomy. These latter measures made enemies of aristocratic young bloods in the city, and the band of pro-Medici young men who stormed the palace of the priors in August 1512 to force Soderini's removal also demanded the revocation of the sentences against persons exiled or deprived of office for sodomy.[11] Soderini's reforms, which appealed to the still vital Florentine traditions of religion and good customs, met with favor among both Savonarola's followers and the rank and file of the Great Council.

Those who have argued that Soderini was bent on establishing personal lordship see Machiavelli as part of a courtier-like group around the *gonfaloniere* and even as his agent or abettor.[12] Starkly different is the view that presents Machiavelli as the neutral public servant loyal to the regime, who steered clear of party politics.[13] The divergence of opinion is made possible in part by a lack of solid evidence. Soderini and Machiavelli must have been in almost daily contact, but we are not privy to their conversations. Before 1512, Machiavelli confined public expression of his political views to foreign and territorial affairs, and his only public comment on Soderini is in the first *Decennale*, where he is referred to (with a play on his name) as the "solid rock [*soda petra*]" on which the Florentines could erect their peace and as the "skillful steersman" of the Florentine ship of state.[14] Ten not particularly informative letters from Soderini to Machiavelli have survived, mostly from the years 1502–3. Interpretations of the relationship between Soderini and the secretary are thus dependent on Machiavelli's later writings (including his claim that he was the tireless and faithful servant of the republic), on comments by contemporaries (particularly Guicciardini and the historian Bartolomeo Cerretani), and on the letters Machiavelli received from Soderini's influential brother Francesco, bishop and soon-to-be cardinal of Volterra.

Piero Soderini's prominent role in foreign affairs and diplomacy before 1502 meant that he and Machiavelli were certainly acquainted from the secretary's early days in office. Soderini's earliest surviving letter to Machiavelli (and Francesco della Casa) is from September 1500, when Machiavelli was serving (with Della Casa) as Florentine envoy to the French court. In the months following his election in 1502, Soderini wrote no fewer than six times to Machiavelli, then in Imola as envoy to Cesare Borgia, in friendly terms giving news and addressing him once (in Latin) as "amice carissime" and twice as "Niccolò carissimo."[15] In September 1502, Francesco Soderini replied to Machiavelli's (now lost) letter of congratulation on Piero's election, expressing gratitude for his "affection for … our family" and assuring him that, as he was "second to none in ability and affection," he would be all the "dearer and more welcome" to the Soderini.[16] Machiavelli and Francesco Soderini had served together as envoys to Borgia earlier that year and were again to collaborate on a mission to the papal court in 1503, and it may have been there that they discussed the idea of the militia. Francesco became an enthusiastic political patron of the militia, which he described in a 1506 letter to Machiavelli as corresponding "to our hope for the welfare and dignity of our country."[17] The relationship between the two men appears to have been close and based on mutual respect, common political interests, and shared views on the realities of the political world. In his 1503 memorandum concerning the rebellion in the Valdichiana, Machiavelli reported, with evident agreement, that he had heard the cardinal argue that among the things for which Pope Alexander and his son Cesare Borgia might be praised was their capacity to recognize opportunities and exploit them well.[18]

Although Machiavelli had often served as an envoy in the four years before Piero Soderini's election, his frequent employment in this capacity after 1502 was sometimes viewed with suspicion because the *gonfaloniere* so openly favored his appointment. Guicciardini and Cerretani both recount the opposition to Soderini's plan to send Machiavelli to the imperial court in 1507, when the emperor's proclaimed intention to enter Italy presented a potential threat to Soderini's adherence to France. *Ottimati* opposed to Soderini's pro-French policy blocked the appointment and had Machiavelli replaced by Francesco Vettori, but Soderini eventually succeeded in having Machiavelli join Vettori with new instructions in January 1508.[19] The Pisan ambassador to Maximilian described Machiavelli as Soderini's agent and reported that one purpose of the mission was to offer Maximilian 40,000 ducats in return for imperial confirmation of Soderini's office and the conferral of an imperial vicariate. This has been seen by some as a major step in Soderini's pursuit of personal lordship. But the ambassador's report, even if true, needs to be placed in context.[20] Among the conditions of the 1509 agreement that Florence eventually signed with the emperor was the preservation of "this present state and dominion." In August 1512 the offer of a subsidy to the Spanish viceroy was similarly dependent on a guarantee of the preservation of "the present government, Council and *gonfaloniere*."[21] It therefore seems plausible that this was also part of Machiavelli's brief in 1508. In an environment in which foreign powers were not averse to exploiting divisions in Florence for their own ends, Soderini's request for confirmation of his position as head of Florentine government does not require sinister explanations. Moreover, a close analysis of Vettori's and Machiavelli's dispatches from the imperial court has also refuted Cerretani's accusation that Soderini sent Machiavelli as his "lackey" to spy on Vettori and ensure that the latter's reports would not threaten the French alliance.[22] Any preference Soderini may have shown for Machiavelli's selection for such missions appears to have been founded on confidence in a trusted and very able civil servant, not on any ulterior motives or designs. In June 1510, when Machiavelli was at the French court with instructions from both Piero and Francesco Soderini in the particularly threatening circumstances of the breakdown of relations between Pope Julius and Louis XII of France, Francesco wrote to his "compatri nostro carissimo" and told him that "in respect to both public and personal feelings, the decision to send you there was very pleasing to us, knowing your skill and prudence, and how useful you can be in all matters."[23]

As to whether this trust and appreciation gave Machiavelli exceptional opportunities to influence government policy, the temptation is always to attribute a variety of initiatives to the better-known secretary famed for his ingenuity. Did the idea of diverting the Arno away from Pisa in 1504 lie with Machiavelli, Leonardo da Vinci, or Soderini? Cardinal Soderini wrote to Machiavelli expressing his commiseration on the failure of the Arno scheme,[24] thus implying that Machiavelli was somehow involved, but no evidence connects him to its origins. Who chose the Florentine victories at Anghiari and Cascina as the subjects for Leonardo's and Michelangelo's murals on the walls of the meeting hall of the Great Council? Given the timing, the murals may have been part of a campaign to gain acceptance of the militia project and encourage Florentine pride in military prowess, but Machiavelli's involvement has never been conclusively demonstrated.[25]

The militia was certainly Machiavelli's project, and he had to persuade a supportive but hesitant *gonfaloniere* who worried about *ottimati* opposition. Fear of both tyranny and the lower classes made arming the city population unthinkable for many *ottimati*, and to assuage their fears the militia was limited to peasants from the surrounding *contado*. Rumors persisted that Soderini might use the militia as a personal force, and it became even more controversial when Don Michele di Coriglia, the ruthless former henchman of Cesare Borgia, was hired to train the soldiers. While it has generally been assumed that Don Michele was Machiavelli's choice, it seems more likely that Francesco Soderini, who concurred with Machiavelli on the need for discipline, was his sponsor. Moreover, it is difficult to envisage how the *gonfaloniere* could ever have taken control of the militia. As Machiavelli himself recommended in his 1506 "Discourse on the organization of the Florentine state for arms," and as the legislation establishing the militia (drafted by Machiavelli) specified, it was to prevent such misuse of the militia that it was placed under the Ten in wartime and in peacetime under a new civilian committee, the Nine, elected for eight-month terms.[26] Critics as well as supporters of Soderini were elected to the Nine.

Machiavelli's later analysis of the republic's deficiencies included the criminal justice system, whose reform he may have influenced. In the "Discourse" outlining the militia project, he peremptorily scolded the government for lacking the twin foundations of any state: "Of justice you have very little and of arms none at all."[27] The 1502 judicial reform introduced a new ad hoc court of appeal, the Quarantia, composed of representatives of the Signoria and its advisory colleges and from twenty to forty citizens drawn from the Council of Eighty. Cases not settled by the internal security and judicial magistracies of the Eight of Ward or the Conservators of the Laws could be referred to the new court. The reasoning behind the reform was that a court of many citizens would be less open to manipulation by the powerful and the play of factional influence.

In 1510 Soderini introduced a proposal that would have strengthened his hand against opponents who colluded with the Medici by extending the Quarantia's competence to cover crimes against the state (*casi di stato*). Rumor had it that the bill had been prepared two years earlier when Filippo Strozzi violated laws against association with the Medici by agreeing to marry Piero de' Medici's daughter, Clarice. Cerretani names Machiavelli among those who drafted the bill.[28] It is possible that Cerretani's information was inaccurate or that Machiavelli's role was only part of his normal duties, but the bill and the issues it addressed are clearly echoed in *Discourses* 1.7, where Machiavelli argues that the laws of a well-ordered republic should include the means to indict citizens who commit offenses "against free government [*contro allo stato libero*]." He also insists that a court of eight citizens is not enough: "it is essential that the judges be many, because a few always act in the normal method of a few." Machiavelli would make the same arguments in his 1520 *Discourse on Florentine Affairs after the Death of the Younger Lorenzo*, written at the behest of Cardinal Giulio de' Medici.[29] If Machiavelli in any way counseled Soderini to deter those who were plotting his destruction, such advice evidently focused on legal procedures and penalties. In any event, the bill failed in the Council, and Cerretani remarked that wise citizens knew that the *popolo* had lost the state.[30] Machiavelli may well have agreed.

Machiavelli's chancery career was therefore not quite normal, both because Soderini often favored him for sensitive diplomatic missions and because Machiavelli sometimes enjoyed a degree of influence not usually allowed to secretaries and chancellors. Machiavelli's closest friends and correspondents among the *ottimati* were for the most part committed supporters of Soderini. But what they shared was not so much personal attachment to Soderini as loyalty to the *governo popolare* and hence to its elected head. This may also have been the essence of Machiavelli's relationship to Soderini. In 1513, after the collapse of the republic, Francesco Vettori tried to persuade Machiavelli that, since he (Machiavelli) had never received favors or rewards from Soderini or his family, he should not feel obliged to visit them if he went to Rome.[31] That Vettori had to impress this on Machiavelli suggests that the former secretary did indeed feel some obligation. Machiavelli had earlier tried to extend his support network beyond the Soderini circle to include some of the *gonfaloniere*'s moderate opponents, including the Salviati cousins.[32] In their case he failed, but his friendship with Vettori endured beyond the fall of the republic and produced their famous correspondence.

Also unusual for a chancery official was the extent of criticism and hostility that Machiavelli aroused. In 1509, following attempts to remove him from office, Machiavelli's chancery assistant Biagio Buonaccorsi informed him that "your adversaries are numerous and will stop at nothing." Indeed, in the next two years Machiavelli was the target of two anonymous, albeit unsuccessful, denunciations to the Eight of Ward.[33] To the many *ottimati* whose advice Soderini ignored, the *gonfaloniere*'s perceived preference for a man of lower status like Machiavelli for diplomatic missions and his at least rumored role in attempts to strengthen the regime's ability to deal with its enemies must have been particularly galling, the more so when the civil servant was prone to voice his opinions with an edge of contempt for the social superiors whom he often saw as blind to the needs of the republic. Once Soderini was gone, Machiavelli was at the mercy of his and the *gonfaloniere*'s enemies. In a memorandum to Cardinal Giovanni de' Medici at the time of his dismissal, Machiavelli vented his hatred for the *ottimati* enemies of the popular government and warned the Medici of the danger they faced from powerful citizens bent on constructing their own oligarchy.[34]

If the attempt on Soderini's life in 1510 was a warning of the extreme measures that some opponents contemplated, his government nonetheless seemed secure and the majority of the Great Council satisfied with his leadership. But in the summer of 1512, French power in Italy collapsed, leaving Florence dangerously exposed to the vengeance of Pope Julius and his allies in the Holy League. To punish the republic for its continuing refusal to repudiate the French alliance, the league sent a Spanish army to Florence in August with demands that included Soderini's removal. At the pope's behest, the terms for peace also required the return of the Medici, ostensibly as private citizens. Acting in his customary manner, Soderini formulated responses to the league's demands, according to Machiavelli's own account, in consultation with "the multitude."[35] A large majority were not prepared, even after the Spaniards sacked Prato, to countenance the removal of the *gonfaloniere*, and although the Spanish viceroy still insisted on the repatriation of the Medici, he ultimately agreed to Soderini's continuation in office. Perhaps fearing that the viceroy and his army might depart leaving the *gonfaloniere* in place, the young pro-Medici conspirators confronted, threatened, and forced Soderini into exile.

The man who faced the conspirators was sixty years old, unwell, worn down by ten years in office, and described by critics like Guicciardini as increasingly irresolute and incapable of action in those last days. But Machiavelli's account of Soderini's reply to the demands for his resignation suggests a stance of some courage and dignity: he had come to his office, he said, neither by force nor by fraud but at the behest of the people, and he would leave only, and then willingly, if the people so wished. After Prato was sacked and fear mounted of an attack on Florence itself, there was little he could do. He had never been prepared to engage in a show of force with his internal enemies and sought above all to avoid violence and bloodshed in the city. On the road to exile, he wrote to his wife that his only wish for the future was to live a private life of peace and quiet.[36]

Departure from the political world was certainly not Machiavelli's wish, but it was his fate as a result of Soderini's overthrow. They were together in the last days of the republic, and one can only wonder what advice the secretary might have given Soderini. He had plenty to say once he himself was also in the political wilderness. In the *Discourses* Machiavelli analyzed the reasons for Soderini's overthrow in both constitutional and personal terms. The fatal flaw of the *governo popolare* was that it lacked the institutional means to indict citizens who "in any way sin against free government" and to "bring charges against the ambition of powerful citizens" (1.7). "If such methods had existed," those who criticized Soderini's conduct could have indicted him and found an outlet for their animosity "without bringing in the Spanish army"; if his conduct was blameless, his enemies would have been reluctant to accuse him for fear of being indicted themselves.[37]

More dramatic in the *Discourses* is Soderini's role as an exemplum of the dire results of the failure "to kill the sons of Brutus," to destroy the allies of the previous regime, the enemies of the present one, and those whom envy provoked to opposition and conspiracy (*Discourses* 3.3 and 3.30). According to Machiavelli, Soderini failed to make bold moves against his enemies because he believed that to do so would have meant going outside the law; even if such actions did not involve violence, the people would have been so alarmed that they would never have permitted another *gonfaloniere a vita*. The reasoning Machiavelli attributes to Soderini in the *Discourses* is thus quite similar to the terms in which the *gonfaloniere* himself justified his refusal to exercise his constitutional right to intervene in judicial proceedings. Machiavelli also saw Soderini's reluctance to act as a reflection of his character and his conviction that, with patience and righteous and correct governance, he could extinguish his enemies' envy and desire to overthrow him. But he nonetheless criticized Soderini's failure to act more forcefully against those enemies on the grounds that an evil should never be allowed to continue out of respect for a good when that good can easily be overwhelmed by the evil: as a result, he lost, "together with his native city, his position and his reputation" (*Discourses* 3.3).[38] Machiavelli makes another reference to Soderini's goodness and forbearance in the chapter (3.9) on the necessity of adapting policies to the times. Soderini and the republic prospered so long as his decent and patient ways were favored by circumstances, but when other methods were called for he and his *patria* were ruined.

Soderini's methods and character loom large in the explanations offered in the *Discourses* of the republic's demise, but Machiavelli also underscores weaknesses in the republican government itself, including its military failures and factionalism. In the 1520 *Discourse on Florentine Affairs after the Death of the Younger Lorenzo* Machiavelli was still of the opinion that a broadly based republic was the most feasible government for Florence, that the Great Council should be restored, albeit with reduced powers, and that the government should have a constitutionally chosen head, a *gonfaloniere*, either for life or for two or three years. But he also believed that some changes would be required if a new Florentine republic were to enjoy greater stability. Looking back at the constitution of 1494–1512, he identified three chief weaknesses. First, it "did not satisfy all the parties among the citizens," and to remedy this he proposed that those citizens with "ambitious spirits" who "think they deserve to outrank the others" be given formal institutional representation in their own council, thus satisfying their ambition and removing the greatest source of instability. The republic's second weakness was its inability to indict and "inflict punishment," and the third lay in the office itself of the lifetime *gonfaloniere*: if the *gonfaloniere* was "intelligent and wicked, [he] easily could make himself prince; if he was good and weak, he could easily be driven out, with the ruin of the whole government."[39]

Not surprisingly, Machiavelli's portrayal of the *governo popolare* and its leader is through the lens of its demise. What is missing in Machiavelli's comments on Soderini is acknowledgment of his successes. Piero Soderini, now associated with Machiavelli's epigram in which he is the "feeble soul" consigned by Pluto to Limbo "with the other babies," maintained his office for ten years in the face of powerful opposition and conspiracy and in an increasingly threatening external situation. Under his leadership many of the problems that had plagued the republic in its early days were resolved. Paolo Vettori, Francesco's brother and one of the conspirators who removed Soderini, later wrote to the Medici that in Soderini's time the city had been in such excellent condition that the memory of that time would always pose a threat to the Medici regime.[40] Perhaps the reason why Machiavelli's analysis is so critical and even bitter is that Soderini, a man of virtue rather than *virtù*, allowed the republic they both served so well to be destroyed.

NOTES

1. Giorgio Cadoni, *Lotte politiche e riforme istituzionali a Firenze tra il 1494 e il 1502* (Rome: Istituto Storico Italiano per il Medio Evo, 1999), pp. 5–17; Alison Brown, "Uffici di onore e utile: la crisi del repubblicanesimo a Firenze," *Archivio storico italiano* 161 (2003): 300–2.

2. Niccolò Machiavelli, *Opere*, ed. Mario Martelli (Florence: Sansoni, 1971), pp. 940–50; trans. Allan Gilbert, in *Machiavelli: The Chief Works and Others*, 3 vols. (Durham, N.C.: Duke University Press, 1965), 3:1445, 1448, 1451–2.

3. Sergio Bertelli, "Petrus Soderinus Patriae Parens," *Bibliothèque d'Humanisme et Renaissance* 31 (1969): 98.

4. Francesco Guicciardini, *Storie fiorentine*, ed. Alessandro Montevecchi (Milan: Rizzoli, 1998), 23, pp. 379, 388; trans. Mario Domandi, *The History of Florence*, (New York: Harper & Row, 1970), pp. 223, 229–30.

5. Guicciardini, *Storie*, 23, pp. 379–80; *History of Florence*, pp. 223–4.

6. Bartolomeo Cerretani, *Storia fiorentina*, ed. Giuliana Berti (Florence: Olschki, 1994), p. 402.

7. *Ibid.*, p. 396.

8. Guicciardini, *Storie*, 25, pp. 411–12; *History of Florence*, pp. 247–8.

9. Bertelli, "Petrus Soderinus," pp. 93–114; also by Bertelli, "Pier Soderini Vexillifer Perpetuus Reipublicae Florentinae, 1502–1512," in *Renaissance Studies in Honor of Hans Baron*, ed. Anthony Molho and John Tedeschi (Florence: Sansoni, 1971), pp. 333–57 (335–9); and "Machiavelli and Soderini," *Renaissance Quarterly* 28 (1975): 1–16. See also Riccardo Fubini, "Introduzione," in *I ceti dirigenti in Firenze dal gonfalonierato di giustizia a vita all'avvento del ducato*, ed. Elisabetta Insabato (Lecce: Conte Editore, 1999), p. 42. For a contrary view: Roslyn Pesman Cooper, "Pier Soderini: Aspiring Prince or Civic Leader?" *Studies in Medieval and Renaissance History* n.s. 1 (1978): 69–126; reprinted in Roslyn Pesman Cooper, *Pier Soderini and the Ruling Class in Renaissance Florence* (Goldbach: Keip Verlag, 2002), pp. 47–126.

10. Cerretani, *Storia*, p. 402; see also Cerretani's *Ricordi*, ed. Giuliana Berti (Florence: Olschki, 1993), pp. 223–34.

11. Michael Rocke, *Forbidden Friendships: Homosexuality and Male Culture in Renaissance Florence* (Oxford University Press, 1996), pp. 228–9.

12. Carlo Dionisotti, *Machiavellerie* (Turin: Einaudi, 1980), pp. 20–30.

13. Robert Black, "Machiavelli, Servant of the Florentine Republic," in *Machiavelli and Republicanism*, ed. Gisela Bock, Quentin Skinner, and Maurizio Viroli (Cambridge University Press, 1990), pp. 71–100.

14. The 1965 English translation of Allan Gilbert (*Works*, 3:1453) follows many Italian editions of the *Decennale* in erroneously rendering the part of the text that refers to the Soderini coat of arms as *"not* so strong" that "on their solid rock you could erect your peace." See Pesman Cooper, *Pier Soderini and the Ruling Class*, pp. 125–6, 141.

15. *Machiavelli and His Friends: Their Personal Correspondence*, trans. James Atkinson and David Sices (DeKalb, Ill.: Northern Illinois University Press, 1996), pp. 29–30, 58, 68–9, 73–7.

16. *Correspondence*, p. 48.

17. *Correspondence*, p. 120.

18. *Opere*, p. 15; *Works*, 1:161–2.

19. Guicciardini, *Storie*, 28, pp. 443–8; *History of Florence*, pp. 271–5; Cerretani, *Storia*, pp. 352, 387–8.

20. Bertelli, "Petrus Soderinus," p. 113; Fubini, "Introduzione," p. 43.

21. Black, "Machiavelli, Servant of the Florentine Republic," pp. 87–8; Pesman, *Pier Soderini*, p. 95.

22. Rosemary Devonshire Jones, *Francesco Vettori, Florentine Citizen and Medici Servant* (London: Athlone Press, 1972), pp. 10–33.

23. *Correspondence*, p. 197.

24. *Correspondence*, pp. 106–7.

25. Nicolai Rubinstein, "Machiavelli and the Mural Decoration of the Hall of the Great Council of Florence," *Musagetes: Festschrift für Wolfram Prinz*, ed. Ronald G. Kecks (Berlin: Gebr. Mann, 1991), pp. 275–84; R. Carlucci, "The Visual Arts in the Government of Piero Soderini during the Florentine Republic," unpublished PhD thesis, Columbia University, 1994, pp. 375–6, 459.

26. Niccolò Machiavelli, *Arte della guerra e scritti politici minori*, ed. S. Bertelli (Milan: Feltrinelli, 1961), pp. 95–115.

27. *Ibid.*, p. 95.

28. Cerretani, *Storia*, pp. 397–8; Cerretani, *Ricordi*, pp. 228–9.

29. *Opere*, p. 30; *Works*, 1:113.

30. Cerretani, *Storia*, p. 398.

31. *Correspondence*, p. 269.

32. See Chapter 4, "Machiavelli and the Medici," by Humfrey Butters.

33. *Correspondence*, p. 193; John Stephens and Humfrey Butters, "New Light on Machiavelli," *English Historical Review* 97 (1982): 54–69.

34. "Ai Palleschi," in Jean-Jacques Marchand, *Niccolò Machiavelli. I primi scritti politici (1499–1512). Nascita di un pensiero e di uno stile* (Padua: Antenore, 1975), pp. 533–5.

35. *Correspondence*, p. 215.

36. Pesman Cooper, *Pier Soderini*, p. 97.

37. *Works*, 1:213.
38. *Works*, 1:425.
39. *Opere*, pp. 25, 27–8; *Works*, 1:103, 107–8.
40. "Ricordi di Paolo Vettori," in Rudolf von Albertini, *Firenze dalla repubblica al principato*, trans. Cesare Cristofolini (Turin: Einaudi, 1970), p. 357.

FURTHER READING

Bock, Gisela, Quentin Skinner, and Maurizio Viroli, eds. *Machiavelli and Republicanism*, Cambridge University Press, 1990.

Butters, H. C. *Governors and Government in Early Sixteenth-Century Florence, 1502–1519*. Oxford University Press, 1985.

Gilmore, Myron P., ed. *Studies on Machiavelli*. Florence, Sansoni, 1972.

Guidi, Guidobaldo. *Lotte, pensiero e istituzioni politiche nella Repubblica fiorentina dal 1494 al 1512*. Florence, Olschki, 1992.

Lowe, K. J. P. *Church and Politics in Renaissance Italy: The Life and Career of Cardinal Francesco Soderini (1453–1524)*. Cambridge University Press, 1993.

Najemy, John M. *Between Friends: Discourses of Power and Desire in the Machiavelli–Vettori Letters of 1513–1515*. Princeton University Press, 1993.

Pesman Cooper, Roslyn. *Pier Soderini and the Ruling Class in Renaissance Florence*. Goldbach, Keip Verlag, 2002.

Polizzotto, Lorenzo. *The Elect Nation: The Savonarolan Movement in Florence 1494–1545*. Oxford, Clarendon Press, 1994.

Ridolfi, Roberto. *Life of Niccolò Machiavelli*, trans. Cecil Grayson. London, Routledge & Kegan Paul, 1963.

4

HUMFREY BUTTERS

Machiavelli and the Medici

The Medici played a central role in Machiavelli's life and works. Until 1494 he lived in a city dominated by them, and from 1498 to 1512 he was employed by a government to which they represented a threat and an alternative focus of allegiance for discontented Florentines. When, after eighteen years of exile, they returned to Florence in 1512, the Medici removed Machiavelli from the chancery and his other posts, but he strove subsequently to win their favor, most famously by dedicating *The Prince* first to Giuliano de' Medici, an idea he had to abandon, and subsequently to Giuliano's nephew, the younger Lorenzo. These efforts were unsuccessful until 1520, when he finally secured their patronage in the form of a commission from the Florentine Studio, arranged by its head, Cardinal Giulio de' Medici, to write a history of Florence, a book that devotes much attention to the deeds of the family's leading members in the fifteenth century. In Machiavelli's last years, Medici favor brought him several minor government posts and assignments.

Little is known of Machiavelli's early connections to the Medici. Apart from the friendship of his father, Bernardo, with the Medici chancellor Bartolomeo Scala, the best evidence for Niccolò's links to the Medici is the poem he addressed to Giuliano, son of the elder Lorenzo.[1] Following the expulsion in 1494 of the Medici regime, which was replaced by the most broadly based constitution in Florence's history, whose core was the Great Council of over three thousand members, and especially during his chancery years from 1498 to 1512, Machiavelli had little to do with the Medici. Published records of his diplomatic missions and personal correspondence from this period contain only a handful of references to them.[2] As a civil servant who enjoyed a close working relationship with the Standardbearer (*gonfaloniere*) of Justice for life, Piero Soderini, from 1502 to 1512, Machiavelli was of course well informed concerning attempts by the Medici to return to Florence and their determination to build a party of friends in Rome and Florence. In the first *Decennale*, Machiavelli's summary in verse of the history of Florence and Italy from the French invasion in 1494 to 1504, he wrote of sixty years of the "yoke" of Medici oppression, of Piero de' Medici's humiliating surrender to the French of important Florentine possessions, including Pisa, and of the resulting downfall of their regime.[3]

Can the *Decennale*'s negative references to the Medici be considered proof that Machiavelli wished to have nothing to do with them? Not necessarily, for the poem was initially dedicated to, and praised the achievements of, Alamanno Salviati, an *ottimate* (member of an elite family) with close ties to the Medici. Alamanno's cousin Jacopo was married to Lucrezia, daughter of the elder Lorenzo and sister of Cardinal Giovanni and Giuliano de' Medici. Alamanno's sister Cornelia was the wife of Giovanbattista Ridolfi, whose nephew Piero was married to Lucrezia's sister Contessina; and in 1507 Alamanno's daughter Caterina married Giovanni Tornabuoni, whose father, Lorenzo, had been executed in 1497 for his involvement in a plot to restore Piero de' Medici to Florence.[4] The Salviati cousins supported Piero Soderini's candidacy for the post of lifetime Standardbearer in 1502, but, like other prominent *ottimati*, they became disillusioned with Soderini, particularly for his failure to implement reforms that would have instituted a more aristocratic constitution by limiting the powers of, though not abolishing, the Great Council. By 1504 Jacopo and Alamanno had emerged as leaders of the opposition to Soderini; and in the following year Florentines were reminded of the continuing influence of the Medici, even in exile, when Lucrezia Salviati and Contessina Ridolfi had a wax model of their brother Giuliano placed in the church of Santissima Annunziata, an act of conspicuous devotion intended to secure his recovery from a long illness. Machiavelli may have hoped, therefore, that by gaining the favor of the Salviati he might win that of the Medici as well. But if this was his aim, it seems not to have worked: in 1506, his chancery colleague Biagio Buonaccorsi reported to him that Alamanno had called him a rogue ("ribaldo") and said he never gave Machiavelli any commissions while he was on the foreign policy magistracy of the Ten.[5] And when Machiavelli published the *Decennale* in 1506, the dedication to Salviati was omitted.

A major political crisis, in which Machiavelli, owing to his closeness to Soderini, found himself at odds with the Salviati cousins and the Medici, was sparked by Filippo Strozzi's pledge to marry Clarice, daughter of Piero de' Medici, in 1508.[6] Most of the Strozzi, together with the Salviati and their allies, sprang to Filippo's defense, conceding that he had been foolish to enter a marriage alliance with the outlawed Medici, but maintaining that he had no ulterior political motive and that the maximum punishment prescribed for such an offence was only a monetary fine. Soderini and his supporters impugned the Salviati and Strozzi, and indictments were drafted against the latter, the most telling of which, an anonymous one, was rumored to have been written by Machiavelli, so skillfully was it worded.[7] Despite the passions aroused on both sides by this episode, it ended with a compromise: Strozzi was banished to Naples for three years and fined 500 florins, but he married Clarice and returned home after less than a year, thanks to a series of special permissions issued by the Signoria (the chief executive magistracy) and the Ten, which Clarice, who was also Soderini's godchild, induced him to accept. This resolution may have persuaded Machiavelli that it was an appropriate moment to make another gesture toward Alamanno Salviati, to whom he wrote a letter in 1509. But this too met with no success.[8]

In the last two years of Soderini's tenure, his relations with Pope Julius II and the Medici became so hostile that his loyal aide Machiavelli had no chance of establishing good relations with the Medici. When, therefore, in 1512 the Medici returned to Florence with the aid of a Spanish army and Soderini was ejected, it was hardly surprising that Machiavelli lost his government posts. But he did not seek to distance himself from Soderini in the months following the return of the Medici. In a memorandum he addressed to the followers of the Medici, written shortly before he was removed from his posts on November 7, Machiavelli warned them to ignore those citizens who were trying to blacken Soderini's name in order to make the people hate him.[9] Machiavelli was clearly referring to the Salviati group, rather than to the *ottimati* as a whole, some of whom had supported Soderini. This group, which included Jacopo Salviati (Alamanno had died in 1510), Giovanbattista Ridolfi, Francesco Guicciardini, and Lanfredino Lanfredini, was willing to retain the Great Council but wanted to reform the constitution along the lines of the more aristocratic Venetian republic. On September 7, 1512, the Great Council approved their proposals, but the Medici were persuaded by their more radical partisans, to whom Machiavelli's piece is addressed, that this offered them insufficient security. On September 16, the Mediceans executed a coup d'état with a show of force and replaced the popular government with a *balìa*, or emergency magistracy. This was a defeat for moderates like Jacopo Salviati, even though he and some of his allies were members of that *balìa*. Machiavelli argued that the loyalty of the Salviati group to the Medici was suspect, because they wished to retain popular support and would not fear a revival of the popular government. He therefore advised in the memorandum that, in order to secure their undivided loyalty, the Medici had to ensure that Salviati and his friends were hated by the people. There are interesting similarities between the points Machiavelli made in this memorandum and what Paolo Vettori, brother of Francesco, wrote to Cardinal Giovanni de' Medici in the *Ricordi* he penned prior to November 7 (since he refers to Machiavelli as still employed in the chancery).[10] He too urged the Medici to shun the moderates and rely on their true and more radical partisans.

Machiavelli's diagnosis may have been intended in part to repay the Salviati for the contempt with which he had been treated by Alamanno. His analysis of the Salviati's political strategy is confirmed by what Francesco Vettori, now Florence's ambassador in Rome, wrote to his brother Paolo about Jacopo Salviati in 1513: when talking to friends of the Medici, Salviati would always stress his longstanding loyalty to that family; but when speaking to supporters of the popular government, he would expatiate upon his devotion to the Great Council.[11] Machiavelli's advice to the Medici may have been perceptive, but it did him no good. Shortly afterwards, he was dismissed and confined to the dominion for a year. When, in February 1513, his name was found on a list of those expected to welcome the plot against the Medici hatched by Agostino Capponi and Pietro Paolo Boscoli, he certainly cannot have expected to receive any help from Jacopo Salviati or other moderate Mediceans, and, in the absence of other influential patrons, no one intervened to prevent his arrest and torture.[12] Giovanni Folchi, who was implicated in the plot, revealed under interrogation that, in conversations about the political situation, Machiavelli had commented that the Medici regime lacked a figure with the elder Lorenzo's gifts of leadership.[13]

While in prison Machiavelli addressed two sonnets to Giuliano de' Medici, and when he was released in a general amnesty after Cardinal Giovanni was elected pope on March 11, 1513, he believed, or affected to believe, that he owed his liberation to Giuliano. During the next two years he tried unsuccessfully to win the favor of the Medici through his friend Francesco Vettori, ambassador to the papal court and among those who had pledged the money for the surety Machiavelli had to post when he was confined to the dominion.[14] In a letter of March 13, Machiavelli asked Vettori to try to get his brother Totto a job in the papal household and five days later expressed the hope that he himself would not be left "on the ground" by the Medici. On April 16 Machiavelli wrote that he believed Vettori would find Giuliano de' Medici "naturally disposed to please me."[15] In all these expectations Machiavelli was to be disappointed. Vettori had less influence with the Medici than Machiavelli supposed, and even to his own brother Paolo he bemoaned his inability to do more for his friends.

The correspondence with Francesco Vettori casts considerable light on Machiavelli's expectations concerning the Medici and also helped Machiavelli work out ideas that found their way into *The Prince*. For example, on April 29, 1513, he gave Vettori an analysis of Ferdinand of Aragon's actions as a ruler of "new states" that he later incorporated in revised form into chapter 21 of *The Prince*. In his famous letter to Vettori of December 10, 1513, Machiavelli refers to his new work *De principatibus* (*On Principalities*) commenting that, because its subject matter ought to be of particular interest to a "new prince," he would "dedicate it [*lo indrizzo*]" to Giuliano de' Medici.[16] In these years there was much talk about Pope Leo's desire to find states for his brother and nephew[17] and, according to the historian Bartolomeo Cerretani, even of making Giuliano king of Naples and Lorenzo duke of Milan.[18] Machiavelli's desire to impress upon the Medici, and especially Pope Leo, the possibilities open to them is one reason why such an important role in the treatise is given to Cesare Borgia, another "new prince" and son of a pope. The emphasis placed in *The Prince* on war and relations between states reflects Machiavelli's experience and interests, but it also consorts perfectly with the final chapter's appeal to Leo to free Italy from the "barbarians." What is absolutely clear is that the book had little to do with the government of Florence. Both in the later *Discourses on Livy* (chiefly in 1.55) and in the little tract on the Florentine constitution following the death of the younger Lorenzo,[19] Machiavelli argued that since Florence lacked a landed nobility it was not suited for princely rule; indeed, in the latter work he dismissed as barbarous and immoral the idea of introducing such a nobility as a prelude to setting up a principate.

Historians have labored to reconcile the author of *The Prince* with the author of the *Discourses*, but the problem is factitious. Machiavelli was interested, not in discussing ideal types of government, but in exploring one of the principal questions Aristotle poses in the *Politics*: what sorts of government are best suited for what sorts of society?[20] He undoubtedly preferred republics to monarchies, but he did not regard the republican model as a panacea. The conspirator Giovanni Folchi had confessed that he and Pietro Paolo Boscoli had been reading Aristotle's *Politics*. Did they discuss it with Machiavelli as well?

Foreign policy and war were the chief topics of the Machiavelli–Vettori correspondence in 1513, not any project to convert Florence into a principate. Thus in *The Prince* Ferdinand of Aragon and Cesare Borgia become suitable models for Giuliano and Lorenzo de' Medici because they carved out "new states" with unconventional methods in difficult circumstances, and because Borgia had the additional qualification of being, like the Medici, a member of a pope's family. But Ferdinand and Borgia lacked the heroic stature of the legendary "new rulers" Machiavelli urges the Medici to emulate in the last chapter of *The Prince* – Moses, Cyrus, and Theseus. What made these the supreme models was not only their personal qualities but the fact that, when they appeared on the scene, the peoples they subsequently led to greatness had reached the nadir of their fortunes: the Hebrews enslaved by the Egyptians, the Persians oppressed by the Medes, and the Athenians scattered. The abject condition of modern Italy was, Machiavelli claims, similar to and indeed, if anything, more dire than that of those earlier peoples. It might seem paradoxical that Machiavelli would see cause for hope in such degradation, and there is certainly a striking contrast between his rather modest recommendation in the summer of 1513 that Pope Leo's best course of action lay in pursuing peace with Spain, France, and Venice and the dramatic appeal to Leo and the Medici for the "redemption" of Italy in the last chapter of *The Prince*. Gennaro Sasso has rightly underscored the "providentialism" and prophetic quality of the last chapter,[21] but Machiavelli may also have been drawing on the less vatic and more historical perspective of the theory of cycles, or anacyclosis, that he knew from (translations of) the sixth book of Polybius and which he deployed more openly in the *Discourses* (1.2 and 3.1) and in the *Florentine Histories* (5.1).

Pope Leo and his family did not accomplish the task set them by Machiavelli, and *The Prince* did not secure Machiavelli the rehabilitation he so desperately wanted. This is hardly surprising, for Vettori had convinced Machiavelli not to come to Rome to present it to Giuliano.[22] In two respects, however, Leo did live up to Machiavelli's expectations. The first is that he established Giuliano and later Lorenzo as new princes in states of their own. In February 1515 Leo installed Giuliano as ruler of a new state consisting of Modena, Parma, Piacenza, and Reggio, and in the following year he deprived Francesco Maria della Rovere of his possessions in the papal state, paving the way for Lorenzo's acquisition of the Duchy of Urbino. Secondly, Leo decided that Florence should reestablish the militia,[23] whose earlier incarnation had largely been Machiavelli's doing. In December 1514, Cardinal Giulio asked Vettori to find out what foreign policy Machiavelli would recommend for the papacy, but, as Vettori told Machiavelli, although Leo expressed his appreciation of the case Machiavelli made for a French alliance, it did not dissuade the pope from joining the anti-French coalition.[24] When rumors reached Cardinal Giulio early in 1515 that Giuliano was thinking of employing Machiavelli in some capacity in his new state, Giulio instructed a papal secretary to warn Giuliano that hiring Machiavelli "does not serve [Giuliano's] needs or ours" and that he should "not get involved" with Machiavelli.[25] Whatever reasons the Medici may have had for shunning Machiavelli and ignoring *The Prince*, there is no evidence that moral disapproval of its more shocking elements was among them.

Machiavelli's dedication of *The Prince*, probably in 1516, to Lorenzo de' Medici, who had replaced his uncle as head of the regime in Florence in the summer of 1513, was no more successful in winning him the patronage or even the interest of the family. He dedicated his next two major works to friends: the *Discourses* to Zanobi Buondelmonti and Cosimo Rucellai (who hosted the discussions in the family gardens where the *Discourses* may have taken shape), and the *Art of War* to Lorenzo Strozzi. But it would be erroneous to conclude that Machiavelli had given up hope of being employed by the Medici. Lorenzo Strozzi's brother Filippo was a close confidant and adviser to Lorenzo de' Medici (who was also Filippo's brother-in-law) and a major figure in papal and Florentine financial administration. Machiavelli's brother-in-law Francesco del Nero was Filippo's agent in Florence.[26] Nor were these the only persons whose friendship could help Niccolò obtain Medici favor. Although Zanobi Buondelmonti played a leading part in the anti-Medici plot of 1522, others who, like him, had gathered with Machiavelli in the Rucellai gardens were on better terms with the Medici. Filippo de' Nerli was the son-in-law of Jacopo Salviati,[27] and by this time Machiavelli's former hostility to the Salviati had dissipated. In a letter to Lodovico Alamanni of December 1517, he referred to a group of the latter's friends that included Jacopo's son Cardinal Giovanni Salviati, Filippo de' Nerli, and Cosimo Rucellai in a manner that suggests that they were friends of his as well.[28] In November 1520, Nerli wrote to Machiavelli asking for a copy of the *Art of War* and informed him that every evening he was reading Justin and Quintus Curtius Rufus to Lucrezia (Medici) Salviati, Jacopo's wife. He conveyed to Machiavelli a request from Lucrezia that he rework and improve a treatise on the life of Alexander the Great that someone had given her.[29] By 1521, as their correspondence makes clear, Machiavelli was on excellent terms with an even more distinguished political ally of the Medici and a relative by marriage of the Salviati, Francesco Guicciardini, papal governor of Modena and Reggio and husband of Maria, daughter of Alamanno Salviati.[30] In September of that year, Cardinal Giovanni Salviati sent the author of the *Art of War* a fulsome letter, praising the work for singling out for discussion and commendation the best features of ancient and modern warfare and describing it as a book for "the common welfare of all Italians."[31]

Jacopo Salviati was now a pillar of the Medici establishment in Florence and Rome, and he used his bank's substantial resources to cater to its needs. But he found Lorenzo de' Medici far too domineering a presence in Florence, and his political views remained moderate. When, after Giulio de' Medici was elected Pope Clement VII in 1523, he sent the Medici bastards, Alessandro (probably his own son) and Ippolito (Giuliano's son), to head the regime in Florence, Jacopo Salviati was among those who opposed the decision and wanted a broader sharing of power. Although by 1520 Machiavelli was on friendly terms with some of the Salviati, rather less is known about his dealings with Jacopo. Battista della Palla reported to Machiavelli in April 1520 that he had thanked Salviati for a letter, probably a recommendation written at Machiavelli's request, and that Salviati was "angry" with Machiavelli for having been too formal in his approach to him about it.[32] Salviati's "anger" is clearly an indication that he considered his relationship with Machiavelli a cordial one.

The subject matter of the *Art of War* made it a relatively safe literary undertaking for an author known for controversial and passionately held views who was trying to regain a role in public affairs. In condemning mercenaries and singing the praises of the Romans as a model for a citizen militia, Machiavelli was not likely to offend his readers and was in any case repeating what he had already said, what other humanists had said before him, and what Vegetius, Frontinus, and Polybius had written centuries earlier. The debt of the *Art of War* to those three classical authors is considerable; indeed, entire passages are sometimes paraphrased or even translated. The Medici regime, moreover, showed its awareness of the value of a militia by reestablishing one in Florence; and when Lorenzo was appointed captain-general of the Florentine forces in 1515, the Otto di Pratica, the foreign-policy magistracy that elected him, recalled that it was Romans who captained the armies that had conquered most of the world and speculated that the Florentines might be able to follow their example, a hope, as has been justly remarked, that could have been expressed by Machiavelli himself.[33]

The *Discourses*, a commentary on the first ten books of Livy's *History of Rome*, undoubtedly offered Machiavelli a broader canvas, but with wider opportunities came more dangerous pitfalls and an increased likelihood of alienating those in power. Significantly, only one of the leading members of the Medici family alive at the time of its composition is named in the *Discourses* – Leo X, whose decision to remain neutral in the conflict between France and the Swiss in 1515 Machiavelli heavily criticizes (2.22). But Machiavelli certainly alludes to the Medici in a particularly dramatic way in the third chapter of the third book, where he reproaches Piero Soderini for not having followed the example, in order to preserve the popular government, of the legendary first Brutus' principled execution of his own sons in defense of the republic. Why did the Medici, who are clearly the "sons of Brutus" in this passage, not punish Machiavelli for this daring suggestion? They may not have read the *Discourses* in manuscript, or perhaps this passage was added in a later revision.[34] Machiavelli's friends certainly knew the *Discourses*, although Nerli remarked, in referring to the failed conspiracy of 1522 in which some members of the Rucellai gardens discussion group were involved, that they should have paid more attention to what Machiavelli wrote (in chapter 6 of book 3) about the dangers and likely failure of conspiracies.[35]

The other Medici mentioned by name in the *Discourses* are the fifteenth-century family leaders, notably Cosimo il Vecchio and the elder Lorenzo. Machiavelli calls Cosimo "prince of the republic," by which he meant "first citizen," not prince de jure. This usage, of classical origin, was current in

Machiavelli's day to refer to leading citizens with a disproportionate degree of power. In *Discourses* 1.33 Machiavelli clearly disapproves of the corrupt means by which Cosimo acquired "more power than is reasonable" and "began to instill fear" in those who had until then controlled the government. But Machiavelli also blames the incompetence of Cosimo's opponents, first for not recognizing the danger, and then for a rash attempt to excise it by exiling him, which only spurred the extensive Medici faction to engineer his recall and to make him "principe della repubblica." Although he considered this first Medici regime deeply flawed, Machiavelli did not believe its opponents should have tried to overthrow it, because conspiracies were rarely successful. In his long chapter on the dangers and frequent failures of conspiracies (*Discourses* 3.6), he includes among the examples the Pazzi conspiracy of 1478 against Lorenzo and his brother, Giuliano, paraphrasing Tacitus' dictum to the effect that people should "wish for good princes but tolerate them however they are." When Machiavelli argues (3.29) that the sins of peoples derive from their rulers (from their "principi"), he supports the idea with two lines from Lorenzo de' Medici's play, the *Rappresentazione di San Giovanni e Paolo*: "And what the lord does is then done by many, for on the lord all eyes are fixed" (lines 789–90).[36] This passage, which offers a key to the interpretation of Machiavelli's account of the Medici in the *Florentine Histories*, occurs in the speech in which the old emperor Constantine exhorts his sons to keep their thoughts fixed on the "common good [*bene universale*]" and to live a "just life [*giusta vita*]," because the ruler's example exerts a powerful influence on the people.

An early example of the advantages Salviati patronage could bestow may have been the commission Machiavelli received in July 1520 to go to Lucca to represent the Florentine creditors, among them the Salviati, of the bankrupt Michele Guinigi. But it was Cardinal Giulio who defined Machiavelli's commission and sent supporting letters to the government of Lucca.[37] After the death of the highly unpopular Lorenzo de' Medici in 1519, Giulio had rushed to Florence to take charge of the regime. Sometime in March 1520 Machiavelli was introduced to him by Lorenzo Strozzi, the dedicatee of the *Art of War*, and other members of the Rucellai gardens circle. Lorenzo's brother Filippo was pleased: "I am very glad you took Machiavelli to see the Medici, for if he can get the masters' confidence, he is a man who must rise."[38] In April another member of the Rucellai circle, Battista della Palla, spoke enthusiastically to Pope Leo about Machiavelli's intellectual merits and the high regard in which the group held him. He praised Machiavelli's new play, *Mandragola*, assuring Leo that he would like it. He also persuaded the pope to entrust him with a message to Cardinal Giulio informing the latter that Leo would be pleased if Machiavelli were given a commission to write something or undertake some other task.[39] These various interventions on Machiavelli's behalf finally bore fruit on November 8, 1520, when the Officials of Florence's university (the Studio), of which Giulio was head, awarded him the commission to write the *Florentine Histories*.

Also in 1520, Giulio invited Machiavelli (as he did others) to draft a proposal on the form of government the Medici should install in Florence now that Lorenzo's death left the ruling branch of the family with no legitimate heirs. Machiavelli's praise for the political virtues of the people (the plebs, or *popolo*) is often contrasted with Guicciardini's preference (and that of many *ottimati*, including the Salviati) for aristocratic republicanism on the Venetian model. The contrast is real but should not be exaggerated, and it is noteworthy that the constitutional prescriptions contained in the *Discourse on Florentine Affairs after the Death of the Younger Lorenzo*, which Machiavelli wrote in response to Giulio's invitation, have much in common with those advanced by Guicciardini in his nearly contemporaneous *Dialogue on the Government of Florence*. Both rejected the idea that the Medici should set up a principate, in Machiavelli's case on the grounds that this form of government was suitable only for societies with a landed nobility, a point he had already made in *Discourses* 1.55. Both men, furthermore, having decided that Florence could only have a republican government, argued that the Medici could not revert to the constitutional arrangements within which their forebears had exercised power in the previous century. One of the reasons for Machiavelli's rejection of the fifteenth-century constitution was that he believed the Medici had become too "grand" to use the relaxed and familiar style of government practiced by Cosimo and the elder Lorenzo. Guicciardini made the same point in his memorandum "On the government of Florence after the restoration of the Medici in 1512."[40] Finally, both men took their inspiration from the idea of mixed government, which Machiavelli had already recommended in *Discourses* 1.2: the combination of the three good kinds of government – monarchy, aristocracy, and polity – that Polybius saw in the Roman republic and Aristotle discussed in the *Politics*.

The 1520 *Discourse* attributes the fall of the popular government of 1494–1512 to its inability to satisfy the ambitions of leading families; it also warns the Medici that the people are hostile to them and will be won over only if the Great Council is restored. Machiavelli's solutions to both these problems were to entrust executive authority to a council of sixty-five, from whose ranks would be selected governing boards of eight to hold office for three months and a *gonfaloniere* (Standardbearer of Justice) to sit for two or three years, and to vest legislative and wide electoral powers in a council of two hundred and a Great Council of a thousand or at least six hundred members. In recommending that the sixty-five and the two hundred be appointed for life, Machiavelli was proposing a constitutional model even more aristocratic than the reform proposals of some of the *ottimati* during the popular government. But he injected a significant element of popular participation into his scheme by stipulating that members of the committee of sixteen standard-bearers (who represented the city's administrative districts) should have the power to transfer the right of deciding particular items of business from the executive committees to the two hundred, or from the latter to the Great Council. To make these changes more acceptable to the Medici and their friends, Machiavelli proposed, first, that the pope could fill the ranks of the sixty-five and the two hundred with Medici supporters; and, second, that during their lifetimes Pope Leo and Cardinal Giulio should enjoy full powers of government. In seemingly reassigning to the Medici the role of lawgiver he had asked them to assume in *The Prince*, Machiavelli went beyond anything Guicciardini recommends in his *Dialogue*. But Machiavelli now added the hope that, once Leo and Giulio were gone from this life, the institutions of their making would function on their own as a republic.[41]

Despite the similarities between Machiavelli's and Guicciardini's reform proposals, one should not lose sight of the fact that Guicciardini's views in the *Dialogue* are expressed by Bernardo del Nero, a devoted Medici partisan executed in 1497 for his involvement in a plot to restore the exiled Piero. In the *Dialogue*'s first book Bernardo defends fifteenth-century Medici government, for which Machiavelli had little enthusiasm. But his suspicions about *ottimati* who cynically declare their allegiance to the cause of liberty in order to get popular support are similar to the views expressed by Machiavelli in his 1512 memoir to the *palleschi*, the Mediceans, in which he urged the Medici not to trust the loyalty of patricians like Jacopo Salviati. In the second book, however, Bernardo is made to assume the mantle of an advocate of the sort of mixed constitution Guicciardini favored and Machiavelli had come to accept.[42] Bernardo's loyalty to the Medici was unimpeachable, since he died for their sake, and it was a peculiarly deft rhetorical trick on Guicciardini's part to have him defend fifteenth-century Medici government in book one and aristocratic republicanism in book two. Bernardo's fictional change of view, therefore, had some features in common with Machiavelli's real one.

The *Florentine Histories* presented Machiavelli with a new and knotty problem: how to produce a work that would please his Medici patrons but not compromise his republican ideals and in which he could tell the truth about the historical Medici and not get into trouble with Giulio/Clement. Never before, after all, had he attempted an extended historical treatment of the family's place in Florence's history. His solution to the dilemma was a subtle blend of several elements. He praises Cosimo and Lorenzo, but sometimes for qualities or achievements that had a negative side. He lauds their patronage of letters, but elsewhere speaks of the flourishing of letters as a sign of corruption. He adverts to their liberality, but indicates that one of its uses was to win partisans and build factions that are the essence of a corrupt society. Concluding his laudatory portrait of Cosimo (*Florentine Histories* 7.6), moreover, Machiavelli notes that he has followed the practice of those who write the lives of princes, not those who write general histories, since Cosimo was a "rare man" and had to be praised in "an extraordinary way." But this warned his readers that the portrait was an exercise in the epideictic rhetoric of public praise, composed of a series of topoi, or commonplaces. And when he writes that Lorenzo was more renowned for prudence than anyone in Florence or Italy had ever been, and more mourned in his *patria*, he was again making use of a topos, that of outdoing, which had been much deployed by Latin and humanist encomiasts and with which most of his readers would be perfectly familiar.

By playing with rhetorical conventions, therefore, Machiavelli was able to please his patrons while allowing other readers to take a less favorable view of his patrons' illustrious forbears. In fact, his "praise" of Cosimo and Lorenzo was mixed with comments and analyses that were far less flattering. Machiavelli made no effort to hide the fact that Cosimo was a very successful faction leader, who used his family, *amici* (friends), and wealth to seize power and retain it. Cosimo's grandson not only followed this example, according to Machiavelli, but was also largely responsible, thanks to his mishandling of the Pazzi, for their conspiracy against him and the subsequent war, from whose dire consequences Lorenzo was saved by the Turkish invasion of Otranto, not by his vaunted prudence. Machiavelli devotes considerable space to the Pazzi War but deals very cursorily with the Barons' War in Naples of 1485–6, even though one of his chief sources for these events, Niccolò Valori's Latin life of Lorenzo,[43] presents the latter's handling of this crisis as one of his great achievements. And whereas some of the writers of the Laurentian circle, and Lorenzo himself, had claimed that a golden age had returned in late-fifteenth-century Florence, Machiavelli by contrast, both in the *Florentine Histories* and in the *Art of War*, emphasized the general corruption of manners in that period.[44] There can be little doubt of Machiavelli's general determination to puncture Cosimo's and Lorenzo's reputations, although often in subtle ways.

Yet Florence's corruption, according to Machiavelli, started much earlier than the fifteenth century, and it is symptomatic of his increasingly aristocratic perspective that he attributed its growth to the excessive ambition of the Florentine *popolo*, manifested in the crushing of the magnates two centuries earlier. Factionalism plagued the city's political life from early on and was not caused by the Medici. He might blame them for doing nothing to cure the disease, because he believed that rulers had to assume responsibility for the sins of those they ruled, and the high opinion he professes to have of their leadership qualities made this failure all the more egregious. Hence, in his *Discourse on Florentine Affairs*, he could offer to their successors, Leo and Giulio, the glittering opportunity to outdo Cosimo and Lorenzo by establishing a constitutional framework that would make Florence a genuine republic for the first time.

Machiavelli's proposals were ignored, but he had succeeded in making himself politically acceptable to the Medici, thanks in part to the efforts of friends who included members of Jacopo Salviati's circle. This stood him in good stead in 1522, while he was writing the *Florentine Histories*, when other close friends of his, in particular Zanobi Buondelmonti and Luigi Alamanni, joined a plot to assassinate Cardinal Giulio. Despite the fact that Buondelmonti allegedly mentioned his name as one who might be approached by the plotters, Machiavelli was not implicated in the affair. The political goodwill he now enjoyed secured Machiavelli a few government posts in the final years of his life, but not without some further disappointments. In 1525 Jacopo Salviati tried, unsuccessfully, to persuade Clement to appoint Machiavelli as secretary to his son Cardinal Giovanni Salviati, whom Clement was sending as legate to Madrid, but the pope refused.[45] In compensation, however, when Machiavelli went to Rome in May of that year to present the *Florentine Histories* to the pope, Clement gave (in addition to a gift of 120 gold ducats) his enthusiastic approval of Machiavelli's recommendation for a militia in the papal Romagna and sent him to Guicciardini, now president of the Romagna, to explain the idea. Guicciardini turned it down, but without losing Machiavelli's friendship. In 1526, as war loomed, Clement sought Machiavelli's advice on Florence's fortifications and approved his appointment as secretary to the new magistracy, recommended by Machiavelli himself, of the Overseers of the Walls. And in 1527, the Florentine government sent Machiavelli as its emissary to Guicciardini, who was by then the pope's lieutenant-general and commander of the papal armies, to make an urgent appeal for help in the city's defense. But Machiavelli never regained the truly important positions he had held until 1512.

The rapprochement of the final years was not purely personal, for it corresponded to a significant shift in Machiavelli's thinking about republican government that brought his views closer to those of Guicciardini. The aim of securing the favor of the Medici had significantly influenced some of Machiavelli's major works. Yet, except on military matters, the Medici largely disregarded his ideas, and after his death their termination of the republic and institution of the principate in 1530–2 represented an even more decisive rejection of his political views.

NOTES

1. Niccolò Machiavelli, *Opere*, ed. Mario Martelli (Florence: Sansoni, 1971), p. 994; Mario Martelli, "Preistoria (medicea) di Machiavelli," *Studi di filologia italiana* (1971): 377–405.
2. Legations in *Opere*, pp. 403, 452; letters, *ibid.*, pp. 1024, 1082, 1096, 1107, 1112. The letters are translated by James B. Atkinson and David Sices, *Machiavelli and His Friends: Their Personal Correspondence* (DeKalb, Ill.: Northern Illinois University Press, 1996), pp. 32–3, 134, 158, 179, 190.
3. *Opere*, p. 940.
4. H. C. Butters, *Governors and Government in Early Sixteenth-Century Florence 1502–1519* (Oxford: Clarendon Press, 1985), p. 65.
5. *Opere*, p. 1087; *Correspondence*, p. 141.
6. Melissa Meriam Bullard, *Filippo Strozzi and the Medici: Favor and Finance in Sixteenth-Century Florence and Rome* (Cambridge University Press, 1980), pp. 45–60.
7. Lorenzo Strozzi, *Le vite degli uomini illustri della casa Strozzi* (Florence, 1892), pp. 96–7.
8. Michele Luzzati and Milletta Sbrilli, "Massimiliano d'Asburgo e la politica di Firenze in una lettera inedita di Niccolò Machiavelli ad Alamanno Salviati," *Annali della Scuola Normale Superiore di Pisa*, ser. 3, 16 (1986): 825–54; Robert Black, "Machiavelli, Servant of the Florentine Republic," in *Machiavelli and Republicanism*, ed. Gisela Bock, Quentin Skinner, and Maurizio Viroli (Cambridge University Press, 1990), pp. 76–7, 90–1, 97–8.
9. "Ai Palleschi," in *Opere*, pp. 16–17.
10. Rudolf von Albertini, *Das florentinische Staatsbewußtsein im Übergang von der Republik zum Prinzipat* (Berne: Francke Verlag, 1955), p. 347; Italian trans. Cesare Cristofolini, *Firenze dalla repubblica al principato* (Turin: Einaudi, 1970), pp. 357–9.
11. Butters, *Governors*, p. 193.
12. Roberto Ridolfi, *Vita di Niccolò Machiavelli*, 7th edition (Florence: Sansoni, 1978), pp. 215–16; earlier edition trans. Cecil Grayson, *The Life of Niccolò Machiavelli* (London: Routledge & Kegan Paul, 1963), pp. 135–6.
13. J. N. Stephens and H. C. Butters, "New Light on Machiavelli," *English Historical Review* 97 (1982): 67.
14. Rosemary Devonshire Jones, *Francesco Vettori: Florentine Citizen and Medici Servant* (London: Athlone Press, 1972), p. 104.
15. *Opere*, pp. 1128–9, 1133; *Correspondence*, pp. 221–2, 228.
16. *Opere*, p. 1160; *Correspondence*, p. 264.
17. Cecil H. Clough, *Machiavelli Researches* (Naples: Istituto Universitario Orientale, 1967), pp. 42–60.
18. Bartolomeo Cerretani, *Dialogo della mutatione di Firenze*, ed. R. Mordenti (Rome: Edizioni di Storia e Letteratura, 1990), p. 81.
19. *Discursus florentinarum rerum post mortem iunioris Laurentii Medices*, in *Opere*, pp. 24–31.
20. Aristotle, *Politics* 1296b.10–14.
21. Gennaro Sasso, "Il 'Principe' ebbe due redazioni?" *La cultura* 19 (1981): 84–5.

22. John M. Najemy, *Between Friends: Discourses of Power and Desire in the Machiavelli–Vettori Letters of 1513–1515* (Princeton University Press, 1993), pp. 286–7.
23. Butters, *Governors*, p. 234.
24. *Correspondence*, pp. 293–307; Najemy, *Between Friends*, pp. 295–312.
25. *Correspondence*, p. 529; Ridolfi, *Vita*, p. 254; Ridolfi, *Life*, p. 162.
26. Bullard, *Filippo Strozzi*, p. 132.
27. Butters, *Governors*, p. 61.
28. *Opere*, pp. 1194–5; *Correspondence*, pp. 317–18.
29. *Opere*, pp. 1200–01; *Correspondence*, pp. 329–30.
30. *Opere*, pp. 1202–7; *Correspondence*, 335–42.
31. *Opere*, pp. 1207–8; *Correspondence*, pp. 342–3. See Pierre Hurtubise, *Une famille-témoin, les Salviati* (Vatican City: Biblioteca Apostolica Vaticana, Studi e Testi 309, 1985), pp. 285–6.
32. *Opere*, pp. 1197–8; *Correspondence*, p. 325.
33. J. N. Stephens, *The Fall of the Florentine Republic, 1512–1530* (Oxford: Clarendon Press, 1983), p. 154.
34. Clough, *Machiavelli Researches*, pp. 92–3.
35. Filippo de' Nerli, *Commentarj de' fatti civili occorsi dentro la Città di Firenze dall'anno 1215 al 1537* (Augusta [Florence], 1728), p. 138.
36. Lorenzo de' Medici, *Opere*, ed. L. Cavalli (Naples, 1970), p. 629.
37. Ridolfi, *Vita*, pp. 281–2; Ridolfi, *Life*, p. 180.
38. Ridolfi, *Vita*, pp. 276–7; Ridolfi, *Life*, pp. 176–7.
39. *Opere*, pp. 1197–8; *Correspondence*, pp. 324–5.
40. Francesco Guicciardini, *Dialogo e discorsi del reggimento di Firenze*, ed. Roberto Palmarocchi (Bari: Laterza, 1932), p. 262.
41. *Opere*, pp. 24–31.
42. The *Dialogue* is in Guicciardini, *Dialogo e discorsi*, pp. 7–172; trans. Alison Brown, *Dialogue on the Government of Florence* (Cambridge University Press, 1994).
43. *Magnanimi Laurentii Medices viri illustris vita per Nicolaum Valorium edita ad Leonem X pontificem maximum*, ed. Enrico Niccolini (Vicenza: Accademia Olimpica, 1991).
44. E.g., *Florentine Histories* 7.28; and the opening exchange between Fabrizio Colonna and Cosimo Rucellai in the *Art of War*, in *Opere*, pp. 303–4.
45. Ridolfi, *Vita*, pp. 330–1; Ridolfi, *Life*, p. 211–12.

FURTHER READING

Anglo, Sidney. *Machiavelli – The First Century: Studies in Enthusiasm, Hostility, and Irrelevance.* Oxford University Press, 2005.
Butters, H. C. "Lorenzo and Machiavelli," in *Lorenzo the Magnificent: Culture and Politics*, ed. Michael Mallett and Nicholas Mann. London, Warburg Institute, 1996, pp. 275–80.
"Political Allegiances and Political Structures in the Writings of Niccolò Machiavelli and Francesco Guicciardini," in *Italy and the European Powers: The Impact of War, 1500–1530*, ed. Christine Shaw. Leiden-Boston, Brill, 2006, pp. 91–106.

Cadoni, Giorgio. *Lotte politiche e riforme istituzionali a Firenze tra il 1494 e il 1502.* Rome, Istituto Storico Italiano per il Medio Evo, 1999.

Gilbert, Felix. *Machiavelli and Guicciardini: Politics and History in Sixteenth-Century Florence.* Princeton University Press, 1965.

Godman, Peter. *From Poliziano to Machiavelli: Florentine Humanism in the High Renaissance.* Princeton University Press, 1998.

Gouwens, Kenneth, and Sheryl E. Reiss, eds. *The Pontificate of Clement VII: History, Politics, Culture.* Aldershot, Ashgate, 2005.

Jurdjevic, Mark. *Guardians of Republicanism: The Valori Family in the Florentine Renaissance.* Oxford University Press, 2008.

Marietti, Marina. "Machiavel historiographe des Médicis," in *Les Écrivains et le pouvoir en Italie à l'époque de la Renaissance*, ed. A. Rochon. Paris, Sorbonne, 1974, pp. 81–148.

"I Medici: immagine e destino," in Marietti, *Machiavelli: l'eccezione fiorentina.* Florence, Cadmo, 2005, pp. 137–86.

Matucci, Andrea. *Machiavelli nella storiografia fiorentina.* Florence, Olschki, 1991.

Najemy, John M. *A History of Florence 1200–1575.* Oxford, Blackwell, 2006.

"Machiavelli and the Medici: The Lessons of Florentine History," *Renaissance Quarterly* 35 (1982): 551–76.

Rubinstein, Nicolai. *The Government of Florence under the Medici (1434 to 1494).* Oxford, Clarendon Press, 1966; revised edition, 1997.

Sasso, Gennaro. *Niccolò Machiavelli*, vol. 2, *La storiografia.* Bologna, Il Mulino, 1993.

Skinner, Quentin. *Machiavelli.* Oxford University Press, 1981.

5

WAYNE A. REBHORN

Machiavelli's *Prince* in the epic tradition

"He who builds on the people builds on mud": Machiavelli cites this saying in *The Prince* (9.272)[1] only to refute it by arguing that the people, if properly managed, will provide a more secure foundation for the Prince's state than fortresses or allies or mercenaries. This important moment in Machiavelli's work does more than elevate the people as well as the Prince who rules them; it also focuses on what must be considered perhaps the key metaphor in the book defining the Prince's activities: he "makes foundations [*fare fondamenti*]." Machiavelli repeats some version of this notion dozens of times in the relatively short text of *The Prince*, encouraging the reader to see the Prince as a cross between an architect and a mason, and illustrating the thesis, argued long ago by Jacob Burckhardt in his classic *Civilization of the Renaissance in Italy* (1860), namely, that people in the period saw the state as a work of art. That Machiavelli should focus on foundations is not surprising since the Prince he describes is "new": he does not inherit a state, but is faced with the challenge of creating one. Machiavelli is thinking of such "new" princes as Hieron of Syracuse, who rose up through the ranks of the army to seize control of Syracuse; the mythical Theseus, who founded Athens; and, perhaps the most memorable of them all, Cesare Borgia, who attempted, but failed, to create an enduring state in Italy. Even established rulers who already possess states, such as Ferdinand of Aragon, can be "new" (21.291), in this case because he is new to those portions of his realm he acquired after his marriage to Isabella of Castile. "New" princes must, of course, begin at the beginning: before they can build a state, they must make its foundations.

Fittingly, *The Prince* is dedicated to Lorenzo de' Medici, a potential new prince, and ends with a clarion call to that prince and his house to apply the political wisdom Machiavelli has offered them and to save Italy from the "barbarians," that is, from the French, the Spanish, and the Swiss, who have overrun the peninsula. Machiavelli's treatise does not begin by discussing the new prince directly, however. In keeping with what may have been his original title, *De principatibus* (*On Principalities*), the first eleven chapters offer a taxonomy of different kinds of princely states, including hereditary, mixed, civil, and ecclesiastical ones as well as those ruled by new princes. Many of the states he discusses nevertheless are, or include, newly acquired realms, and in most of the chapters Machiavelli discusses princely rulers rather than, say, political structures, constitutions, and the like. After two chapters (12 and 13) condemning mercenary armies, the rest of the book is focused on the new Prince, on how he must have real expertise in military affairs, avoid dependence on fortresses for his security, and make sure he controls his subordinates. In the most "scandalous" section of the work, chapters 15–19, Machiavelli discusses the Prince's relationship to conventional virtues such as liberality, mercy, trustworthiness, and piety, arguing that he need only *appear* to have these qualities, since his actual embracing of them might cost him his state. Finally, after devoting his twenty-fourth chapter to explaining that contemporary princes have lost their states because of their indolence and lack of foresight, Machiavelli focuses the twenty-fifth on Fortune, insisting that the new Prince can indeed defeat her through a combination of prudence and force, thus setting the stage for his calling upon the Medici in the last chapter to begin laying the foundations for a new Italy.

To say that Machiavelli's Prince makes foundations is to describe how he intervenes in the world of history. In this context, Machiavelli's metaphor is, however, somewhat unexpected, since he typically describes the movement of history using organic metaphors of birth and growth. Thus, one might think he would imagine the Prince as a farmer who plants seeds or a father who engenders and then cares for a child. Such notions do, in fact, appear fleetingly in *The Prince*, but they are not central to Machiavelli's thinking the way laying foundations is. This chapter will explain why Machiavelli would prefer to think in such terms, why the vision of the Prince as an architect and mason had such a hold on him. As we shall see, this vision is about freedom and power, and it connects the Prince to the tradition of the epic and to one important ancient epic hero in particular, Virgil's Aeneas. As we shall also see, however, Machiavelli's Prince is very different from his epic prototype: a hero like Aeneas, he is an Aeneas without a Rome.

To understand the meaning of Machiavelli's insistence on the metaphor of "laying foundations," it is necessary to examine first the way in which he imagines the movement of history. Occasionally, Machiavelli chooses fairly neutral, colorless verbs to describe what "happens" or "occurs," verbs such as *avvenire* (once), *occorrere* (twice), and *succedere* (four times). More frequently, however, and more suggestively, as he imagines historical events as going through a cycle, as being born, growing, and – although he hesitates to say so – dying, he rehearses a conceptual vocabulary that went back to the ancient Greek historian Polybius (d. 118 BCE).[2] Thus, Machiavelli uses forms of the verb *nascere*, "to be born," no fewer than twenty-seven times in *The Prince*. For example, in chapter 23, he says the Prince should avoid flatterers and never vacillate, because from such things there "arises [*nasce*] the low opinion others have of him" (294). At one point Machiavelli replaces this metaphor with a similar one when he worries that, if the Prince is miserly, it "will give birth to [*partorisce*] infamy" (16.281). Machiavelli may be using such verbs because he wishes to stress the logical, cause-and-effect, nature of events, especially since his project in *The Prince* is to offer rational explanations for history and then to formulate general rules to guide princely action. Thus, in the seventeenth chapter, Machiavelli writes that the good discipline Hannibal preserved in the huge army he led into Italy should not be seen as one of his "miraculous actions," that is, as something inexplicable, but rather as resulting from (*nascere*) the "inhuman cruelty" (282) he used to discipline his troops. However, as Machiavelli explains effects by supplying causes for them, the verb *nascere* that he uses to tie the two together never stops having its literal meaning: events as effects, in other words, are always "born" out of events as causes.

If Machiavelli's *nascere* makes history an organic process, so do the verbs *crescere* (to grow) and *accrescere* (to cause to grow), each of which appears six times in *The Prince*. For instance, Machiavelli talks at one point of how the Florentines and Venetians had "increased [*cresciuto*]" their states by employing mercenaries (12.276). Using the verb *accrescere* in chapter 11, he says that Pope Julius II did everything he could "to cause the Church to grow" (274), and in chapter 3 he praises the Romans for not allowing the states of the Achaeans or the Aetolians "to grow" (260). Moreover, although Machiavelli does not apply the verb *morire* (to die) to states, reserving it for individuals, he does think of the state as succumbing to potentially fatal illnesses, faulting rulers, for instance, who do not spot those illnesses when they "arise [*nascono*]," because they will then "grow [*crescere*]" and will be "incurable" (3.260).

If one ponders Machiavelli's Polybian conception of the state as an entity that is born, grows, and may finally die, then one might expect he would conceive of it either as a plant or as an animate being. In one striking passage, Machiavelli does indeed talk about its being like "all the other things in nature that are born and grow [*nascono e crescono*]" (7.266). Moreover, as the last example in the previous paragraph indicates, he does sometimes talk of how the Prince finds "remedies" for illnesses afflicting the state, as if it were human. In fact, on two occasions the Prince creates the state by "introducing form into matter" (6.264, 26.296–7), a conception harking back to the Scholastics and Aristotle that was used to describe, among other things, procreation. Considering the fact that Machiavelli repeatedly sums up the unpredictable, contingent nature of history in the personified, female figure of Fortune, it is not surprising that he would represent the Prince's introduction of the form of the state into the matter of history in such sexual terms – which is just what he does suggest at the end of chapter 25. If the Prince is to master Fortune, Machiavelli writes, he must "beat her and knock her about" and make her into his "amica," his "friend," ally, and lover (296). Nevertheless, neither conception – of the state growing like a plant or being produced through the Prince's sexual union with *Fortuna* – is as central to Machiavelli's thinking about the Prince as is the notion of his making foundations.

How can we account for such a preference? The best answer may be that, whether the Prince is planting the seed of the state in the ground or inseminating Fortune with his own seed, he effectively loses control over the process. By contrast, if the creation of the state involves the laying of foundations, then the Prince-as-architect has full responsibility over its design just as the Prince-as-mason does over its actual construction. Through this metaphor, in other words, the Prince takes charge of the world of history. Machiavelli might, of course, acknowledge that the making of foundations must be adapted to the nature of the terrain, depends on the availability of building materials, and involves a host of subordinate workers who may have very different agendas than the Prince does. Indeed, Machiavelli's consistent preoccupation with what the Prince must do in order to make his people loyal and obedient subjects might lead one to conclude that the foundations metaphor is an over-simplification. Nevertheless, Machiavelli does insist on it, and this insistence, coupled with the disconnect between the metaphor and reality, suggests that what we are dealing with here comes close to myth or fantasy despite Machiavelli's claim that he is writing about the "effectual truth" of things rather than "imaginary republics and principalities" (15.280). In fact, we can specify one particular myth that his metaphors suggest. As Machiavelli's imagination turns the people into inert blocks of stone and makes the Prince himself immensely powerful as he puts them in place by flexing his will, the Prince becomes something like a version of Amphion, the legendary founder of Thebes, whose eloquence, according to the Roman poet Horace, was so powerful that he was able to build the city, "moving the rocks and putting them where he wanted by means of the sound of his lyre."[3] Particularly relevant to what the Prince is doing is the fact that writers on rhetoric throughout the Renaissance identified Amphion's magical power with eloquence, with the orator's ability to move his listeners.

Machiavelli's Prince is an epic hero as well as a figure out of myth. His defining attribute, his *virtù*, means "valor," "cunning," "prowess," and "manliness" – all attributes of the hero – and his primary activity, waging war, drives the action of almost all ancient and Renaissance epics. I have argued elsewhere that one epic prototype for the Prince is Homer's Odysseus, a hero who unites in himself both cunning and martial prowess, eloquence and violence, the fox and the lion.[4] However, a good case can be made for a very different epic hero as the inspiration for the Prince, a hero whose story Machiavelli certainly knew very well. While uniting some aspects of both Odysseus and Achilles, this hero was seen as transcending both of them in virtue and was especially admired as the founder of the state that Machiavelli and the rest of the Renaissance took as the model for their own. That hero was, of course, Virgil's Aeneas.

Before examining the ways in which Machiavelli's Prince resembles – and, more importantly, differs from – Virgil's Aeneas, it is important to see that, in shaping his Prince as a hero, Machiavelli also followed Virgil's lead in setting up an implicit generic opposition in *The Prince*, contrasting the Prince's epic action with the idleness of pastoral. Virgil himself was not merely aware of this generic opposition, but transmitted it to posterity through his Sixth Eclogue by having the singer of the poem begin in the epic vein with kings and battles, and then having the god Apollo rebuke him for attempting to go beyond the "slender" poetry of pastoral. In fact, the generic opposition between pastoral and epic structured Virgil's career, for he began with the low genre of pastoral and ascended to the heights of epic in *The Aeneid* during the last decade of his life. In general, pastoral – including Virgilian pastoral – embraces pleasure, assumes a benevolent, even protective, natural world that exists apart from the world of time and history, and presents characters who play and sing rather than work. It celebrates happiness as they take their ease, enjoying the *otium*, the idleness and lack of striving, that is, perhaps, the defining feature of the genre. This pastoral *otium* stands at the opposite extreme from the *negotium* – the "work," "business," "trouble," or "labor" – that defines the life of the epic hero. Unlike pastoral swains who never worry about tomorrow, the heroes of epic dwell in a potentially hostile universe and live lives of unremitting effort and constant strife; they are obsessed with time, often looking back to the past with nostalgia, but driven forward in a quest for the future. And if any epic hero embodies these traits, that hero is Virgil's Aeneas.

Machiavelli structures his thought in *The Prince* in terms of this Virgilian opposition between pastoral *otium* and epic *negotium*. Just as Aeneas' life is one of ceaseless toil in pursuit of future goals, so is that of Machiavelli's Prince. He may create spectacles to satisfy his people, but he cannot stop to enjoy them himself. Never idle, he is always busy founding the state, working to maintain it, striving desperately to avoid its collapse. In chapter 14, Machiavelli offers a vision of the Prince that explicitly defines him in epic terms: he is a warrior who commits every moment of his life to "training [*esercizio*] for war" (279). Machiavelli ends the chapter by placing his Prince in the company of such epic conquerors as Cyrus the Persian and Alexander the Great, whose lives were characterized by "industriousness" and who rejected the defining feature of pastoral by refusing to be "idle [*ozioso*]," even "in times of peace" (280).

If the Prince's commitment to *negotium* connects him to Aeneas, so, as we have noted, does his laying the foundations of his state. The creation of Rome is, of course, central to *The Aeneid*, although the actual founding of the city occurs well after Aeneas' death and is not described in the poem. In fact, Virgil actually pays more attention to the *fall* of cities. That of Troy preoccupies Aeneas throughout the first half of the poem and is described in detail in book 2, at whose climax Venus grants Aeneas a vision in which he sees "Neptune with his great trident shak[ing] the walls, dislodg[ing] them from their base, and tear[ing] the entire city down off of its foundations" (*Aeneid* 2.610–12). Moreover, there is another city in Virgil's poem whose destruction is at issue, although that destruction, like the building of Rome, is merely anticipated in the poem. That city is Carthage, whose "walls" are "rising" (1.437) when Aeneas comes upon it, and whose ultimate destruction is foreshadowed by Dido's tragic death. As her body burns, her people wail "as if all of Carthage had fallen to an invading enemy" and the furious flames were already burning through the "roofs of houses ... and temples" (4.671). Dido's sister, Anna, says it directly: with her suicide, Dido has destroyed herself, her people, and her "city" (4.683).

Although the actual building of Rome, like the burning of Carthage, does not occur in Virgil's narrative, Aeneas does have glimpses of what is to come. When he meets his father in the underworld, he is allowed to view his descendants, including Romulus, who is identified with a Rome not merely imagined as extending its "empire" over the earth but as a city that "will have seven hilltop citadels surrounded by a wall" (*Aeneid* 6.782–3). Later, in book 8, when Aeneas' shield is described, he can see Augustus on it, "borne in triumph through the walls of Rome" (8.714–15). This is the Rome, of course, for which and in which Virgil is writing his poem. Looking forward to a glorious future, Aeneas' son declares that the spot where they make their first camp in Italy is the "home," the *patria* or "fatherland," they were destined to reach (7.122), and shortly thereafter they identify a site to build their "city" (7.149), a city Aeneas himself designs (7.157–9). In all the examples just cited, Virgil clearly links Aeneas and the Trojans to the imperial city their descendants will found. What is more, he identifies that city with its walls at least as much as its buildings. The brief opening paragraph of Virgil's poem covers the entire arc of this history: beginning with Aeneas, an "exile because of fate" (1.2), who suffers and fights until he can found his "city" (1.5), it ends by anticipating what Aeneas' descendants will build one day, the "altae moenia Romae [the walls of lofty Rome]" (1.7).

If Machiavelli's Prince resembles Aeneas as a builder, he also resembles his Roman model as the potential creator of a powerful, independent Italian state that will expel the "barbarian" invaders from the north, showing, in the words of Petrarch with which *The Prince* ends, that "ancient valor is not yet dead in Italian hearts" (26.298). Machiavelli's Prince will thus create anew the Roman Empire in the modern world. There are, however, many differences between the Prince and his Roman predecessor. One of the primary ones involves Aeneas' concern for morality and religion, a concern summed up in the concept with which he is associated throughout Virgil's poem, his *pietas*, which meant piety toward the gods, toward ancestors and family, and toward the state in general, and duty, the duty Aeneas displays, for example, by fighting for his people and their future. The medieval Christian tradition later identified *pietas* with love of God, and the word eventually came to mean not just religious piety, but mercy and even pity, so that being pious finally became incompatible with warfare. Writing at the end of this historical transformation, Machiavelli considers *pietas* in chapter 17 of *The Prince*, using the Latin word in its title, "De crudelitate et pietate," "On Cruelty and Piety [or Mercy]" (281). In fact, since this chapter also contains *The Prince*'s only citation from *The Aeneid* – and one of the rare mentions of Virgil in all of his writings – it seems clear that he is here inviting readers to think back to Virgil's poem and to compare and contrast his Prince with Aeneas.

Machiavelli's conception of princely *pietas* is an inversion of Virgil's as well as a rejection of the Christian identification of it with piety, mercy, and pity. Although Machiavelli does say the Prince should be pious, a show of religiosity is all that is required. In fact, Machiavelli is convinced that princes who are truly pious will, like the unarmed prophet Savonarola (6.265), come to a bad end. Thus Machiavelli argues that, since "it is much safer to be feared than to be loved" (17.282), "cruelty" is by far a greater virtue than "piety." Moreover, the model princes who appear in Machiavelli's book also display little or none of Aeneas' loyalty to family, let alone his concern for retainers, friends, and allies. Nevertheless, Virgil's hero and Machiavelli's Prince do seem similar in one way: both are dedicated to the states they found. Aeneas' Rome, however, is an impersonal, transhistorical entity to which he subordinates himself and his desires – he is the agent of a community larger than himself – whereas the Prince treats his state as his personal possession and rules it with an iron fist. As princes and leaders, then, both men may be, in Virgil's words, "renowned for piety" (1.10), since both feel a keen sense of duty to the state. Each is, however, pious in his own way.

Machiavelli's Prince differs even more fundamentally from Aeneas in terms of what he is imagined as building. Aeneas, as we have noted, builds walls and even designs a city that points toward the ultimate *urbs*, Rome itself. The Prince, by contrast, is seen as a maker of foundations. Indeed, at virtually no point in *The Prince* does Machiavelli talk about the *walls* of the Prince's city, let alone imagine him building a castle or residing in a palace. Rather than think of him as an Aeneas *redivivus*, then, it might be better to style him an Aeneas *manqué* – for he seems unable to imagine the building constructed on the foundations he is laying. For example, although words such as *fondare* and *fondamenti* sound from one end of *The Prince* to the other, words related to edifices and buildings make themselves scarce. *Casa* (house), for instance, appears only twelve times, but four of these involve the houses of the people, not of the Prince, and seven are metaphorical, identifying the "ruling house" of a family. Only once, when Oliverotto da Fermo has been "fuori di casa," "away from home" (8.270), is the word used in reference to a prince's abode, although here it is not a structure this would-be Prince is building so much as one he hopes to usurp from the uncle who raised him. Significantly, while Machiavelli celebrates Romulus, the *founder* of Rome, as a model prince (6.264–5), in *The Prince* he never mentions Augustus, who brought peace to the Roman world and was responsible for building the city of which Virgil sings.

Ironically, nowhere is the absence of princely buildings from Machiavelli's vision more noticeable than in the twentieth chapter, which asks whether princes ought to "build fortresses" (289). Although Machiavelli presents this question at the start, he spends the bulk of the chapter reviewing the relationship the Prince has with his subjects, returning to the issue of building fortresses only in the last paragraph. There he begins by endorsing the building of fortresses because it has been done from ancient times. However, he immediately supplies no fewer than three examples of princes whom he praises for having wisely torn down fortresses in order to ensure their hold on their states. He then generalizes that fortresses are useful, or not, depending on circumstances: if the Prince has more fear of his own people than of foreigners, he should build fortresses, but if the situation is reversed, he should not. Having thus presented a seemingly "balanced" judgment of the matter, Machiavelli again criticizes fortress building, speaking of how the Sforzas' huge "castle" (291) in the center of Milan has done them more harm than good. Finally, only at the end of the paragraph does Machiavelli seem to offer a positive example of a fortress, that of the Countess of Forlì (Caterina Sforza) who was able to take refuge in hers when her people rebelled, waiting there until aid arrived from Milan. Machiavelli quickly takes back this last example, however, noting that her fortress was useless to her later when

Cesare Borgia attacked her, for her people, who hated her, joined with Borgia and drove her away. When, in the very last sentence of the chapter, therefore, Machiavelli restates his earlier "balanced" opinion of fortresses, he must be speaking ironically: the conclusion he wants the reader to reach is that the best fortress is not a fortress, but the people. Revealingly, although the people implicitly constitute the Prince's fortress, Machiavelli never says that explicitly. An earlier passage reveals what he really thinks: if the Prince manages the people correctly, they will be the "good foundation" of his state (9.272).

To say that Machiavelli cannot imagine the palace or the city his Prince will build is not to say that he does not imagine specific political goals for him. Fundamentally, his goal is to create and maintain *lo stato* (the state), a word which in Machiavelli's lexicon designated both a geographical and a political entity. To accomplish this goal, he will act to establish a citizen army, institute laws and *ordini*, enforce a sometimes brutal form of justice, create a system of rewards for his citizens to increase their loyalty to the state, and put on spectacles to entertain them. Clearly, in addition to the Prince's own energy and acumen, what is crucial for the state that Machiavelli would establish is the people on whom it will be built. And yet, despite his insistence that they are not to be thought of as mud but as the stone blocks moved by a Prince with Amphion-like abilities, it may well be that he cannot envisage a house or castle or city actually being erected on the foundation they supply precisely because his work also contains a very different vision of them.

This vision appears intermittently in the text whenever Machiavelli stresses the people's egocentric pursuit of their own interests, their undependability, their cowardice, their resistance to innovation. Machiavelli sums it up in chapter 17 of *The Prince*:

> This can be said of men in general: that they are ungrateful, fickle, hypocrites and dissemblers, avoiders of dangers, greedy for gain; and while you benefit them, they are entirely yours, offering you their blood, their goods, their life, their children, as I said above, when need is far away, but when you actually become needy, they turn away. (17.282)

Although the good Prince hopes to be able to shape such beings to serve his ends, they are by their nature an unstable, rather slippery lot – so slippery, in fact, that from this angle they actually do seem more like yielding mud than solid stones. To put the matter less metaphorically: since the Prince cannot truly depend on the people to remain faithful to him, to love him no matter what, he can never rest secure with the foundations he has laid down. Those foundations only seem to be solid; in reality they are always threatening to disintegrate, forcing the Prince to build and rebuild them over and over again.

If Machiavelli, unlike Virgil, cannot imagine the state his hero would create as a city with walls and buildings, he does share with his great forebear a fear that that state, like Aeneas' Troy, can be destroyed. Not surprisingly, to talk about that destruction, Machiavelli consistently uses the verbs *rovinare* and *ruinare* and the noun *ruina*, which appear more than forty times in *The Prince*. All these words derive from the Latin *ruere*, which means "to fall or tumble or rush down," the result of which is, of course, *ruins*. Occasionally, Machiavelli applies one of the verbs to actual buildings, as when he speaks of how people who have taken refuge in a fortified city might find that their possessions outside have been "destroyed [*ruinate*]" (10.273) by their besiegers. Even more strikingly, he uses the two alternate forms of the verb in the same sentence when he compares Fortune to "one of these destructive [*rovinosi*] rivers" that "destroy [*ruinano*] trees and buildings" (25.295). Machiavelli also thinks of ruins on a grander scale, as when he refers to the hiring of Goths as soldiers as the "first cause of the fall [*ruina*] of the Roman Empire" (13.278). Although Machiavelli does not write here or elsewhere of physical ruins, his use of *rovinare*, *ruinare*, and *ruina* cannot help but suggest them.

Normally, when Machiavelli uses some form of these words, he is talking about the fall, that is, the failure or death, of people, and in particular, of princes. Thus, in chapter 15, he says that anyone who assumes human beings will be good will only achieve "his ruin [*ruina*] rather than his preservation" (280). Similarly, at the end of the long chapter 19, Machiavelli sums up what he has been saying about a host of Roman emperors, most of whom failed and were murdered, by explaining how either hatred or scorn was the cause of their "ruina" (289). And in chapter 26 he speaks of how the seemingly invincible Swiss were "defeated [*rovinati*]" by the Spanish infantry (298). However, the literal, architectural sense of those words, though often buried, is never too deep that it cannot be brought into the light, as when Machiavelli says, "It is necessary for a prince to lay good foundations; otherwise, he is certain to come to ruin [*che ruini*]" (12.275). In these two short clauses Machiavelli identifies the fundamental opposition that defines the Prince's life: he either lays foundations or crashes down in ruins. Any life he might have between these two states, a life, that is, in which he would build the walls of his house and city, and then live in them, is simply omitted.

Reinforcing this sense of an absent center between extremes is the one quotation that Machiavelli takes from *The Aeneid* and uses in his discussion of princely *pietas*. In chapter 17 he argues that cruelty is the best policy for rulers, especially new princes, because too much mercy will lead to political chaos. To underscore this point, Machiavelli cites Dido's words from Virgil's poem: "Harsh necessity and the newness of my reign force me to take such measures and to watch over my borders with a widespread guard" (17.282, quoting *Aeneid* 1.563–4). Note what Machiavelli does *not* do here: he does not cite a passage about the difficulties the Trojans have in establishing themselves in Italy, even though the second half of *The Aeneid* is devoted to that very subject. Instead, he cites the words of Dido, whose Carthage is just being built when Aeneas arrives, the sight of which is, ironically, the only glimpse Aeneas has of the building of a great city, like the Rome his descendants will create. It is, however, a Carthage that will eventually be turned into ruins. In other words, when Machiavelli seeks an analogue in Virgil's poem for his Prince's situation, he does not find it in Aeneas' successful journey from the ruined city of Troy to Italy, where the "walls of lofty Rome" will rise one day, but in Dido's Carthage, whose initial construction and final destruction, its foundations and its ruins, must have haunted Machiavelli's imagination.

The imaginary landscape of the Prince's world has very few features. There are open fields in which the Prince hunts and travels and fights; the odd castle or city; many foundations; and plenty of ruins. These last two landmarks tend to become one, for ruins, in their most extreme form, amount to little more than foundations. Machiavelli plays on this similarity when he speaks of how Duke Guidobaldo of Urbino "ruinò funditus," "razed to the ground," the fortresses his enemies used against him (20.290). *Funditus* is a Latin word that means "to the *fundus*," that is, "to the bottom," or "to the foundations." The imaginary landscape of the Prince is thus full of foundations that uncannily anticipate the ruins they will eventually become. The real landscape of Machiavelli's Italy was also filled with ruins, real ruins, the vestiges of the Roman empire whose success Machiavelli may want contemporary Italian states to imitate, but whose fall is equally present in his book. He devotes the longest chapter of *The Prince*, the nineteenth, to a description of the decadence, not the triumph, of Rome, discussing a long series of emperors who failed as rulers and were murdered. However, the clearest sign of Rome's fall in Machiavelli's work is the Italy that it has become, an Italy "without a head, without order, beaten, despoiled, torn apart, overrun . . . [which has] endured every sort of ruin" (26.297). Machiavelli's last term here, "ruina," may refer to the devastation wrought by the French, Spanish, and Swiss, but it cannot help but evoke the *ruins* of the ancient empire that perished a millennium earlier.

In Machiavelli's vision of princely activity, his Prince thus seems trapped in an endless cycle of beginnings and endings. No sooner has he made his foundations than they seem to metamorphose into the ruins that threaten the end of his state. Moreover, his ruin is, in a sense, inevitable, as inevitable as the failure of Cesare Borgia, the fall of Rome, and the death of princes in general, a ruin that forces the Prince to pick up his stones and start laying foundations again – and again and again. Machiavelli's vision of princely action and defeat here must betray his sense of the radical instability of the political world in which he lived, an Italy that, since the French invasion of 1494, seemed always in a state of crisis, its cities conquered one day by one power and then retaken the next day by their original rulers or overrun by someone else. Both the Prince's world and Machiavelli's Italy are ultimately under the sway of Fortune, Machiavelli's symbol of the instability of the world of history. Machiavelli often imagines Fortune as a woman, whom the Prince can beat into submission, although what gets built as a result of that beating remains unclear. When Machiavelli compares Fortune to "one of these destructive [*rovinosi*] rivers," perhaps he does so in order to imagine the Prince as actually *building* something in opposition to it, although what he builds consists of "dikes and embankments" (25.295), not houses, let alone cities. Strikingly, in *The Prince* Machiavelli does not use what was perhaps the most familiar image for Fortune in the Middle Ages and the Renaissance, namely the "wheel of Fortune" (which he had, however, used in his poem "Fortune"). Nevertheless, in the seemingly endless cycle of making foundations, collapsing in ruins, and making foundations again, the Prince does seem caught on some diabolical version of Fortune's wheel.

If one can imagine the Prince as a figure like Amphion, the powerful mythical builder of Thebes, the constant moving of stones as he lays, and lays again, the foundations of his state evokes a very different figure. This figure is not the builder of a city, but a malefactor who has been sentenced to hell where he is condemned to push heavy stones up a steep hill, only to have them roll down to the bottom once he reaches the summit, thus forcing him to repeat the whole process over and over again. This figure is, of course, Sisyphus, and although Machiavelli does not refer to Sisyphus in his writings, he surely knew the story. Homer recounts it in *The Odyssey* (11.593–600), which Machiavelli might have read in Latin translation; Virgil alludes to it in *The Aeneid* (6.616); and Dante in his *Inferno* (7.16–66) makes Sisyphus' punishment the basis for that of the avaricious and the prodigal. Ezio Raimondi has argued that the Sisyphus myth informs a famous statement Machiavelli makes in the letter of December 10, 1513, to Francesco Vettori, in which he describes the wretchedness of his daily life on his farm, speaks of how he has just written *The Prince*, and reveals how desperate he is to return to Florence, so desperate that he would be willing to serve the Medici "even if they would begin by having me roll a stone around [*voltolare un sasso*]."[5] Raimondi claims that the Roman poet Lucretius, in his *De rerum natura* (3.995–1002), provided Machiavelli with the crucial, political reading of Sisyphus' stone rolling as an allegory of the torments men endure, not in the afterlife, but in this world, in their desperate, futile pursuit of political office.

Although Machiavelli's reference to rolling a stone certainly expresses the frustration defined by Lucretius' allegory, Raimondi argues that Machiavelli did not share Lucretius' negative view of political activity, which, however frustrating, was immensely valuable to Machiavelli, indeed his means of self-definition.

Raimondi's argument provides a useful perspective from which to view the Prince's endless laying of foundations, and thus to connect Machiavelli's life with that of the hero he imagines in his book. One may call the Prince's activity Sisyphean, but, as Raimondi suggests, to do so without further qualification would be to see it as hell-on-earth and to make *The Prince* a grim and pessimistic book. To be sure, the Prince's labors will never – can never – cease, but that does not mean he is unhappy as he rolls his stones. In this regard, he is, again, very different from Virgil's Aeneas, for sadness, a melancholy regret over what has been lost, is precisely what the Roman hero feels throughout *The Aeneid*, especially when he goes to war in the second half of the poem, which often turns into an elegy for the loss of youth and beauty. What Aeneas says when he is viewing scenes of the Trojan war carved on the walls of Dido's temple really sums up what Virgil wants his readers to feel about the history of Rome and the burdens its great leaders bear: "Sunt lacrimae rerum," "there are tears in [the very heart of] things" (1.462). While *The Aeneid*, unlike Machiavelli's treatise, can imagine the city of Rome as the end that fulfills and justifies its hero's striving and suffering, Virgil's vision is always tinged with melancholy because of the enormous losses that empire building demands.

Unlike Aeneas, Machiavelli's Prince may never achieve a vision of the house or city whose foundations he is making, but he is certainly not melancholy as he makes them. That does not mean he indulges in the carefree happiness of pastoral as he enjoys the moment and its pleasures. In fact, the verb *godere* (to enjoy), always seems slightly suspect to Machiavelli. He rejects, for instance, the supposed wisdom of his fellow Florentines, who sum it up in a favorite proverb: "to enjoy [*godere*] the benefit of time" (3.260). Machiavelli is warning against temporizing here, but his language implicitly pits princely action, the decisive action he admires in the Romans, against the notion that one might stop and *enjoy* anything. One cannot do so simply because time, which "drives all things on" (3.260), will not permit it. In Machiavelli's analysis of Italy's political crisis, he says its rulers have lost their states precisely because they thought they could tarry in the pleasure of the moment; they have failed because they are just like most men: "when they find things good in the present, they enjoy them (*vi si godono*]" (24.294) rather than worrying about future difficulties. The closest Machiavelli comes to endorsing this kind of happiness is what he says about the successors of

Alexander the Great: "if they had been united, they might have enjoyed at their leisure [*godere oziosi*]" (4.263) the state that Alexander left them. Here, but only fleetingly, Machiavelli comes close to endorsing the enjoyment of the moment that the adjective "oziosi" links directly to pastoral. Such a moment did not occur, of course, because those rulers did not remain united, nor is it ever a possibility for the Prince, who must always be vigilant, alert, and active.

If the Prince cannot stop and smell the roses of pastoral, that does not mean he is unhappy. On the contrary, happiness essentially defines what he feels. For if princes do what they are supposed to do, if, that is, they succeed – and princes are only Princes if they succeed – then they will be not only "powerful, secure, honored," but also, as Machiavelli adds, "happy [*felici*]" (6.265). Revealingly, although he typically defines princely activity through the opposition of *fondare* and *ruinare*, at one point in chapter 25 he substitutes the verb *felicitare* for *fondare*, remarking on how people are unnecessarily puzzled "when they see this prince happy [*felicitare*] today and in ruins [*ruinare*] tomorrow." Two sentences later, Machiavelli explains that a prince who adapts his actions to suit Fortune will be "felice," whereas he who does not will be "infelice" (25.295). In fact, the entire twenty-fifth chapter resounds with variants on *felice* and *felicitare*. Although editors and translators want to turn *felice* into "prosperous" and *felicitare* into something like "to prosper" or "to succeed," the words have those senses only metaphorically. Basically, *felice* mean "happy," although, to do the editors and translators justice, there may also be a trace of the Latin sense of *felix* as "fruitful" or "fortunate" in Machiavelli's *felice*.

To sum up, then: Machiavelli's successful Prince is not filled with a melancholy determination like that of Aeneas, nor does he tarry among the pleasures of pastoral idleness. Forced to move his stones into place over and over again, he resembles Sisyphus, but not the Sisyphus of Homer and Virgil, Dante and Lucretius, the Sisyphus who suffers the pains of hell. Machiavelli's Prince recalls, at least in one important way, another, more modern Sisyphus, the Sisyphus whom Albert Camus describes in his existentialist essay, *The Myth of Sisyphus*. To be sure, Camus's Sisyphus moves his stones around as an act of rebellion, embracing what he does as a way of creating meaning in a meaningless universe in which foundations, not to mention buildings, are unthinkable. By contrast, Machiavelli's Prince thinks he can find meaning in the world as he lays the foundations of the state, even though he may never see the building that would be erected on top of them. Nevertheless, Machiavelli's Prince does join hands with Camus's Sisyphus in that both are committed to action, and in this regard what Camus concludes about his hero's feeling can be said about Machiavelli's hero as well: "One must imagine that Sisyphus is happy."[6]

NOTES

1. Citations of Machiavelli's works are from Niccolò Machiavelli, *Tutte le opere*, ed. Mario Martelli (Florence: Sansoni, 1971); all translations are my own. Citations of *The Prince* provide chapter and page from Martelli's edition.
2. On Machiavelli's knowledge of Polybius' cyclical view of history, see, among others, Felix Gilbert, *Machiavelli and Guicciardini: Politics and History in Sixteenth-Century Florence* (Princeton University Press, 1965), pp. 320–1; and Gennaro Sasso, *Studi su Machiavelli* (Naples: Morano, 1967), chap. 5.
3. Horace, *Ars poetica* 394–6. Although Machiavelli does not refer to Amphion, he no doubt knew the myth from Horace or Dante (*Inferno* 32.11).
4. Wayne A. Rebhorn, *Foxes and Lions: Machiavelli's Confidence Men* (Ithaca, N.Y.: Cornell University Press, 1988), chap. 4.
5. *Opere*, ed. Martelli, p. 1160; Ezio Raimondi, "Il sasso del politico," in Raimondi, *Politica e commedia* (Bologna: Il Mulino, 1972), pp. 165–72.
6. Albert Camus, *Le Mythe de Sisyphe* (Paris: Gallimard, 1942), p. 168.

FURTHER READING

Ascoli, Albert Russell, and Victoria Kahn, eds. *Machiavelli and the Discourse of Literature*. Ithaca, N.Y., Cornell University Press, 1993.
Bárberi Squarottti, Giorgio. *Machiavelli, o la scelta della letteratura*. Rome, Bulzoni, 1987.
Chabod, Federico. *Machiavelli and the Renaissance*, trans. David Moore. New York, Harper & Row, 1958.
Coyle, Martin, ed. *Niccolò Machiavelli's* The Prince: *New Interdisciplinary Essays*. Manchester University Press, 1995.
Fleisher, Martin. *Machiavelli and the Nature of Political Thought*. New York, Atheneum, 1972.
Garver, Eugene. *Machiavelli and the History of Prudence*. Madison, University of Wisconsin Press, 1987.
Gilbert, Felix. *Machiavelli and Guicciardini: Politics and History in Sixteenth-Century Florence*. Princeton University Press, 1965.
Hale, John R. *Machiavelli and Renaissance Italy*. New York, Collier, 1963.
Hörnqvist, Mikael. *Machiavelli and Empire*. Cambridge University Press, 2004.
Hulliung, Mark. *Citizen Machiavelli*. Princeton University Press, 1983.
Kahn, Victoria. *Machiavellian Rhetoric: From the Counter-Reformation to Milton*. Princeton University Press, 1994.
Mansfield, Harvey. *Machiavelli's Virtue*. University of Chicago Press, 1996.
McCanles, Michael. *The Discourse of* Il Principe. Malibu, Undena Publications, 1983.
Najemy, John M. *Between Friends: Discourses of Power and Desire in the Machiavelli–Vettori Letters of 1513–1515*. Princeton University Press, 1993.
Parel, Anthony. *The Machiavellian Cosmos*. New Haven, Conn., Yale University Press, 1992.
Pitkin, Hanna F. *Fortune Is a Woman: Gender and Politics in the Thought of Niccolò Machiavelli*. Berkeley, University of California Press, 1984.

Pocock, J. G. A. *The Machiavellian Moment: Florentine Political Thought and the Atlantic Republican Tradition*. Princeton University Press, 1975.

Rebhorn, Wayne A. *The Emperor of Men's Minds: Literature and the Renaissance Discourse of Rhetoric*. Ithaca, N.Y., Cornell University Press, 1995.

Skinner, Quentin. *Machiavelli*. New York, Hill & Wang, 1981.

6

JOHN M. NAJEMY

Society, class, and state in Machiavelli's *Discourses on Livy*

The *Discourses* and *The Prince*

In the *Discourses on the First Ten Books of Titus Livy* Machiavelli undertook a wide-ranging comparison of ancient and modern states and societies, enlivened by a running contrast between the ancient Roman republic and modern Florence that gives the work much of its polemical force. The proem to book 1 announces a search for "new methods and institutions [*modi e ordini nuovi*]" for "organizing republics, maintaining governments, ruling kingdoms, organizing militias, conducting wars, rendering justice to subjects, and extending territorial power." Machiavelli chose Livy's history of Rome as his textual interlocutor because of its abundant material on the early history of the ancient republic, which was, for Machiavelli, the exemplary state by which all others, ancient and modern, should be assessed. This was not a purely theoretical inquiry. Motivated by the "inborn desire I have always had to work, without fear or hesitation, for those things I believe will benefit everyone" (proem, book 1), Machiavelli hopes that "those who read these analyses of mine may more easily draw from them that utility for which knowledge of history should be sought." Asserting (proem, book 2) that ancient "virtù" and modern "vice [*vizio*]" are "clearer than the sun" and that the modern debasement of religion, laws, and military training has reached extreme levels of corruption, particularly among those holding the reins of power, he must "boldly" say what he understands of "past and future times, so that those, still young, who will read these writings of mine can reject the present and prepare themselves to imitate those former times whenever fortune gives them the opportunity." Machiavelli must have felt some affinity across the ages with Livy, who similarly wanted to show (book 1, preface) not only "what life and morals were like" in Rome's earliest times and "through what men and by what policies ... empire was established and enlarged," but also "how, with the gradual relaxation of discipline, morals first gave way, as it were, then sank lower and lower, and finally began the downward plunge which has brought us to the present time, when we can endure neither our vices [*vitia*] nor their cure."[1] For Livy too, history was "wholesome and profitable," because in it "you behold the lessons of every kind of experience [from which] you may choose for yourself and your own state what to imitate."

To the extent that the *Discourses* follow Livy's text, Machiavelli's attention is chiefly on the first ten books (the first "decade"), which recount Roman history from the origins to 293 BCE, but with frequent references to the third and fourth decades, which take the narrative to 179. (The second decade and the rest of the huge work were lost, and books 41–45 were discovered shortly after Machiavelli died.) But the *Discourses* are not a systematic commentary on Livy. Some sections roughly follow the order of Livy's chapters, while others, most notably the first eighteen chapters of book 1, draw from or allude to scattered bits of Livy in no apparent order.[2] The uneven relationship to Livy has prompted speculation that Machiavelli may have written the parts that do and do not follow Livy as separate works and then loosely combined them. Some believe that, because in chapter 2 of *The Prince* Machiavelli says he "will omit discussion of republics," having "analyzed them at length on another occasion," he must have drafted the first eighteen chapters of book 1 (the part of the work that comes closest to a systematic "discussion of republics") before *The Prince*, which was mostly written in the second half of 1513. All such speculation is built around the *Discourses*' apparent contradictions and awkward transitions, and, while it is certainly possible that portions of the work were drafted at different times, the only external evidence of when it was written is the statement by contemporary historian Filippo de' Nerli that "Machiavelli composed that book of his discourses on Titus Livy at the request" of his friends who gathered in the Orti Oricellari in 1516–17 to read and discuss works of ancient history.[3] The *Discourses* apparently did not receive the final editing Machiavelli may have planned, but their 142 chapters – which exactly match the number of Livy's books and thus pay homage to him – suggest that, even if the work had been revised, the overall structure would not be much different from what we now have.

That the *Discourses* followed *The Prince* also seems likely in view of the critical, deconstructive dialogue they establish with that work. In the dedicatory letter to two friends from the Orti, Zanobi Buondelmonti and Cosimo Rucellai, Machiavelli departs from the "common practice" of those who dedicate their works to princes and, "blinded by ambition and avarice," praise them for many virtues when they ought to condemn them for every censurable fault. He dedicates his *Discourses* "not to those who are princes, but to those who . . . deserve to be princes." If this is self-reproach for having dedicated *The Prince* to a prince, it alludes to the possibility that the *Discourses* critically revisit other aspects of *The Prince*. To note such revisions is not to affirm that the two works represent opposing political philosophies (e.g., that Machiavelli advocated monarchy and the pursuit of power in *The Prince* and republican liberty in the *Discourses*). Their differences lie rather in the way Machiavelli wrote about themes they both address. Three of these differences are particularly noteworthy.

The Prince is famous for its rigid categories and either/or constructions, in which terms define themselves by opposition to one another.[4] Its opening chapter assumes a strict and mutually exclusive opposition between "republics" and "principalities" ("All governments [*stati*] and all dominions ... have been and are either republics [*republiche*] or principalities [*principati*]"). Following a series of other oppositions, including that between hereditary principalities and new ones, the chapter culminates with the statement that all new principalities "are acquired either with the arms of others or with one's own, either through *fortuna* or through *virtù*," thus establishing the dramatic distinction between dependence on others (fortune) and autonomy (*virtù*) that is the foundation of *The Prince*'s advice to, and judgment of, princes. Early in the *Discourses* (1.2) Machiavelli revisits these categories and insists on their instability and mutability. Discussing the classical typology of good and bad forms of government, which Machiavelli knew from Plato, Aristotle, and particularly Polybius ("principato" [monarchy], "ottimati" [aristocracy], and "popolare" [popular government]; and their corrupt counterparts tyranny, government by the few, and anarchy ["licenzioso"]), he asserts the precarious nature of all three good types, which are "so easily corrupted that they come themselves to be pernicious." The three bad forms "depend on" the good ones, and "each is so much like the one closest to it that they easily jump [*saltano*] the one into the other ... If, therefore, an organizer of a republic establishes one of these three governments in a city, he establishes it for a short time only, because no remedy can prevent it from slipping into its contrary [*che non sdruccioli nel suo contrario*], on account of the likeness" of the good and bad forms. The inevitable degeneration of good forms into bad opposites introduces a principle that recurs throughout the *Discourses* and is clearly about more than forms of government. The terms of differential pairs no longer mutually exclude each other; indeed, bad forms inevitably and quickly evolve from their good counterparts on account of their "similarity" to them, and good forms are complicit in generating their negative opposites. Machiavelli later (*Discourses* 3.11) underscores the ubiquity of this principle: "As we have said several times before, in everything is hidden some evil of its own [*qualche proprio male*] that causes new contingencies to emerge." In the *Discourses*, in short, things are *not* either this or that, but sooner or later both.

The inevitable slippage of all things into their contraries implants change, instability, mutability, and, therefore, time and history at the center of the

Discourses in a way that is conceptually precluded in *The Prince*, where Machiavelli had used historical examples, with little attention to context, largely as parables of the constant tug-of-war between *virtù* and *fortuna*. The *Discourses* are predicated on the impermanence of forms, and thus on time and change. The opening chapter of book 3 also theorizes change in terms that recall and elaborate the "slippage into contraries," but now with a medical metaphor: "mixed bodies" like republics and religions, says Machiavelli, must periodically return, or be returned, to their beginnings and original principles if they are to live out their natural lives. All bodies necessarily possess some goodness in the beginning, but "in the process of time that goodness is corrupted, and unless something intervenes to bring it back to the mark, [this corruption] kills the body," for, "as the medical doctors say" (Machiavelli paraphrases the ancient medical theorist Galen), "every day something is added [to the body] which at one time or another requires a cure." The body politic is similarly corrupted from within.

A second idea of *The Prince* subjected to critical scrutiny and historical perspective in the *Discourses* is the myth of heroic founders. In *Prince* 6 the "most admirable" founders are Moses, Cyrus, Romulus, and Theseus, who founded states with their own arms and needed from Fortune only the opportunity to show their "excellent *virtù*" and persuade their peoples to accept new laws and institutions. In *Discourses* 1.2 Machiavelli reprises the myth by characterizing as "happy" those "republics" lucky enough to get all their laws at once from a single lawgiver, as Sparta did from Lycurgus. But Lycurgus was yet another figure of myth-history. His example underscores the legendary, semi-fictional status of (three of) *The Prince*'s four founders, and the improbability of solitary, heroic founding is further emphasized in this same chapter by the acknowledgment that Rome had no Lycurgus. What no single founder did for Rome was accomplished by chance ("il caso"), as we shall see, in the conflicts of its social classes. In *Discourses* 1.9 the figure of the "fondatore" reemerges with the example of Romulus and the "general rule" that "never or rarely does it happen that a republic or kingdom is well organized from the beginning, or its old constitution completely reformed, unless this is accomplished by one man." Two chapters later, however, Machiavelli admits that Romulus' foundations were incomplete. Although, as its "first founder," Romulus gave Rome birth, beginnings, and a senate, it was Numa, Rome's second king, who, "finding the Romans a most bellicose people and wishing with the arts of peace to make them respect the laws," introduced religion and such reverence for God that the Romans feared breaking oaths more than breaking the laws. So powerful were Numa's religious institutions in disciplining the army and instilling courage in the people that, in any "debate" about whether Rome owed more to Romulus or to Numa, Machiavelli avers that "Numa would be first." So Rome had at least two founders, and the first, who arrogated all authority to himself, was not the more important, which casts some doubt on the "rule" that founders must act alone. In *Discourses* 1.49, asserting that Rome's experience shows "how difficult it is in organizing a republic to endow it with all the laws that will keep it free," and that, despite all the good laws instituted by Romulus, Numa, and subsequent kings, "new necessities constantly arose that called for new *ordini*," Machiavelli declares in effect that founding requires constant revision, evolution, and many lawgivers: founding is a long historical process that is never quite complete. The need for constant refounding suggests to Machiavelli the superiority of republics over princes: whereas hereditary monarchies always face the risk of a weak or bad king, well-ordered republics can produce "infinite numbers of very able leaders" (*Discourses* 1.20), each with the talents or temperament required by particular circumstances. Rejecting the "common opinion," shared even by Livy, that condemns the "multitude" as fickle and inconstant, Machiavelli concludes that "governments of the people are better than those of princes." Princes might be more efficient in instituting laws, establishing polities, and creating new *ordini*, but the people are much better at preserving and maintaining a state because they are "more prudent, more constant, and of superior judgment than a prince" (1.58).

In the *Discourses* Machiavelli likewise exposes the Prince-redeemer, theorized in *Prince* 26 as Italy's liberator from foreign invaders, restorer of its lost *virtù*, and promulgator of new *ordini*, as an improbability and perhaps a fantasy. He ponders (in *Discourses* 1.17) the difficulty corrupt republics face in preserving liberty: in a completely corrupt state, not even the best laws can help unless they are "implemented by someone who, with exceptional power [*estrema forza*], makes people obey." But Machiavelli says he does "not know if this has ever happened or is even possible," because no one can live long enough to consolidate such reforms. Theoretically, the only hope is for someone to give the city a "new birth, amidst much danger and blood," using "*grandissimi straordinari*, which few men know how to use or would even want to." "Straordinari" are measures literally "outside" (Latin *extra* = vernacular [e]*stra*) the "ordini," which is Machiavelli's term for the public institutions, laws, and customs that sustain healthy states (whether republican or monarchical). Ambitions pursued in violation of the *ordini*, whether by individuals or groups, are, in Machiavelli's lexicon, either a negation of the *ordini* (hence producing *disordine* or plural *disordini*) or methods and ways "outside" the *ordini*: *modi straordinari*, *vie straordinarie*, or simply *lo straordinario* – a degeneration of the *ordini* that he also calls "corruption." The cluster of terms deriving from *ordini*, including the *Ordinanza*, the militia

Machiavelli helped create; the verb *ordinare* (to establish or institute *ordini*); the adjective *ordinario* and past participle *ordinato* (as in well-organized, *bene ordinate*, republics); and the various forms of its negation (*disordini*, *straordinario*, etc.) are, collectively, the central and most frequent element of Machiavelli's political vocabulary, with no fewer than 1,700 occurrences throughout his works, and over 600 in the *Discourses* alone. The only words that approximate this frequency have a wider variety of often non-political meanings: *parte*, *modo*, and *stato*. After *ordini*, the political terms that appear most often are "city" (over 1,100) and "citizen(s)" (*c.* 600); "prince(s)" (approximately 1,000); *popolo*, *popolare*, and related terms (almost 1,000); and "king," "kingdom," and "to reign" (over 1,000).[5]

In *Discourses* 1.18, still pondering the possibility of applying "straordinari" to corrupt republics, Machiavelli suggests that new *ordini* can be instituted either gradually or all at once. But he immediately asserts the "near impossibility" of both ways. Prudent reformers who proceed gradually are rare and they "never" succeed in persuading others. For the sudden introduction of comprehensive reform, "modi ordinari [lawful, constitutional means]" are useless in conditions of complete corruption; it would be "necessary to have recourse to *lo straordinario*, in other words, to violence and arms, and before all else to become prince [*principe*] of that city in order to do with it as one wishes." This is the moment where the *Discourses* come closest to the figure of the Prince-redeemer, and critics who believe that Machiavelli began the *Discourses* before *The Prince* see in these lines the "discovery" of the redeemer-reformer of a corrupt state who employs "lo straordinario," setting aside laws and conventional ethics to heal the state and impose new *ordini* – a "discovery" that allegedly prompted Machiavelli to interrupt the *Discourses* and give the idea fuller treatment in *The Prince*. Yet the next few lines argue the *impossibility*, in terms of human psychology, that a prince could ever be capable of both amoral methods and moral objectives: "Because reinstituting in a city a government of laws [*vivere politico*] presupposes a good man [*uomo buono*], and becoming prince of a city through violence presupposes a bad man [*uomo cattivo*], it is extremely rare that a good man will want to make himself prince through evil means, even if his objective is good, or that an evil man, having become prince, will want to do good things or that it will ever occur to him to use for a good end the authority he has acquired by evil means." Far from "discovering" the Prince-redeemer, this passage dismantles the very possibility of achieving "good" ends through "bad" means. Good men are unwilling to use evil measures, even for good ends, and bad men, perfectly willing to use evil measures to acquire power, will not turn that power to good ends. In *Discourses* 1.18 Machiavelli finally buries the fantasy of good princes capable of redeeming states with the "violence and arms" of "grandissimi straordinari," which he now relegates to the pathology of political corruption.

Republics between the nobles and the people

The "path not yet trodden by anyone" that Machiavelli claims to enter in the proem to book 1 of the *Discourses* is a revolutionary inquiry into the social bases of politics, government, and territorial expansion, and into the social structures, class interests, and conflicts underlying the success and failure of states. Each of the three books, Machiavelli says (in *Discourses* 1.1; proem, book 2; and 3.1), focuses on a particular theme. The first explores Rome's domestic political arrangements to identify the laws and *ordini*, both political and religious, "that sustained *virtù* for so many centuries" (1.1). The second deals with the growth of Rome's empire and discusses mostly military topics, including methods of warfare, infantry and cavalry, fortresses, relations with conquered peoples, colonization, army discipline, and, in 2.19, the damage conquests can do to a conqueror (a hint of what comes later). This book also contrasts successful Roman methods of incorporating conquered peoples into the empire with Florence's faltering attempts to preserve its regional domin-ion in Tuscany. Among the most memorable chapters of the *Discourses* is 2.2, in which Machiavelli attributes to ancient religion the love of freedom that caused the Romans' earliest antagonists to resist them so obstinately – especially the ferocity and grandeur of the ceremonies that instilled greatness of spirit, strength of body, the high estimation of worldly honor and obliga-tion toward one's country – and contrasts this with the debilitating meekness of Christianity, with its preaching of humility rather than glory, abjectness rather than *virtù*. The third book explores the contributions of individuals to Rome's greatness, particularly in military tactics and commands, but it frequently departs from its assigned themes to deal with other issues, for example, the long chapter (3.6) on conspiracies.

Amidst many digressions and detours, the unifying theme of the *Discourses* is the precariousness of republics and their vulnerability to the ambition of noble and elite classes. The motor driving the history of republics, their forms of government, and their capacity for survival, defense, and expansion is the perpetual antagonism between the nobles and the people: in Rome between the senatorial nobility and the plebs, and in Florence between the *grandi* (or *ottimati*) and the politically organized middle classes called the *popolo*. In *Prince* 9 Machiavelli had already distinguished the aims of these classes: whereas the *popolo* desires only not to be oppressed by the *grandi*, the latter actively seek domination over the *popolo* and equality with the prince: because *grandi* consider themselves the prince's equals, he cannot satisfy their demands "honorably and without damaging the interests of others." Princes will therefore be more secure in alliance with the *popolo*, whose loyalty they can win because the objective of the *popolo* "is more honorable than that of the nobles."

The antagonism between the classes assumes more dramatic significance in the *Discourses*. It appears early in the book: in 1.2 Machiavelli claims that the conflict ("disunione") between the plebs and the Senate drove the Roman state toward "perfection." Under the monarchy of the Tarquins, the nobles had been restrained, but with the establishment of the republic they began to "spit out their poison against the plebs" (1.3) and provoke hostilities. The "security of the plebs" thus required the institution of the Tribunes of the plebs, guarantors of the *ordini* with power to veto laws that threatened the plebs. In praising the Tribunes for making Rome an even "more perfect republic," Machiavelli polemically dissented from prevailing opinion among the Florentine *ottimati*, who admired Venice for its domestic peace and condemned Rome as a "chaotic [*tumultuaria*]" republic. In 1.4, Machiavelli not only defends the Roman republic from such criticism but also argues – in the most strikingly revolutionary idea of the *Discourses* – that "those who condemn the conflicts [*tumulti*] between the nobles and plebs are, it seems, criticizing the chief reason why Rome remained free." Contemporaries were well aware of Machiavelli's penchant for challenging conventional wisdom; but to Francesco Guicciardini the notion that conflict between Rome's classes was not an obstacle to and nothing less than the foundation of Rome's liberty seemed so preposterous that he famously mocked it, saying that "praising discord is like praising a sick man's illness because the remedy that has been used on him is the right one."[6] Guicciardini had the weight of tradition from Augustine to the Renaissance civic humanists on his side: a millennium of political thought had assumed that good states must have internal peace and that discord is a poison to be eradicated. But Machiavelli argued that competition between Rome's classes yielded the supremely beneficial effect of containing the overweening ambition of the nobles by giving the people a share of political power. Rome's detractors, he continues in 1.4, "do not properly consider that in every republic there are two divergent classes [*umori*], the *popolo* and the *grandi*, and that all the laws made in favor of liberty result from their conflict [*disunione*] ... Every city ought to have ways in which the people can express its aspirations," for "the desires of free peoples are rarely damaging to liberty." The Tribunes represented and protected the plebs and restrained noble ambition and insolence; for making Rome a popular republic they merit the highest praise.

The people, Machiavelli says in 1.5, are better "guardians of liberty" than the nobles because (as he had written in *The Prince*) the *grandi* have a "great desire to dominate" whereas the people have "only the desire not to be dominated" and thus a "greater longing to live free." He qualifies this by saying that in republics (like Rome) seeking expansion and empire the people are more effective guardians of liberty, whereas in republics that aim only at self-preservation without expansion (like Venice and Sparta) nobles will best fulfill that role. But he then reformulates the distinction between the classes, no longer emphasizing the difference in their desires, by asking "which kind of men are more dangerous in a republic, those who seek to acquire [the people], or those who fear losing what they have acquired [the nobles]." His answer is that the *grandi* are more dangerous because those who "possess much" are able to "upset things [*fare alterazione*]" "with greater power and impact [*con maggiore potenza e maggiore moto*]." "Alterazione" here means more than disturbance or trouble: "fare alterazione" means overthrowing or undermining a government. This is the kernel of the analysis that he subsequently develops throughout the *Discourses*: whereas the people, lacking the resources of the *grandi*, need the state to resist being oppressed, the *grandi* subvert the state in ways made possible by their wealth, which permits them to do more than dominate the people. The very means with which they pursue this end undermine the institutions of the state itself; they are the more dangerous class because they inevitably corrupt and destroy republics. Only from constant discord between the classes can laws emerge to safeguard liberty by giving the people the power to keep the nobles in check. Machiavelli defends "tumultuous" Rome because its conflicts ensured both liberty and territorial expansion by giving the people a decisive role in government (through the tribunes) and the army.

In Florence, by contrast, Machiavelli asserts that these features of a vigorous popular republic were either lacking or incompletely achieved. After affirming in 1.5 that the "guardianship of liberty" is better entrusted to the *popolo* than to the *grandi*, in 1.7 he gives a prime example of such "guardianship": "Those appointed *per guardia* of a city's liberty can be given no power more useful or necessary than that of bringing accusations before the people or the magistrates against citizens who in any way commit offenses against free government [*contro allo stato libero*]." Formal indictments are necessary to restrain offenses committed by nobles against the people (his example is Coriolanus, an "enemy of the popular party" in Rome, who tried to punish the plebs for creating the Tribunes by withholding grain, and whose indictment by the same Tribunes saved him from an angry mob) and also to force those who slander their enemies (slanders being "one of the ways citizens gain great power" [1.8]), to defend and prove such "calumnies" in court. The absence of such procedures, says Machiavelli, led to the assassination in 1498 of Francesco Valori, leader of the Savonarolan party, and to the expulsion and exile of Piero Soderini in 1512, in both cases because the slanders directed against them by their enemies could not be formally adjudicated and, as Machiavelli presumed in Soderini's case, dismissed. Soderini's *ottimati* enemies therefore resorted, not only to "private forces [*forze private*]" – to factions and conspiracies – but also to the intervention of "foreign forces [*forze forestieri*]" – an explicit allegation that the anti-Soderini *ottimati* conspired to bring in the Spanish army to overthrow him and the republic. Machiavelli again underscores Florence's need for an institution akin to the Tribunes in observing (1.49) that Florentine courts were always vulnerable to bribery and pressure from "the few and the powerful."

In *Discourses* 1.33, Machiavelli returns to Florence's failure to contain its *grandi*. Problems afflicting republics, he says, "more often emerge from internal than external causes," and the internal causes can be divided into two categories: citizens who are "allowed to take more power than is reasonable" and corruption of the laws. But both causes converge on elite subversion of the state. The first danger occurs when a "young noble" of "virtù istraordinaria" emerges – and the "straordinaria" nature of his "virtù" is already a clue to the danger – and citizens "compete to honor him, so that if he has any ambition at all ... he quickly achieves such power that, when the citizens realize their error, they have few options to stop him." Machiavelli's example is none other than Cosimo de' Medici, the founder of the family's political fortunes, who, "thanks to his prudence and the ignorance of his fellow citizens, acquired such reputation that he began to cause fear within the *stato*." Cosimo's rise to power and victory over his rivals was achieved with his "parte," his faction, which made him "principe della republica" (first citizen, although the allusion to princely pretensions is unmistakable), just as happened, Machiavelli adds, "with Caesar in Rome." This is a stunning juxtaposition, especially in view of Machiavelli's judgment that the ancient historians who praised Caesar had been "corrupted" and intimidated by his power (1.10) and that Caesar became the "first tyrant in Rome" (1.37). The daring comparison exposes the full implications of what had seemed (to the Florentines) the innocuous appearance of a popular "young noble" of "virtù istraordinaria." Machiavelli later (1.52) attributes Cosimo's success to his strategy of favoring the people, but this follows a chapter about the Roman Senate's attempt to win the gratitude of the plebs by instituting regular pay for the army and hoping thereby to weaken the Tribunes, who opposed the gesture as a trick to increase taxes. Cosimo's seemingly unobjectionable tactic of favoring the people takes on a different meaning when placed in the context of attempts by "nobles" to deceive the people.

Elite subversion of the state acquires another dimension in *Discourses* 1.46: ambitious citizens, says Machiavelli, seek to protect themselves from being harmed by private citizens or punished by the magistrates by "seeking friend-ships [*amicizie*]" in "ways that have the appearance of being honorable, such as helping people with money or shielding them from the powerful. And because this seems virtuous [*pare virtuoso*], it easily fools everyone and nothing is done to prevent it, until, forging ahead without opposition, [a citizen] attains such power that private citizens and the magistrates alike fear him." Republics ought therefore to have among their *ordini* some method of "preventing citizens from doing evil under the camouflage of good." Machiavelli elaborates on this in *Discourses* 3.28, recounting from Livy the episode of Spurius Maelius, not a patrician but "very rich," who "acquired a huge following among the people" by stockpiling grain and distributing it "privatamente" in order to win the people's gratitude. Fearing this "liberal-ity," the Senate appointed a dictator (a special prosecutor) who put him to death. Machiavelli has a larger point here (announced in the chapter title) about how "the beginning of tyranny often hides under a pious deed," which leads him to the paradox that, while "citizens of repute" are indispensable to republics ("a republic without citizens of repute cannot last"), they are at the same time "the cause of tyranny." Reputation is acquired in two ways, "public" and "private," and republics must distinguish between them and curb the latter. The "private" methods include doing favors "to this and that citizen by lending money or arranging marriages for their daughters," and they are dangerous because "such things make men *partigiani* [faithful clients of factional leaders] and embolden those distributing favors to corrupt public institutions [*il publico*] and transgress the laws."

These "private" ways of acquiring reputation are available only to wealthy *grandi*, who gather clients and build powerful factions that make them more feared than the magistrates. The privatization of politics begins with acts of seeming friendship and culminates in forms of extra-legal power that over-whelm the state. Machiavelli repeatedly emphasizes that nobles and *grandi* carry out their subversion of republican *ordini* through "private methods" that reflect the practices and inclinations of their class, through the very virtues, we might say, of "nobility" and what we now call patronage. Twice (*Discourses* 1.16 and 3.3) he admonishes free governments, especially newly liberated ones, to prevent factions and the corruption and tyranny they breed by "killing the sons of Brutus," a reference to the conspiracy against the fledgling Roman republic hatched by the legendary founder's sons, who plotted to restore the monarchy. In Machiavelli's reading, the "sons of Brutus" are not simply enemies of the state; they are nobles who seek to overthrow the new republic because it did not allow them to profit "straordi-nariamente," as they had under the kings, "so that it seemed to them that the people's liberty became their servitude" (1.16). The "sons of Brutus" stand for all *grandi* ready to scuttle republics to secure the "extra-legal" privileges they expect from alliances of mutual advantage with princes. A "free *stato*" makes "partigiani" – factions – its enemies, not its friends, for those who once benefited from a "stato tirannico" by "feeding on the prince's wealth cannot live happily if deprived of the chance to reap such benefits and will feel constantly impelled to re-impose tyranny to regain" them (1.16). Tyranny, as Machiavelli analyzes it in chapters 29, 34, 35, and 40 of book 1, is not simply the excessive authority of one man: the institution of the dictator in Rome did not cause tyranny, because it was generally done "according to the *ordini publici*" (1.34). Tyranny originates instead from the temptation by either class to have recourse to a protector. When the *popolo* does so, even if provoked by the need to protect itself from the nobility's desire to "tyrannize," Machiavelli says it is always an error (1.40). But more often it is the *grandi*, the "sons of Brutus," who bring on tyranny.

Machiavelli attributed Rome's collapse into tyranny to two principal causes. The first was the enraged response of the nobility to the revival of the agrarian laws by the Gracchi late in the second century BCE (*Discourses* 1.37). By limiting the landed wealth of nobles and distributing the conquered lands of the expanding empire to Rome's soldiers, the original agrarian laws had enabled the plebs to "hold in check the ambition of the nobles" and protect Rome's liberty. But their revival sparked such bitter enmity between patricians and plebeians that both classes resorted to "private remedies," raising armies and plunging Rome into civil wars that "brought the destruction of the republic ... and ruined Roman liberty." Machiavelli acknowledges that this analysis "might seem inconsistent" with his earlier contention that conflicts between the Senate and the plebs had preserved liberty, but he explains the apparent contradiction, partly by claiming that the plebs themselves changed and became more determined "to share honors and wealth with the nobles," but mostly by asserting that the "ambition of the nobles is so great that, if it is not resisted in various ways, it quickly brings a city to ruin." Even though the agrarian laws could not permanently contain the ambition of Rome's nobles, liberty would not have lasted as long as it did without those laws: "If the contention over the agrarian law took three hundred years to enslave Rome," without such laws "the city would have lost its liberty much sooner," and nothing could have prevented complete dominance by the nobles. Even as Machiavelli castigates the aims and methods of the nobles, he concedes that the nobility's furious reaction goaded the plebs – who were not always innocent victims – into "illegalities [*straordinari*]" of their own. But when noble ambition, particularly in defense of property and wealth, caused the conflict to descend into the "private remedies" of factions and civil war between armies led by the warlords Sulla,

Marius, and ultimately Caesar, Rome became a thoroughly "corrupt" republic and tyranny was inevitable.

The culmination of Machiavelli's polemic against the *grandi* comes in *Discourses* 1.55. Praising the uncorrupted "goodness" of the free cities of Germany, he explains that they retain their virtuous way of life because they permit no one to live "in the style of a gentleman [*gentile uomo*]" and thus maintain among themselves a "balanced equality [*una pari equalità*]." These "gentlemen," defined as those "who live idle, on income from landed possessions, unconcerned with cultivating the land or other activities to support themselves," are "pernicious" to republics. But "still more pernicious are those who, besides enjoying this landed wealth, command walled towns and have subjects who obey them" – quasi-feudal lords who exercise jurisdiction over rural populations. Both groups are "hostile to all *civiltà*" – the customs and institutions of republican government – and their preponderance in the Kingdom of Naples, around Rome, in Lombardy, and in the Romagna explains why republics do not exist in those regions. By contrast, in Tuscany, home to three republics (Florence, Siena, and Lucca) and other cities eager to recover (from Florence) their lost liberty, the absence of "gentlemen" guarantees "equality" before the law and compels the elite class to live within the political and legal framework established by republics. Machiavelli is not arguing here the theoretical superiority of one or the other form of government. His point is analytical: a city's (or region's) form of government is determined by the power and legal status of its elites. Republics are possible only where there is no powerful class of landed gentlemen or feudal lords; where such "gentlemen" predominate, only princedoms are possible, because only a monarchy (a "mano regia") has the "absolute and overwhelming power" needed to restrain the "extreme ambition and corruption" of the nobles. To institute a republic in a region dominated by "gentlemen" would require their elimination; conversely, installing a princedom in an area of great "equality" would require creating a class of "gentlemen" and giving them landed possessions and jurisdiction. "Gentlemen" and feudal lords are incompatible with republics because they exercise autonomous jurisdiction and create hierarchical forms of power manifested by the obedience they command from their factions; they are the most visible and unrestrained form of "private" power and "corruption."

The "gentlemen" of *Discourses* 1.55 and the urban *grandi* who in every republic contend with the people are two quite different categories of nobles: "gentlemen" prevent republics from coming into being at all, whereas urban *grandi* compete with the people in a republican framework and do not exercise formally autonomous jurisdiction. But a closer look at the argument reveals that the two kinds of nobles represent different points, indeed moving points, on a continuum of danger to republics. The link is suggested in Machiavelli's observation that "he who wishes to construct a kingdom or a princedom where there is much equality can do so only if he draws out of this equality many men of ambitious and restless temperament and makes them gentlemen ... endowing them with fortified towns and landed possessions and giving them grants of property and men, so that, placed among them, he maintains his power through them and they fulfill their ambitions through him." Despite declaring it nearly "impossible" to accomplish this, Machiavelli here in effect explains how republics can be transformed into principalities. The key element is the presence in republics of "men of ambitious and restless temperament" whom the prince can turn into "gentlemen." These can only be the urban *grandi* whose ambition, so Machiavelli assumes, makes them always and already disposed to accept privileges from princes and become the "gentlemen" needed to sustain a monarchy. Their overweening ambition, in other words, makes *grandi* potential "gentlemen," prepared to turn their backs on the republic and become pillars of a princely order in return for money, property, and prestige. The passage alludes to what Machiavelli no doubt feared the Florentine *grandi* were in the process of doing (and what the Medici principate achieved some years after he died).

The second cause of Rome's corruption was the privatization of military commands. Vast territorial conquests were made possible by the "full powers [*commissioni libere*]" (2.33) the Senate gave to consuls and other commanders, reserving to itself only the right to start or end wars. This policy was predicated on the assumption that broad discretionary authority to make battlefield decisions would enhance the determination of commanders to win glory for themselves and thereby instill greater discipline and motivation. But the very expansion that proved its wisdom turned a good practice into a fatal flaw (3.24). Unlike the virtuous Cincinnatus, who refused the Senate's invitation to extend his consulship (in violation of its own decree against reelection), the consul Publilius Philo was offered and accepted reappointment, because it was thought unwise to change commanders in the middle of a war. Machiavelli finds in this episode the beginning of Rome's ruin: "although decreed by the Senate for the public good, in time this destroyed Roman liberty." It became a bad thing, ironically, because the practice of giving commanders greater autonomy and longer terms had been so successful: "The farther the Romans took their armies, the more such extensions of command seemed necessary to them, and the more they did it." One result was that fewer men had experience of command and the prestige of victory. Even worse, "when a citizen commanded an army for a long time, he won it for himself and made it his private army [*partigiano*], for in time that army forgot the Senate and recognized him as its leader." "In this way," Machiavelli adds, now linking the extension of commands and the privatization of military power to the civil wars sparked by the agrarian laws, "Sulla and Marius were able to find soldiers to follow them against the public good; in this way Caesar was able to seize his country." Rome's liberty slipped into its contrary by a process that was difficult to recognize before it was too late. Expansion transformed its armies from expressions of the state's, or the people's, authority into instruments of the personal ambition of dangerous warlord-generals. Both Rome and Florence, despite their differences, fell victim to dangerously powerful citizens: as Roman commanders made armies their "partigiani," so Florentine factional bosses, above all the Medici, similarly made citizens their "partigiani."

The *Discourses* are much more than fulsome praise of Rome's liberty, power, and territorial conquests. Woven into this acclaim and admiration is the story, equally exemplary in its negative portrayal, of how the *ordini* that made Rome powerful and free were eventually corrupted and "slipped into their contraries," a corruption that turned *ordini* into *disordine* and *modi straordinari*. Machiavelli believed that the decline of Roman liberty that resulted from the spread of different forms of private power reached its nadir in the late republic and not, as the civic humanists had held, under the emperors. Indeed, he saw the disease to which Rome fell victim as peculiar to republics, precisely because the open class antagonisms permitted by healthy republics are easily corrupted and "slip into" factional and private power. What makes the *Discourses* so compelling is the effort to understand how and why strong states and peoples destroy themselves. *The Prince* tried to theorize the success and failure of individuals in terms of the struggle of *virtù* against an external, malevolent, and ultimately inexplicable *fortuna*. In the *Discourses*, by contrast, the evolution and transformation of political institutions and social structures govern historical change in processes that, while not easily predictable, have a logic and an etiology that can be understood, at least in retrospect. Whether Florence could learn from Rome's errors was a matter for the next generation to decide.

NOTES

1. Livy, *Ab urbe condita*, ed. and trans. B. O. Foster (Cambridge, Mass.: Harvard University Press, 1988), 1:6–7.
2. Felix Gilbert, "The Composition and Structure of Machiavelli's *Discorsi*," *Journal of the History of Ideas* 14 (1953): 136–56. See also appendix 2, by Cecil H. Clough, "Machiavelli's Use of Livy in His *I Discorsi*," in *The Discourses of Niccolò Machiavelli*, ed. and trans. Leslie J. Walker, 2 vols., new edition (London and Boston: Routledge & Kegan Paul, 1975), 2:323–7.

3. Filippo de' Nerli, *Commentari de' fatti civili occorsi dentro la città di Firenze* (1728), p. 138; Gilbert, "Composition and Structure," p. 151.
4. Michael McCanles, *The Discourse of* Il Principe (Malibu: Undena Publications, 1983).
5. Counted from the Intratext website: www.intratext.com/IXT/ITA1109/_FA.HTM
6. Francesco Guicciardini, *Considerazioni sui* Discorsi *del Machiavelli*, in *Opere*, vol. 1, ed. Emanuella Lugnani Scarano (Turin: UTET, 1970), p. 616; trans. James B. Atkinson and David Sices, in *The Sweetness of Power: Machiavelli's* Discourses *and Guicciardini's* Considerations (DeKalb, Ill.: Northern Illinois University Press, 2002), p. 393.

FURTHER READING

Baron, Hans. "Machiavelli the Republican Citizen and Author of *The Prince*," in Baron, *In Search of Florentine Civic Humanism*, 2 vols. Princeton University Press, 1988, 2: 101–51.
Bausi, Francesco. *I "Discorsi" di Niccolò Machiavelli. Genesi e strutture*. Florence, Sansoni, 1985.
Coby, J. Patrick. *Machiavelli's Romans: Liberty and Greatness in the* Discourses on Livy. Lanham, Md., Lexington Books, 1985.
Mansfield, Harvey C., Jr. *Machiavelli's New Modes and Orders: A Study of the* Discourses on Livy. Ithaca, N.Y., Cornell University Press, 1979.
Pocock, J. G. A. *The Machiavellian Moment: Florentine Political Thought and the Atlantic Republican Tradition*. Princeton University Press, 1975.
Richardson, Brian. "The Structure of Machiavelli's *Discorsi*," *Italica* 49 (1972): 460–71.
Sasso, Gennaro. *Machiavelli e gli antichi e altri saggi*, 4 vols. Milan, Naples, Ricciardi, 1987–97.
   Niccolò Machiavelli. Storia del suo pensiero politico, 2nd edition. Bologna, Il Mulino, 1980.
Skinner, Quentin. *The Foundations of Modern Political Thought*, 2 vols. Cambridge University Press, 1978, 1: 139–89.
   "Machiavelli's *Discorsi* and the Pre-Humanist Origins of Republican Ideas," in *Machiavelli and Republicanism*, ed. Gisela Bock, Quentin Skinner, and Maurizio Viroli. Cambridge University Press, 1990, pp. 121–41.
Whitfield, J. H. "On Machiavelli's Use of *Ordini*," *Italian Studies* 10 (1955): 19–39.

Three editions with excellent commentary:

Machiavelli, Niccolò. *Discorsi sopra la prima deca di Tito Livio*, ed. Giorgio Inglese. Milan, Rizzoli, 1984.
   Discorsi sopra la prima deca di Tito Livio, ed. Francesco Bausi, 2 vols. Rome, Salerno Editrice, 2001.
   Opere, ed. Rinaldo Rinaldi, 2 vols. Turin, UTET, 1999.

7

MIKAEL HÖRNQVIST

Machiavelli's military project and the *Art of War*

The military occupies a paradoxical, if not controversial, place in Machiavelli scholarship. Most commentators agree that Machiavelli's concern with military affairs was at the heart of his political thinking and that the military crisis of contemporary Italy crucially influenced his views. It is widely recognized that Machiavelli considered force and military strength to be determining factors in relations among states. Scholars also concur that his involvement with the new Florentine militia ordinance of 1506 was an important formative experience during his chancery days and that the idea of a conscript army or citizen militia was a key element in his classically inspired republicanism. Despite this widespread acknowledgment of the role of the military in Machiavelli's thought, the *Art of War* (1521), his most systematic and detailed treatment of military organization and the methods of war, remains by far the least studied of his major works. How can this paradox be explained, and is this relative lack of interest in the *Art of War* justifiable? This chapter analyzes Machiavelli's military experience and writings on military matters and takes a critical look at the *Art of War*. By comparing this late work to the earlier memoranda Machiavelli composed in connection with the militia project and his theorizing on military affairs in *The Prince* and the *Discourses*, we will ask how and to what extent the *Art of War* contributes to our overall understanding of Machiavelli's political and military project, and in what way his military experience and the role he played in the militia ordinance of 1506 prepared, or anticipated, his views on military affairs in the major works.

Machiavelli's military experience and theories must be seen in the context of the Italian wars and the general crisis that the Italian military system underwent at the turn of the sixteenth century. At a time when gunpowder weapons, including field artillery and hand-held arms, were beginning to play a more significant role on the battlefield, medieval military organization and methods of warfare were rapidly becoming obsolete. The situation was particularly alarming for Florence, since the city had stubbornly refused to introduce the necessary military reforms that other Italian states began to adopt in the fifteenth century. While their neighbors experimented with new methods of government control over the military, created specialized administrative organs for military matters, and raised new taxes enabling the establishment of standing forces, the wealthy merchants of the Florentine republic, reluctant to provide the fiscal resources needed for maintaining a permanent military organization, continued to rely on mercenary companies hired on a short-term basis for the city's defense. This policy impeded Florence's expansion and thrust for hegemony in Tuscany and central Italy and left the city unarmed, weak, and defenseless in the face of foreign aggression. After the French invasion in 1494, which resulted in the expulsion of the Medici and the loss of the republic's most important subject town, the seaport of Pisa, many critics, foremost among them Machiavelli, bitterly accused the elite of a failure of leadership and neglect of military affairs.

As his government's envoy to Pistoia and Arezzo between 1499 and 1503 and as second chancellor responsible for administering Florence's relations with its subject territories, Machiavelli experienced firsthand the military crisis and breakdown of the Florentine territorial state. Inspired by the Swiss attempt to imitate the ancient Roman militia, by Cesare Borgia's effort to fashion himself into a modern equivalent of ancient warlords, and by his own reading of ancient historians and military treatises, Machiavelli began to develop ideas for a new militia ordinance for Florence. The idea begins appearing in his correspondence from May 1504, and later that year he addressed Florence's military weakness in the first *Decennale*, the chronicle in verse of Italian history since the French invasion of 1494. Having from early on understood that it would be impossible to arm a faction-ridden city, Machiavelli accepted the compromise of a peasant militia drawn from the immediately surrounding countryside (the *contado*). What was radically novel in his proposal was the idea of creating a permanent military organization throughout the territory based on part-time soldiers who would continue to be enrolled and trained even in peacetime.

Poor showings by hired mercenaries at the Pisan front in the summer and fall of 1505 paved the way for the militia. After some clever maneuverings by *gonfaloniere* Piero Soderini and his brother Francesco, the cardinal of Volterra, the proposal was piloted through the legislative councils. On December 30, 1505, Machiavelli was dispatched to the Mugello and Casentino regions to begin recruiting, equipping, and training conscripts aged fifteen to forty. During this early stage, he was closely involved in the project at all levels. Perhaps on Machiavelli's recommendation, Cesare Borgia's former henchman, the notoriously cruel Spanish condottiere Don Miguel de Corella (known in Italy as Don Michele or Micheletto), was hired as "Captain of the Guard of the Contado and District" to enforce discipline in the new militia and throughout the *contado*. In 1506, Machiavelli wrote the "Cagione dell'Ordinanza," also known as the "Discourse on the organization of the Florentine state for arms," in which he justified and outlined the structure of the new militia and explained why recruitment, for reasons of security, had to begin in the *contado*, and not in the city proper or in the outlying district. The councils formally approved the militia on December 6, 1506, and entrusted oversight in peacetime to a new magistracy, the Nine of the Militia, and in wartime to the foreign policy and military affairs committee of the Ten. The first committee of the Nine was elected on January 10, 1507, with Machiavelli as its chancellor, an office he held, alongside his positions as head of the second chancery and secretary of the Ten, until 1512.

Although Machiavelli never commanded troops in battle, in his capacity as chancellor of the Nine he gained broad and direct experience of military affairs. In addition to managing the official correspondence with civilian commissioners who oversaw military operations, his regular duties included hiring captains and training and equipping the militia companies. He spent the winter of 1508–9 at the Florentine camp outside Pisa. On March 7, 1509, he was at Piombino to negotiate the handing-over of that seaport, and when the official act of Pisa's surrender was signed on June 4, 1509, he was one of the countersigners. After the recovery of Pisa, arguably the high point in his chancery career, Machiavelli's attention seems to have shifted away from the militia, and, apart from two more memoranda on the subject of relatively minor interest, there are few indications of involvement in military activities during his last years in office. He was apparently not present when the Florentine army, consisting largely of militia conscripts, was routed by Spanish troops at Prato on August 29, 1512, the event that cleared the way for the return of the Medici and the dismantling of the republic – and his militia – in September.

The introduction of the militia is one of the best documented episodes from Machiavelli's years in office. Published and unpublished sources of various kinds allow us to glimpse the thinking behind the project and follow its implementation in some detail. In addition to the above-mentioned "Cagione," Machiavelli wrote several memoranda dealing extensively with the recruitment of conscripts, the organization of the militia companies, the authority of the commanders, the meting-out of penalties, disciplining of troops, cavalry reform, the methods to be used in the siege of Pisa, and the election of a new infantry captain. His correspondence and retrospective comments in the *Discourses* and the *Art of War* offer a good understanding of his role in the endeavor. Other valuable accounts are provided by contemporaries, especially Francesco Guicciardini in his *Storie fiorentine*.

In the militia memoranda we encounter for the first time the central idea underlying Machiavelli's military thinking: the importance for every state of having its own arms ("arme proprie"). Drawing on this humanist common-place, he argued that experience shows that troops raised among the subjects of one's own dominion are better and more reliable than foreign mercenaries. In these early writings, Machiavelli declares "arme proprie" to be the corner-stone of all successful states. The preamble to the "Cagione" affirms that in all empires, states, principalities, republics, and wherever power is exercised, the foundations must be "justice and arms," polemically accuses Florence of having "little justice and no arms at all," and decries the republic's weak foundations and vulnerability in the face of outside threats. The fact that the Florentines had lived "without arms" for a century while somehow main-taining their independence should not lead them to believe they could go on doing so in the future. Times have changed, Machiavelli asserts, and to stay free the city must arm itself and adopt a new military structure by public decree.[1] Machiavelli returned to the theme of the republic's foundation in arms in the December 1506 law that instituted the militia, with a slight, but important, modification in its application to Florence. Here too he says that all republics that have maintained themselves and expanded have had as "their principal foundation two things, that is, justice and arms."[2] But con-trary to what he wrote in the "Cagione," Florence is now said to have "good and holy laws" and a well-organized administration of justice, and to lack only arms. The change was no doubt prompted by the need not to offend his political superiors if the proposal was to have any chance of being approved in the councils.

But how could "arme proprie" and the recruitment of infantry conscripts in the *contado* contribute to a refounding of the Florentine state? To trace this line of Machiavelli's thinking, it is necessary to look more closely at how the militia was organized and employed during its first years and the language of the laws passed in connection with it. From these texts it appears that the policing and law-enforcement functions of the project were equally important to, or more important than, that of raising a fighting force. There is a constant concern in these writings with the problem of disobedience, unruly behavior, and the fear of outright rebellion among the militias and in the *contado* population in general. Whatever its broader aims, there can be little doubt that the militia's organizers conceived of it, at least in part, as a powerful tool by which to bind the subjects of the *contado* closer to the republic. A key to understanding this aspect of the militia is that "proprie" in Machiavelli's concept of "arme proprie" refers not to the individuals who carried the weapons, but to the state or city commanding them. It is also important to keep in mind that Machiavelli's militia companies did not consist of city dwellers or well-to-do rural property holders coming together for the mutual defense of their republic. Instead, they were peasants with no, or limited, political rights, forced to serve as soldiers by legal decree. Placed under the authority of the republic and its commanders, the conscripts were equipped with arms that were not their private possessions but belonged instead to the republic of Florence. In this way, so it was hoped, arms and the discipline and organization they entailed would serve as a unifying element binding together the heretofore loosely structured Florentine territorial state.

The campaign to create loyal subjects in the *contado* was also conducted in several other ways. Much attention was paid to the authority of the commanders and their right to punish conscripts who did not respond to call-up notices or failed to follow orders. Penalties varied from fines for minor offences to capital punishment for desertion and participation in armed political factions. Dispatches tell of heavy-handed disciplining of the *contado*, including even the burning of houses. Unsurprisingly, given Machiavelli's involvement in the project and the recent impact of Savonarola's preaching, religion and fear of God were also mobilized to exact obedience and create ties of loyalty. The December 1506 law required conscripts to take an oath on the gospels, with words that "would most effectively bind them body and soul," while a catalog of the punishments to which they were liable was read to them. Through the use of various insignia, the organization and division of the *contado* into territorially based militia companies were made visually manifest. The introduction of the new ordinance also meant that the Florentine banner with the heraldic lion, the Marzocco, would be seen flying high all over the countryside, especially during holidays, when the companies were expected to train. In the light of this evidence, Machiavelli can hardly be accused of exaggerating when, in a letter to the Ten of January 1506, he refers to the ordinance as "a project designed to reform a province [*una impresa di riformare una provincia*]."[3] But would the subsequent arming of the city proper, as projected in the "Cagione" (but never realized), have meant the extension of this disciplining reform to the capital?

Machiavelli clearly viewed the introduction of new military orders in the Florentine state as a step-by-step process. Since the original ordinance of 1506 limited conscription to the *contado* peasants and did not include Florentine citizens, it bore little likeness to the ancient Roman militia. However, Machiavelli's intention and that of his closest associates was to extend the ordinance to the city proper and also to the subject cities of the district. The reasons he offers in the "Cagione" for not arming the cities of the district at the outset seem genuine and well founded. While the inhabitants of the *contado* could be relied upon because they had nowhere to turn for protection except Florence and therefore "recognize no other patron," the subject cities in the *distretto*, like Arezzo, Sansepolcro, Cortona, Volterra, Pistoia, Colle Valdelsa, and San Gimignano, were often openly hostile to Florence and desired nothing more than to reclaim their independence. If Florence were to furnish them with arms, they would most likely use them not to defend the republic against foreign powers, but to rebel against it. Hence the arming of the *distretto* would have to wait until the *contado* had been properly organized militarily. As for why the arming of Florence itself should also be postponed, Machiavelli becomes more evasive. Since the role of the city is to command and provide cavalry troops, and since it is more difficult to learn to command than to obey, he argues, it is preferable to begin by imposing obedience on the *contado* rather than by appointing commanders from the city. This is hardly a satisfactory explanation, but what seems an uncharacteristically weak argument should instead in all likelihood be regarded as deft handling of a sensitive issue. According to Guicciardini, one of the major obstacles to the acceptance of the militia was the widespread fear among Florence's leading citizens that it would be used by Soderini and his supporters to seize tyrannical power.[4] To defer the arming of the city to a distant and unspecified future was one of several strategic master strokes that helped make the militia possible.

The militia's humiliating defeat at Prato in 1512 and Machiavelli's subsequent dismissal from office did nothing to dampen his interest in military matters, which remained unabated through his last years, when he was appointed inspector of Florence's fortifications. His major works put this interest on prominent display. Although scattered comments in diplomatic reports and memoranda strongly suggest that Machiavelli had already begun before 1512 to develop a comprehensive theory linking politics and military concerns, it is to the theoretical writings of his post-chancery period that we must turn for more systematic treatments.

The Prince's arguments on military affairs can largely be summarized in the three main points identified in connection with the militia documents: the state's foundation in arms, the concept of "arme proprie," and the introduction of new military orders as a step-by-step process. *The Prince* echoes the "Cagione" in claiming that "good arms," in combination with good laws and good customs, are the foundation of all strong states. Good arms, according to chapter 12, are even more fundamental than good laws, since there "cannot be good laws where there are no good arms, and where there are good arms there must be good laws." In *The Prince*, whose explicit aim is the founding of a new militarily strong principality in central Italy, Machiavelli alludes to Florence's lack of arms in the famous reference to Savonarola, the Dominican friar who in 1494–8 influenced Florentine politics from the pulpits of San Marco and the cathedral. At the beginning of his ascendancy,

Savonarola gained widespread support for his political and religious reforms by claiming divine inspiration as a prophet. But when the Florentines began to doubt him, comments Machiavelli in chapter 6, the friar lacked the means necessary to keep "the support of those who had believed in him" and to "make unbelievers believe." In a memorable passage, Machiavelli says that, like all "unarmed prophets," Savonarola "came to ruin in his new orders." Had Savonarola been able to buttress his innovations and divine inspiration with armed force, he would have remained "powerful, secure, honored, and successful." The lesson Machiavelli draws from this episode, and to which he would return in the *Discourses* (3.30), is that religion (and rhetorical manipulation in general) can surround and infuse power with legitimizing and mobilizing gestures but cannot replace arms as a viable and lasting foundation for power itself.

In chapters 12 and 13 of *The Prince*, Machiavelli loudly proclaims his belief in the superiority of "arme proprie" over hired troops and attacks the Italian mercenary system. Dividing arms into three broad categories, "arme proprie," auxiliaries, and mercenaries, he dismisses the latter two as completely useless. In most cases they are outright harmful, because they are disloyal, greedy, excessively ambitious, and lack unity, discipline, and fear of God. Even when they prove to be militarily effective, they are dangerous because their self-interest and thirst for power make them a threat to the state that hires them. Native troops are more loyal, more reliable, and fight with greater determination and are therefore to be preferred by republics and princes alike. "Arme proprie" are a mark of *virtù* and thus a means to combat and control fortune. A principality lacking its own arms cannot be secure because "it is completely dependent on fortune" and has no *virtù* with which to defend itself "in times of adversity."[5]

Having a strong foundation in "arme proprie" is not an end in itself in *The Prince* but the starting point of a process. This is most evident in Machiavelli's lengthy account of Cesare Borgia's struggle to free himself from dependence on the arms of others. Having disposed of his own warlords, the Orsini, Vitelli, Oliverotto da Fermo, and others, by ruthless fraud, and perhaps with the blessing of the king of France, Borgia began to put distance between himself and the French, seeking new allies and strengthening his power base in the Romagna. Machiavelli believes that by the time Borgia's father, Pope Alexander VI, died unexpectedly in 1503, the duke had come a long way in laying solid foundations for his future power. Although unable to bring his military and political project to completion, his uncompromising pursuit of a strong foundation based on his own arms made him in Machiavelli's eyes a model for new princes to emulate.

In the *Discourses* Machiavelli repeats his conviction that a good militia is the foundation of every strong state and that nothing good can last if not supported by arms. His primary example is the legendary founding of Rome, in which Romulus committed fratricide to make himself the city's sole ruler, delegated power to the Senate, and reserved to himself only the right to convene this assembly and command the armies (*Discourses* 1.9). According to Machiavelli, this Roman example teaches that the exercise of military command and the control of arms should be regarded as the exclusive prerogative of the prince. The message that one should not trust in the arms of others is further endorsed in his account (*Discourses* 2.4) of Rome's victory in the Social War in 91–89 BCE. For some time the Romans had allowed their Italian allies to live as their equals under the law and to participate in their conquests, while reserving for themselves "the seat of the empire and the right of military command." The wisdom of this mode of proceeding became clear when the Italian allies later rebelled against Rome's growing power. Rome's newly conquered non-Italian subjects had, upon submitting to Roman generals, come to regard Rome, and not its allies, as their protector and lord. Therefore the Romans could now equip them with Roman arms and use them in a pincer movement to quell the uprising. The example further highlights the expansive, and inherently imperialist, nature of Machiavelli's notion of "arme proprie," and its connection to sovereignty, conquest, and territorial control.

If the ancient Roman republic exemplifies in the *Discourses* the virtues of "arme proprie," modern Florence illustrates the cost of neglecting this founding principle. Having originated as an unfree colony under Roman domination, so Machiavelli argues, Florence struggled for a long time to climb out of the shadow of its mighty founder. When the city finally began to shape its own institutions, this was done in an ad hoc manner, resulting in a confused mixture of old and new elements. As a result, Florence had never become a truly sovereign state or a republic worthy of the name (*Discourses* 1.1, 1.49). Treating Piero Soderini, Florence's lifetime *gonfaloniere* and Machiavelli's superior and protector, as a potential founder, the former secretary explains why Soderini failed to give Florence the foundation it so badly needed. While Savonarola's ambitious project had been defeated because the friar lacked arms, Soderini's downfall was caused by his reluctance to employ the arms placed at his disposal. Although he had been exhorted to use force against the supporters of the old Medici regime, to "kill the sons of Brutus" as Machiavelli puts it, Soderini's attachment to peaceful ways and civic institutions prevented him from following this advice. Instead, he tried to win over his adversaries "with patience and goodness," with the result that they finally ousted him from power (*Discourses* 3.3). Soderini's failure clarifies what action Machiavelli thought was required if the arming of Florence and the introduction of the militia ordinance were to give the republic strong foundations. The disciplining of the *contado* was an important, but of itself insufficient, step in a process that would also require the uncompromising enforcement of law and brutal suppression of the regime's opponents, including the supporters of the Medici and the intransigent *ottimati*, who are stigmatized in the *Discourses* as enemies of liberty.

In the *Discourses* Machiavelli develops his step-by-step approach to the introduction, through the militia, of good arms and good laws into a full-fledged theory. "New laws and institutions" can be introduced in either of two ways, either all at once ("a un tratto") or little by little ("a poco a poco") (*Discourses* 1.2, 1.18). While the founding of the Roman republic and subsequent killing of the sons of Brutus could be seen as an example of the first strategy, the second way is epitomized by the long-term constitutional development of Rome, which, although described by Machiavelli as a "perfetta republica" after the institution of the Tribunes completed its mixed constitution, nevertheless went on changing its laws and institutions as necessity required. Gradual development is also evident in Rome's imperial strategy, which Machiavelli wanted Florence to imitate in its dealings with subject cities and neighboring states. The militia project of 1506 fits well into this theory, since its ultimate aim was not merely to provide Florence with arms but also to constitute the initial step in a grand strategy designed to bring the rule of law to the city and, in a perhaps not too distant future, imperial greatness to the republic.

The militia project aimed at the creation of obedient, loyal, and patriotic subjects through the introduction of "arme proprie," and the *Discourses* can be said to offer the theoretical foundation for this plan. In Machiavelli's classically influenced republicanism, the republic is not a coming together of independent individuals or free citizens. Instead, good and civic-minded citizens are *created* out of obedient subjects, who have learnt to respect the laws, to serve their country, and to place the public good over their own private good. Among such citizens, who realize that they have no rights other than those granted by the state, arms can be introduced and a native militia of free citizens created. In such a republic, disciplined citizens can be expected to use their arms not to fight each other or to compete for power *within* the republic, but to contribute to its expansion and territorial growth by seeking glory *beyond* its borders. Arms are now in the hands of citizens, but more important still is the fact that they are commanded and directed by the republic and its leaders. Such arms can be used in the defense of republican liberty and the pursuit of imperial greatness. Without them there can be no sovereignty. This is the larger meaning of Machiavelli's "arme proprie."

How does the *Art of War* (written probably in 1519 and published in 1521 and the only one of Machiavelli's major works to be printed during his lifetime) contribute to his theory of "arme proprie" and military reform? Does it represent a further development of his military thinking? Dedicated to Lorenzo Strozzi, who played a role in Machiavelli's reconciliation with the Medici around this time, the *Art of War* is Machiavelli's only attempt in the genre of the humanist dialogue. It is set in 1516 in the Rucellai gardens, the Orti Oricellari, where in the years after the Medici restoration of 1512 humanists and young *ottimati* with republican leanings met to discuss literature, philosophy, ancient history, and politics. Its main speaker is the renowned military captain and condottiere, Fabrizio Colonna, who, we are told at the beginning of book 1, passed through Florence while returning south from Lombardy, where he had served Ferdinand of Spain in the recent wars, and was invited to the Rucellai gardens to discourse on war. Fabrizio is welcomed by his host, Cosimo Rucellai, and by Zanobi Buondelmonti, Battista della Palla, and Luigi Alamanni, who appear in minor roles in the dialogue. Machiavelli says he was present on the occasion, but he does not take part in the discussion. The dialogue thus purports to offer a realistic account of an actual meeting in the Orti Oricellari, but, as we shall see, this narrative frame is deceptive.

As promising as its setting and cast may sound, the *Art of War* is an awkward attempt to combine the form of the humanist dialogue, inspired by Plato and Cicero, and the subject matter of ancient military treatises, notably that of Vegetius (late fourth century CE). Due to the dominant and lecturing posture of Fabrizio, it lacks the dramatic qualities and multivocal charm of other Renaissance dialogues like Leonardo Bruni's *Dialogi ad Petrum Histrum*, Poggio Bracciolini's *De avaritia*, Lorenzo Valla's *De voluptate*, and Francesco Guicciardini's *Dialogo del reggimento di Firenze*. In its monological reliance on the voice of the main speaker, it comes closer to resembling Matteo Palmieri's *Vita civile*, in which a wise elder lectures two young members of the Florentine ruling class on the ethical principles underlying republican citizenship.

The manifest aim of the *Art of War* is to provide a blueprint for a revival of ancient Roman military methods and values and to define the proper place of war and a correctly organized military in a state's political and civic culture. Divided into seven books and preceded by a short preface, it deals in great technical detail with many aspects of ancient and contemporary military life. The first book begins with an intriguing exchange between Fabrizio and Cosimo Rucellai on the possibility of imitating the ancients (and why Fabrizio himself has not put into effect the methods he lauds) and the performance of the Florentine militia, to which we will return. In books 1 and 2 Fabrizio offers his views on how to recruit, pay, arm, train, and discipline troops. There is also a fascinating note in book 2 on the effect of military music on soldiers' morale. Books 3 and 4 discuss the order of battle, including marching and combat formation, tactics and the coordination of infantry and cavalry. Book 5 says more about the order of march, provisioning, communications and intelligence. In book 6 Fabrizio addresses problems involved in setting up camp and decamping, with a detailed account of the organization of the Roman military camp, and comments on the use of spies and the importance of discipline. Book 7 deals with fortifications, sieges, and the advantages and disadvantages of artillery and concludes with a lament over the failures of Italy's princes and their responsibility for its continued vulnerability.

Interspersed between these lengthy discourses are elaborations on well-known Machiavellian themes. Following the line of reasoning established in the militia writings and continued in *The Prince* and the *Discourses*, the *Art of War* subscribes to the doctrine that a state's foundation must be in arms. We are on familiar ground when Fabrizio claims in book 1 that "no one has ever founded a republic or a monarchy without seeing to it that those who live there have arms to defend themselves"[6] and that all human endeavors and institutions would be futile if not buttressed and defended by military force. Having in *Prince* 25 compared the military defenses needed to ward off foreign invasions to dams and dykes built to keep a rising flood at bay, Machiavelli likens them in the preface of the *Art of War* to the roof of a palace without which all the fancy interiors would be devastated by heavy rains.[7] Yet again we learn that the strength of an army consists in its infantry. The ideal is the ancient Roman republic and its citizen army, imitated with relative success by the modern Swiss. Machiavelli evidently took pleasure in putting his exaggerated and often rather spurious criticism of condottieri and his arguments in favor of "arme proprie" in the mouth of Fabrizio, a hired gun whose professional military career contradicted the ideals of the citizen army he lauds.

The technical nature of the *Art of War* goes a long way toward explaining why the work has attracted comparatively little critical attention. Another reason could be the fact that, by comparison with *The Prince* and the *Discourses*, it takes a more conventional view of politics and military affairs, and especially of the means necessary for pursuing an expansionist foreign policy. Having in *The Prince* advocated a calculating and self-interested use of fraud and cruelty and exhorted his princely reader to devote himself exclusively to the methods and practices of war, in the *Art of War* Machiavelli has Fabrizio condemn war as a full-time profession (the "arte" of war as against the part-time citizen-soldier) because it obliges the warrior at all times "to be rapacious, fraudulent, and cruel."[8] In the *Discourses* he had heaped praise on the great conquerors of the ancient Roman republic, men like Manlius Torquatus and Furius Camillus, whose bravery, ruthlessness, and ability to deceive had been instrumental in the Roman republic's rise to imperial greatness. In the *Art of War*, by contrast, he commends the military captains of the early republic for having acquired glory, not by a calculated use of force and fraud, but by acting as "valiant and good men [*valenti e buoni*]."[9] This censoring of the Machiavellian warlord could be seen in relation to the work's general downplaying of the role of the resourceful individual in military affairs. In the *Art of War*, the quality of *virtù* is attributed to orders, institutions, collectivities, actions, and horses, and only rarely to individuals. Emphasis on conventionally acceptable means and on collective and institutional aspects of warfare has the intended, or unintended, effect of taking much of the edge off Machiavelli's earlier arguments.

Rather than assuming that in the *Art of War* Machiavelli was backtracking from his previous positions, it might more reasonably be speculated that this sudden conventionality was an attempt to defuse the controversy that had come to surround his name. For it is difficult to ward off the impression that the former secretary was here writing with an eye to the Medici, cleansing his theory of the features that might offend their sensibilities, anxious to safeguard, or at least not endanger, future commissions or appointments (although this does not necessarily preclude subversive subtexts in the *Art of War*).[10] The commission to write the *Florentine Histories* awaited him, and it is not far-fetched to assume that he was also envisaging a role for himself in connection with the new militia reinstituted under the Medici in 1515. While this strategy could possibly be excused as a prudent adaptation to circumstances, it contributed to making the *Art of War* a more conventional and less bold enterprise than its predecessors.

As this hypothesis implies, one of Machiavelli's main objectives in writing the *Art of War* was to promote himself in the role of military expert, not unlike the way he had presented himself in *The Prince* as an authority on political affairs and a potential Medici adviser. It is also against this background that the references in the *Art of War* to the Florentine militia need to be understood. As soon as Fabrizio begins presenting his program for military reform in book 1, Cosimo Rucellai interrupts him to point out how closely it resembles the Florentine militia ordinance of 1506. This comment gives rise to an interesting exchange between Fabrizio and Cosimo on the pros and cons of Machiavelli's militia:

> COSIMO: Then you would set up a militia ordinance similar to the one that exists in our villages?
>
> FABRIZIO: What you say is right. But to tell the truth, I would arm, officer, exercise, and order them in a manner that I am not sure you have used.

COSIMO: Then you praise the ordinance?

FABRIZIO: Why would you like me to condemn it?

COSIMO: Because many wise men have always condemned it.

FABRIZIO: You contradict yourself when you say that wise men condemn the ordinance. One could easily be held wise and be misjudged.

COSIMO: Its consistently poor performance makes us hold this opinion.

FABRIZIO: Beware that it isn't your own fault, not that of the militia; as you will come to understand before the end of this discussion.[11]

When Cosimo confronts Fabrizio with the criticism that the idea of arming the people commonly receives, the latter, echoing Machiavelli's "Cagione" of 1506, retorts that it can never be harmful to arm one's own citizens and subjects, as long as it is done in a legal and orderly manner. Having repulsed Cosimo's attack, Fabrizio goes on the counteroffensive, criticizing "these wise men of yours [questi vostri uomini savi]," Machiavelli's sarcastic term for the opponents of the militia among Florence's leading citizens, who, instead of condemning the ordinance, ought to dedicate themselves to correcting its weaknesses. How this can be done, Fabrizio promises to demonstrate in the course of their discussion.[12]

In a brief memorandum, written in connection with Lorenzo de' Medici's plan for a new militia in 1514–15, Machiavelli looked back to the ordinance of 1506, attributing its shortcomings to the fact that the soldiers were too few and insufficiently armed.[13] In the Art of War he has Fabrizio say that he would "arm, officer, exercise, and order" his conscripts in a manner different from that previously used. This open criticism of how the first militia project was realized should not come as a surprise, since Machiavelli, from his position as chancellor of the Nine, could have had only limited control over its implementation. Given that the exchange between Fabrizio and Cosimo serves as a preamble to the proposal for military reform set forth in the Art of War, we have every reason to assume that the methods advocated by Fabrizio would have resembled those Machiavelli might have preferred in 1506 if he had had final say in the matter.

Noting how little the fictional Fabrizio Colonna has in common with the historical figure of that name, most readers of the Art of War tend to view the former as a thinly disguised mouthpiece for Machiavelli's opinions. If this is correct, Fabrizio's ideas in the dialogue allow us to situate Machiavelli more firmly in relation to his intellectual and political project. Of particular interest in this context are the reasons Fabrizio gives for not having put his own theories into practice. Great undertakings and designs, he explains, require careful preparations so that when the opportunity arises one is ready to seize it. Careful preparations, however, are presumably made cautiously and quietly, and he who does so cannot be accused of negligence unless the opportunity arrives and he fails to act either "due to lack of preparation or for not having thought of it at all." By his own admission, Fabrizio has never had "any such opportunity to show what preparations he has made in order to be able to bring the militia back to its ancient orders."[14] In book 7, toward the end of the dialogue, he challenges his young interlocutors to judge for themselves whether he has given sufficient thought to the reforms he proposes, convinced that they will recognize his expertise and realize how much time he has spent considering these things.[15]

Fabrizio's comments suggest that he regards himself not merely as an expert in the ancient art of war and military affairs in general, but also as a potential founder of a new, but classically inspired, military establishment in Italy. Throughout Machiavelli's works, arms are considered the foundational element of all states, and we may therefore surmise that this military reform implies the founding of a new political order as well. Fabrizio's problem, however, is that he cannot act on his own, or in his own name, but only through others, and through those whom he is called upon to serve. In this regard, he bears a canny resemblance to his creator, highlighting the particular constraints under which the latter operated.

If the *Art of War* succeeds in promoting Fabrizio, alias Machiavelli, as a military expert – praise that the work was later to receive from the likes of Voltaire and Clausewitz – ultimately it fails to bridge the gap between theory and practice and between means and ends. Whereas the militia project, *The Prince*, and the *Discourses* had all been animated by a strategic step-by-step approach tying small beginnings to great things to come, in the *Art of War* Machiavelli does not even attempt such a link. Here there is no process, no introduction *a poco a poco*, no intermediate stages, no disciplining of the countryside, no combined use of diplomacy and force, and no enemies to overcome. In the end, Fabrizio leaves his young interlocutors with the promise that the first Italian state that adopts the methods originally introduced with the Florentine militia, as perfected however by the lessons Fabrizio himself imparts during the course of the dialogue, "will become master of this whole province [*signore di questa provincia*]." To press home his point, he cites the example of the ancient Macedonians, who, while the other Greek states were idle and "occupied with reciting comedies," made preparations and founded a military establishment capable of making them "rulers of the world [*principe di tutto il mondo*]." Such are the power and glory, he implies, that await Florence if it follows his advice. But Fabrizio is old and tired, and the task of reviving the might and glory of the ancients will fall on the young. Finishing his long discourse, he bows out and reproaches "nature" for having made him aware of all he has said without giving him the opportunity or power to put it into practice.[16] As Fabrizio exits the stage, we are left with the impression of having heard Machiavelli acknowledge more openly and in less guarded terms than ever before the ultimately imperial objective of his political and military project.

NOTES

1. "La cagione dell'Ordinanza, dove la si truovi, et quel che bisogni fare," in Niccolò Machiavelli, *Tutte le opere*, ed. Mario Martelli (Florence: Sansoni, 1971), pp. 37–40 (38).
2. "Provvisione prima per le fanterie, del 6 dicembre 1506," in *Opere*, pp. 40–7 (40).
3. Niccolò Machiavelli, *Legazioni e commissarie*, ed. Sergio Bertelli, 3 vols. (Milan: Feltrinelli, 1964), 2:927.
4. Francesco Guicciardini, *Storie fiorentine*, ed. Alessandro Montevecchi (Milan: Rizzoli, 1998), 26, pp. 417–28.
5. *Opere*, p. 278.
6. *Opere*, p. 312.
7. *Opere*, p. 301.
8. *Opere*, p. 305.
9. *Opere*, p. 306.
10. See Marcia Colish, "Machiavelli's *Art of War*: A Reconsideration," *Renaissance Quarterly* 51 (1998): 1151–68.
11. *Opere*, pp. 310–1.
12. *Opere*, p. 311.
13. "Scritto sul modo di ricostituire l'Ordinanza," in *Niccolò Machiavelli, Istorie fiorentine e altre opere storiche e politiche*, ed. Alessandro Montevecchi (Turin: UTET, 1986), pp. 129–33 (131).
14. *Opere*, pp. 304–5.
15. *Opere*, p. 387.
16. *Opere*, p. 389.

FURTHER READING

Burd, L. Arthur. "Le fonti letterarie di Machiavelli nell'*Arte della guerra*," *Atti della Reale Accademia dei Lincei*, ser. 5, 4 (1896–7): 187–261.
Fachard, Denis. "Implicazioni politiche nell'*Arte della guerra*," in *Niccolò Machiavelli politico storico letterato*, ed. Jean-Jacques Marchand. Rome, Salerno Editrice, 1996, pp. 149–73.
Gilbert, Felix. "Bernardo Rucellai and the Orti Oricellari: A Study on the Origin of Modern Political Thought," *Journal of the Warburg and Courtauld Institutes* 12 (1949): 101–31.
  "Machiavelli: The Renaissance of the Art of War," in *Makers of Modern Strategy from Machiavelli to the Nuclear Age*, ed. Peter Paret, Gordon A. Craig, and Felix Gilbert. Princeton University Press, 1986, pp. 11–31.
Hörnqvist, Mikael. *Machiavelli and Empire*. Cambridge University Press, 2004.
  "Perché non si usa allegare i Romani: Machiavelli and the Florentine Militia of 1506," *Renaissance Quarterly* 55 (2002): 148–91.

Lynch, Christopher, ed. and trans. with commentary, Niccolò Machiavelli, *Art of War*. University of Chicago Press, 2003.

Mallett, Michael. *Mercenaries and Their Masters: Warfare in Renaissance Italy*. Totowa, N.J., Rowman & Littlefield, 1974.

"The Theory and Practice of Warfare in Machiavelli's Republic," in *Machiavelli and Republicanism*, ed. Gisela Bock, Quentin Skinner, and Maurizio Viroli. Cambridge University Press, 1990, pp. 173–80.

Najemy, John M. "'Occupare la tirannide': Machiavelli, the Militia, and Guicciardini's Accusation of Tyranny," in *Della tirannia: Machiavelli con Bartolo*, ed. Jérémie Barthas. Florence, Olschki, 2007, pp. 75–108.

Pieri, Piero. *Il Rinascimento e la crisi militare*. Turin, Einaudi, 1952.

Vegetius, *Epitome of Military Science*, trans. N. P. Milner. Liverpool University Press, 1993.

Verrier, Frédérique. "Machiavelli e Fabrizio Colonna nell'*Arte della guerra*: il polemologo sdoppiato," in *Niccolò Machiavelli politico storico letterato*, pp. 175–87.

Wood, Neal. "Introduction" to Niccolò Machiavelli, *The Art of* War, trans. Ellis Farneworth (1965). Revised edition: New York, Da Capo Press, 1990, pp. ix-lxxix.

8

ANNA MARIA CABRINI

Machiavelli's *Florentine Histories*

Machiavelli's *Florentine Histories* originated under Medici patronage at a moment in which, after the death of Lorenzo the younger in May 1519, Cardinal Giulio de' Medici controlled Florence (on behalf of Pope Leo X) and the regime seemed open to the possibility of major constitutional overhaul. In March 1520, Machiavelli was introduced to Giulio through the good offices of his friends in the Orti Oricellari and was warmly received. One result of the changed attitude of the Medici toward Machiavelli was the commission, finalized on November 8, 1520, and approved by the Officials of Florence's university (the Studio), headed by Giulio himself, to "compose the annals and chronicles of Florence [*ad componendum annalia et cronacas florentinas*]." The *Florentine Histories* thus owe their existence to these external circumstances, but the conceptualization and design of this last of Machiavelli's great works reflect long-standing interests integral to the development of both his political theory and the pragmatic requirements of his persistent critique of Florentine politics.

This was not the first time Machiavelli had donned the historian's mantle. The first *Decennale*, written in 1504, is a verse summary of Italy's history in the decade 1494–1504, in which events involving Florence are tightly bound into the unfolding political situation. Moreover, if we accept the assertion of Machiavelli's friend and chancery colleague Agostino Vespucci in the dedication of the 1506 printed edition of the *Decennale*, a "more extensive" history of the same events was then "being forged" in Machiavelli's "workshop"[1] – a work that was not realized.

After Soderini's fall and the return of the Medici in 1512, in the absence of the urgency that had accompanied Machiavelli's role as secretary and chancellor, the general development of his political thought modified his approach to Florence's history. An important moment of these reflections is *The Prince*'s analysis (chapter 9) of the unavoidable divisions within cities caused by the "contrasting humors" of the *popolo*, who seek not to be "commanded or oppressed" and the *grandi*, who desire to command. This discussion of the "civil principate" (how a private citizen becomes prince "with the favor of his fellow citizens") alludes more than once to the Medici conquest of power, but explicit references in *The Prince* to Florentine history are infrequent and generally serve only as examples.

Much different, quantitatively and qualitatively, is the weight of Florence's history in the *Discourses on Livy*. In Machiavelli's theoretical approach to republics, Florence is defined in contrast to the ancient model of Rome; but Florence also affects Machiavelli's reading of Livy's history and the lesson he derives from it: Florence's history and the search for solutions to its political problems constitute an important foundation of Machiavelli's reflections on Roman history. One of the most original themes of the *Discourses* (1.4) is the dynamic relationship linking Rome's liberty and greatness to the conflicts between the *popolo* and the *grandi*. Despite Rome's "tumultuous" history, the outcome of these struggles rarely led to banishments or violence "against the common good"; instead they contributed decisively to implanting laws and good *ordini*. In the *Discourses*, the contrast between the exemplary model of Rome and the negative model of Florence, hinging on the condition of their respective *ordini*, is pursued chiefly with regard to contemporary Florence, but with growing interest for the past, especially the fifteenth century and the Medici.

The only chapter of the *Discourses* that takes a broad overview of Florentine history is 1.49, which argues that, because Florence was born subject to a greater power (its "principio" thus being "servo"), it never achieved a political constitution allowing it to live "civilmente" and in peace: so that "in the two hundred years of which we have secure historical memory," Florence "has never had a government for which it could genuinely be called a republic." To this original defect was added another critical source of corruption, already identified in the *Discourses* as an endemic disease and further cause of the impossibility of reform, namely, factions that subordinated the general good of the state to their own interests. Chapter 55 of book 1 reconsiders the question of reform from the different perspective of the "great equality" that results from the nearly complete absence in Tuscany of a feudal nobility: a condition that would make it "easy for a prudent man who has knowledge of the ancient republics [*antiche civiltà*] to introduce a republican form of government [*uno vivere civile*]." These are but a few of the themes concerning Florence's history in the first book of the *Discourses* that are essential for understanding the *Florentine Histories*, but it should be noted that the importance of Florence's negative exemplarity becomes even more acute in books 2 and 3, where references to the city's history and its faulty development – caused in large part by the inability of its "wise" citizens to draw lessons from history, Rome's, of course, but also Florence's – become more numerous. In sum, although the *Discourses* show some interest in extending the analysis of Florence's negative historical and political conditions beyond contemporary events, they do so only episodically. This is the task Machiavelli takes on in the *Florentine Histories*.

The *Discourses* took shape in the literary and political circle of the Orti Oricellari. In August 1520, while Machiavelli was in Lucca representing certain Florentine merchants, he sent the *Life of Castruccio Castracani* he had just written to his friends at the Orti, who welcomed it as a "model of a history,"[2] a characterization to be understood chiefly in literary and stylistic terms. Indeed, writing Florence's history confronted Machiavelli with the problem of engaging the standards and traditions of Florentine historiography, especially its humanist branch, with regard to language, structure, and the period to be covered. First of all, he wrote his history in Tuscan, not Latin; he also decisively rejected an annalistic format and opted for a direct polemical challenge to the prestigious fifteenth-century humanist historians ("two most excellent historians," he calls them) Leonardo Bruni and Poggio Bracciolini, authors, respectively, of the *Historiarum Florentini populi libri XII* (Twelve Books of the Histories of the Florentine People) and the *Historia Florentina* in eight books, both written in Latin but quickly given Tuscan translations (Bruni's by Donato Acciaiuoli and Poggio's by his son Jacopo Bracciolini) that assured them a wide readership.

Bruni's history, written between 1415 and his death in 1444, inaugurated and founded humanist historiography by taking classical historians, particularly Livy, as models for both form and substance. As he meticulously explains the causes of events and their connections, Bruni constructs his history according to the canons of classical rhetoric, with invented speeches in direct discourse and an emphasis on the exemplarity of illustrious deeds. Linguistically and conceptually innovative with respect to the Florentine chronicle tradition and mainly for its critical–philological methods and use of documentary sources, Bruni's history aspired to be the sole true history, not merely of Florence, but of the Florentine people, from a perspective that transcended local concerns and anchored the dignity of the subject in the city's glorious inheritance as the daughter of Rome, the proud assertion of her liberty, and her memorable accomplishments. He aimed to rewrite Florence's history from the beginning, reconstructing its essential unity against the fragmented treatment of the chronicles and fashioning an image of the city that erased its more violent features and downplayed its commercial and guild elements. Not that internal politics and civic disorders are lacking in the narrative; but their weight is unevenly distributed throughout the work, which ends with the death of Giangaleazzo Visconti in 1402. Poggio's history takes the Roman historian Sallust as its model to narrate the wars fought by

Florence, mainly against Milan, until the 1454 Peace of Lodi. Here the space devoted to Florence's domestic history is very limited: not a word, indeed, on the exile and return of Cosimo de' Medici in 1433–4. In Poggio's case, Machiavelli's criticism that the humanist historians neglected Florence's internal history occasions no surprise; with regard to Bruni, however, who was also a major source for Machiavelli, the polemic is justified less by Bruni's alleged lack of attention to domestic matters than by his history's ideological framework.

In the preface to the *Florentine Histories* Machiavelli claims he modified his original intention to begin with the rise of the Medici in 1434 after "diligently" reading Bruni and Poggio to see how they organized their histories, so that, by imitating them, his own would "gain greater approval from readers." He found that, while they were "most diligent" in narrating Florence's wars, they either passed over in silence the "civil discords and internal conflicts and the consequences that resulted from them," or described some of them so briefly as to provide "neither profit nor pleasure to their readers." Thus, far from imitating his predecessors, Machiavelli unleashes a hard-hitting and sarcastic indictment of their methods, insisting that pleasure comes from a thorough and detailed narration and that the utility of history depends on the "*lezione* that reveals the causes of hatreds and divisions in cities," addressed to "citizens who govern republics so that they can maintain unity through the [examples] of others who gained wisdom from the dangers they experienced." A useful "lezione" should produce efficacious political application, all the more for Florentines because of the exceptional character of the civil conflicts of their city. The theme of civil discord, crucial to the *Discourses* and reprised in the *Histories* again in contrast with ancient republics, above all Rome, is the keystone of Machiavelli's approach to Florentine history. But it also confronted him with a more complex picture than that yielded by the *Discourses*, for Florence's uniqueness, in its negative exemplarity, consisted in the distinctive way in which the divisions of the body politic occurred and the consequences they produced. As Machiavelli asserts in the preface,

> In Florence, first the nobles divided amongst themselves, then the nobles and the *popolo* came into conflict, and finally the *popolo* and the *plebe*; and many times it happened that when one of these parties emerged victorious it divided into two factions. From these divisions came as many deaths, exiles, and destroyed families as ever occurred in any city whose history is known to us.

Yet, paradoxically, these numerous and severe conflicts, far from destroying Florence, did not prevent its power from "becoming ever greater." To the historical reality of these domestic conflicts Machiavelli now contrasts the failed potential of a united Florence (apparently no longer conditioned by its "servile" origins) that would have reached exceptional greatness if, after its liberation from the empire, "it had adopted a form of government that kept it united." If that had happened, "I don't know what republic, modern or ancient, would have been greater." Such praise underscores even more strikingly Florence's memorable domestic divisions and Machiavelli's critique of his humanist predecessors.

These then, says Machiavelli, were the reasons that caused him to "change course": to begin his history from the beginning, to narrate "in depth [*particularmente*]" domestic events down to 1434 (which thus remains the work's central divide), and thereafter to include external events as well "down to our own times." In book 1 Machiavelli provides a summary of Italian history from the fall of the Roman Empire to 1434, a succinct overview noteworthy for the pan-Italian perspective into which the city's history is integrated and for its elucidation of the Church's role in Italy's history (along lines that recall *Discourses* 1.12). Machiavelli's initial plan is indicative of the expectations that defined the context in which the *Histories* were written. Starting in 1434 would have meant giving the onset of the Medici domination the status of a watershed so decisive as to require a new periodization of Florentine history. Making the Medici ascendancy the work's central axis, endorsed by the official standing implied in the public commission, would have put Machiavelli in an uncomfortable position. Modifying the plan thus served his purposes in this regard as well. But the deeper motivation, which had its roots in the *Discourses*, was to identify and examine the causes that led to the crisis of the republic and the rise of the Medici: the crucial outcome toward which the narrative converges in books 2 through 4.

The fundamental interpretive framework of the *Histories* is its analysis of the kinds and frequency of civil conflicts, closely connected to the problem of the absence or defective nature of Florence's *ordini*. Both themes underscore the intimate tie between past and present that runs throughout the *Histories*: not only as a *lezione* to be conveyed, but also as the direction and driving force of political action and/or as polemical recrimination. The discussions concerning institutional reform in the years after Lorenzo's death in 1519 are an important element of the historical and political background in which Machiavelli began writing the *Histories*. In the famous opening lines of the *Discourse on Florentine Affairs after the Death of the Younger Lorenzo*, presumably written in late 1520 and addressed to Pope Leo, Machiavelli explained the city's constantly changing governments by observing that Florence had never been "either a republic or a principate with the requisite qualities." The *Discourse*'s comparison of the "stati" (governments or regimes) since 1393 marks a significant step toward the *Histories*. Because of Florence's "great equality" (by which Machiavelli means the absence of a titled, feudal nobility), a stable "stato" would require the establishment of "a republic with all its [necessary] parts."[3] After Leo died, Machiavelli again took part in renewed discussions of political reform, as we see from an April 1522 draft in Machiavelli's own hand of a proposal for constitutional reorganization.[4] But the discovery in June of that year of a plot to assassinate Cardinal Giulio put an end to all talk of reform.

Writing the *Histories* occupied Machiavelli for several years, and various hypotheses, based in part on autograph fragments of the draft, have been offered concerning the phases of composition. The eight books of the work we have were finished by the spring of 1525, and Machiavelli presented them to Giulio de' Medici, now Pope Clement VII, with a carefully worded dedication. The closing in 1522 of the tentative window of reform may have contributed to the increasing pessimism of the *Histories* as they took shape, but without in any way dimming their intellectual tension, as the prefaces to books 3 and 4 and the speeches in direct discourse make clear. The dual inspiration that characterizes the *Histories* forcefully emerges from such passages: on the one hand, an intimate connection with political theory; on the other, as a field of action and critical, polemical persuasion. Because of Machiavelli's stated distance from the illustrious humanist predecessors, in his hands the exemplarity of Florentine history turns on the narration and analysis of the republic's civil conflicts. He took on the task of completely rewriting, from this angle, the city's history from the beginning.

Machiavelli did not make use of official documents; his sources were mostly fourteenth- and fifteenth-century histories and vernacular chronicles. Despite his criticism of Bruni in the preface, the latter's work provided not only a constant point of polemical contrast, but also significant interpretations of key events down to 1400 and a model of narrative construction that the fragmentary and unstructured chronicle accounts lacked. From the chroniclers, Giovanni Villani, Marchionne di Coppo Stefani, Alamanno Acciaiuoli, the so-called pseudo-Minerbetti, Domenico Buoninsegni, Neri Capponi, Giovanni Cavalcanti and the Dominican Giovanni di Carlo (author of a Latin account of the Medici regime), Machiavelli took the vivid details of events and their protagonists for Florence's domestic history, particularly concerning institutional changes and civil conflicts, whereas for foreign and military affairs he relied chiefly on the humanist historians. Identifying the sources and the ways in which Machiavelli used them is crucial to interpretation and a complex problem to which only in-depth analyses can do justice, especially because, instead of relying on one source at a time, it was from the juxtaposition and comparison of different sources that he drew the building blocks of the narrative. His sources were on the one hand objects of inquiry and, on the other, material that he utilized freely without philological concerns. Indeed, for Machiavelli history entailed the construction of para-digms and plausible models and a rationalization of events according to an interpretive logic. Scrupulous verification of facts was of little interest to him; he often modified details, sometimes without apparent explanation. His aim was to identify the causes and consequences of events, to study the motivations and undertakings of individuals and groups, and to shed light on short- and long-term effects. For these reasons Machiavelli did not adopt the annalistic framework characteristic of chronicles and humanist histories, preferring to delineate a synthesis of Florence's history with attention only to the most significant and crucial facts.

After his analysis of its Roman foundation, in the second book Florence's history assumes independent significance worthy of memory with the first of its divisions, attributed by both poetic and chronicle traditions to the Buondelmonti murder of 1215 (2.3): a division between factions led by the noble Buondelmonti and Uberti families, whose chief political conse-quence was the conflict between the Guelf and Ghibelline parties. This is Machiavelli's point of departure for the entire subsequent course of develop-ments. Some key points of particular interest may be considered in order to highlight the interaction, which is not without its problematic aspects, of Machiavelli's theoretical concerns with his approach to writing history. One of the focal points of the narrative is the always looming risk of ruin and loss of liberty that endemic recurrences of civil conflict entailed, in relation to both external dangers and wars and the threat of domestic tyranny. In two crucial episodes of the second and third books Machiavelli highlights the dramatic reality of these risks: the tyranny of the duke of Athens in 1342–3 and the revolt of the Ciompi in 1378.

Machiavelli integrates the episode of the duke of Athens into the over-arching theme of book 2, the struggles between the nobles and the *popolo* that emerged, after the Guelf–Ghibelline wars ended, from "those humors that naturally exist between the nobles [*potenti*] and the people [*popolo*]," who cannot coexist harmoniously "since the people wish to live according to the laws and the nobles want to dominate the laws" (2.12). Machiavelli's recon-struction of this conflict emphasizes the *popolo*'s resistance, beginning with the anti-magnate laws, to the nobles' "insolence" and abuse of power. Even as he never wavers from his assessment of the motivations behind these struggles and the ultimate responsibility of the nobles, Machiavelli underscores the radicalization of the conflict and the exasperation and hatred to which the nobles were driven by the growing arrogance and thirst for domination among the more powerful elements of the *popolo*. He sees the culmination of the long conflict in the dramatic events of 1343: in the tyranny of Walter of Brienne, duke of Athens, and its tragic end; in the failure of yet another attempt at reconciling the parties; and in the decisive clash that resulted in the nobles' crushing defeat. Brienne had been sent by King Robert of Naples to help Florence through severe military and financial crises, and the Florentines appointed him military commander just when popular indignation against the ruling class was at its height because of military failures. The nobles expected that Brienne's arrival in this explosive situation would provide the occasion for the revenge against the *popolo* they had been waiting for. Machiavelli attributes to the nobles a plan of action that appeared successful at first but would prove a total failure: unconcerned about the fate of the city and persuaded that they had the duke's favor, they supported his assumption of a "signoria," or lordship, as the only way "to subdue the *popolo* which had so afflicted them" (2.33). In encouraging Brienne, the nobles only became the instruments of his ambition, which was also sustained by the favor he gained with the working class with his draconian punishments of the leaders of the failed war policy. A third protagonist thus enters the scene between nobles seeking revenge and the upper ranks of the *popolo* terrified of Brienne: the *plebe*, which alone benefited from the duke's rule and subsequently came into conflict with the *popolo*.

Machiavelli inserts into his account of Brienne's rise an invented last-hour dramatic appeal to the duke by the communal priors in defense of Florentine liberty (2.34), to which Brienne brusquely replies (reversing and hiding his true intentions and echoing what the *Discourses* say about corrupt and divided cities) that "if through his reforms Florence were freed of factions, vain ambition, and antagonisms, its liberty would be restored, not taken away" (2.35). The reality of Brienne's tyranny and the tragic consequences of Florence's irreducible disunity are mirrored in the uprooting of republican institutions and the city's oppression and loss of "civic modesty" (2.36). Only the *plebe* enjoyed the duke's favor, following and acclaiming him when he rode through the city with his armed guard.

The events that follow Brienne's violent expulsion in July 1343 demonstrate that this dark page of Florentine history would never serve, then or later, as a salutary lesson, for soon the "insolence" of the nobles revived, leading to the final confrontation in which the *popolo* emerged victorious. Yet, according to Machiavelli, the defeat of the nobles meant that Florence was deprived of their "military valor [*virtú dell'armi*]" and "nobility of spirit [*generosità di animo*]." This theme marks the crucial introduction to book 3, where Machiavelli again compares Florence's and ancient Rome's internal divisions, but with significantly different emphases from those of *Discourses* 1.4, beginning with his explicit underscoring of the gravity of those "natural enmities." The contrast seeks to demonstrate the destructive character assumed by Florence's conflicts, in which the *popolo* pursued its objectives in a "harmful and unjust" way, resulting in laws "not for the common utility but entirely in favor of the victor" and in the downfall of the old nobility, which now had to adopt attitudes and ways of living similar to those of the *popolo* if it wanted any role in government. For Machiavelli, the paradox of the outcome is Florence's "remarkable equality," which nonetheless did not compensate the high price (the loss of the magnates' military valor and nobility of spirit) that Florence paid for the opportunity – always missed yet constantly and urgently needed – to be "easily reorganized into any form of government by a wise lawgiver" (3.1).

The persistently negative dimension of Florence's history is confirmed in Machiavelli's account in book 3 of the eruption of "enmities between the *popolo* and the *plebe*." Machiavelli here faced the double problem of defining the character and evolution of these conflicts and of delineating the nature of the "plebeian party [*parte plebea*]" and how it was like and unlike the "lesser *popolo* [*popolo minuto*]" and the "lowest plebs [*infima plebe*]." Machiavelli attributes to these classes, for the first time in Florentine historical writing, genuine political importance. He presents the Ciompi Revolution as a coherent and coordinated project for the conquest of power and as the central and most dramatic event of book 3. In passages that forcefully reveal the logic and dynamic of these conflicts, but not without radical and bold simplifications by comparison with the less coherent but more complex picture presented in the chronicles, Machiavelli delineates the agonizing strife that led the city once again into an explosive situation. He highlights the decisive role of Salvestro de' Medici (3.9), no doubt also because of the family to which he belonged, assigning him responsibility for having incautiously and unwittingly created an unstoppable chain reaction during his term as Standardbearer of Justice in 1378, by encouraging the *popolo* and the guilds to rise up, thus sparking a first wave of arson and pillaging which led within days to the revolt of the unskilled workers, the Ciompi, who until then had been subject to the powerful Wool Guild.

The pages on the Ciompi Revolution are among the most memorable in the *Florentine Histories*, above all for the depth of their analysis of the motivations behind the hatred of the men of the plebs against "the wealthy citizens and leaders of the guilds." Machiavelli synthesizes the history of Florence's guild organization, clarifies the tension between major and minor guilds, and, for the first time, provides an overview of the circumstances of the classes excluded from political participation, denied their own guilds, and deprived of any possibility of appeal or redress, to which was now added their fear of punishment for acts of arson and pillage already committed. Machiavelli gives a remarkable picture, through the voice of an anonymous *ciompo*, of the radically subversive potential (on both the theoretical–ideological and hortatory–political planes) inherent in, and resulting from, the condition of the *plebe*. The powerfully suggestive invented speech of the anonymous worker is laced with themes from Machiavelli's theoretical writings, here taken to extreme consequences from the perspective of a lucid, discerning consciousness of dire poverty and oppression and a savage, violent conception of nature and human action. Attributing to the Ciompi the deliberate intention of taking up arms, seizing the republic, and persevering in the evils already committed, Machiavelli vividly depicts the revolt by selecting, condensing, and substantially reworking the details of his chronicle sources and by highlighting the impotence and weakness of Florence's political institutions and the "malice," fear, and pursuit of private interests by citizens who might have prevented the disorders (3.15). In this dramatic frame, Michele di Lando, the wool-carder elected Standardbearer of Justice by the revolutionaries, assumes ideal and heroic stature in Machiavelli's account for leading the battle in the streets against the unskilled Ciompi, contrary to their expectations, and for rescuing the city from the risk of a "tyranny greater than that of the Duke of Athens." Machiavelli's final comment on the Ciompi is a stinging one: "These events frightened the plebs and caused the major guildsmen to realize how ignominious it was for those who had suppressed the arrogance of the nobles to have to endure the stench of the plebs" (3.17).

If the Ciompi Revolt represents the pinnacle of the lacerations of Florence's social and civic fabric, Machiavelli nonetheless shows that, after its suppression, the endemic evil of factions resurfaced almost immediately, displaying contrasting forms of abuse of power: first, the brief and violent rule of the minor guilds (1378–82); then the counterrevolution of the elite families, who imposed, with methods no less injurious and severe, the oligarchic regime whose long life (1382–1434) and success in expanding Florence's territorial state Machiavelli acknowledges, but side-by-side with its corruption and failure to extinguish the factionalism that eventually re-exploded and led, as shown in book 4, to the Medici domination.

From book 4 to the end, writing the *Histories* became more problematic because Machiavelli had to narrate the rise and domination of the Medici in a work whose commission had been approved by a Medici. He expressed his anxiety in a 1524 letter to Francesco Guicciardini, saying he wished he could speak with him "because, since I am about to come to certain details, I would need to learn from you whether or not I am being too offensive in exaggerating or in understating the facts."[5] According to a famous letter of Donato Giannotti in 1533, Machiavelli had confided to him both the difficulty he faced in writing the *Histories* and the necessity of proceeding cautiously by leaving out "the larger causes of things" and without discussing "the methods and tricks by which one attains such power." Giannotti also related the important clue Machiavelli himself provided for reading these books: "and if anyone nevertheless wants to understand this, let him observe well what I shall have [Cosimo's] opponents say, because what I am not willing to say as coming from myself, I shall have his opponents say."[6] The reader is thus given the task of reconstructing Machiavelli's assessment of the Medici through the text's allusions, the speeches of Medici adversaries, and the roles of the various protagonists.

Particularly relevant in this context is that the introduction to book 4 polemically returns to the typology of republican governments: republics not "bene ordinate" (lacking good *ordini*) are destined to alternate, not between "liberty" and "servitude [*servitù*]," "as many think," but between "servitude" and "license [*licenza*]," because of the ruinous effects of the antagonism between the "ministers of license" (the *popolo*) and those of servitude (the nobles). Without the intervention (which "very seldom happens") of a "wise, good, and powerful citizen who establishes laws" that can restrain this antagonism, such a republic, not being "founded on good laws and good *ordini*," oscillates only between "tyranny" and "license" and can be sustained, precariously at best, only by the "virtù" and good "fortune" of one man, who, however, "could be removed by death or rendered ineffective by difficulties."

This, says Machiavelli, was Florence's condition during the long domination of the pre-Medici oligarchy. He attributes the revival of factionalism to the "insolence" of the ruling citizens and their mutual envy and suspicion (4.2), which made them oblivious to the hatred their wicked ways provoked among the people and to the growing power of the Medici, beginning with Giovanni, Cosimo's father (4.3). Machiavelli paints an ideal portrait of Giovanni: he was politically able and astute in gaining the people's favor, yet reluctant to engage in factionalism and determined not to exceed the limits of his private station (4.11, 4.16), thus preventing the growing conflict from coming to a head in his lifetime. This picture of Giovanni prepares the way for a deliberate contrast with Cosimo, highlighting the latter's partisanship, his corrupting liberality, and the well-orchestrated campaign of slander against his enemies in military and foreign affairs (e.g., 4.26), which sparked the open conflict with Rinaldo degli Albizzi, the most determined of all the oligarchs to eradicate Cosimo's growing power and the favor he cultivated among the non-noble classes. What was actually at stake here, and what the two factions, different only in name, really stood for, Machiavelli makes clear in a crucial speech attributed to Niccolò da Uzzano, one of the wisest and most influential of the oligarchic leaders, who explains his reasons for rejecting an attempt to persuade him to join Rinaldo in banishing Cosimo. Niccolò's speech takes its cue from a passage in Giovanni Cavalcanti's fifteenth-century

Istoria fiorentina (an important source for book 4), which Machiavelli transforms into a full-fledged political analysis of the opposing parties. He has Uzzano explain why Cosimo's party had the advantage in a city "which, naturally given to factions and having always lived with them, is corrupt." Although Niccolò da Uzzano recognizes Cosimo's methods as those that "propel men aiming for princely rank," he nonetheless firmly opposes the idea of intervening to stop him, because things had reached the point where the inevitable outcome would be to liberate the city from one factional leader only to subject it to another, and Rinaldo degli Albizzi was no better than Cosimo. Alluding to Cosimo's great wealth and its corrupting power, he concludes that "all these citizens, partly from ignorance and partly from malice, are ready to sell this republic; and so much is Fortune their friend that they have found a buyer" (4.27). His speech takes on a quality of cogent but unheeded foresight, for Cosimo's expulsion, after Uzzano's death, caused the ruin of the old oligarchy. Their fates reversed, Rinaldo was forced into exile and Cosimo returned in triumph, acclaimed as the "benefactor of the people and father of the fatherland" (4.33), an outcome about whose significance Niccolò da Uzzano's speech leaves no doubt.

In books 5 through 8 of the *Histories*, the space devoted to internal politics lessens by comparison with the attention to foreign policy and wars. As announced in book 5's opening chapter, the narrative reprises, with undiminished negative judgment, the wider Italian context and the "cowardice" with which wars were then fought, extinguishing "virtù" and paving the way for the invasions of the "barbarians" beginning in 1494: a stinging denunciation, modeled on the *Art of War*, of "this ruined world [*questo guasto mondo*]" (5.1), whose negative exemplarity, however, could be as useful as the knowledge of ancient glories. Internal developments are unevenly represented in the second half of the *Histories*: limited to a few chapters in books 5 and 6; concentrated in book 8 in an extensive treatment of the Pazzi conspiracy; but more fully treated in book 7. Machiavelli's hurried treatment in books 5 and 6 of the first two decades of the Medici regime again exposes the difficulties of the commission, for which he adopted two shrewd strategies. First, he attributes direct responsibility not to Cosimo, but to his supporters and lieutenants (5.4), for the serious abuses of power by the Medici in securing their hold on government. Second, he establishes contrasts between Cosimo and key figures, especially the exiled Rinaldo degli Albizzi (who bitterly denounces Cosimo's regime in an attempt to draw Filippo Maria Visconti of Milan into a war), and the internal rival Neri Capponi. Neri is depicted as an acclaimed citizen who owed his great reputation to meritorious public service and not to private methods and manipulation of government: the anti-Cosimo, in sum, who had "many friends and few partisans," always suspect to the Medici and resisted by them until his death in 1455 left Cosimo's faction without major enemies.

Here the narrative enters a new phase. Having recounted foreign affairs to the mid-1460s in book 6, in the introductory chapter of book 7 Machiavelli declares it necessary to turn back in time to analyze the last decade of Cosimo's control of internal politics as a prelude to discussing his son Piero's regime (1464–9) and that of Piero's son Lorenzo (1469–92). Reprising the theme of Florence's divisions, Machiavelli reaffirms their inevitability and harmful consequences when, as always happened, they generated factions and partisans and triggered the ineluctable process that led each victorious faction to divide as soon as its adversary was crushed. Book 7 begins with the split in Cosimo's party in 1455 after fears of old adversaries, which had kept the party "united and humane" and thus not hated by the people, had dissipated (7.1–2). Machiavelli underscores Cosimo's superior political skills in defeating and humiliating former allies who contested his leadership in 1458, but he characterizes the regime that emerged from that confrontation as "intolerable and violent," dominated by Cosimo's powerful chief lieutenant Luca Pitti and others "no less violent and rapacious than he": "even without a foreign war to destroy it, Florence was destroyed by its own citizens" (7.4). In depicting Cosimo as old, tired, and unable to prevent these abuses, Machiavelli relieves him of primary responsibility for this state of affairs. Nor is the extensive and apparently laudatory eulogy of Cosimo, inserted in the narrative to mark his death in 1464, without its ambiguities. Machiavelli justifies "having imitated those who write the lives of princes" with the notion that, because Cosimo "was a rare man in our city," it was "necessary to praise him in an extraordinary way" (7.6). But the fact remains that Machiavelli avoids discussing the specifics of the Medici regime's electoral manipulations and methods of control.

The rest of the narrative focuses on the weaknesses that undermined Medici power from within and pushed the city to the brink of civil war in 1465–6 after Cosimo's death. Machiavelli discusses in detail the attempt of a group of elite former Medici lieutenants to block Piero's succession by exploiting for their own ends the general desire for a government run by elected officials rather than by the advice of a few influential men. Among the movement's leaders only Niccolò Soderini, according to Machiavelli, genuinely shared the wish to revive republican government; for the others (Dietisalvi Neroni, Luca Pitti, and Agnolo Acciaiuoli), it was a deceitful manipulation whose real motives were personal ambition and hatred. Machiavelli injects both drama and sarcasm into his account of the confrontation, and, although Piero emerged victorious, the emphasis on the great jeopardy in which the Medici regime found itself underscores its defective foundation and inadequate stabilization. No less serious were the consequences of the Medici victory: the complete takeover of government by Piero's faction (7.17) and a new and dangerous war provoked by exiled former allies. As he had done for Cosimo, Machiavelli excuses Piero's alleged inability, because of illness, to prevent excesses and abuses (7.21), but he nonetheless has Piero paint a terrible picture of the regime in reprimanding his own partisans for their violence and avarice (7.23).

As Machiavelli explains at the beginning of book 8, the Medici assumed so much authority after their triumph in 1466 that no possibility of overt opposition remained. Whereas earlier they "had fought [for power] on a basis of equal authority and reputation with some other families" of the elite, the final defeat of the *ottimati* completely changed the situation. Malcontents now had no avenue for dissent except conspiracy. As Machiavelli had already argued in *Discourses* 3.6, most conspiracies are doomed to failure, and he now shows how, ironically, the Pazzi plot became the instrument by which the Medici "took sole power in the city" (8.1). Machiavelli's extensive narration of the conspiracy makes clear the tangle of reciprocal fears and resentments that led Lorenzo to deny the Pazzi the honors appropriate to their status and the Pazzi to conclude that they had to avenge such intolerable insults. Here too Machiavelli makes use of contrasts, this time between Lorenzo, "hot with youth and power" (8.3) and the desire to rule, and his moderate, prudent brother Giuliano. (Into his brief, admiring profile of Giuliano, Machiavelli inserted an encomiastic mention of Giuliano's natural son, Giulio, the dedicatee of the *Histories* [8.9].)

The detailed account of the conspiracy's structure, organization, and execution culminates in the attack in the cathedral on Giuliano and Lorenzo, in which the former was murdered and the latter wounded. It then shifts to the streets and the conspirators' botched attempt to seize the government palace, followed by the tragic succession, briefly but powerfully described, of the summary executions of the plotters. Particularly revealing is Machiavelli's remark concerning the desperate and pathetic attempt of Jacopo Pazzi to appeal to the *popolo* and *libertà*: "but because the one had been made deaf by Fortune and by the liberality of the Medici, and the second was unknown in Florence, no one answered his call" (8.8). By then the entire city had taken up arms on behalf of the Medici (8.9). The failure of the plot was followed by declarations of war, specifically against Lorenzo, from the chief foreign conspirators, Pope Sixtus IV and King Ferrante of Naples. Machiavelli has Lorenzo deliver an oration before the Signoria and three hundred eminent citizens that is noteworthy for its skillful mystification but also for its appeal to a more than individual responsibility. Lorenzo defends the ascendancy of the Medici in terms of the "unito consenso" he claims it enjoyed on account of the gratitude acquired for the many benefits bestowed on the Florentines. Identifying Florence's cause with his own and exploiting to the full the attack he and his brother had suffered, he succeeds in winning, amid the emotion of the moment, unconditional support and a permanent armed guard (8.10).

Machiavelli's account of the Pazzi war of 1479–80, from which Lorenzo emerged with notable success, occupies much of the rest of book 8. But about Lorenzo's domestic political control Machiavelli is increasingly reticent, as he also is in the famous eulogy of Lorenzo (8.36), more carefully crafted and detached than that of Cosimo, and in the conclusion, which nonetheless makes clear the general sorrow of the Florentines and of Italy's rulers over Lorenzo's death and the loss of his wisdom and good counsel. The book ends with Lorenzo's death in 1492 and a foreshadowing of those "bad seeds" that soon thereafter, "because there was no one who knew how to extinguish them, brought ruin and continue to bring ruin to Italy," but without reaching the year 1494, in which Italy's crisis began with the French invasion and the first period of Medici rule came to an end with the expulsion of Lorenzo's son Piero. The *Florentine Histories* end without any conclusion. If Machiavelli thought of continuing beyond 1492, he would have found it exceedingly difficult to reach "these present times of ours," as announced in the preface, and to narrate the rise and fall of the republic for which he had labored and suffered so much, without failing to honor the obligations incurred with the commission, without renouncing his own dignity as a man and an historian.

NOTES

This chapter was translated from Italian by the volume editor.
1. Niccolò Machiavelli, *Opere*, ed. Corrado Vivanti, 3 vols. (Turin: Einaudi-Gallimard, 1997–2005), 1:93.
2. Niccolò Machiavelli, *Lettere*, ed. Franco Gaeta (Turin: UTET, 1984), pp. 511–12; *Machiavelli and His Friends: Their Personal Correspondence*, trans. James B. Atkinson and David Sices (DeKalb, Ill.: Northern Illinois University Press, 1996), pp. 328–9.
3. *Discursus florentinarum rerum post mortem iunioris Laurentii Medices*, in Niccolò Machiavelli, *L'arte della guerra. Scritti politici minori*, ed. Jean-Jacques Marchand, Denis Fachard, and Giorgio Masi (Rome: Salerno Editrice, 2001), pp. 624–41 (624); trans. Allan Gilbert in *Machiavelli: The Chief Works and Others*, 3 vols. (Durham, N.C.: Duke University Press, 1965), 1:101–15 (101, 106).
4. Machiavelli, *L'arte della guerra. Scritti politici minori*, ed. Marchand *et al.*, pp. 645–54.
5. Machiavelli, *Lettere*, ed. Gaeta, p. 539; translation (slightly modified) in *Correspondence*, p. 351.
6. Donato Giannotti, *Lettere italiane*, ed. Furio Diaz (Milan: Marzorati, 1974), p. 35; translation (slightly modified) in Gilbert: *Works*, 3:1028.

FURTHER READING

Anselmi, Gian Mario. *Ricerche sul Machiavelli storico*. Pisa, Pacini, 1979.

Bock, Gisela. "Civil Discord in Machiavelli's *Istorie fiorentine*," in *Machiavelli and Republicanism*, ed. Gisela Bock, Quentin Skinner, and Maurizio Viroli. Cambridge University Press, 1990, pp. 181–201.

Cabrini, Anna Maria. *Interpretazione e stile in Machiavelli. Il terzo libro delle "Istorie"*. Rome, Bulzoni, 1990.

Per una valutazione delle "Istorie fiorentine". Note sulle fonti del secondo libro. Florence, La Nuova Italia, 1985.

Di Maria, Salvatore. "Machiavelli's Ironic View of History: The *Istorie fiorentine*," *Renaissance Quarterly* 45 (1992): 248–70.

Dionisotti, Carlo. "Machiavelli storico," in Dionisotti, *Machiavellerie*. Turin, Einaudi, 1980, pp. 365–409.

Gilbert, Felix. *Machiavelli and Guicciardini: Politics and History in Sixteenth-Century Florence*. Princeton University Press, 1965.

Hatfield, Rab. "A Source for Machiavelli's Account of the Regime of Piero de' Medici," in *Studies on Machiavelli*, ed. Myron P. Gilmore. Florence, Sansoni, 1972, pp. 317–33.

Marchand, Jean-Jacques, ed. *Machiavelli politico storico letterato*. Rome, Salerno Editrice, 1996.

Marietti, Marina. "Machiavel historiographe des Médicis," in *Les écrivains et le pouvoir en Italie à l'époque de la Renaissance (deuxième série)*, ed. A. Rochon. Paris, Université de la Sorbonne Nouvelle, 1974, pp. 81–148.

Martelli, Mario. "Machiavelli e la storiografia umanistica," in *La storiografia umanistica*, vol. 1. Messina, Sicania, 1992, pp. 113–52.

Najemy, John M. "*Arti* and *Ordini* in Machiavelli's *Istorie fiorentine*," in *Essays Presented to Myron P. Gilmore*, ed. Sergio Bertelli and Gloria Ramakus. Florence, La Nuova Italia, 1978, pp. 161–91.

"Machiavelli and the Medici: The Lessons of Florentine History," *Renaissance Quarterly* 35 (1982): 551–76.

Phillips, Mark. "Barefoot Boy Makes Good: A Study of Machiavelli's Historiography," *Speculum* 59 (1984): 585–605.

Quint, David. "Narrative Design and Historical Irony in Machiavelli's *Istorie fiorentine*," *Rinascimento* 43 (2003): 31–48.

Raimondi, Ezio. "Machiavelli and the Rhetoric of the Warrior," *Modern Language Notes* 92 (1977): 1–16.

Richardson, Brian. "Notes on Machiavelli's Sources and His Treatment of the Rhetorical Tradition," *Italian Studies* 26 (1971): 24–48.

Rubinstein, Nicolai. *The Government of Florence under the Medici (1434 to 1494)*. 2nd edition. Oxford, Clarendon Press, 1997.

Sasso, Gennaro. *Niccolò Machiavelli*, vol. 2, *La storiografia*. Bologna, Il Mulino, 1993.

Struever, Nancy S. *The Language of History in the Renaissance: Rhetoric and Historical Consciousness in Florentine Humanism*. Princeton University Press, 1970.

Wilcox, Donald J. *The Development of Florentine Humanist Historiography in the Fifteenth Century*. Cambridge, Mass., Harvard University Press, 1969.

9

J. G. A. POCOCK

Machiavelli and Rome: the republic as ideal and as history

I

To write about Machiavelli and republicanism is to expose both writer and reader to a series of temptations and misunderstandings. There was an ideal of government to which we are used to applying the terms "republic" and "republicanism," and Machiavelli addressed himself to it; but how far he or his contemporaries employed a vocabulary readily translated by these terms is another question, since *res publica*, or its English translation "commonwealth," could be used to mean any political body, irrespective of whether it was ruled by a monarch or not. There is a historical process by which "republic" and "commonwealth" came to be used in English as denoting kingless government, and "republicanism" came to be opposed to "monarchism"; and as this happened, the two terms came to denote opposed political norms, each supported by a theory of government and even a philosophy of political life. For these reasons it is possible to use "republicanism" as denoting an intellectually complex and historically continuous ideology, and to assign Machiavelli his place in its history. A history of "Machiavelli and republicanism" can in principle be written as a history of how it became possible to see him and his role in this way. The history may well prove to have been going on for a long time, and even to have begun taking place in his lifetime and affecting his thoughts and intentions. We know, however, that he was a complex and deliberately enigmatic writer, who lived in a highly distinctive political environment and wrote with intentions peculiar to it. Machiavelli the Florentine has to be assessed – as "republican" or not – in the terms permitted by Florentine history between 1494 and 1530. But the posthumous Machiavelli – the figure created when his works were read on the print networks of Europe at large – may have had other histories and have been "republican" in other senses.

Machiavelli himself wrote (*The Prince*, chapter 1) that "states" could be classified as either republics or principalities, and from this we see that he found it possible to use "republic" as the opposite of single-person government. It is important, however, that he wrote of "princes" – *principi* in Tuscan, *principes* in Latin – and not of kings, although his category "princes" is at times extended in various ways to include kings and what they were doing. Kings and their apologists were all too keenly aware that sacred and hereditary monarchs often behaved in the same ways as did Machiavellian usurpers. He was not, however, a critic or analyst of kingship, or even of monarchy, if by that term we mean the form of rule developed in the territorial kingdoms of Spain, France, or England, and it would be a mistake to associate him with a "republicanism" whose opposite was "monarchism" in any generalized form. In France or England there was an ideology of kingship with a vocabulary of its own, juristic, ecclesiastical and even political; Machiavelli did not write in this vocabulary or have occasion to examine the problems arising within it. His study of the "cose di Francia"[1] shows him interested in the character of territorial monarchy, but as a phenomenon other than those of his Italian world. He was interested – indeed, urgently and immediately involved – in an opposition between "republican" and "princely" government in quite another sense, more Italian than transalpine and more Tuscan and Lombard than papal or Neapolitan; and this instantly divides into two further settings, one historically immediate and experienced, the other historically distant and studied with intellectual passion.

The historical setting in which Machiavelli's thought should be situated is that of the *Regnum italicum*, the region in which Lombardy and Tuscany were conceived as being situated. This was a term already paradoxical, of which there already existed a sophisticated historiography. To call it a *regnum* was paradoxical, for the reason that no ruler had successfully reduced it to the kingdom it had been (perhaps) under the Carolingians or had been claimed to be by the Hohenstaufen emperors. The many wars of papacy and empire had so turned out that neither pope nor emperor ruled the *Regnum italicum* as principality or state. There had emerged a number of powerful trading cities, uneasily interacting with local military nobilities, and the popes had joined with these cities in the alliance against the Hohenstaufen that became known as Guelf. All Florentine writers (Machiavelli included) were Guelf, not Ghibelline, in their accounts of history and celebrated the victories of the papacy and (at first, in the thirteenth century) its French allies. With the humiliation of the papacy by Philip the Fair and its withdrawal to Avignon in the early fourteenth century, the cities of Tuscany and Lombardy each evolved in its own way, and when the popes returned to Rome in 1377 and set about the consolidation of their temporal power, they became in some cases the chief threat to the power and autonomy of the cities. So, at least, historians in the fifteenth century presented matters. They agreed that, under those circumstances, the politics of the cities had become factious and unstable, and that this had led, in not a few cases, to the power of single lords – *podestà, signori,* and *principi* – some of whom could be regarded as usurpers and even tyrants, and some of whom sought to set up dynasties and legitimize hereditary rule.

Such was the image of Italian politics – it is a separate question how far we choose to regard it as the reality – within which a conceptual opposition between "republican" and "princely" governors took shape. It is vitally important to realize that this was a mental world in which both forms were doubtfully legitimate and historically fragile; the republics because they were liable to break up into warring factions, the princes because their acquisition of power was recent and legitimized by neither law nor religion. Machiavelli is therefore a student of power as fragile and morally questionable. He distinguished between *principi naturali,* whose rule had been legitimized, and *principi nuovi,* whose origins were recent, remembered, and resented. *The Prince* is focused on an imaginary member of the latter class, and what Machiavelli has to say about *principi naturali* (in *Prince* 2 and 3) tends to dwell on situations in which they are nearer to *principi nuovi* than they care to admit. (The Medici of Florence, who were a mercantile rather than a military family in their origins, occupy a category of their own.) Machiavelli is therefore more a historian of government as contingent than a philosopher of government as norm or ideal.

In the *Regnum italicum* of the fourteenth to the sixteenth centuries, papacy and empire, republic and princedom could be viewed either as sacred and secular ideals – the form in which they all preferred to explain and justify themselves – or as the products of a none-too-secure history. The *Regnum* was a world of its own, in which no form of government had finally been established, and it could be said of any regime that it had come into being as the result of historical circumstances and might or might not persist. It is important to keep this in mind when studying both Machiavelli and "republicanism." In the circumstances in which the Lombard and Tuscan cities – Venice is a special case – found themselves, the rule of a state by its citizens, whether these were a restricted group (*governo stretto*) or a more comprehensive one (*governo largo*), became a form of government opposed to the rule of a single man or family, however this might have been established. There arose a discourse and even a philosophy presenting the self-government of citizens as the political society best and most natural for man (in the abstract; it was restricted to "man" in the sense of males). By a process still not completely studied, this ideal annexed the word *res publica,* so that "republic" became, and has remained, a term denoting both a political ideal and an opposition to monarchy in every form. Machiavelli's distinction between "republics" and "principalities" shows this process far advanced by his time, though it must be kept in mind that his *principi* were *principi nuovi* as the cities knew them. Kingdoms were few in his world, none nearer than Naples, though the kings of France and Spain were increasingly threats to Italy from lands transalpine or transmarine.

The rule of a state by its citizens – the *vivere civile, vivere politico, governo del popolo*, to give some of the many alternatives, of which "republic" was one – was an ideal supported, and at the same time attacked, in a body of literature – rhetoric, history, political philosophy – traceable back to ancient Athens and Rome, and powerfully attractive to humanists. We have – for reasons lying outside the scope of this chapter – become accustomed to give philosophy (in a broad sense of the word) primacy among the intellectual disciplines focused on the study of politics, and to use "political theory" as a term ancillary to it. In a world deeply concerned with the study of Greek and Roman literature, however, there were other discourses of politics; jurisprudence was one, although the "republic" is more a moral than a juristic idea. As Lombard and notably Tuscan cities – Florence among the latter – found themselves in a world where rule by citizens was liable to be replaced by that of *signori* and *principi*, the *vivere civile* or republic sought for a philosophic foundation. In a memorable work of the last generation, *The Crisis of the Early Italian Renaissance*, Hans Baron singled out the experience of Florentine humanists in a war of 1400–1402 against the Visconti of Milan as a moment when this search achieved results, and "liberty" was defined in participatory terms as the active involvement of the citizen in rule and self-rule among his equals. Subsequently, the author of this chapter gave, in *The Machiavellian Moment*, an emphasis partly heuristic and partly historical to the statement of this ideal found in Aristotle's *Politics*, a work certainly not unknown among Florentine humanists and translated into Latin by Leonardo Bruni. Since these works were published, the narrative suggested by Baron has been subjected to considerable revision and criticism, partly by those, chiefly Quentin Skinner, seeking a deeper and more contextualized narrative, partly by those, like James Hankins, who have questioned the prevalence of the "republican" ideal itself, and in some degree as a result of a debate between "positive" and "negative" conceptions of "liberty" in which historians as well as political theorists have become involved (Isaiah Berlin and Skinner). The revision of Baron's historical narrative has had two major effects: it has traced the foundation of the ideal of rule by citizens to times as early as the thirteenth century, thus removing the crisis of 1400–1402 from a central or pivotal role; and it has grounded this formation in sources more rhetorical than philosophical and more Latin than Greek (Skinner). If there is a central figure among the great men of antiquity who now stands as the "philosopher" of an Italian-constructed "classical republicanism," it is Cicero rather than Aristotle; and Cicero's standing as "philosopher" now rests on the perfection of his rhetoric, and on his speeches in defense of the senatorial order, no less than on his expositions of civic virtue and natural law.

There is a move here from philosophy to rhetoric, of great importance in recent scholarship; and the concept of rhetoric may be applied to Machiavelli. The contention of this essay, however, is that the circumstances of the *Regnum italicum* were conducive to seeing all political forms in contexts of historical contingency and instability. With the veneration of Cicero, or any other classical Latin author, there arrived – or rather, was seen as always and ancestrally prevalent – the veneration of ancient Rome; but this veneration had always been challenged from within. There was the Christian challenge levelled by Augustine, who claimed that Roman liberty had never been other than the love of power, *libertas* the expression of *libido dominandi*. This might be answered by the Aristotelian claim that political life entailed the acceptance of equality among citizens, so that ruling became inseparable from being ruled. But Latin (unlike Attic) literature conveyed and was part of a great historical narrative of Decline and Fall, in which Rome had been destroyed, not by a mere vicissitude of temporal affairs, but by causes inherent in its own greatness, even in its own liberty. Sallust, one of the key authors on whom the rhetoric of Italian "republicanism" relied, had followed the Greek Polybius and preceded the Greeks Plutarch and Appian in developing the theme of *libertas et imperium*, a historical dialectic which, more than any politics of shared authority or civic virtue, is republican Rome's chief legacy to Western political thought.[2] The primeval kings had jealously restricted the *libertas* of their chief men; but under the rule of Senate and people their *virtus*, or civic energy, exploded as a force of conquering freedom, which either destroyed the *libertas* of others or harnessed it in an *imperium* that was the expression of the *libertas* of Rome. Polybius foretold, Sallust began to witness, and Tacitus, Plutarch, and Appian completed narrating the demise and suicide of this system; *libertas* had conquered an *imperium* greater than it could maintain, and the institutions of the latter had replaced those of the former. Sallust emphasized the luxury and corruption that empire had induced in Rome; Appian passed beyond the moral to the material, narrating how the rise of great estates destroyed the class of citizen-warriors, reducing them to the instruments of their generals in the civil wars that ended in the victories of Caesar and Augustus. The historian and chancellor of Florence Leonardo Bruni completed the grand narrative, recounting how the Caesars had destroyed *libertas* and *virtus* and condemned Romans to impotence in the face of barbarians. Here began a new history of empire and papacy, culminating in the exhaustion of them both and in the *libertas* – but probably not the *imperium* – of the *Regnum italicum*.[3]

There were tensions, therefore, between the Roman republic as norm or ideal and the same republic as history. An Italian city wishing to continue as a government by citizens might uphold, and eloquently expound, a Ciceronian ideal of public virtue, prosperity, and liberty. It might identify the threat of a usurping prince with Caesar or Augustus, narrating dark stories of civil war and tyranny. A recurrent trope in the literature is Sallust's account of the debate between Cicero, Caesar, and Cato over what was to be done with the accomplices of Catiline after the unmasking of his conspiracy; in this debate Caesar plays a dubious and suspect role, urging that the conspirators be spared for reasons possibly his own.[4] But the narrative opened by Sallust and continued by other historians led to the violent deaths of all three men: Cato by suicide and the others by murder, with Cicero perishing in the wars that followed Caesar's assassination and led to the principate of Augustus. Here the overall narrative changed abruptly from history to political ideality, as "Caesar" and "prince" became terms denoting the benign world-ruler found in the grand visions of Roman law and Christian empire. Aspiring *signori* and *principi* in the *Regnum italicum* might draw on this imagery if they could; but it was firmly in the hands of popes and emperors, whose power bases lay outside the *Regnum* but who in the end conquered it and gave the princes legitimacy as their creatures. Machiavelli saw the subjugation of the Italian republics begin; others witnessed its completion.

Roman history did not present a simple opposition between republic and monarchy, less still between republic and empire. It could not be detached from the narrative begun by Sallust and continued by Bruni, in which the republic had destroyed itself and the emperors had failed to save empire: a story to be told in secular terms, though continued into Christian history. An Italian republic could not fail to see itself in the setting of Roman history; yet none of them played the role of Rome.[5] No city of north or central Italy had any prospect of subduing all the others and incorporating them in a universal empire that would prove fatal to its own liberty; no republic had made its citizens soldiers and then seen them become, first the mercenaries of a condottiere, then the professionals of a military state. Yet this was the history all humanists studied; a history greater than any they could take part in, from which they had to learn what they could. Machiavelli's perception of the history of Rome is one thing, his narrative of the history of Florence another; whether either makes him an exponent of "republicanism" is a third problem.

II

We may, then, oppose a "Ciceronian" idealization of the republic to a "Sallustian" relation of its decline and fall. The two are not incompatible, since it was open to pagans and Christians alike to believe that the works of humankind in the world were mortal, however good; but they are distinct generically. The former would be the creation of rhetoricians and philosophers, concerned with the question of the best form of government; the latter of historians, concerned to narrate the vicissitudes of things in time. We have seen why humanists in the Italian republics and the *Regnum italicum* developed a particular interest in the latter question and in the "Sallustian" approach, above all when writing of Rome itself; to model the history of any actual republic on that of Rome was difficult, since the element of empire was lacking. When Machiavelli wrote of republics, he wrote of Rome; we should look for the balance or imbalance between the normative and the narrative, between the question of the best form of government and the question of any government's prospects of maintaining itself in time.

The Prince lays it down that governments are either republics or principalities, but proceeds to concentrate on the peculiar instability of the *principato nuovo*, in the none-too-hopeful prospect of rendering it permanent. The *Discourses* open (1.1–2) with an elaborate comparison between republics perfect in their origin and republics, at first imperfect, which attain a greater stability in time; but this is soon reshaped as the contrast between commonwealths aiming at self-preservation and those aiming at expansion (1.5–6). This theoretical question must stem in part from the "Sallustian" presentation of Roman history as problematic, but there are diversities of value already present in it. Commonwealths for preservation are stable but oligarchic, since they do not aim at conquest and do not arm many of their citizens; Sparta relied on the formidable infantry of the few, mercantile Venice on contracts with mercenaries. There has appeared the fundamental link between citizenship and the bearing of arms, but also the question whether government is to be *stretto* or *largo*; is it the test of a republic's goodness that it does or does not extend citizenship, and arms, to the many? Rome now appears as the archetypal, almost the only, commonwealth for expansion; it armed the plebeians, who manned the legions, defeated other cities, and incorporated them in Rome's expanding *imperium*. *Ex imperio libertas*, however: because the plebeians were armed, they could assert their civic demands not by civil war but by the threat of secession. Arms were not everything; with them went a sacrosanct and religious discipline, civic as well as military, ensuring that the threat would be withdrawn if the demands were negotiated or an enemy became dangerous. The point about the secession of the plebs was that they did not secede; the point about the disorders and tumults of early Rome was that they were instruments of political negotiation. Machiavelli focused his *Discourses* on Livy's first ten books, with their legendary portraits of heroic action and civic virtue, in order to present the image of a commonwealth that succeeded in preserving itself by means of expansion, and therefore needed the means of expansion.

From this point on, ethical and moral debate could develop. *Virtù*, the quality of mind dear to Machiavelli, was suited to a commonwealth for expansion, more democratic to the extent that it gave arms to the people; it was aggressive, audacious, daring, aiming at the masculine domination of a feminized *fortuna*. The commonwealth for preservation was necessarily more cautious and *disarmata*, in need of the prudence of oligarchic government. Prudence, the virtue most recommended by the statecraft of kings and counsellors, ranked among the Christian virtues; but Machiavellian *virtù*, associated with the commonwealth for expansion, was as pagan as most such commonwealths had been, and in any debate between the two, prudence would be favored by king and church. Much of Machiavelli's probably well-deserved reputation as a neo-pagan in conflict with Christian values arises, not from the *ragion di stato* (reason of state) he was thought to have recommended to princes, but from the preference for commonwealths aiming at expansion that lies at the heart of his theory of republics – a preference, besides, for the *libertas* that resulted in *imperium*. But here we return, as he did, to the "Sallustian" narrative. The heroic *virtù* of the first ten books of Livy ended in the civil wars and the principate of Augustus, and Bruni had already condemned the Caesars for destroying republican liberty and Rome's capacity for empire with it. Like Bruni, Machiavelli knew that the history of the republic was both ironic and tragic, and in the *Discourses* he did not fail to narrate it. The version of history he selected was centered on the agrarian laws and the failure of the Gracchi, and although he condemns the Gracchi it is more for imprudence and bad timing than for the supposed injustice of their proposed reforms. The agrarian crisis ended with land and power in the hands of the nobility, but Senate and people in a condition of civil war that made the armies the instruments of their commanders and not of the *res publica* (*Discourses* I.37). The full story of the republic's disintegration and of the weaknesses of the principate that succeeded it is not to be found in the *Discourses*, and it is not clear how this catastrophe might have been avoided.[6] Did he perhaps agree that a republic of citizen warrior farmers could only have been maintained by perpetual expansion and the seizure of new lands? This thought had been expressed by Tiberius Gracchus in Appian's history.[7] Ironically, however, the final extensions of empire had been achieved first by the legions of Pompey and Caesar seeking new provinces in the contest for power, then by those of Augustus and Trajan aiming to consolidate the frontiers after the contest had ended.

If we are to think of Machiavelli as a normative writer, recommending certain political forms and ethical values above others, his account of Rome might appear critical of the republic as an ideal structure. When we survey his attitude toward the changing political forms in his own Florence, it is hard to avoid feeling that, although he thought of republic and principate as alternative possibilities, was critical of both, and would have served either, his heart was with some form of republic if one could be achieved. (What might have happened had he lived through the siege and final collapse of the Florentine republic in 1529–30 is a vain if fascinating conjecture.) If we turn to the *Discourses* in search of signs for or against the republic as a preferred form of government, we find ourselves within the problem of duration and survival. The *governo largo*, which arms its people and must listen to their voices, is a commonwealth for expansion, and Machiavelli concedes that the commonwealth for preservation (by definition a *governo stretto*) is more stable and will last longer. Nevertheless, Rome is to be preferred to Venice, because, in choosing to expand, it chose "la parte più onorevole [the most honorable course]" (*Discourses* 1.6) and glory over length of days. Glory is a pagan value, and Machiavelli may be read as consciously reversing the morality of Augustine, for whom *libertas* and *imperium* were expressions of the *libido dominandi*. Or is he indicating that pagan and Christian values were both open to Europeans of the Renaissance, but could never be reconciled? If so, the republic is a pagan rather than a Christian polity. Machiavelli apparently preferred the ancient religion that worshipped the gods of the city, as more conducive to political *virtù* than were Christian meekness and pacifism. In the century following his, Thomas Hobbes and many others are to be found saying that the sovereign – prince or republic, Leviathan or Oceana – should control both religion and *virtù* and lessen the subversive force of a Christianity seen as fanatical rather than passive. But this was a product of the Reformation and the Wars of Religion, which Machiavelli did not live to see. His criticism of Christian values is the expression of a strong antipathy to the politics of the papacy; he did not anticipate the Enlightened irreligion that was to make use of him.

The ancient republic and Machiavelli's admiration of it in the early sixteenth century are both to be set within specific historical conditions. It is still history, although in a more general sense, that is operative when we consider Machiavelli's judgment (*Discourses* 1.58) that the people are, on the whole, wiser than their rulers. Here we have Aristotle's opinion that, although individuals know little, their collective judgment knows more than the most prudent few ever can; but a more Machiavellian perception emerges when we hear that, in the unpredictable world of fortune and contingency, it is necessary to know when to act daringly and when cautiously, and how to turn rapidly from the one to the other. Individuals, conditioned by birth and experience, find it hard to do this; but the republic, having many leaders among its people, has a diversity of personality types at its disposal, and the few and many together know how to choose them: for example, the choice between the daring Scipio and the cautious Fabius the Temporizer (Cunctator), each the right man at the right moment (*Discourses* 3.9). The republic, therefore, is more adaptable and better fitted to survive than the prince.

III

Insistently, therefore, we find ourselves returning to the context of history, survival, exterior danger, and interior weakness, which may be opposed to the context of good and bad, just and unjust, redeemable and sinful, in which ancient and Christian political philosophy pursued its enterprise. It has always been argued that Machiavelli's choice of this context – in which the criteria are failure and success, audacity and prudence, ruthlessness and clemency – was of itself a political choice although not a moral one. He chose to enjoin these values, it is supposed, because he preferred them to those of justice or redemption. Arguably, he did; but it seems fair to ask whether recommending this choice was the sole purpose he had in writing. There was, and had been since Sallust in the last century of the Roman republic, a literature of *libertas et imperium*, which pointed out, almost exclusively in the context of Roman history, that these values might be both interdependent and incompatible. Machiavelli continued this literature, and we may say that he continues to write according to its assumptions and criteria. It may follow that his decision is primarily a matter of genre; he is writing political history, not political or Christian philosophy, and we should not read the former as a repudiation of the latter, the philosophical choice of an anti-philosophy. Alternatively, we may say with Isaiah Berlin that he is pointing out that Renaissance Europeans lived according to two irreconcilable value systems, the one ancient and the other Christian;[8] Machiavelli's apparent reversal of Augustine's choice is a way of saying that the choice between them remains open and inescapable. From here we can proceed in a historical direction; the republic is a pre-Christian ideal, and to opt for it is to opt for the problematic of pre-Christian history. The republic exists among the problems it sets for itself; if the author of this chapter may say so, every republic occupies a Machiavellian moment.

There remains the question of the applicability of Roman history to Florentine history. Certainly, Machiavelli's history of Florence tells another story: that Florence was never fully autonomous and consequently never confronted the problem of republican stability in a soluble form. No Italian republic was in a position to repeat the history of Rome; but why is this? Here we may turn back, as Machiavelli in some sense did, to the narrative of how popes and emperors had left the cities of the *Regnum italicum* free but faction-ridden and therefore liable to fall under the rule of princes. This is a post-Roman and post-Carolingian story; but behind it Leonardo Bruni had discerned something deeper, the failure of Tuscan cities to return to what they had been in the Etruscan period, before the Roman conquest. A league of free cities, he suggested, preserved more republican virtue than did the empire of a single republic. Machiavelli investigates this question (*Discourses* 2.4), and his admiration of the free and warlike Swiss cantons may hint at his answer; but he thought the Romans had had, or had left themselves, no alternative to the pursuit of empire, its glory and its shame. By the time he was writing, however, princes were ineradicable from the political landscape, and he could imagine an expulsion of the French and Spaniards from Italy only as the work of some Caesar-like figure who should be both conqueror and legislator. The problem of *libertas et imperium* was unlikely to recur in its ancient form.

Here we may venture upon the afterlife of Machiavelli's writings, and with it the afterlife of the problems of Roman history and the history of republics. As "Machiavellism" was invented by his readers after his death, his style of thought was replaced by "Tacitism," as Italian, Spanish, and French authors employed Tacitus' history of the Roman emperors from Tiberius to Nero to teach courtiers and counsellors how to serve absolute rulers, and "princes" in this sense how to avoid becoming tyrants. At the same time, Machiavelli was refashioned as an amoral counsellor to tyrants, as the atheist he may have been, and increasingly as a forerunner of the subjection of religion to the state: increasingly but misleadingly, as the issue had scarcely arisen in his lifetime, and his Prince – an insecure usurper in a culture formerly republican – does not stand for the state and has none of its apparatus (judicial, ecclesiastical, bureaucratic) behind him. In these debates the recoverable as opposed to the mythical Machiavelli was an ancestral figure rather than an immediate parti-cipant; he lived before the Wars of Religion and the eighteenth-century Enlightenment's attempt to supersede them with a commercial society, both civil and cosmopolitan; but Rome and the republic recur as the Enlightened order is itself the target of criticism. The *républiques fédératives* that inter-ested Montesquieu were Dutch and Swiss rather than Roman, mercantile rather than military; but was not Napoleon Bonaparte, condottiere and legislator, the hero of a republic and its Caesarist betrayer, the last and even the only Machiavellian Prince in European history?

Enlightenment presupposed the transfer of armed power to the state and a commercially active citizenry controlling the state's capacity to finance armies; but from its first appearance this development was feared as reducing and corrupting the *virtù* of the disarmed citizen.[9] Here Machiavelli reemerged – still as a figure somewhat ancestral – whose stress on the need for citizens to be armed and active placed him (at least before the democratic revolutions) on the "ancient" side of the debate. Here we may examine one of his more normative and less historical statements: the generalization that the few wish to rule over others, the many to avoid being ruled by them (*Discourses* 1.5). Developed in a certain direction, this becomes an anticipation of the "liberal" thesis that citizens desire negative liberty rather than positive: less a share in free action for themselves than laws that will protect their privacy and property against either private or public interference. Privacy and property enlarge into society and culture, realms of being that are or should be immune from politics and which replace the ancient idea that the *res publica*, by defending *virtù*, defines the human as the political. Here we have a kernel of the debate between "republicanism" and "liberalism," liberty as positive (and ancient) or negative (and modern). It is usual to suppose the triumph of modernity and liberalism; but from the militias and standing armies of eighteenth-century debate we go on to the conscript citizen armies of the two world wars, and in their aftermath we find ourselves enquiring what manner of war the state should make and how its soldiers are to be citizens or its citizens soldiers. This chapter has sought to locate Machiavelli and his use of history in the history of his own time; but there is a narrative, continuing into a present, in which he is still at least quotable.

NOTES

1. "Ritratto di cose di Francia," published in Niccolò Machiavelli, *Tutte le opere*, ed. Mario Martelli (Florence: Sansoni, 1971), pp. 55–63; Jean-Jacques Marchand, *Niccolò Machiavelli: i primi scritti politici (1499–1512)* (Padua: Antenore, 1975), pp. 507–24; *Edizione nazionale delle opere di Niccolò Machiavelli*, vol. 3, *Arte della guerra. Scritti politici minori*, ed. Jean-Jacques Marchand, Denis Fachard, and Giorgio Masi (Rome: Salerno Editrice, 2001), pp. 546–66.
2. J. G. A. Pocock, *Barbarism and Religion*, 4 vols. (Cambridge University Press, 1999–2005), vol. 3, *The First Decline and Fall* (2003), parts 1 and 3. Readers of *The Machiavellian Moment* are invited to consider this work as a sequel.
3. Sallust, *Catilinae conjuratio* 50–5; Leonardo Bruni, *History of the Florentine People*, vol. 1, books 1–4, ed. and trans. James Hankins (Cambridge, Mass.: Harvard University Press, 2001); Pocock, *Barbarism and Religion*, vol. 3, *The First Decline and Fall*, pp. 60–78.
4. Pocock, *Barbarism and Religion*, vol. 3, *The First Decline and Fall*, pp. 37, 140.
5. For a rather different view, see Mikael Hörnqvist, *Machiavelli and Empire* (Cambridge University Press, 2004).
6. Pocock, *Barbarism and Religion*, vol. 3, *The First Decline and Fall*, pp. 210–20.
7. *Ibid.*, pp. 46–7.
8. Isaiah Berlin, "The Originality of Machiavelli," in *Studies on Machiavelli*, ed. Myron P. Gilmore (Florence: Sansoni, 1972), pp. 149–206; Berlin, *Against the*

Current: Essays in the History of Ideas, ed. Henry Hardy (New York: Viking, 1980).

9. J. G. A. Pocock, *Virtue, Commerce, and History: Essays on Political Thought and History, Chiefly in the Eighteenth Century* (Cambridge University Press, 1985).

FURTHER READING

Baron, Hans. *The Crisis of the Early Italian Renaissance: Civic Humanism and Republican Liberty in an Age of Classicism and Tyranny*, 2 vols. Princeton University Press, 1955; revised, one-vol. edition, 1966.

In Search of Florentine Civic Humanism: Essays on the Transition from Medieval to Modern Thought, 2 vols. Princeton University Press, 1988.

Berlin, Isaiah. *Four Essays on Liberty*. London, Oxford University Press, 1969.

Two Concepts of Liberty. Oxford, Clarendon Press, 1958.

Hankins, James. "The 'Baron Thesis' after Forty Years and Some Recent Studies of Leonardo Bruni," *Journal of the History of Ideas* 56 (1995): 309–38.

Hankins, James, ed. *Renaissance Civic Humanism: Reappraisals and Reflections*. Cambridge University Press, 2000.

Pocock, J. G. A. "Machiavelli and the Rethinking of History," *Il pensiero politico* 27 (1994): 215–30.

The Machiavellian Moment: Florentine Political Thought and the Atlantic Republican Tradition. Princeton University Press, 1975; reissued with an afterword, 2003.

Skinner, Quentin. *The Foundations of Modern Political Thought*, vol. 1, *The Renaissance*. Cambridge University Press, 1978.

"Machiavelli's *Discorsi* and the Pre-Humanist Origins of Republican Ideas," in *Machiavelli and Republicanism*, ed. Gisela Bock, Quentin Skinner, and Maurizio Viroli. Cambridge University Press, 1990; pp. 121–41.

Visions of Politics, 3 vols. Cambridge University Press, 2002, vol. 2, *Renaissance Virtues*.

10

ALISON BROWN

Philosophy and religion in Machiavelli

Writing to Machiavelli in June 1509, his friend Filippo Casavecchia warned him that his "philosophy" ("la vostra filosofia") would never be comprehended by fools and that there were not enough "wise" people who did understand it.[1] Casavecchia was referring to Machiavelli's foresight in contributing to the recapture of Pisa through the institution of the militia, which is not what we mean by philosophy today. Nevertheless, Casavecchia put his finger on the quality that contemporaries admired about Machiavelli, namely, the originality of his thinking in a broader context. Machiavelli never wrote systematically about his understanding of philosophical issues, to which ancient thinkers contributed as much as contemporary politics and religion, nor are we sure that his ideas can be described as a coherent whole. On the contrary, his view of the cosmos and of man's nature as unchanging seems difficult to reconcile with the flexibility he demanded in the field of politics, where his ideas about republicanism, princely rule, and religion seem equally at odds.

The starting point for describing Machiavelli's outlook has always been his letter to Francesco Vettori on December 10, 1513, describing the origins of *The Prince* as the outcome of both practical political experience and the influence of the classics.[2] The practical experience consisted of his work in the chancery and diplomatic missions, which stressed the importance of rules, models, and necessary procedures and encouraged in him a skeptical and somewhat fatalistic approach to life. The literary works that influenced him included his school texts, the books in his father's library (among them Livy's history of Rome), the poets mentioned in the letter to Vettori (including Ovid, Dante, and Petrarch), and the newly discovered texts of Lucretius' *De rerum natura* (*On the Nature of Things*) and the sixth book of Polybius' *History*. Underpinning these was the influence of the milieu in which he grew up: Florence under the political and cultural hegemony of Lorenzo de' Medici, in which popular belief in astrological determinism combined with sophisticated Platonic idealism to praise Lorenzo as the wise man ruling above the stars.

This combination of ideas about the influence of the stars and the role of the Platonic wise man attracted and repelled Machiavelli in equal measure. It accounts for what I shall call "the puzzle" of Machiavelli, by which I mean the apparent conflict in his thinking between traditional belief in ancient astrology and belief in man's freedom to act independently, which in turn raises the question of his attitude to religion. Although belief in prodigies and the influence of the stars coexisted with Christian providentialism in the outlook of many contemporaries, Machiavelli's unconventional thinking about religion and Christianity makes his position less than fully clear. Yet there are clues to help us. Discussing the influence of upbringing and education, Machiavelli wrote in *Discourses* 3.46 that what one hears as a young man "of necessity makes an impression and then regulates one's behavior for the whole of one's life." This suggests that Machiavelli's early writings can serve as a guide to understanding his "philosophy" or wider outlook in later life.

The puzzle of Machiavelli

A good place to start is Machiavelli's famous letter of September 1506 to Piero Soderini's nephew Giovanbattista Soderini, commonly called the "Ghiribizzi" (musings). This revealing letter anticipates nearly all the themes of Machiavelli's later writings and uniquely reveals him thinking, as it were, aloud about philosophical problems, weighing them up and having second thoughts that he added in the margin, providing what Gennaro Sasso has called "a harsh counterpoint, the beginning of a negation, the temptation – even more than the attempt – to overcome" the problem.[3] The problem he addressed concerned the difficulty of formulating rules about political behavior after he witnessed Pope Julius II's amazing success, against the odds and contrary to the rules of conventional wisdom, in recapturing the rebel city of Perugia by entering it unprotected and with seemingly inadequate armed forces. The episode suggested to Machiavelli that, while success was sometimes the result of careful preparation, at other times it was a matter of chance. Since it is impossible to take a middle course between kindness and cruelty, or between having fortresses and not having them, and because we cannot change our natures in order to adapt to the constantly changing "times and the order of things," which affect both states and individuals ("in general and in particular"), Machiavelli concluded that "wise men" who are capable of adapting to changing circumstances and who could thus, according to the well-known adage, "command the stars and the fates" do not exist. Successful rulers are simply those whose character suits the times and are lucky enough, like the impulsive Julius, not to live long enough to experience changes that require accommodation and adaptation.[4] In the poem on "Fortune," also addressed to Giovanbattista Soderini around the same time, Machiavelli struck the same negative note in speculating that, if only we could leap from top to top of fortune's wheels, we would always be happy and successful, but that because "this is denied by the occult force that rules us" and we cannot change the disposition we are born with, we are helpless in the face of fortune (lines 115–20).[5] Since Machiavelli repeatedly expressed similar ideas in both chapter 25 of *The Prince* and in the *Discourses*, where he also acknowledged the role of prodigies and prophecies in predicting "great events," it has been argued that natural astrology played an important role in his "philosophy," casting "a dark shadow on his attempt to safeguard free will."[6]

The conflict between natural determinism and free will is indeed the crux of the matter, but there is an alternative solution to this puzzle about the ability of the man of *virtù* to act freely in Machiavelli's circumscribed cosmos. Two years before writing the "Ghiribizzi" to Giovanbattista Soderini, Machiavelli sent a now lost letter to Bartolomeo Vespucci, a Florentine teacher of astrology at the University of Padua, in which he evidently entertained a more positive view of the individual's freedom to act. For in his reply to this missing letter, Vespucci wrote:

> Your opinion is absolutely right, since all the ancients agree that the wise man can himself change the influences of the stars. This should be understood not with respect to the stars, since nothing can change what is eternal, but rather with respect to the wise man himself, who, by changing his step this way and that, can change and alter himself.[7]

Machiavelli's opinion seems to have been that, although the wise man cannot change the course of the stars and the universe (as the adage had it), he could change his own actions and, in so doing, change himself. We should not be surprised, then, that in the "Ghiribizzi" Machiavelli added afterthoughts in the margins that form a counterpoint ("the beginning of a negation," as Sasso calls it) to the mainly negative drift of the letter:

> each man must do what his mind [*animo*] prompts him to – and do it with daring [*audacia*], then try his luck [or tempt fortune: *tentare la fortuna*], and, when fortune slackens off, regain the initiative by trying a different way of proceeding from his customary one.

"Trying a different way" or "changing one's step" was the "tempting" solution to the problem of free will at this stage of Machiavelli's life. It might still be difficult to integrate the dynamism of these afterthoughts into his overall philosophy but for one new piece of evidence: Machiavelli's

ALISON BROWN

marginal notes in his transcription of Lucretius' *De rerum natura*, written around 1497. For in book 2 Machiavelli marked several passages referring to the "atomic swerve," which, by causing atoms to collide, introduces an element of unpredictability into an otherwise predetermined universe. This suggests he had picked up Lucretius' association of the swerve with free will. If so, Lucretius may provide the missing link in our understanding of Machiavelli's philosophy, "the compass" (to adopt the phrase he used in writing to Giovanbattista Soderini) of his "navigation."

The influence of Lucretius

Machiavelli never refers to Lucretius by name, but we know from the surviving transcription, in Machiavelli's own hand, of Lucretius' book-length philosophical poem, *De rerum natura*, that he read and commented on this work at an early stage of his life, doubtless before he entered full-time employment in the chancery in 1498.[8] He may have undertaken the task as a student of Marcello di Virgilio Adriani, a professor at the University of Florence (the Studio), or as his amanuensis. Adriani's inaugural lecture in 1497 had been strongly influenced by Lucretius – as its title, *Nil admirari*, "Wonder at nothing," suggests, since Lucretius' purpose in his poem (like Adriani's in 1497), had been to eradicate superstitious fear and wonder by explaining "the causes of things."[9] It is likely, as we shall see, that Machiavelli was familiar with the lecture, and only nine months later, in June 1498, he was appointed to serve under Adriani in the chancery, four months after Adriani had himself been elected first chancellor.[10] So, although Machiavelli's early years remain tantalizingly obscure, Adriani and Lucretius were clearly major influences – and their importance is still undervalued.

Adriani had been lecturing on poetry and oratory in Florence's university since the death of Poliziano in late September 1494, just before the French invasion and the fall of the Medici regime. Initially he quoted Lucretius to show the relevance of the latter's description of primitive life "before the founding of cities" to Florence's turmoil after the fall of the Medici, but by 1497 he developed a new tack to make his lectures relevant to a commercial city that, as he put it, "reacted to everything by calculating the dividend it would bring." Adriani offered the teaching of ancient philosophy, and especially Lucretius, in order to alleviate the fear of change and the unknown created by the play of fortune. In 1496 his predecessor in the chancery, Bartolomeo Scala (a friend of Machiavelli's father), had found Lucretius relevant for the same reasons, and in his official (and printed) *Defence* of the new republican regime he openly named "the amazing Lucretius" as one of the ancient philosophers who believed the world was created by "the fortuitous clash of individual

160

atoms," and whose poem even Virgil, "the king, we might say, of Latin poets," was not embarrassed to quote.[11] When Adriani responded the following year to Savonarola's attack on ancient philosophers who believed the world "was made of atoms," he emphasized themes that later became central to Machiavelli's philosophy: novelty, fortune, and fear as the underpinnings of superstitious religion.

There are other clues to the influence on Machiavelli of Adriani's 1497 Lucretian lecture in words and phrases Machiavelli used in later writings. Machiavelli's ambition in the preface to book 1 of the *Discourses* to follow a path as yet untrodden by anyone ("non essendo suta ancora da alcuno trita") in order to find "new ways and methods" clearly echoes Lucretius' intention to traverse paths not yet trodden (*trita*) by any foot in order to gather "new flowers";[12] but it also echoes the opening of Adriani's lecture, which refers to the difficulty, in the current state of intellectual life in Florence, of finding anything "new" to say without repeating well-worn platitudes (*trita*).[13] Reflecting on novelty and the human faculty of wonder that it generates, Adriani goes on to describe how we enter life like "alpinists who descend into an elegant and magnificently built city" astonished by what we see, whether due to our mental "oblivion of things" as described by Plato (*Timaeus* 23a, *Laws* 682), or because everything *is* new (as Lucretius, although unnamed by Adriani, says in *De rerum natura* 5.330–1).[14] Machiavelli clearly echoes Adriani in his controversial chapter on whether or not the world is eternal (*Discourses* 2.5), when he asserts that our ignorance of the past is due not only to the role of religions in destroying records of the past but also to the "oblivion" caused by natural disasters like floods, from which the only survivors are "uncouth mountain dwellers." And although, like Adriani, Machiavelli does not name Lucretius or attribute our oblivion of the past to the world being new, Lucretius is nevertheless very germane to the argument of this much disputed chapter, not simply because of his hostility to religion but because he suggests that the absence of historical evidence earlier than "the Theban War and the ruin of Troy" (5.324–31) is a reason against the world being eternal.

More substantial influences on Machiavelli, however, are the two key themes that Adriani went on to develop in his lecture concerning fortune and the superstitious origins of religion. As we shall see, Adriani's attack on propitiatory religion for holding men in bondage until the final day of settlement, and thereby increasing instead of assuaging their fears, exerted a strong influence on Machiavelli. Equally important is the theme of fortune and the need to react to it with flexibility, or "mental mobility" as Adriani calls it, by understanding its joint role with Nature and God as the authors of all events. Fortune is much discussed in Machiavelli scholarship, and recently its sound

Christian credentials, especially in *Prince* 25, have been asserted.[15] But Adriani's and Machiavelli's emphasis on mental flexibility is a new response to fortune that stems from the very different tradition of Lucretian atomism. And since it is Lucretius who describes how the atomic swerve gives us freedom in wresting not only our movements but also our minds from the fates, it seems likely that Adriani had him in mind in lecturing on the need for flexibility or "mental mobility" to enable us to adjust to change "like reeds bending in the breeze."[16]

That Lucretius' passage on the swerve influenced Machiavelli is further suggested by markings in Machiavelli's hand in his transcription of *De rerum natura*. Following a pointing hand in the margin at line 82 of book 2 (on the mistake of not believing in the spontaneous movement and collision of atoms in the void), two passages on free will (literally "a free mind") are marked with marginal comments. The first is on the atomic swerve, which, by breaking the decrees of fate, enables us to enjoy free will. Without this "free will wrested from the fates [*libera ... fatis avulsa voluntas*]," asks Lucretius (2.256–60), how would living creatures all over the world be able to go where pleasure leads them, "swerving our motions not at fixed times and fixed places, but just where our mind [*mens*] takes us?" Here Machiavelli wrote in the margin: "from motion there is variety and from it we have a free mind [*liberam habere mentem*]." The second, at lines 284–7, concerns our ability to resist external pressure to act against our will, and Machiavelli noted in the margin: "weight, blows and the swerve are in the seeds," condensing Lucretius' argument that motions are caused by something other than the external force of weights and blows, thanks to the freedom given to us by the swerve of the very first atoms.[17] These are followed by the marginal comment on lines 294–5, "nothing is more closely packed or more widely spaced than at its beginning," for (as Lucretius continues in lines 296–303) nothing can increase or decrease the mass of matter or the sum total of things: not only are atoms permanent and unchanging but so too is their motion, which is the same now as it used to be and will be in the future, everything being born under the same conditions and developing in the same way according to the laws or "pacts" of nature. To this world the gods contribute nothing, moved neither by propitiation nor by wrath as they "enjoy a life of deepest peace" (lines 646–8, 651), which Machiavelli summed up in the margin with the comment, "the gods don't care about the affairs of mortals."[18]

These marginal comments testify to the particular importance Lucretius had for Machiavelli, concentrated as they are in book 2 on the structure of the universe and focusing on the topics of free will, motion, matter, and the indifference of the gods to human affairs. They all contribute key ideas to

Machiavelli's philosophy that have hitherto seemed difficult to reconcile. The first is the notion of an unchanging universe, in which the "things that are now, were before in the past, and will move in the same way in the future," as Lucretius has it (2.297–9), or, as Machiavelli will rephrase it in the preface to book 2 of the *Discourses*, "the world has always been in the same condition" (*cf. Discourses* 1.39 and *Asino* 5.103–4: "And it is and always has been and always will be that evil follows after good, good after evil"). The second key idea is that of a world "in constant motion" (Lucretius, 1.995), which Machiavelli also echoes in the preface to book 2 of the *Discourses*: "since human affairs are always in motion" (*cf. Asino* 5.100–2). The third is the theory of a natural cycle of development governed by laws to preserve the species and "the sum total of things" (Lucretius 2.302–3 and 5.923–4; Machiavelli, *Discourses* 1.2, *Florentine Histories* 5.1), and, within this life cycle, the possibility of change and the exercise of free will through the swerve, enabling a man wise and energetic enough to "change his step" or, as he puts it in *Prince* 25 and 26, to exercise his free will ("libero arbitrio") in the half of his actions not controlled by fortune or by God, who "does not want to do everything." Other hints of Lucretius' presence in Machiavelli, apart from this account of the physical universe and critique of religion (more on this later), include his account of evolution in *Discourses* 1.2, which adopts Lucretius' contractual explanation of justice; his attack on ambition and avarice; his interest in animal morphology; and the allusion in the December 1513 letter to Vettori to the myth of Sisyphus, to which Lucretius (3.995–1002) gives a specifically political twist that must have appealed to Machiavelli.[19]

Another important influence on Machiavelli came from the fashionable debates on the eternity of the world that were taking place just as Machiavelli was writing the *Discourses*, particularly at the university of Pisa (whose provost, Francesco del Nero, was related to Machiavelli by marriage and employed his brother, Totto, as an assistant). The major discrepancy between Lucretius and Machiavelli concerns precisely the issue of the eternity of the world: are both the world and the universe eternal, as Machiavelli is said to have believed, or is it only the universe that is eternal and not the world, as Lucretius held? The eternity of the world is an Aristotelian-Averroist belief, and, according to the "Lucretian philosopher" in Pisa, Raffaele Franceschi, the debate in Pisa in 1517 on the soul "could not have been livelier if Pietro Pomponazzi [the Paduan Averroist] had been there."[20] So Machiavelli would certainly have known about it, and it may well have influenced the ambiguous opening to *Discourses* 2.5. Gennaro Sasso reads this chapter as a scholastic question, or *quaestio*, for debate on whether the world has always existed and concludes that Machiavelli was an Aristotelian-Averroist. It is more likely that the chapter's ambiguity reflects Machiavelli's open approach to the question, influenced by Adriani's 1497 lecture in the way suggested above, as well as by the later debates in Pisa. What concerned both Adriani and Machiavelli, with differing emphasis, was why almost all knowledge of antiquity (which Adriani called "an almost untouched treasure-chamber") had been lost. This is the context in which Machiavelli pursued what seems to be the main point of the chapter, an attack on all religions, including Christianity, for destroying evidence of the past.[21] In 1513, just as Machiavelli was beginning his major writing period, both the Epicureans and the Aristotelian-Averroists were condemned as heretical by the Fifth Lateran Council for believing "in the mortality or in the unity of the soul and the eternity of the world."[22] To understand better where he stood on this issue, we need to turn to the equally contentious question of Machiavelli's attitude to religion and the Church.

Religion and the Church

Although in *Discourses* 2.5 Machiavelli treats Christianity "relativistically" as one of a succession of religions with a limited life cycle, in *Discourses* 2.2 he calls it "our religion," which "teaches us the truth and the true way." It is of course difficult to know what Machiavelli's personal religious beliefs may have been, but given the tradition of skepticism in the chancery (where Bartolomeo Scala had already adopted an anthropological approach to religion in his 1496 *Defence* of Florence) we need to explore his reputation for nonconformity to see what light, if any, it throws on the place of religion more widely in his philosophy. Every year from 1500 until 1513 Niccolò and his brother Totto (who was a priest) paid the friars of Santa Croce money to commemorate the death of their father, Bernardo, and also to complete a bequest from their great-uncle to the friars. But in May 1513, shortly after Machiavelli's removal from office and brief imprisonment, payments for their father's bequest were terminated.[23] Although Bernardo was apparently devout and belonged to a confraternity, there is no evidence that Niccolò was a member of a religious company. Indeed, he parodied such companies in his "Statutes for a pleasure company," and, despite writing an "Exhortation to Penitence" (perhaps for someone else, it has been suggested), he tells us he never made a practice of listening to sermons.[24] Other evidence of Machiavelli's religiosity is retrospective and not fully reliable, such as his famous dream about preferring to be with the damned in Hell than with the saved in Heaven, and his reported death-bed confession to a friar, which, even if it happened, might – like the baptism of his children, evidently arranged by his wife and family – reflect the wishes of others as much as his own.[25]

In the opinion of his friends, Machiavelli was certainly not typically devout. Francesco Vettori told Machiavelli in November 1513 that he attended mass at the church near where he lived in Rome "since I am religious, as you know... I do not do as you do, who sometimes do not bother."[26] When the Wool Guild appointed Machiavelli to select a Lenten preacher for Florence in 1521, Francesco Guicciardini likened it to appointing Pachierotto, a well-known homosexual, to choose a wife for a friend, adding that if Machiavelli at his age started thinking about his soul it would be attributed to senility, not goodness, "since you have always lived in a contrary belief."[27] Further evidence of the "contrariness" of Machiavelli's religious beliefs is his post-humous role in the dialogue "On free will" written by a close friend, Luigi Guicciardini, who told his brother Francesco in 1533 that (the now deceased) Machiavelli represented "someone who finds it difficult to believe the things that should be believed, not just those to laugh about." But Luigi seems to have been aware of the originality of Machiavelli's thought in using him to challenge Luigi's own efforts in the dialogue to reconcile Christian free will and astrology, although without grasping "the inner unity" of Machiavelli's thought.[28]

This brings us to the question of the mortality of the soul, for, if Machiavelli really did not believe in the soul, it would imply that he supported Lucretius and the Epicureans in the debate over whether the world or the universe was eternal. He revealingly deleted the word "soul" (*anima*) from his draft preface to the *Discourses*, and in a letter written to Vettori in April 1527 he famously declared that he loved his country more than his own soul, just as he praised the Florentines who fought against the papacy in 1375–8 for valuing their country more than their souls.[29] Nor did the soul play any part in Machiavelli's physiology, where imagination (*fantasia*) replaces the soul or "spirit" (*anima*) in its relationship with the mind or intelligence (*animo*). Despite the recent emphasis on the role of imagination in Machiavelli's plays in creating the self, or "self-fashioning," in his letters it describes a process of critical psychological and political analysis that distinguishes the "effectual truth" of a situation from appearance, much as Lucretius distinguished the reality of a man, "the thing itself," when his mask is ripped away through adversity.[30]

If the beginning of this process can be seen in Machiavelli's 1506 letter to Giovanbattista Soderini, its culmination is the letter he wrote in March 1526, a year before he died, to Francesco Guicciardini. He told Guicciardini his head was full of "ghiribizzi" that might seem "either rash or ridiculous," but in fact his musings produced a last, consistent statement of the political philosophy he had outlined twenty years earlier. In this letter he presents the valiant Giovanni de' Medici (Giovanni delle Bande Nere) as the hero with exactly the qualities needed to outstep the fates.[31] And between these two letters Machiavelli resorted to another imaginative (and partly autobiographical) writing, the poem *Asino*, to present an equally consistent account of his unorthodox philosophy, combining the issue of the individual's independence with criticism of traditional Christianity in order to defend the naturalistic right of all living creatures to act freely. In so doing he overturned not only the Christian terminology of providence and grace and even the power of Christ, but also the idea of propitiatory religion (and by implication Savonarola), since, "To believe that without effort on your part God fights for you, while you are idle and on your knees, has ruined many kingdoms and many states."[32]

Religion as superstition based on fear of punishment, *metus poenarum*, is of course the great theme of *De rerum natura*, and Adriani developed it at length in the 1497 lecture *Nil admirari*, where he also attacked the idea of propitiatory religion that had God playing the role of pawnbroker.[33] "Fear of God" based on fear of punishment is also a central theme for Machiavelli, who often represents God as a judge to be feared or a "friend" to be placated and almost never as the providential creator of the universe.[34] All wise legislators claim to derive their authority from God, Machiavelli wrote in *Discourses* 1.11, "because otherwise their laws would not have been accepted." Where "fear of God is lacking," a kingdom will fall unless religion is replaced by fear of a prince. "Fear is the greatest master there is," he told Francesco Vettori several times,[35] for, as he wrote in chapter 17 of *The Prince*, it is "sustained by a dread of punishment that never leaves you." In *Discourses* 1.14 he explains how the Romans inculcated fear and superstition for political purposes through blood-curdling ceremonies, oath taking and the manipulative use of soothsayers and diviners and interpreted "their auspices according to necessity," by which he meant that their leaders were never deterred by adverse auguries from doing what they needed to do, at the same time managing to manipulate the rituals to avoid showing any disrespect for religion.[36]

Machiavelli's interest in the political value of religion to rulers was, of course, very different from Lucretius' wish to liberate men from its thrall through enlightened teaching (as Adriani attempted to do in his lectures) and was much closer to Polybius and Livy than to Lucretius. As several historians have noted, Machiavelli's attitude to religion presents two quite different faces. One sees it as a form of political control; the other follows Lucretius in describing religion anthropologically as the expression of the deeply rooted beliefs and fears of ordinary people, which Machiavelli, unlike Lucretius, saw as the basis of their respect for law and civilized behavior.[37] Both approaches are present in the *Asino* (5.106–27), where Machiavelli criticizes the idea that prayers alone can save kingdoms but also acknowledges the value of ceremonies and devotions in keeping people happy and united. The second view of religion underlies a passage in the *Florentine Histories* (1.5) that describes the impact of the barbarian invasions of Italy in overturning "the laws, customs, way of life, religion, language, dress and the very names of things," for not only did old beliefs fight with "the miracles of the new," but Christianity itself was divided into different churches with different heresies, leaving people to die miserably not knowing to which God to turn for help, "as all unhappy people are accustomed to do."[38] Machiavelli saw religious disunity as symptomatic of political disunity and popular distress, both of which needed addressing in order to achieve the ordered society that he strove for.

These two aspects of religion also help to explain Machiavelli's attitude to Christianity and the Church of his day. He attacked the papal court in *Discourses* 1.12 for its impiety and immorality before attacking Christianity more broadly in *Discourses* 2.2 for having the wrong ethos in glorifying "humble and contemplative men rather than active ones" and in suffering injuries passively instead of reacting to them boldly as the Romans did in their bloody and victorious wars. For the same reasons, he criticized the friars (*Discourses* 3.1) for teaching the people passivity in not speaking out against evil, which allowed their dishonest prelates and leaders to do whatever they wanted, unafraid of punishment that "they cannot see and do not believe." Yet he admired the friars' founders, Francis and Dominic, for reviving the idea of primitive Christianity "in the minds of the people," who saw it as their authentic culture.

The Dominican friar Girolamo Savonarola was an especially emblematic figure for Machiavelli, for he integrated both facets of ancient religion that fascinated Machiavelli: as a political force based on fear, and as the expression of the deeply rooted culture of ordinary people. He admired Savonarola for using religion to support political necessity in persuading the Florentines (who, Machiavelli adds, were far from stupid) that he "spoke with God," and for reading the Bible "judiciously" when it was necessary to break its commandments. But he criticized him for misusing his influence with the people: instead of preaching boldness, he encouraged passivity by suggesting that they would be saved through fasting and prayers alone, "idle and on their knees," and, worse, he lost their respect through his hypocrisy over the law of appeal.[39] There is little evidence that Machiavelli believed in Christian revelation or even in the special authority accorded to religious states and holy men. His writings provide instead a remarkably consistent account of a world in which religion played a supporting but subordinate role in the essential art of politics.

Conclusion

If we attempt to draw the threads together, Machiavelli's philosophy was both coherent and original, built on cornerstones laid early in his life. Although he apparently accepted an important role for fortune and, at times, a certain determinism in his view of the world, thus following the view of many ancient philosophers and contemporaries, he was novel in allowing unexpected room in this deterministic universe for a bold and clever person to exercise his free will, whether a political leader like Scipio, a young Medici prince, an imaginative teacher like Machiavelli himself, or even the upstanding boar in the *Asino*. This freedom was not due to God's providence or to the traditional Christian explanation of man's free will; it was, rather, a natural characteristic, shared by animals and humans – by "living creatures all over the world," as Lucretius put it (2.256) in the passage highlighted by Machiavelli – in a universe that allowed for the play of free will within its regulated cycles of development.

When Machiavelli wrote *The Prince* in 1513–15, he argued that it was Italy's descent to the bottom of the cycle that provided Pope Leo and his nephew Lorenzo with the opportunity to exercise the "free will" allowed by Fortune and by God, who, as he says in chapter 26, "does not want to do everything."[40] In a republic, the opportunity for the "good man" to act when his country was at the bottom of the cycle was to teach others, based on the lessons of history, what to do when the wheel of fortune turned upwards; for, despite appearances to the contrary (sometimes one's own declining life cycle makes the past seem better than the present, and sometimes the downturn of one's country makes the past genuinely better than the present), "the world has always gone on in the same way."[41] A decade later, in 1526, a similarly low moment in his country's cycle (as a menacing imperial army began its descent into Italy) gave Giovanni delle Bande Nere the opportunity to fight for his country. As Machiavelli told Francesco Guicciardini, here was a man who everyone said was "brave and impetuous, has great ideas and is a taker of bold decisions," qualities that precisely define him as Machiavelli's man of *virtù*.[42] Even the boar in the *Asino* (8.22–8) shows its innate free will by rearing up on its hind legs and contemptuously dismissing any return to human life: "I don't want to, and I refuse to live with you." The poetic episode evokes Machiavelli's real-life advice, shortly before he died, to his son Guido to let their mad mule free to "go wherever it likes to regain its own way of life."[43]

In this scheme of things, God and providence had no special role to play, nor did religion or Platonic idealism contribute to the civic and patriotic morality of Machiavelli's "good man," who would be judged not in a final court of appeal or Last Judgment, but only by his success in providing for the security and "common good" of his country. As his friends acknowledged, Machiavelli was a quirky and unconventional thinker who laughed at matters both serious and frivolous. Yet underlying his humor was a consistent and novel philosophy for his times. Admiring good behavior and respecting personal belief-systems, his philosophy was not immoral. But neither was it religious, maintaining as it did that religion was based on fear and should be used in the service of politics and not as its master.

NOTES

1. Machiavelli, *Tutte le opere*, ed. Mario Martelli (Florence: Sansoni, 1971), p. 1108. Machiavelli's literary writings are cited from Allan Gilbert's English translations in Machiavelli, *The Chief Works and Others*, 3 vols. (Durham, N.C.: Duke University Press, 1989), and his letters from James B. Atkinson and David Sices, *Machiavelli and His Friends: Their Personal Correspondence* (DeKalb, Ill.: Northern Illinois University Press, 1996). Unless otherwise indicated, translations of Lucretius are by W. H. D. Rouse in Lucretius, *De rerum natura* (Cambridge, Mass.: Harvard University Press, 1982).

2. *Opere*, p. 1160; *Correspondence*, pp. 264–5.

3. *Opere*, pp. 1082–3; *Correspondence*, pp. 134–6. Gennaro Sasso, "Qualche osservazione sui 'Ghiribizzi al Soderino'," in *Machiavelli e gli antichi e altri saggi*, 4 vols. (Milan and Naples: Ricciardi, 1987–97), 2:52. Also Anthony Parel, *The Machiavellian Cosmos* (New Haven, Conn.: Yale University Press, 1992), pp. 76–7.

4. *Opere*, p. 1083; *Correspondence*, p. 135. On the adage "The wise man commands the stars [*sapiens dominabitur astris*]," see Parel, *Cosmos*, p. 11, and on "general and particular" fortune, pp. 12 and 69–70.

5. *Opere*, p. 978; *Works*, 2:747.

6. Anthony Parel, "Human motions and Celestial Motions in Machiavelli's Historiography," in *Machiavelli politico storico letterato*, ed. Jean-Jacques Marchand (Rome: Salerno Editrice, 1996), p. 382; Parel, *Cosmos*, pp. 37–41. For these ideas in the *Discourses*: book 1, preface, chaps. 39 and 56; book 2, preface, chap. 29; in the *Florentine Histories*, book 5, chap. 1.

7. *Opere*, p. 1064; my translation. On Vespucci, see Sasso, "Qualche osservazione sui 'Ghiribizzi'," pp. 32–46.

8. Machiavelli's transcription is in Rome, Vatican Library, Rossi 884, first described by Sergio Bertelli and Franco Gaeta, "Noterelle machiavelliane: un codice di Lucrezio e di Terenzio," *Rivista storica italiana* 73 (1961): 544–53; also by Bertelli, "Noterelle machiavelliane: ancora su Lucrezio e Machiavelli," *Rivista storica italiana* 76 (1964): 774–90.

9. Adriani's lecture is in Florence, Biblioteca Riccardiana, MS 811 (hereafter R), fols. 18r–26r; see Alison Brown, *The Return of Lucretius to Renaissance Florence* (Cambridge, Mass.: Harvard University Press, 2010), pp. 50–6; and Armando Verde, *Lo Studio fiorentino*, 4.3 (Florence: Olschki, 1985), pp. 1309–18.

10. Nicolai Rubinstein, "The Beginnings of Niccolò Machiavelli's Career in the Florentine Chancery," *Italian Studies* 11 (1956): 72–91.

11. Referring to Virgil, *Georgics* 2.490–2, in *Apologia contra vituperatores civitatis Florentiae* (Florence, 1496), published in Bartolomeo Scala, *Humanistic and Political Writings*, ed. Alison Brown (Tempe, Ariz.: Medieval and Renaissance Texts and Studies, 1997), pp. 395–6; now translated by Renée Neu Watkins in Bartolomeo Scala, *Essays and Dialogues* (Cambridge, Mass.: Harvard University Press, 2008), p. 237.

12. John M. Najemy, *Between Friends: Discourses of Power and Desire in the Machiavelli–Vettori Letters of 1513–1515* (Princeton University Press, 1993), pp. 337–8.

13. Adriani, "Nil admirari," R, fol. 18v; Lucretius, *De rerum natura*, 1.926–8; *cf.* 4.1–2.

14. Adriani, "Nil admirari," R, fol. 20r. Cf. Verde, *Lo Studio fiorentino*, 4.3, p. 1313.

15. E.g., Cary Nederman, "Amazing Grace: Fortune, God, and Free Will in Machiavelli's Thought," *Journal of the History of Ideas* 60 (1999): 617–38.

16. Lucretius, *De rerum natura* 2.251–60; Adriani, "Nil admirari," R, fol. 19r–v: "necessarium in nostris animis mobilitatem."

17. Vatican Library, Rossi 884, fols. 22r; 25r: "motum varium esse et ex eo nos liberam habere mentem"; fol. 25v: "in seminibus esse pondus plagas et clinamen."

18. *Ibid.*, fol. 26r: "nil esse suo densius aut rarius principio"; fol. 32r: "deos non curare mortalia."

19. Ezio Raimondi, "Il sasso del politico," and "Il politico e il centauro," in Raimondi, *Politica e commedia. Il centauro disarmato* (Bologna: Il Mulino, 1998), pp. 37–43, 125–43.

20. Armando Verde, "Il secondo periodo de Lo Studio Fiorentino (1504–1528)," in *L'Università e la sua storia*, ed. Paolo Renzi (Siena: Protagon, Editori Toscani, 1998), pp. 111–12 and 123–4, note 18. On Totto, who in 1520 sent Del Nero transcriptions of lectures in Pisa: p. 112 and note 12, p. 122; on Franceschi: pp. 117–18; also Verde, *Lo Studio*, 4.3, pp. 1458–60.

21. Gennaro Sasso, "De aeternitate mundi," in Sasso, *Machiavelli e gli antichi*, 1:167–399, esp. 172–3 on the radicalism of Machiavelli's "relativizzazione" of sects and religions and his rejection of Christianity as the "vera religione."

22. Giovan Domenico Mansi, *Sacrorum conciliorum nova et amplissima collectio*, 33 (reprinted Graz, 1961), p. 842.

23. Archivio di Stato di Firenze, Corporazioni religiose soppresse, 92, no. 69, fol. 99r-v; cf. Archivio di Stato di Firenze, Notarile antecosimiano 6234, fol. 153r-v. The 1483 testament of Machiavelli's father, Bernardo, and the contents of Bernardo's library are published by Catherine Atkinson, *Debts, Dowries, Donkeys: The Diary of Niccolò Machiavelli's Father, Messer Bernardo, in Quattrocento Florence* (Frankfurt: Peter Lang, 2002), pp. 164–71.

24. Letter to Francesco Vettori, December 19, 1513: *Opere*, p. 1162; *Correspondence*, p. 267. On the "Statutes" and the "Exhortation" (*Opere*, pp. 930–4; *Works*, 2:865–8 and 1:170–4), see Emanuele Cutinelli-Rèndina, "Riscrittura e mimesi: il caso dell'*Esortazione alla penitenza*," in *Cultura e scrittura di Machiavelli* (Rome: Salerno Editrice, 1998), pp. 413–21; also by Cutinelli-Rèndina, *Chiesa e religione in Machiavelli* (Pisa and Rome: Istituti Editoriali e Poligrafici Internazionali, 1998), pp. 279–84.

25. Gennaro Sasso, "Il 'celebrato sogno' di Machiavelli," in Sasso, *Machiavelli e gli antichi*, 3:211–300 (211–20, 269–94); Giuliano Procacci, "Frate Andrea Alamanni confessore del Machiavelli?" in Procacci, *Machiavelli nella cultura europea dell'età moderna* (Rome and Bari: Laterza, 1995), pp. 423–31. On baptisms: letter of Biagio Buonaccorsi to Machiavelli, November 17, 1503, *Opere*, p. 1058, and *Correspondence*, p. 91; *cf.* Agostino Vespucci to Machiavelli, October 20–9, 1500, *Opere*, p. 1023 ("tametsi non baptizes"), and *Correspondence*, p. 32.

26. *Opere*, p. 1158; *Correspondence*, p. 261.

27. *Opere*, p. 1202; *Correspondence*, p. 335.

28. Felix Gilbert, "Machiavelli in an Unknown Contemporary Dialogue," *Journal of the Warburg Institute* 1 (1937): 163–6.

29. Parel, *Cosmos*, pp. 27–8; Machiavelli to Vettori, April 16, 1527, *Opere*, p. 1250, *Correspondence*, p. 416; *Florentine Histories*, 3.7, *Opere*, p. 696, *Works*, 3:1150.

30. Lucretius, *De rerum natura* 3.58: "eripitur persona, manet res." On imagination or *fantasia* in Machiavelli, *cf.* Najemy, *Between Friends*, pp. 185–97, especially 190, note 23, citing Lucretius (4.51–2) on images.

31. *Opere*, pp. 1228–30, *Correspondence*, pp. 380–3.

32. *Asino* 1.84, 3.115–25, 5.106–27, 8.16–18; in *Opere*, pp. 956, 962, 967, 973; *Works*, 2:752, 758, 763–4, 770. *Cf.* Gennaro Sasso, "L' 'Asino' di Niccolò Machiavelli: una satira antidantesca: considerazioni e appunti," *Annali dell'Istituto Italiano per gli Studi Storici* 12 (1991–4): 457–552 (459, 467–8, 471–2); reprinted in Sasso, *Machiavelli e gli antichi*, 4:39–128.

33. Brown, *The Return of Lucretius*, pp. 52–6 and notes 30–8 (on Savonarola at 54); Lucretius, *De rerum natura* 5.1151, 1161–1240 (esp. 1161–8 and 1194–1203); Adriani in R, fols. 20r-v, 25r-v.

34. Sebastian de Grazia, *Machiavelli in Hell* (Princeton University Press, 1989), pp. 220–1 and 50–4 ("divine friendship," although missing any allusion to Lucretius and propitiation).

35. As Vettori reminded Machiavelli (August 5, 1526): *Opere*, p. 1238; *Correspondence*, p. 395. See also Cutinelli-Rèndina, citing the influence of Lucretius as well as Averroes, in *Chiesa e Religione*, p. 165, note 275; also Cutinelli-Rèndina, *Introduzione a Machiavelli* (Rome and Bari: Laterza, 1999), p. 80, note 14.

36. John M. Najemy, "Papirius and the Chickens, or Machiavelli on the Necessity of Interpreting Religion," *Journal of the History of Ideas* 60 (1999): 659–81 (674–8).

37. Gennaro Sasso, *Niccolò Machiavelli: storia del suo pensiero politico* (Bologna: il Mulino, 1980), p. 510, calls it a "contradiction"; Cutinelli-Rèndina, *Chiesa e religione*, pp. 212–14, sees it as an "oscillation between two poles."

38. Najemy, "Papirius and the Chickens," pp. 666–7.

39. *Discourses*, 1.11, 1.45, 3.30; *Asino*, 5.106–27.

40. On the "opportunity," see Hugo Jaeckel, "What Is Machiavelli Exhorting in His *Exhortatio*? The Extraordinaries," in *Machiavelli politico storico letterato*, ed. Marchand, pp. 59–84.

41. *Discourses*, book 2, preface, and 2.30; *cf. Florentine Histories*, 4.1.

42. See note 31 above.

43. Machiavelli to his son Guido (April 2, 1527): *Opere*, pp. 1248–9; *Correspondence*, p. 413.

FURTHER READING

Brown, Alison. "Lucretius and the Epicureans in the Social and Political Context of Renaissance Florence," *I Tatti Studies* 9 (2001): 11–62.

    The Medici in Florence: the Exercise and Language of Power. Florence and Perth, Olschki, 1992.

    "Platonism in Fifteenth-century Florence and Its Contribution to Early Modern Political Thought," *Journal of Modern History* 58 (1986): 383–413.

    The Return of Lucretius to Renaissance Florence. Cambridge, Mass., Harvard University Press, 2010.

    "Savonarola, Machiavelli and Moses," in *Florence and Italy: Renaissance Studies in Honour of Nicolai Rubinstein*, ed. P. Denley and C. Elam. London, Westfield, 1988, pp. 57–72. Reprinted in Dunn, John, and Ian Harris, eds. *Machiavelli*, 2 vols. Cheltenham, Elgar, 1997, 2:425–40.

Ginzburg, Carlo. "Diventare Machiavelli: per una nuova lettura dei 'Ghiribizzi al Soderini'," *Quaderni storici* 41 (2006): 151–64.

    "Machiavelli, l'eccezione e la regola: linee di una ricerca in corso," *Quaderni storici* 38 (2003): 195–213.

Godman, Peter. *From Poliziano to Machiavelli: Florentine Humanism in the High Renaissance*. Princeton University Press, 1998.

Martelli, Mario. "I 'Ghiribizzi' a Giovan Battista Soderini," *Rinascimento* 9 (1969): 147–80.

Niccoli, Ottavia. *Prophecy and People in Renaissance Italy*. Princeton University Press, 1990.

Rahe, Paul. *Against Throne and Altar: Machiavelli and Political Theory under the English Republic*. Cambridge University Press, 2008.

    "In the Shadow of Lucretius: The Epicurean Foundations of Machiavelli's Political Thought," *History of Political Thought* 28 (2007): 30–55.

Santoro, Mario. *Fortuna, ragione e prudenza nella civiltà letteraria del Cinquecento*. Naples, Liguori, 1966.

Sasso, Gennaro. *Machiavelli e gli antichi e altri saggi*, 4 vols. Milan and Naples, Ricciardi, 1987–97.

Also the five papers by John Geerken, Marcia L. Colish, Cary Nederman, Benedetto Fontana, and John M. Najemy in the Forum on "Machiavelli and Religion: A Reappraisal" (with valuable bibliographies) in *The Journal of the History of Ideas* 60 (1999): 579–681.

11

VIRGINIA COX

Rhetoric and ethics in Machiavelli

I have not adorned this work nor filled it with long periodic sentences or pompous and magnificent words or any of the other elegant niceties and super-ficial ornaments with which many writers like to adorn and elaborate their matter; for it was my intent that it should either be entirely unembellished, or that the variety of the argument and the weightiness of the subject matter should alone constitute its appeal.[1]

Machiavelli's scornful dismissal of verbal ornament in the dedicatory letter of *The Prince* can look to modern eyes like a rejection of "rhetoric," in the reductive sense that word is often given today, namely, overripe verbal bombast. Within Machiavelli's culture, however, rhetoric was understood in a broader and more positive sense as a comprehensive practice of persuasion, embracing the conceptual as well as the verbal, and as an art with a particular political vocation. Machiavelli's writings are heavily indebted to this rhetorical tradition, not only for the form in which they cast their arguments, but also for their substance. We might even describe political practice, in the distinctive way Machiavelli frames it, as a creative adaptation of rhetoric. In Machiavelli's Florence, as in the classical world, rhetoric offered a sophisticated model for a complex, power-oriented civic practice: power-oriented in the sense that the orator's mission was to mold his listeners' responses and work on their wills. Machiavelli's genius lies in the transfor-mative political use he proposes for this practice. His, however, is an innova-tion with long historical roots.

Machiavelli's rhetorical culture

Rhetoric in Machiavelli's day was conceived of as more than the cultivation of a correct and elegant verbal style; much of its prestige derived from its claims to teach a mode of acting effectively through speech within the public sphere. This political conception of rhetoric was an inheritance from classical Greece and Rome, where the "science" of public speaking was elaborated in the theoretical works of Aristotle, Cicero, and Quintilian and powerfully embodied in the applied rhetorical culture represented by Cicero's and Demosthenes' political and judicial orations. Also important for Renaissance readers were the fictionally recreated speeches by statesmen and generals found in historians like Livy and Sallust and poets like Homer and Virgil, which contributed seductively to the political charisma attaching to the practice of eloquence. This classical rhetorical legacy found a particular imaginative purchase in Italy in the twelfth and thirteenth centuries in city-states, among them Florence, that recalled in their political organization the great republics of classical antiquity. Among the earliest translators of Cicero's rhetorical theory and political speeches was the Florentine chancellor Brunetto Latini (c. 1210–94), unfortunately now best remembered as a damned soul in Dante's *Inferno*. Latini's writings on rhetoric vividly recreated in the vernacular the Ciceronian ideal of the orator-statesman capable of conjuring political order, Orpheus-like, from primal anarchy. More practically, Latini theorized the utility of eloquence in negotiating a political realm characterized by conflict and dissent, stressing rhetoric's original adversarial character as the art of the law court and civic assembly.[2] This was a vision that had lasting appeal in Florence through the ensuing age of classical cultural revival known as humanism, as the rhetorical heritage of the ancient world was further absorbed and internalized and knowledge of Greek came to enrich the existing Latin base. Latini's fourteenth- and fifteenth-century successors, especially chancellors Coluccio Salutati (1331–1406) and Leonardo Bruni (1370–1444), continued to assign a crucial role to eloquence in civic life, as did Machiavelli's colleague Marcello Virgilio Adriani (1464–1521), who became chancellor in 1498. Nor was the study of rhetoric limited to those, like Machiavelli, who received a humanistic education: numerous fifteenth-century Florentine manuscripts combine vernacular paraphrases of Ciceronian rhetorical theory with collections of modern and translated classical speeches, offering evocative testimony to the importance of rhetoric and its perceived practical utility.[3] A Florentine citizen might be called on to participate in the consultative committees known as *pratiche*, to hold one of the rotating offices of government, to assist in the governance of his guild, and perhaps to undertake diplomatic service. All these activities required rhetorical competence, sometimes seen almost as synecdochic for political ability. Machiavelli was no exception in this regard; indeed, as an employee of the republic's rhetorical nerve center, the chancery, he was regularly involved in rhetorical activity. Although not eligible for political offices himself, in the chancery he ghostwrote political speeches, drafted official letters, and participated in diplomatic missions. More than a discrete "discipline," rhetoric for Machiavelli was a defining feature of his intellectual and professional environment.

What, concretely, did the art of rhetoric consist in for Machiavelli? In Aristotle's formula, rhetoric is essentially the art of reasoning on subjects "such as seem to present us with alternative possibilities" (*Rhetoric*, 1.2): negotiable subjects, in other words, as opposed to those where scientific certitude is possible. More specifically, rhetoric was customarily defined as concerned with civic matters, predominantly judicial and political. A division, again dating to Aristotle, was made into the three genres of forensic, deliberative, and demonstrative rhetoric: the first was the rhetoric of the law courts, the second of political assemblies, the third of ceremonial oratory such as funeral orations and victory celebrations. Five separate technical skills were identified as making up the art, of which three applied to both spoken and written uses of rhetoric: the "discovery" of arguments (*inventio*), their organization or structuring (*dispositio*), and their casting in appropriate language (*elocutio*). The two other skills were more specific to oratory: *memoria*, the disciplining of memory to allow for a fluent presentation; and *actio* or *pronuntiatio*, the art of delivery, embracing gesture and facial expression as well as verbal articulacy and voice management. Especially important here is the co-presence in rhetoric of the conceptual element of *inventio* along with the more formal and stylistic elements of *dispositio* and *elocutio*. Classical rhetoric emphatically did not limit itself to verbally embellishing a rational "substance" deemed the province of some other science; rather, it laid claim to the prerogative of originating argument, a feature of the art that often earned it the hostility of philosophers. More generally, a defining feature of classical rhetoric as an art of discourse was its holistic character: especially in its originally envisaged context of oral performance, it was a practice that sought to work simultaneously on the audience's reason, imagination, and emotions, drawing both on elements of logical argument – Aristotle pairs it with dialectic – and on the sensual dimensions of rhythm, spectacle, and sound. Oratory was also typically conceived of in antiquity as combative and adversarial in character, and attuned to particular circumstances of delivery; an orator's skill was perceived as lying in the swiftness and sensitivity of his response to ambient conditions, both the status and character of his audience and its more intangible mood. The harmonization of a speech with the "moment" was theorized by the earliest Greek rhetorical theorists, the sophists, as *kairos* and foregrounded by the Roman theorist Quintilian (35–95) in a passage of his *Institutio oratoria* that also nicely illuminates, through its military analogy, the pugnacious tone of much classical rhetorical theory:

> In practice [in oratory], almost everything depends on causes, times, opportunity, and necessity. Hence a particularly important capacity in an orator is a shrewd adaptability [*consilium*], since he is called upon to meet the most varied emergencies. What if you should instruct a general, every time he marshals his troops for battle, to draw up his front line, advance the two wings, and station

his cavalry on the flanks? This may indeed be the best plan, if circumstances allow, but it may have to be modified owing to the nature of the ground ... or again it may be modified by the character of the enemy or the nature of the immediate danger... So, too, with the rules of oratory.[4]

A further aspect of classical rhetoric that deserves to be highlighted is its overwhelming emphasis on persuasion as the objective. Words were regarded not as the orator's ends, but as his means; the raw material on which he worked was his audience's "hearts and minds." This view was not uncontested. Writing after the fall of the Roman Republic, when rhetoric had lost much of its practical political role as an instrument of deliberation, Quintilian proposed a more aesthetic and less functionalist definition of the art: rhetoric as "correct speech" (*bene dicere*), rather than persuasion. This more apolitical conception of rhetoric had gained ground in Italy by Machiavelli's day, especially within princely regimes in which participatory institutions and civic councils had been eliminated or reduced to political irrelevance, and where deliberative practices of rhetoric had been displaced by demonstrative or ceremonial oratory. Within the surviving republics, however, including Florence and Venice, the notion of rhetoric as persuasion remained a potent one. This was especially true in Machiavelli's Florence, following the reestablishment of popular republicanism in 1494 after the ejection of the Medici. Machiavelli's own imaginative allegiance to the notion of rhetoric as persuasion finds vivid expression in a passage at the end of the fourth book of his dialogue, the *Art of War*, where the main speaker, the general Fabrizio Colonna (*c.*1450–1520), laments the decline of military oratory in his day. The great military leaders of antiquity, Colonna argues, were distinguished by their capacity to control armies through the power of speech. His prime example is Alexander the Great, whose abilities in this regard were legendary. Colonna's treatment of the value of rhetoric is decidedly functionalist: oratory is not a decorative "accomplishment" for a general, but part of his essential battery of leadership competences. Verbal persuasion is presented as an instrument of power, in a continuum with other, more tangible means: Colonna tellingly opens his disquisition, in fact, by noting that "it is easy to persuade a few men of something, or to dissuade them from it, for, if words are not sufficient, you can use authority or force. The difficulty lies in removing a dangerous opinion ... from a multitude, where words are the only means available."[5] Following his comments on oratory, Colonna goes on to discuss the utility to military leaders of a strategic use of religious auguries and claims to supernatural assistance; he also approvingly mentions the use of visual persuasion, as when the Spartan king Agesilaus displayed Persian captives naked to reassure his men of the "womanly" physical softness of the enemy they had to meet. In leadership contexts verbal rhetoric is thus intriguingly located as part of a more generalized science of persuasion that also embraces religious ritual and political spectacle. Analogies are found to this holistic approach in classical rhetorical theory, which incorporates among the instruments of persuasion nonverbal elements, such as gesture, and effects created only partially through verbal means, such as the evocation of character (*ethos*) and the ability to arouse emotion (*pathos*). Indeed, oratory could on occasion include the kind of dramatic visual spectacle the *Art of War* envisages as part of a general's motivational rhetoric. A memorable passage in Cicero's discussion of *pathos* in his dialogue *On the Orator* (2.195–6) describes the orator Marcus Antonius narrating his successful defense in the embezzlement trial of the ex-consul Manius Aquillius, which climaxes in his spontaneous ripping aside of his aging client's garments to reveal the wounds he had endured for the republic.

In its long medieval history of transmission, classical rhetoric had proved a remarkably multivalent body of doctrine. Over a thousand years, ancient rhetorical theory was quarried as a source of materials in formulating a series of spin-off disciplines, ranging from literary hermeneutics and memory theory to the arts of preaching and letter writing. New impetus was given to this process in the fifteenth century, when the dry and rule-based textbooks of rhetoric used by medieval scholars were supplemented by the more sophisticated and vivid ancient practice-oriented treatises rediscovered in this period, including Cicero's *On the Orator*. The fifteenth and early sixteenth centuries in Italy proved a particularly productive time for creative reapplications of rhetoric: in the 1430s the humanist Leon Battista Alberti (1404–72) famously reworked rhetoric as art theory in his treatise *On Painting*, and in the 1450s the earliest surviving treatises rhetorically codifying the popular courtly activity of dance inaugurated a trend toward the application of rhetorical theory to the field of social practice, a trend that saw its mature realization in the dialogue *The Book of the Courtier* by Machiavelli's contemporary Baldassare Castiglione (1478–1529). Castiglione takes Cicero's dialogues *On the Orator* as the formal model for his work and draws liberally on rhetorical theory in formulating his model of successful elite behavior. Essentially, Castiglione teaches the Renaissance courtier how to shape his *ethos* persuasively in such a way as to gain the goodwill of his audience; rhetoric is here definitively extended from its verbal base to become an art of behavioral persuasion. Castiglione deserves special notice in this context because his project in *The Courtier* may be seen as in some sense historically parallel with that of Machiavelli's *Prince*, which can also be located within this history of rhetorical reinvention, although it does not wear its rhetorical credentials on its sleeve. Both Castiglione and Machiavelli seek to train their protagonists, courtier and prince, in the skills necessary to thrive in a competitive and potentially treacherous environment. Both recognized in the quintessentially adversarial art of classical oratory a generative model for their new "arts."

Political ethics and the orator's ends

If we return to the passage from *The Prince* quoted at the beginning of this chapter, in which Machiavelli states his intention to abjure pompous verbal adornment, it should be clear by now that it would be misleading to see this as a global rejection of rhetoric. Indeed, this passage may perhaps be better seen as itself a piece of rhetorical self-positioning on Machiavelli's part. In the division among three genres of classical rhetoric, a florid and elaborate style was conventionally seen as appropriate principally to the demonstrative genre, the least functional and most "decorative" of the three. Deliberative or political rhetoric, by contrast, was better served by a self-consciously lean style, more consonant with the importance of its subject matter: to show excessive concern with form would be indecorous and counterproductive when the health of the republic was at stake. In rejecting verbal ornament in his dedicatory letter, then, Machiavelli was signaling the urgency of his forthcoming argument and casting himself emphatically as an engaged political actor and not as an apologist or intellectual cheerleader.

Machiavelli's positioning of *The Prince*'s rhetoric as deliberative rather than demonstrative is a gesture of far-reaching significance.[6] Within princely regimes, the processes of political deliberation were characteristically "private," while the public face of political discourse was demonstrative. Humanist advice books for princes reflect this dynamic, being typically framed according to the canons of demonstrative rhetoric. Rather than genuinely advising (the task of deliberative rhetoric), such advice books set themselves the task of reaffirming societal values through the practice of praise and blame, following classical prescriptions for the demonstrative genre. This had implications for ethics. Along with a distinctive stylistic level, classical rhetoric allocated to each genre a distinctive ethical character, defined by the *fines* or "ends" to which the three genres were seen as directing themselves. The object of a forensic orator was to demonstrate that his cause was just and his opponent's unjust; hence, the end of forensic rhetoric was justice. The end of demonstrative rhetoric was correspondingly defined as the honorable or decent (*honestum*), while that of deliberative rhetoric was advantage or *utilitas*: what was materially beneficial to the state. The proper concern of the deliberative orator was thus not regarded as justice or decency, but what was conducive to the republic's survival and strength. Roman rhetorical theorists tended to mitigate this position by allowing some place for the *honestum* in deliberation. In its starkest form, however, as Aristotle formulates it, deliberative rhetoric was decidedly about power rather than morality: "political orators often make any concession short of admitting that they are recommending their hearers to take an inexpedient course or not to take an expedient one. The question whether it is not unjust for a city to enslave its innocent neighbors often does not trouble them at all."[7]

This tradition of ethical "realism" within deliberative rhetoric is, of course, of the greatest significance for Machiavelli, as it allows us to contextualize his own political realism more accurately. Rather than the absolute innovation *The Prince* may seem when we plot it solely against those texts conventionally labeled as "political," within a rhetorical perspective it appears as more of a relative innovation involving context and tone as much as substance. It had long been countenanced in rhetorical theory that in political deliberation considerations of power and security might outweigh considerations of moral decency if the two were in conflict. Rhetoric was intrinsically relativistic in that it ascribed differing ethical "ends" to its context-differentiated genres. Machiavelli's radicalism in *The Prince*, from a rhetorical point of view, lies in his flouting of the rules of decorum, in lifting the language of deliberation out of its "proper," circumscribed sphere within the councils of state, and placing it on display in a work intended for general circulation and dressed in the formal trappings of a treatise on government. It is this, in fact, more than any particular discrepancy in moral perspective, that differentiates *The Prince* from the private advice-papers we find addressed to the Medici in this period by Florentine patricians such as Paolo Vettori, some of which approach the problem of how the family should consolidate its power in a similarly hard-headed way.[8] Interestingly, *The Prince* seems to have met with no particular moral opprobrium during the initial period of its manuscript circulation in Florence; it was only following its posthumous publication in 1532 that its shock value began to be registered.[9]

Beyond deliberative rhetoric in general, especially illuminating as a context for Machiavelli's ethics is its treatment in the anonymous first-century BCE treatise entitled *Rhetoric to Herennius* (*Rhetorica ad Herennium*). Now relegated to a secondary position within the pantheon of classical rhetoric below the more sophisticated writings of Aristotle, Cicero, and Quintilian, in the Middle Ages and the Renaissance the treatise was attributed to Cicero and regarded with great respect, its status as the principal rhetorical textbook of the time assured by its didactic clarity and concision. *Ad Herennium* follows Roman practice in seeing the end of deliberative oratory not as advantage *tout court*, but rather as *utilitas* mitigated by considerations of *honestas*. More precisely, *Ad Herennium* (book 3, 3.2.3–3.3.6) proposes as the principal values of deliberative rhetoric security (*tutum*) and the honorable (*honestum*) and suggests that, because these two values will often be in tension, political deliberation is essentially the art of negotiating between the two.[10] Nor is this conflict presented as merely apparent, as in the Stoic philosophical position espoused by Cicero in *On Moral Duties*, which regards nothing as genuinely advantageous in politics unless it is also compatible with honor. The author of *Ad Herennium* is fully prepared to countenance situations where the honorable will need to be sacrificed to security and to provide instructions for how an orator should argue in such cases. The contributory components of security are defined as force (*vis*), broken down into military and naval resources, and deception (*dolus*), defined as encompassing "money, promises, dissimulation, unexpected swift action [and] lies." Of course, as *Ad Herennium* is quick to note, only an orator who did not know his job would step forth bluntly and counsel the utility of *dolus*: when addressing an audience, he should prefer the more euphemistic term *consilium* (strategy). Similarly, in arguing against an adversary who bases his case on an appeal to decency, the orator should not respond by counseling that virtue be abandoned, but should rather seek to shift the terms of the discussion to undermine his opponent's moral claims, showing that the qualities the opponent calls justice, liberality, or courage are better described as pusillanimity, financial irresponsibility, and recklessness.[11]

Within its apparently technical rhetorical prescriptions, *Ad Herennium* encapsulates a miniature manual of political realism that has a great deal in common conceptually with Machiavelli's *Prince*. The immediately striking point of coincidence is, of course, *Ad Herennium*'s deadpan definition of *vis* and *dolus*, "force" and "fraud," as the components of security and thus as legitimate resources within political deliberation. As any reader of *The Prince* will recall, this anticipates Machiavelli's notoriously transgressive argument in chapter 18 where he advises the ruler of the frequent need in politics to "depart from the human" and model his behavior on the "lion and the fox." Equally illuminating for the interpretation of *The Prince*'s ethics is another aspect of *Ad Herennium*'s treatment of deliberative ethics: its division of the category of the decent (*honestum*) into two components, one substantive and objective, the "right" or "correct" (*rectum*), the other subjective, the *laudabile* or "praiseworthy," defined as "that which is conducive to present praise or future reputation." Although seemingly minor, the distinction is an important one, in that it allows the orator to present value conflicts in political deliberation in terms of a tension not between advantage and decency (*utile* and *honestum*), as was usual in philosophical discourse, but, more narrowly, between security and reputation (*tutum* and *laudabile*). This had obvious strategic benefits, in that it allowed what was conventionally conceived of as the toughest of ethical dilemmas in political deliberation to be massaged into a more easily soluble technical conflict between what were essentially two kinds of "advantage."[12] With *Ad Herennium*'s dialectic pairing of *tutum* and *laudabile*, we seem very close to the rhetorical norms obtaining in *The Prince*, especially when we look closely at the terminology Machiavelli adopts in discussing political ethics. In chapter 15, after listing what are conventionally considered princely virtues and vices, Machiavelli says:

> I know everyone will agree that it would be a *most praiseworthy thing* for a prince to possess, out of all the abovementioned qualities, those that are *held to be good*. However, since it is not possible to possess them all, or to observe them completely, as the condition of humanity does not allow it, it is necessary rather that he should be sufficiently prudent to *avoid the infamy of those* [*vices*] that would deprive him of power. He should also keep away from the others, if he can, but, if he cannot, he need not be too concerned about indulging himself. Moreover, he should not worry about *incurring the infamy of those vices* without which he can with difficulty *safeguard his state*; for, if he thinks the whole thing through properly, he will find some things that seem like virtues, but that would bring about his ruin if he were to adhere to them, and others that seem like vices, that will ensure his *security* and well-being. (Emphases added)

The opposition here is not between *utile* and *honestum* but rather between *tutum* and *laudabile*; it is not the "wrongness" of vice that Machiavelli presents as its downside, but rather the infamy it may bring on its practitioner. He will later say in *Discourses* 2.13 that fraud is "the less censurable the more it is concealed." The strategy of presenting the morally good under the guise of the *laudabile* continues in chapters 16 and 17 of *The Prince*, where Machiavelli speaks of the desirability of being "considered" generous or clement, or of having "the reputation," or "name," of being liberal, before regretfully concluding that the conditions of political life do not always allow the ruler this indulgence. When the choice is framed in this way, he says in *Discourses* 3.41, the decision cannot be difficult:

> Wherever one is deliberating ultimately about the survival [*salute*] of the fatherland, there must be no consideration of what is just or unjust, or merciful or cruel, or praiseworthy [*laudabile*] or ignominious; on the contrary, putting aside all other considerations, we must cleave to that policy that saves the life of the republic and maintains its liberty.

The arts of the orator and the arts of the prince

Up to this point, we have been looking specifically at the ways in which rhetorical conventions informed the structure of Machiavelli's arguments on political ethics. There are also broader and more diffuse ways in which the classical conception of oratory shaped Machiavelli's framing of his own "art." One example is the emphasis he places upon flexibility of response and adaptation to circumstance in political actors. Castiglione's similar emphasis on flexibility for his courtier clearly shows the rhetorical genetic inheritance he shared with Machiavelli. The need for adaptation is brought to the fore in chapter 25 of *The Prince*, where Machiavelli argues that success in politics is determined by "consonance with the times" and might in theory be assured in perpetuity to the ruler capable of adjusting his procedure to the needs of the moment. The same notion appears in *Discourses* 3.9, where the need for flexible response is seen as one reason for the superiority of republican government, since it is more likely that such a need can be met by a multitude of leaders than by a mythical chameleon-like prince. Dynamism and improvisation are primary characterizing elements of Machiavellian politics, while rigidity of thought or practice is frowned upon; success arises less from any rationally calculable universal formula than from an ability to seize the opportunities offered by Fortune. We are close here to the dialectical relationship of agency and context embodied in the sophistic–rhetorical notion of *kairos*, or harmonization with the moment: as with Quintilian, the orator's art is seen to rest crucially in his capacities of adaptation and response.

The quality of existential flexibility that characterizes the Machiavellian political actor cannot, of course, be divorced from the question of moral flexibility. In *Prince* 25 and *Discourses* 3.9, Machiavelli illustrates the prince's need to change with the times by invoking the morally neutral qualities of "impetuosity" and caution. There are times when the heedless rashness of a Pope Julius can effect miracles, others when it would bring disaster. In the 1506 letter to Giovanbattista Soderini in which Machiavelli first elaborates this theory, the examples he selects are more morally implicated; comparing the clemency for which the Roman general Scipio was traditionally celebrated with the "barbarity" of his Carthaginian opponent Hannibal, he concludes that the success or failure of these two modes of procedure will depend not on their intrinsic "rightness" or "wrongness" but on the circumstances in which a leader operates.[13] The implications of this reasoning, spelled out in chapter 18 of *The Prince*, are that to be consistently virtuous is inimical to a prince's survival; rather, one should "seem merciful, trustworthy, humane, dependable, and religious, and be so," but also be "set up in your mind in such a way that, when it is necessary for you not to be so, you are capable of shifting to the contrary [*mutare el contrario*]."[14] In this emphasis on elasticity and the ability to sustain contraries, we have here something like a behavioral transcription of the oratorical skill of arguing both sides of an issue (*in utramque partem*), an exercise that held a fundamental place in classical and humanistic rhetorical training. Argument *in utramque partem* implies a degree of epistemological relativism and an instrumental, rather than a philosophical, attitude to truth; what the orator seeks is not what is true by some putatively universal standard but what is persuasively functional to his case. Substituting "virtue" for "truth," we have something similar in Machiavelli. As is truth for the orator, so *virtù* for Machiavelli is not determined by universally defined norms. Rather, it is mobile, contingent, and functionally defined: essentially, "what the occasion demands."

Machiavelli's emphasis in *Prince* 18 on the importance of *seeming* virtuous points us to another respect in which his prince may be compared to an orator. Character or *ethos* was accorded great importance within the orator's persuasive arsenal; hence Quintilian's definition of the orator as "a respectable man [*vir bonus*] skilled in speaking." Rather than a natural given, the orator's *ethos* was thought of as something created with conscious artistry and an eye to audience reaction; perhaps more than to "character," this points to "image" in the modern political sense. In keeping with this, Cicero and Quintilian frequently make comparisons between orator and actor, although they are quick to assert the greater social dignity of the former: Antonius in Cicero's *On the Orator* describes himself, in a neat piece of wordplay, as "neque actor ... alienae personae, sed auctor meae [not the actor of an alien *persona* but rather the author of my own]."[15] This notion of *ethos* as something composed with an eye to persuasive efficacy is, again, a feature shared by Castiglione's courtier and Machiavelli's prince; both simultaneously recognize the importance of appearances and their susceptibility to manipulation. As chapter 18 of *The Prince* makes clear, the prince must know how to act his part, crafting his *ethos* to meet his audience's conventional expectations of princely virtue: he must "appear in all he says and does the epitome of piety, faith, integrity, humanity, and religion."[16] Machiavelli's language in this chapter intriguingly and quite explicitly draws on rhetorical terminology, as when he speaks of the need for the prince to "color" (*colorire*) his nature for public consumption and remarks on the ease with which princes who renege on agreements may find pretexts to "color" their bad faith. The metaphor of color as embellishment, though evidently originating in painting, had long been fully naturalized within rhetorical theory, to the extent that *colores* had become the standard technical term for the rhetorical "figures of speech."

In addition to *ethos*, Machiavelli also incorporates into his art of government the further oratorical component of *pathos*, or the arousal of emotion. More than the mild sentiments of reverence excited by political ceremonies and rituals, he seems chiefly interested in the keener emotions mobilized by dramatic events. Paradigmatic here is his praise in *Discourses* 2.2 of the Roman practice of animal sacrifice, whose gory character is credited with instilling a corresponding ferocity in the Roman soul. A modern-day equivalent, though rather different in its emotional effects, would be the kind of striking exemplary punishment Machiavelli recommends to rulers in *Prince* 21, citing as an example of an expert practitioner in the field the notoriously cruel Bernabò Visconti (1323–85). Machiavelli gives some idea of what he means in chapter 7, where he recounts Cesare Borgia's deft public scapegoating of his lieutenant Ramiro de Lorqua. After employing de Lorqua as the agent of a harsh but necessary imposition of law and order in the Romagna, Borgia successfully purged the resentment that had accrued to him for his subordinate's cruelty by having his lieutenant "found one morning in two pieces on the main square in Cesena with a piece of wood and a bloody knife by his side." The choreographic and visual panache Machiavelli associates with this exemplary exercise of power has analogies with the rhetorical technique of *enargeia*, the powerful visual evocation of experience through language, such that it seems to "come alive before the eyes."[17] The power of Machiavelli's prince is not exercised technocratically behind the scenes, but "brought to life" for the watching public through an imaginatively compelling visual representation. The effectiveness of the spectacle is measurable by its reported impact on Borgia's subjects, whom "the ferocity of the sight," as Machiavelli comments coolly, left simultaneously "satisfied and stupefied [*sodisfatti e stupiti*]."[18] Similar language is used in chapter 19 concerning the "audience response" to the exploits of the tyrannical emperor Septimius Severus.[19]

Reading *The Prince* as a rhetorical text

There are reasons why the exemplification of this chapter is drawn predominantly from *The Prince*. While rhetoric may profitably be adduced as a context for Machiavelli's writings in general, as it can for all thinkers of his humanistic formation, *The Prince* has a special place within Machiavelli's political *oeuvre* on account of its peculiar foregrounding of the act of rhetorical persuasion. Both *The Prince* and the *Discourses* are prefaced by dedicatory letters, but the dedicatees of the *Discourses* are invoked as an ideal audience only in the relatively attenuated way common in literary works. The dedication of *The Prince*, by contrast, taken in conjunction with the concluding peroration of chapter 26, establishes a concrete, quasi-dramatized persuasive agenda for the book. The aim of *The Prince* is to inspire Machiavelli's dedicatee, Lorenzo de' Medici, to undertake the salvation of Italy, and to teach him the means to achieve this. At the same time, secondarily, it is to persuade him of Machiavelli's exceptional qualifications as a political adviser. The extent to which these purported objectives were feasible, or genuinely pursued by Machiavelli, need not concern us here: what is important is that the work stages itself so compellingly as an act of political counsel, delivered by a "real" political adviser to a "real" political actor possessed of the power to translate theory into practice. Moreover, in this rhetorical scenario the prince is positioned as a neophyte. Implicitly, indeed, the logic of the work demands that we see Lorenzo as initially a victim of the debilitating teachings of conventional wisdom. Machiavelli's task as counselor is to disabuse him of these mistaken convictions and thus unlock his impeded political potential. Such is the rhetorical "plot" of the treatise, which we, as readers, are invited to observe as a spectacle, while, at the same time, and in a manner that notably complicates our reception, we are subjected mimetically to the same persuasion ourselves.

All this needs to be borne in mind when attempting a rhetorical reading of *The Prince*. It has particular bearing on our reading of the treatise's teachings on political ethics, since this is the area in which Machiavelli's task of corrective disabuse is chiefly concentrated. The first principle we must observe, when reading *The Prince* rhetorically, is to resist the urge to infer Machiavelli's position from isolated sound bites: his argument, instead, needs to be seen holistically, as a process unfolding throughout the book. Teachings on oratorical strategy are useful guides in this regard, particularly those portions of rhetorical theory devoted to the problem of how an orator may go about arguing a case that his audience is likely to find morally repugnant, a scenario to which classical theorists devoted considerable attention and for which they provided detailed advice. In such circumstances, they taught, an orator should not seek to confront his audience's prejudices head-on; rather, he should use an "indirect approach" (*insinuatio*), at first showing that he shares his listeners' values, before gradually going on to suggest that the case he is making is less morally scandalous than it initially appears.[20] It is useful to remember this, especially when gauging the import of *The Prince*'s moral pronouncements. To cite a much-discussed example, nothing could seem clearer on the surface than Machiavelli's statement in chapter 8 that the atrocities of the Sicilian tyrant Agathocles were such as to disqualify him from the accolade of *virtù* or the prospect of glory. It may be mistaken, however, to take this as signaling the kind of moral "line in the sand" it is sometimes interpreted to be. Machiavelli is here broaching for the first time explicitly the controversial questions of political morality that lie at the heart of his treatise. At a point in his argument where a degree of "insinuation" is so rhetorically predictable, we should be wary of placing too much weight on his words. The division between *scelleratezza* (wickedness) and *virtù*, which seems relatively clear-cut in chapter 8, becomes progressively more nuanced as we learn the extent to which successful political action may on occasion require a suspension of morality. By chapter 18, we are compelled to confront the fact that a prince may often find himself called on to act "contrary to faith, contrary to charity, contrary to humanity, contrary to religion" – and may yet, if he duly polishes his presentational skills, escape with his reputation intact.

If a consideration of the rhetorical character of *The Prince* should counsel caution in evaluating Machiavelli's more conciliatory ethical pronouncements, this does not mean that we should necessarily take his most morally provocative statements as definitive. *The Prince* stages itself as a form of initiation rite, a gradual induction into what Machiavelli implies is the hidden doctrine of political realism. The structure of its argument demands an escalation from discretion to explicitness, while its task of breaking down what are implicitly presented as deeply engrained ethical assumptions in the reader-initiate makes strong language appropriate when we have finally reached the "moment of truth." A rhetorical reading of *The Prince* also counsels against taking the treatise as representing Machiavelli's considered position on the question of political ethics, without taking into account the particular pressures imposed by the rhetorical structure of the work. Within the rhetorical microclimate of *The Prince*, Machiavelli's princely addressee does not need to be persuaded of the imperative to govern for the benefit of his subjects, or reminded that good government is preferable to tyranny. Rather, Lorenzo is implicitly positioned at the outset as a political idealist, presumably steeped in the teachings of traditional princely advice books. What he needs is not further instruction on sound government, but a confrontation with harder political truths. This premise is Machiavelli's rhetorical point of departure in *The Prince*, and this inevitably influences the *inventio* of the treatise, both in terms of what is said and what is unnecessary to say. It is partly as a consequence of its rhetorical structure that *The Prince* presents a vision of such singular ethical starkness: what we have here is a powerful *pars destruens* (the destructive or critical part of an argument, in Bacon's terminology) attacking conventional thinking on political morality, unbalanced by any very substantial *pars construens* (or constructive part) of the kind we see in the *Discourses*. Any interpretation of *The Prince* as a statement of political ethics must take this calculated disequilibrium into account. More generally, it may be helpful in reading this deceptively simple and straight-talking text to set aside modern notions of Machiavelli as "political theorist" and to think of him instead under the more historically consonant heading of "orator" (a term often used in this period generically to designate any writer of prose). Reading *The Prince* as a rhetorical performance, rather than a conventional work of political theory, usefully alerts us to the dynamic and manipulative qualities of the text, as well as its singularity within Machiavelli's political *oeuvre. The Prince* merits its designation as a "neglected rhetorical classic"[21] not least for the mastery it displays of *ethos* and *pathos*: Machiavelli's highly characterized "voice" is a key element in the text's impact on its reader, as is the emotional suasion effected through its forceful and often visceral language. To ignore these elements in our analysis and concentrate solely on the third, and more rational, rhetorical component of *logos*, or argument, is to reduce this incomparably rich and unsettling text to something much flatter and more jejune.

NOTES

1. Machiavelli, *Tutte le opere*, ed. Mario Martelli (Florence: Sansoni, 1971), p. 257. Translations are mine unless otherwise stated.
2. Virginia Cox, "Ciceronian Rhetoric in Italy, 1260–1350," *Rhetorica* 17 (1999): 239–88 (259–66).
3. Stephen J. Milner, "Communication, Consensus, and Conflict: Rhetorical Precepts, the *Ars Concionandi*, and Social Ordering in Late Medieval Italy," in *The Rhetoric of Cicero in its Medieval and Early Renaissance Commentary Tradition*, ed. Virginia Cox and John O. Ward (Leiden: Brill, 2006), pp. 411–60 (399–400, 402–8).
4. *Institutio oratoria* 2.13. Translation adapted from the Loeb editions by H. E. Butler and Donald A. Russell (Cambridge, Mass.: Harvard University Press, respectively 1920–1922 and 2001).
5. *Opere*, p. 354.
6. As John F. Tinkler showed in a breakthrough article, "Praise and Advice: Rhetorical Approaches in More's *Utopia* and Machiavelli's *The Prince*," *Sixteenth Century Journal* 19 (1988): 187–207.
7. *Rhetoric* 1.3, 1358b; trans. W. Rhys Roberts, in *The Complete Works of Aristotle*, ed. Jonathan Barnes, 2 vols. (Princeton University Press, 1984), 2:2160.
8. *Ricordi di Paolo Vettori al cardinale de' Medici sopra le cose di Firenze* (1512), in Rudolf von Albertini, *Firenze dalla repubblica al principato* (Turin: Einaudi, 1970), pp. 357–9; translation by Russell Price in *Cambridge Translations of Renaissance Philosophical Texts*, ed. Jill Kraye, 2 vols. (Cambridge University Press, 1997), 2:238–44.
9. Brian Richardson, "*The Prince* and Its Early Italian Readers," in *Niccolò Machiavelli's* The Prince: *New Interdisciplinary Essays*, ed. Martin Coyle (Manchester University Press, 1995), pp. 18–39.
10. Virginia Cox, "Machiavelli and the *Rhetorica ad Herennium*: Deliberative Rhetoric in *The Prince*," *Sixteenth Century Journal* 28.4 (1997): 1109–41 (1119–20).
11. On the prescribed techniques, see Quentin Skinner, *Reason and Rhetoric in the Philosophy of Hobbes* (Cambridge University Press, 1996), pp. 139–53.
12. Cox, "Machiavelli," pp. 1126–7.
13. *Opere*, pp. 1082–3.
14. "parere pietoso, fedele, umano, intero, religioso, ed essere; ma stare in modo edificato con l'animo, che, bisognando non essere, tu possa e sappi mutare el contrario"; *Opere*, p. 284.

15. *De oratore*, II.47.194b. On the element of "imposture" in *De oratore*, see Michelle Zerba, "The Frauds of Humanism: Cicero, Machiavelli, and the Rhetoric of Imposture," *Rhetorica*, 22.3 (2004): 220, 227–8.
16. "paia, a vederlo e udirlo, tutto pietà, tutto fede, tutto integrità, tutto umanità, tutto religione"; *Opere*, p. 284.
17. On the utility of the term *enargeia* in analyzing political spectacle in Livy, see Andrew Feldherr, *Spectacle and Society in Livy's History* (Berkeley: University of California Press, 1998), pp. 4–12.
18. *Opere*, p. 267.
19. *Opere*, p. 287; compare chap. 21 (p. 291) on Ferdinand of Spain.
20. On *insinuatio* in Machiavelli, see Cox, "Machiavelli," pp. 1131–2; and Mikael Hörnqvist, *Machiavelli and Empire* (Cambridge University Press, 2004), pp. 26–30.
21. Eugene Garver, "Machiavelli's *The Prince*: A Neglected Rhetorical Classic," *Philosophy and Rhetoric* 13 (1980): 99–120.

FURTHER READING

Ascoli, Albert Russell. "Machiavelli's Gift of Counsel," in *Machiavelli and the Discourse of Literature*, ed. Albert Russell Ascoli and Victoria Kahn. Ithaca, N.Y., Cornell University Press, 1993, pp. 219–57.
Colish, Marcia. "Cicero's *De officiis* and Machiavelli's *Prince*," *Sixteenth Century Journal* 9.4 (1978): 81–93.
Connolly, Joy. *The State of Speech: Rhetoric and Political Thought in Ancient Rome*. Princeton University Press, 2007.
Garver, Eugene. "After *Virtù*: Rhetoric, Prudence, and Moral Pluralism in Machiavelli," in *Prudence: Classical Virtue, Postmodern Practice*, ed. Robert Hariman. University Park, Penn., Pennsylvania State University Press, 2003, pp. 67–98.
Geuna, Marco. "Skinner, Pre-Humanistic Rhetorical Culture and Machiavelli," in *Rethinking the Foundations of Modern Political Thought*, ed. Annabel Brett and James Tully. Cambridge University Press, 2007, pp. 50–72.
Habinek, Thomas. *Ancient Rhetoric and Oratory*. Oxford, Blackwell, 2005, esp. chap. 1 and 4.
Hariman, Robert. *Political Style: The Artistry of Power*. University of Chicago Press, 1995, esp. chap. 2.
Kahn, Victoria. *Machiavellian Rhetoric: From the Counter-Reformation to Milton*. Princeton University Press, 1994.
Kennedy, George A. *A New History of Classical Rhetoric*. Princeton University Press, 1994.
Mack, Peter. *Elizabethan Rhetoric: Theory and Practice*. Cambridge University Press, 2002, esp. chaps. 6 and 7.
Olmstead, Wendy. "Exemplifying Deliberation: Cicero's *De officiis* and Machiavelli's *Prince*," in *A Companion to Rhetoric and Rhetorical Criticism*, ed. Walter Jost and Wendy Olmstead. Malden, Mass., Blackwell, 2004, pp. 173–89.
Rebhorn, Wayne A. *Foxes and Lions: Machiavelli's Confidence Men*. Ithaca, N.Y., Cornell University Press, 1988.

Richardson, Brian. "Notes on Machiavelli's Sources and his Treatment of the Rhetorical Tradition," *Italian Studies* 26 (1971): 24–48.

Skinner, Quentin. "Machiavelli's *Discorsi* and the Pre-humanist Origins of Republican Ideas," in *Machiavelli and Republicanism*, ed. Gisela Bock, Quentin Skinner, and Maurizio Viroli. Cambridge University Press, 1990, pp. 121–41.

Stacey, Peter. *Roman Monarchy and the Renaissance Prince*. Cambridge University Press, 2007, esp. chap. 6.

Viroli, Maurizio. *Machiavelli*. Oxford University Press, 1998, chap. 3.

12

ALBERT RUSSELL ASCOLI &
ANGELA MATILDE CAPODIVACCA

Machiavelli and poetry

Machiavelli's reputation rests above all on his political-historical writings, and secondarily on his notable contribution to the re-emergence of classicizing comic drama. Yet, as scholarship has increasingly shown, he was also profoundly engaged with poetry and poets, as reader and writer. This chapter focuses attention on four interrelated dimensions of Machiavelli's engagement with poetry: the "poetic" dimensions of the nonpoetic works (citations of and allusions to poetry, use of poetic devices and strategies); the poems he wrote; the poets he read (and more or less obliquely rewrote); and his "poetics," that is, his concept(s) of what poetry is and what it does, and its relationship to other modes of discourse, particularly the political-historical.

What Machiavelli's "realism" consists of is a source of ongoing scholarly debate. The general perception that he had little patience for the world of imaginative fictions remains alive and well among readers of *The Prince* and the *Discourses*. For such readers, the fact that Machiavelli frequently names poets and allusively echoes poetry in these nonpoetic works has commonly been dismissed as attributable, on the one hand, to the fundamentally literary-rhetorical character of upper-class education in his time (which was immersed in classical Latin literature), and, on the other, to the increasing importance assigned by Florentine culture to its vernacular literary heritage, above all the newly canonized "three crowns" of the fourteenth century: Dante, Petrarch, and Boccaccio. But these factors are insufficient in themselves to account for the critical role poetry and poets play in Machiavelli's works, along with the topoi, myths, and narrative and rhetorical strategies they deploy, particularly in the textual economy of the best known of those works, *The Prince*.

Machiavelli's famous letter to Francesco Vettori of December 10, 1513, culminating in the announcement of the composition of a "little work" entitled *De principatibus*, is shot through with literary references. Machiavelli speaks of walking with a book under my arm, either Dante, Petrarch, or one of the minor poets, Tibullus, Ovid, or the like. I read of their amorous passions and their loves, remember mine, and take pleasure for a while in these thoughts.

He also compares himself to the classical comic character Geta and to the mythological Sisyphus, suggesting in subtle ways the hopelessness of his predicament and the complexities of his relationship with the Medici as potential patrons on whom he both must and cannot rely for employment. In announcing the decision to turn his political-historical studies into a text for the benefit of others, he cites the authority of Dante, who represents for Machiavelli the fusion of historical-political investments with poetic artistry, even as Dante's providential-prophetic view of history is the target of some of the Florentine secretary's most biting irony.

The Prince itself is no less fruitfully "poetic," despite its avowed commitment to the "effectual truth of things" (chapter 15) and to believing only what one can "touch with one's hands" (chapter 18). For example, Machiavelli's famous dictum that the prince must know how to use the beast in himself as well as the man, and in particular partake of both the lion and the fox, alludes not only to Cicero but also to Dante's Guido da Montefeltro (*Inferno* 27.74–5) and serves as the oblique – figurative, allegorical – vehicle for stationing himself in relationship to his ultimate addressee, Pope Leo X. The text of *The Prince* is repeatedly charged with figurative language whose exact sense is far from evident, but whose emotional, persuasive power is clear: the Prince must be like the fox and the lion, his teacher like the centaur (chapter 18); the art of governance is like the art of medicine (chapter 3); the prudent man "is like an archer" (chapter 6); Italy herself is personified as a much mistreated woman in dire need of her "redeemer" (chapter 26).

Two well known but not necessarily well understood examples from the end of *The Prince* may give an idea of how Machiavelli both turns poetry to his specific rhetorical and conceptual purposes and himself writes "poetically" in a treatise that seemingly faults the role of the imagination in traditional political discourse. The work closes with an exhortation lifted from Petrarch's great political *canzone*, "Italia mia" (My Italy):

> Virtue [*virtù*] against madness [*furore*], / will take arms and let the battle be short: / because the ancient valor / is not dead in Italian hearts. (*Canzoniere* 128.93–6)

If the citation is simply dismissed as a rhetorical flourish, one would then have to note that such devices explicitly contradict Machiavelli's claim in the dedication that

> I have not filled this volume with pompous rhetoric, with bombast and magnificent words, or with the unnecessary artifice with which so many writers gild their work. I wanted nothing extraneous to ornament my writing.

Such departures from this (anti-)rhetorical program may suggest Machiavelli's awareness that his political pragmatics is actually utopian, to the degree that it depends upon persuading inept and/or hostile members of the Medici family to listen to "those who know [*quelli che sanno*]" (a phrase in chapter 26 that ironically echoes Dante's characterization of Aristotle, the political philosopher par excellence, as "the teacher of those who know" [*Inferno* 4.131]).

Furthermore, Machiavelli's use of the Petrarch quotation changes its sense simply by displacing it into a new discursive context. On the one hand, he appears to treat Petrarch's poetry as nothing more than a vehicle for (proto-) patriotic political ideas and values. On the other, the passage from "Italia mia" was chosen not simply because it advocates Italian solidarity against "barbarian" invaders (French, Spanish, and Swiss), but because it echoes terms that take on particular weight as the text of *The Prince* progresses. "Arms," needless to say, are the focus of Machiavelli's urging of "new modes and orders" on the feckless Italian princes: the eschewing of mercenary armies and fighting with "one's own arms" (chapters 12, 13, and 24).

More telling still is the use of the passage to reprise Machiavelli's own revisionary treatment of the *virtù–furore* opposition. In Petrarch's poem, *virtù* suggests both moral virtue and political-military prowess; Machiavelli, having specifically separated these two senses of the word (see, e.g., chapters 8 and 18), thus at once echoes and radically contradicts his chosen precursor, and with him two millennia of Western thought that had sought to reconcile ethics and politics. Even as Machiavelli incorporates poetry into a political discourse, he does so in a "poetic" way: not as part of an overt, rational, and linear argument, but obliquely through the thematic accretion of meaning by the repetition in difference of key words and images.

The second example comes from the penultimate chapter, the culmination both of the central *virtù–fortuna* opposition and of the treatise's avowed goal to make and dispense pragmatic rules for political praxis. The chapter reveals three steps in Machiavelli's project: (1) to prove that *virtù* (human ability) can overcome fortune (the universe of contingent circumstances); (2) to define two types of *virtù* – prudent foresight and impetuous violence – that can be brought to bear on fortune; and (3) to specify that different circumstances call for different types of *virtù* (while the same type of *virtù* may have different results under different circumstances).

The logic of the chapter suggests, on the one hand, that there are in fact no universal rules of princely conduct and, on the other, that, even if there were, the rigidity of human temperaments would prevent one from adapting one's behavior in accordance with such rules. In other words, the chapter undoes precisely what it purports to propound. This tension is intimately bound up with figurative, "poetic" images, which serve both to give substance to

Machiavelli's claims and to register the strain within them. Specifically, fortune is figured in two different ways: as a raging river in flood, whose power can only be tamed if provisions are made ahead of time through prudent foresight (the first kind of *virtù*), and, more famously, as a woman who can be subdued with violence (the second sort of *virtù*).

The disparity between the two images of fortune is notable, suggesting both the complexity of concepts subtending the apparently self-explanatory word *fortuna*, and also Machiavelli's dependence on a literary-iconographic tradition in his treatment of those concepts. What the two figures have in common is that they materialize and delimit an otherwise boundless concept and serve to create the impression that *fortuna* is susceptible to both the understanding and the mastery of the "virtuous" political subject. At the same time, by employing two such different figurative representations of *fortuna*, Machiavelli reveals how the strategic choice of which image to use in a given moment may determine the direction of an argument and its conclusions, rather than the other way around.

To put it otherwise, deliberately or not, Machiavelli reveals that the notion of an unadorned language, transparent to historical reality, emptied of "poetic" devices, is itself utopian, because "reality" is always mediated by the imposition of narrative order and the deployment of rhetorical figures, while politics is in many ways the art of the spectacular (for example, Cesare Borgia's execution of Ramiro de Lorqua in chapter 7) and the fictive (lies offered as truths, as discussed in chapter 18).

In turning from the role of poets and poetic language in the "nonpoetic" works to the place of poetry itself within Machiavelli's *oeuvre*, the first difficulty to overcome is the tendency either to trivialize this type of writing or to turn it into a cadet branch of his political-historical project. To the extent that there is a visibly "literary" Machiavelli, he is the author not chiefly of poetry, but of two plays, *Mandragola* (c. 1518) and *Clizia* (1525). Machiavelli himself now and then suggested, regarding both his drama and his poetry, that these literary pursuits ran a poor third behind active political life, his true vocation, and political-historical writing, the preferable alternative. In the same vein, he frequently characterizes the scene of theater and poetry as the location of "maldicenza" – the degraded and degrading banter that he enters into with adversarial interlocutors, real and imagined (as can be seen especially in the prologue to *Mandragola* and the invocation to the *Asino*). Finally, there is the preponderance of critical views that see in the literary and theatrical Machiavelli merely a projection of his primary concerns into verse and onto the stage, and which attribute, in other words, no specificity to poetry as a mode of discourse beyond the ornaments of style.

Direct evidence of Machiavelli's sense of a specifically poetic vocation, and of the specificity of poetry as discourse, is scattered, but significant. In a letter of April 2, 1527, to his son Guido, in which he urges him to study "letters and music" (evoking a canonical definition of poetry as a "musical art"), Machiavelli adduces the honor that his own "little bit of *virtù*" in these fields has brought him.[1] Writing to Lodovico Alamanni on December 17, 1517, Machiavelli famously acknowledged the greatest Italian poet of his day, Ludovico Ariosto:

> These last few days I have read the *Orlando furioso* of Ariosto, and truly the poem is beautiful [*bello*] throughout, and in many places it is marvelous [*mirabile*]. If you see him there, give him my regards, and tell him I only regret that, having recalled so many poets [in the proem to the *Furioso*'s last canto], he left me out like a prick, and that he has done to me in his *Orlando* what I will not do to him in my *Asino*.[2]

This passage tells us that Machiavelli was *au courant* with poetic events (the *Furioso* had appeared just a year earlier); that he understood poetry in the key aesthetic terms of the *beautiful* and the *marvelous* (more in due course on the importance of the latter category); and that he considered himself worthy of inclusion among the poets of the day. It also announces his own major poetic project, the *Asino*, comparable at least in some respects to Ariosto's *Furioso*. There is additional evidence, both in the plays and in the *Dialogue Concerning Our Language* (*Discorso o dialogo intorno alla nostra lingua*; date uncertain and attribution contested), that Machiavelli also saw Ariosto as his principal competitor in the field of comic drama.

Machiavelli's poetic production is not large by the standards of his day. It consists, principally, of his two versified historical accounts, the first and second *Decennali* ("Ten-Year Chronicles") written in 1504 and *c.* 1514, the second left incomplete; four *capitoli* in *terza rima* (the interlaced triple rhyme scheme invented by Dante for the *Divine Comedy*) between 1506 and 1518; a pastoral eclogue also in *capitolo* form; his jocular "Carnival Songs," written over at least a twenty-year period; a remarkable "Serenata" in *ottava rima*, the eight-line stanza usually used in narrative poetry (after 1517); three "tailed" sonnets to Giuliano de' Medici on Machiavelli's imprisonment and banishment from politics (probably 1513); and some late poems written for performances of his plays and for his young beloved, Barbera Salutati. Last, but by no means least, is his *Asino*, the ambitious, and ostensibly incomplete, longer poem on which he staked his reputation as a poet.

The *Decennali* and four *capitoli* give at least superficial support to the notion that Machiavelli's poetry was merely a vehicle for conveying historical-political commentary. The first *Decennale*[3] synthetically conveys what Machiavelli considered the principal events in Italy of the ten years from the invasion of Charles VIII of France (1494) to the death of Alexander VI and the fall of Cesare Borgia. The second declares an intention to cover the subsequent ten years, but breaks off, unfinished, in 1509. Many of the events treated in these poems are taken up again in *The Prince* and later prose works, though with encomiastic references to the deposed Piero Soderini deleted, no doubt in order not to offend Soderini's enemies, the Medici, and with an apparently far more positive view of Cesare Borgia and his father, perhaps because they were meant to serve as a model for Lorenzo the younger and his uncle, Pope Leo.

The *Decennali*'s adoption of *terza rima* at first suggests a direct Dantean filiation, given also its highly critical view of Florentine, French, and papal politics. Yet *terza rima* had already been widely adopted by poets after Dante, and in more than one case by versifying chroniclers of Italian history. Nor, as it will soon appear, should we discount the mediating influence of Petrarch's highly influential adaptation of Dante's verse form in his *Triumphs* (*Trionfi*), which could be said to stand at an intermediate point between the overtly Trinitarian implications of the *Commedia*'s rhyme scheme and Machiavelli's resolute focus on historical contingency.

The "poetic" and rhetorical dimensions of the *Decennali* deserve closer scrutiny than can be given here. Among the suggestive features of the first (complete) *Decennale* are its recurrent use of often-punning animal imagery (Vitellozzo Vitelli is "the veal"; France is "the cock," "Gallo" meaning both "rooster" and "Gaul"; Milan is the "viper"; and so on); and its intermittent personification allegory whose most obvious example is found in the recurrent addressing of the poem to a "voi" who is clearly not the dedicatee, Alamanno Salviati, but rather political-military Florence. What is ostensibly a review of Italian history consistently interprets peninsular events in terms of their effects on Florence, highlighting matters of concern to Florentines (the exile of the Medici, the rise and fall of Savonarola, the loss and botched recovery of Pisa, the fears raised by Borgia's adventurism, and so on).

Also noteworthy are the narrative-generic characteristics of the poem. On the one hand, after a (mock) epic invocation of Apollo and the Muses in lines 1–9 ("I sing the travails of Italy"), the poem becomes in effect an anti-epic, complete with antiheroes (Charles VIII, Alexander VI, the Florentine political class) and, in place of the foundation or affirmation of a political culture, its peninsula-wide undoing. This effect is reinforced by the overlay of a few epic conventions – including the intimation of Hell visiting this world rather than a heroic *descensus ad inferos* – in what otherwise seems a chronicle of events. Seen from another angle, however, the first *Decennale* has a clearly, if intermittently, focused plot, which can be seen as following the pattern of tragedy, for example in the rise and precipitous fall of Cesare Borgia with which the poem concludes.

Machiavelli wrote three of his *capitoli*[4] between 1506 and 1512. These too are in *terza rima* and they also lend themselves to being read as an apprenticeship in preparation for the major prose works. Each treats a theme central to Machiavelli's conceptual vocabulary: Fortune, Ingratitude, and Ambition (with her running mate, Avarice). Lines like the following from the *capitolo* on Ingratitude seem "ripped from the pages" of *The Prince* (written some years later):

> Because, when you help to change a state, he whom you have made prince will fear that you will take from him what you have given, and so he will not observe faith or pact with you, because his fear of you is more powerful than the contracted obligation. ("Ingratitude" 172–7)[5]

In the *capitoli* one also finds anticipations of the imagery (fortune as a river) and exemplary figures that reveal the poetic-rhetorical antecedents of *The Prince* and the *Discourses*.

Perhaps most intriguing is the possibility that, despite being addressed to specific interlocutors, these three *capitoli* appear to form a complex, motivated textual sequence, not unlike the series of Petrarch's *Triumphs* (Love [Lust] overcome by Modesty overcome by Death overcome by Fame overcome by Time overcome by Eternity). Although not hierarchical or "vertical" like Petrarch's, Machiavelli's sequence is similarly progressive and symptomatic of his tendency to create carefully structured relationships among his texts (for instance, the first four of the so-called "Carnival Songs" can similarly be read as a sequence oriented around the theme of love, sacred and profane). The depiction of *fortuna* as an impersonal force governing and overwhelming all human endeavor (this fortune is a raging river, never a pliant mistress), gives way to two commentaries on human attempts to cope with *fortuna*. "Ingratitude" suggests the way in which collaborative efforts between princes and their supporters to master fortune with *virtù* break down in an endemic lack of trust between those who initially cooperate, thus leading to further "reversals of fortune."

"Ambition" is perhaps the most significant of the *capitoli*, providing a theory of human nature constantly driven by desire for more power and possessions and revealing fortune to be, not an external force, but a direct product of human behavior. "The insatiable human mind" (55), which first and most vividly expressed itself in Cain's fratricidal envy of Abel (46–8), is the root of all mutations of circumstance, personal and historical: "From this comes the fact that one rises while another falls, / from this depends, regardless of law or contract, / the variability of every human state" (64–6).[6] At the same time, ambition used well, that is, in concord with the members of one's community and directed against external enemies, can become "armed virtue" and thus also a source of Machiavellian *virtù*, which is fortune's opposite and nemesis, and, implicitly, the remedy for ingratitude. In other words, as a complex, the *capitoli* posit the fundamental problem of earthly mutability and parse the modalities by which human agency both produces and, in rare instances, controls the seemingly arbitrary flow of history.

The "Serenata"[7] at first seems quite distinct from the *capitoli*: it is written in a different verse form (*ottava rima*); is of significantly greater rhetorical complexity than the individual *capitoli*; and, most notably, exchanges a political-historical thematic for the more traditional lyric topic of sexual love. Nonetheless, this poem is similarly preoccupied with changeability and gives additional evidence for Machiavelli's literary sophistication, both in its intertextual debts to Italian and classical precursors (specifically Poliziano's "O trionfante sopra ogni altra bella," and Ovid) and in its organizational complexity. It begins in the direct address of a first-person lover-narrator to a beloved lady, which then modulates into a relatively faithful rehearsal of Ovid's recounting in *Metamorphoses*, book 14, of the seduction of the virgin goddess Pomona by the shape-shifting Vertumnus, who comes to her in the form of an old and ugly woman. Within this tale, as in the Ovidian original, Vertumnus' efforts culminate in the recounting of yet another myth, the unhappy love of Iphis for the unyielding Anaxerete. Pomona finally yields to Vertumnus. The poem returns to the Machiavellian "I," who recounts two more tales not found in the Ovidian original; they are offered, respectively, as examples to be imitated and avoided by his beloved. This addition reflects both fascination with, and keen understanding of, the Ovidian tactic of framing tales within tales, further reinforced by the addition of a third degree of framing.

From his earliest poetic endeavors, then, Machiavelli was driven to the elaboration of complex forms which, both intratextually and intertextually, position themselves as representations of history and the radical historicity of the human condition. The recurrent theme of mutability, whether at the historical-political or the personal-erotic level, may also suggest what it is about poetry, the domain of figurative displacements (metaphor as *translatio*) and structured narrative reversals, that appealed to Machiavelli and linked his "rational" practical concerns to the world of imagination. The historicity of human experience is not simply personified in Fortune, but also dramatized in the artful perspectivalism implied by the multiplication of subjective narrative voices adopted by Machiavelli, both in themselves and as they are positioned in relation to interlocutors (Florence in the *Decennali*, the beloved in the "Serenata," various friends in the *capitoli*, Lorenzo the younger in *The*

Prince, and so on). The historicity of literature itself is made clear both in the deliberate reuse of precursor texts and in the transformations of significance effected thereby (as in the use of "My Italy" in *The Prince*, the ironization of epic conventions in the first *Decennale*, and the celebration–subversion of Dante throughout the Machiavellian *oeuvre*).

In the terms just sketched, Machiavelli's longest and most complex poetic endeavor, the *Asino*, may be seen as the formal and thematic climax of his career as "poet" proper. Despite its ambitions, the poem has been understandably, if regrettably, neglected, for a number of reasons: the far greater popularity of Ariosto's chivalric poem and of the nascent neo-Petrarchan lyric collection fostered by Pietro Bembo; the greater importance attributed to Machiavelli's other works, both dramatic and political-historical; and the apparently incomplete state of the *Asino* itself, which suggests that it may have been abandoned by its author. Most likely written around 1517, the *Asino*[8] spans eight chapters that recount the adventures of a first-person-singular protagonist in the land where Circe, the Homeric enchantress who turns men into beasts and who is herself overcome by the charms of Odysseus/Ulysses, has established an Amazonian reign of women. The text begins with a tripartite proem in which the poet (1) stages his refusal to invoke the Muses (extending the anti-epic stance of the *Decennali*) or to dedicate the poem to any patron (unlike *The Prince* and the *Discourses*) (lines 1–30); (2) tells the story of a Florentine youth who couldn't restrain himself from unseemly running (31–90); and (3) offers a conclusion that flouts the rhetorical-poetic convention (*captatio benevolentiae*) of wooing the reader's sympathy (91–121).

The subsequent chapters are similarly divided into three parts. The first section (chapters 2 to 4) treats the protagonist's awakening in a Dantesque "dark wood"; his rescue by Circe's lovely handmaiden; and his "sexual healing" in her tender hands. The second section (chapter 5) is a protracted meditation on political affairs. The third (chapters 6 to 8) dramatizes an encounter with the animals transformed by Circe, who are both "typical" of different types of political and cultural behavior (foxes, lions, dragons, and so on) and topically allegorical of specific individuals. A contemporary commentator claims they are "all friends of the Medici," but does not say which ones,[9] and although the topical character of the episode is certain (6.28–34), it has proven difficult to match the animals with specific persons. The most memorable and eloquent of these animals is a pig who rejects his former humanity and with it civic life. With the disillusioned rejection of political humanity, the poem ends at a clearly climactic moment, without, however, dramatizing the protagonist's own anticipated metamorphosis into an ass – unless it be figuratively in the narrator's declaration that in his satiric "braying" he has "taken on the nature of him whom I sing" (1.13–18) – much less completing the promised Apuleian, Dantean, and/or Ulyssean journey.

As its title suggests, the poem takes its initial inspiration from Apuleius' classical, satirical romance of the same title, even as its (extant) contents are not conspicuously Apuleian. Moreover, it synthesizes a considerable range of literary and specifically poetic sources, both vernacular and classical. Like the *Decennali* and the *capitoli*, the *Asino* is written in *terza rima*, the verse form invented by Dante and, as noted, subsequently adapted by Petrarch and many others. In its colloquial diction and often scabrous humor, the poem also has affinities with the genre of colloquial and "jocose" poetry, associated particularly with the Quattrocento poet Burchiello, and evident debts to the *novella* tradition identified with Boccaccio.

Dante, however, is undoubtedly Machiavelli's most powerful poetic influence, here as elsewhere. The debt is registered not only in prosody, but also in innumerable verbal echoes, which, however, are consistently "contaminated" by Machiavelli's desacralizing, satiric tendencies, frequently expressed by a structured juxtaposition with the words of other vernacular precursors. For instance, like the *Divine Comedy*, the *Asino* begins its narrative with a first-person-singular protagonist who, lost in a dark wood at a critical moment in his life, encounters a guide. But this guide, Circe's unnamed handmaiden, is a sensualized, terrestrial conflation of Dante's Virgil and Beatrice. Symptomatic is the passage in which the narrator tells his guide, at the climactic moment of their lovemaking, how she has restored his "smarrita virtù" (4.129), echoing Dante's "lost [*smarrita*] way" in *Inferno* 1.3. The protagonist exclaims:

> Blessèd be your beauties [*Sian benedette le bellezze tue*]! / Blessèd the hour [*Sia benedetta l'ora*] when I set / foot in the forest [*il piè ne la foresta*], as well as whatever things / I have done or written [*feci né scrissi*] that you took to heart. (*Asino* 4.132–5)

This passage begins with words taken from *Purgatorio* 29.86–7 where the twenty-four elders, representing the books of the Old Testament, anticipate the arrival of Beatrice in words usually reserved for the Virgin Mary: "blessed be your beauties" ("benedette / sieno ... le bellezze tue"), followed by an echo of *Canzoniere* 61, in which Petrarch adapts the form of the biblical beatitudes to his less than spiritual love for Laura: "Blessèd be ... the hour [*Benedett[a] sia ... l'ora*]," as well as by an obscene double entendre ("I set foot in the forest") more typical of the randy "jocose poets." In other words, the conflation of the intertexts mischievously resignifies the Dantean "selva" as a locus of sensual pleasure that renders blessed both the protagonist's actions ("things I have done") and his writings ("or written"). This intertextual game is highlighted by the reference to writing, which points to the poem's meta-literary reflections on the nature of the aesthetic imagination.

Machiavelli's debts to vernacular precursors mingle with other classical sources in addition to Apuleius. As the name Circe makes clear, Machiavelli also connects his work to the allegorized tradition of Homeric and Virgilian epic and particularly to the motif of the female temptress who turns men into beasts. Plutarch's *Gryllus*, which stages Odysseus'/Ulysses' colloquy with one of the animals transformed by Circe, is the primary source for the protagonist's concluding interchange with the pig. Implicit both here and in the lovemaking with a Circe stand-in is the identification of the narrator with the wily Greek adventurer, who is also the central character of a famous episode in Dante's *Comedy*. The *Asino*, then, represents a synthesis, or at least a pastiche, of literary genres, and especially of two major literary traditions: the classical Greek and Latin on the one hand, and the Italian vernacular on the other, especially the by-now canonical "crowns" of the Trecento. Unmistakably, and very much like Jacopo Sannazaro and Ariosto, Machiavelli in the *Asino* sets out to reunite the Latin-humanist and vernacular traditions after a century in which the two had largely been kept separate (with some notable exceptions, chiefly Poliziano). Finally, the *Asino* also has (as foreshadowed in Machiavelli's letter to Alamanni) its contemporary poetic competitors obliquely in view. Notable is the retelling of the mock coronation of the so-called Abate of Gaeta (Giacomo Baraballo) with the poet's laurels on the Capitoline Hill in 1514 (6.109–26), which might be interpreted as an allusive fling at the formidable Ariosto's own self-coronation at the end of his poem, thus fulfilling, with a bitter twist, Machiavelli's promise not to "exclude" his rival as he himself had been excluded in the *Furioso*.[10]

In a sense, then, the *Asino* presents us with Machiavelli's ideal poetic library and represents his broadest and most ambitious exploration of the nature and value of the "literary." Yet it also has, like the *Decennali* and the *capitoli*, a high degree of historical-political content, containing numerous verbal echoes of the major political works and addressing many of their key concepts (e.g., the cyclicality of history; fortune vs. *virtù*; the dangerous consequences of territorial expansion). Perhaps most importantly, both the *Discourses* and *The Prince* are evoked in the *Asino* as the narrator identifies the genesis and genealogy of Machiavelli's political reflections:

> And because one thought calls for another, / the mind ran off [*corse*] to those past events / that time has not yet hidden from us, / and, thinking now of this and now of that, discoursed [*discorse*] / upon how Fortune [*fortuna*] often first caressed, / then savaged, the ancient peoples: / and so marvelous [*meravigliose*] did these

things seem to me, / that I wished to discourse [*discorrere*] with myself / about the variability of all earthly things [*variare de le mondane cose*].   (*Asino* 5.28–36)

By presenting political reflection as originating in an imaginative conversation with the past, this passage recalls the letter to Vettori of December 10, 1513, while the sequence *corse-discorse-discorrere* (in which the first two words are in the emphatic position of rhymes) obviously alludes to the *Discourses*. These lines also crucially link reflection on the past to an understanding of the operations of change in the present and make both originate in the pleasures of an aesthetic experience – that of the marvelous – which is consistently associated with the imagination. In other words, the passage implicitly proposes the faculty of imagination as the best way to enter into an understanding of the dynamic processes of human society, politics, and history. Coping with the "variability" of existence entails recognizing the power of the imagination to understand and shape the realities around us and the historical conditions that contribute to creating it.

The point becomes clearer as we consider that this passage also functions as an allegorical key for interpreting the proemial fable of the running boy. The rhyme of *corse* (ran) with *discorse* (discoursed) evokes the etymology of the verb *discorrere*, whose Latin origin (*discurrere*) means "to run here and there." Thus, the youth who cannot control his passionate compulsion (specifically called a *fantasia*, 1.80) to run "without any consideration for propriety [*senza alcun rispetto*]" (1.35–6), and who in the end continues to do so despite the sanctions of his father and the ministrations of a learned doctor (*medico*), figures the unarrestable political imagination of Machiavelli himself.

Significantly, the ministrations of the *medico* not only fail to cure the boy, but also provide the very occasion for the *Asino*'s political satire, as the narrator suggests in commenting on the story:

> [The doctor] promised the boy's father to make him sane [*sano*] again. / But as it happens that one always believes / in whoever promises a good (which is why / one always puts so much faith [*fede*] in doctors [*medici*]) / and often, by believing [*credendo*] in them, one is deprived / of the good (and thus it seems that this profession alone / battens on and lives off the ills of others) /, thus the father was in no doubt / and put this case [*caso*] in the doctor's hands, / having believed [*credette*] in his words.   (*Asino* 1.48–57)

This passage underlines how belief in the prescriptive science of "doctors" is not grounded in reason, but rather sustained by their imaginative capacity to elicit "fede" through promises (*Mandragola* deals with a similar theme, as does *Prince* 18). By analogy, politics is thus an art of imaginative persuasions.

That "medici" is a pun concealing a topical allegory becomes evident when the boy loses control and begins running again precisely when he finds himself in via Martelli gazing down "Broad-way," that is, via Larga (1.74), where, as any Florentine of the time knew, stands Palazzo Medici, the emblem of Medici hegemony since Cosimo the elder built it:

> The youth, seeing this straight and wide street [*via dritta e spaziosa*], / could not hold himself back / from returning to his old pleasures / and, having set aside all other things, / his *fantasy* turned back to *running* [*di correr gli tornò la fantasia*], / which, whirling like a mill [*mulinando*], never rests. (*Asino* 1.76–81)

Like the youth's impulsive reaction to the spacious via Larga, which explicitly allegorizes Machiavelli's compulsion to critical thought, the poet's political *fantasia* is set in motion by the Medici, who provide the former secretary with such ample (again "largo") material for his satire:

> whence, if I now scatter some poison [*veleno*], / though I have lost the habit of speaking ill [*dir male*], / I am forced into it by these times, so abundant in grist for my mill [*di materia largo*]. (*Asino* 1.100–2)

In other words, the metonymical figuration of Medici power by the "via Larga" calls forth that very Machiavellian satire that it had sought, through the figure of the "medico," to restrain.

The force of the allegory is heightened because it is surrounded by a tissue of allusions to the way in which poetic imagination may either serve the powers that be or attack them. The subsequent reference to "our Ass, who has traced his steps over so many stairs [*scale*] of this our world" (1.103–4) in order to acquire the knowledge of humanity that permits his braying, recalls Cacciaguida's prophecy of Dante's political exile from Florence ("you will learn how the bread of others tastes of salt, / and what a hard path it is to descend and ascend the stairs [*scale*] of others") and his vision of Dante's decision to "be a party unto himself" (*Paradiso* 17.58–60, 69), much like the "asinine" poet of the proem. It also evokes Cacciaguida's forceful insistence to Dante to "make all your vision manifest" (128) and "strike the highest peaks," that is, men in highest positions, with his poetic criticisms (134).

Finally, we should note the references to Machiavelli's fruitless attempts to "earn rewards [*fare acquisto*] in other ways" (*Asino* 1.95) once deprived of political office. This undoubtedly points to the writing of *The Prince* and its failure to win him Medici favor. But it is also a clear verbal echo of the episode of John the Evangelist in canto 35 of the *Orlando furioso*, where, with deep, desacralizing irony, Ariosto probes the relation of poets, including himself, to powerful patrons. In the episode's scandalous culminating lines, John claims to have been granted eternal life as a reward for praising his patron, Christ, and says: "beyond all others I earned a reward [*io feci acquisto*]" (35.29.1). St. John's good fortune, however, stands in stark contrast to the depiction (with an allusive, but patent, attack on Ariosto's own masters, the Este dukes of Ferrara) of the ingratitude of the powerful and the revenge taken on them by poets through fictionalizing verbal portraits.

Machiavelli, whose appeals for Medici patronage had repeatedly gone unanswered, thus allusively warns the Medici that their regime is subject to the subversive critique of the poetic imagination and that the ingratitude of princes is not without consequences. Indeed, the *correre* of the youth is almost certainly meant to echo the *capitolo* on Ingratitude, where Machiavelli uses the same verb as a metaphor for the free play of the imagination that propels his poetry:

> Therefore, by singing I seek to arrest / and remove from my heart the sorrow of adverse fortunes / that courses through [*corre*] my maddened soul.
>
> ("Ingratitude" 16–18)

In both the *capitolo* and the *Asino*, the moment of autobiographical reference is not an end in itself; it appears in the context of a more general reflection upon the power of the artistic imagination. This is, remarkably, even the case in the brilliant sonnet, addressed to Giuliano de' Medici, restored as master of Florence in 1512, in which Machiavelli recounts his imprisonment and torture by suspicious Medici functionaries:

> Giuliano, I have on my legs a pair of snares [*geti*], / together with six pulls of the rope on my shoulders / – I'll spare you the recounting of my other miseries – / since poets are always treated thus.[11]

The passage dramatizes the impotence and victimization of poets, with whom Machiavelli already identified in 1513 when he wrote the poem, but it also implies their special status and ability to make visible the violent abuses of those who rule.

Machiavelli articulates his poetics in relation to his vocation as historian and political thinker and emphasizes the necessary intrication of power with imagination through several key terms. Central to the comparison of the running boy and the satirical poet of the *Asino* is *fantasia*, which traditionally designates the inventive power of imagination. For Machiavelli, the word fuses several meanings. It designates the obsessive nature of individuals, the way of seeing and being that prevents them from adapting to changing circumstances. In 1506 he had written that "each man governs himself according to his own ingenuity [*ingegno*] and imagination [*fantasia*]."[12] *Fantasia* is thus like *ambizione* (in the *capitolo*): the intrinsic *fortuna* of humanity, which cannot help but follow its own natural impulses, blind to consequences, a point also made explicitly in the *Asino* (1.88–90). *Fantasia* is also a power, a special form of *virtù*, which enables the poet, moved by wonder ("tanto a me parver maravigliose") to see and represent in its full and true range "the variability [*variar*] of all earthly things" (*Asino* 5.34–6). Writing to Francesco Vettori on January 31, 1515, Machiavelli addressed the *varietà* of his own writings, connecting it directly to the production of wonder:

> Anyone who saw our letters, honored *compare*, and saw their variety [*diversità*] would wonder greatly [*si maraviglierebbe assai*] … This way of proceeding, though it might seem worthy of vituperation to some, to me seems praiseworthy because we are imitating nature, which is variable [*varia*].[13]

By associating wonder, in this letter as in the *Asino*, both with stylistic variety and with the variety of human affairs, Machiavelli sketches a theory of aesthetic pleasure not as a utopian escape but as the expression of his most profound realism. Change is an integral and inevitable feature of human history; and therefore one cannot hope ever to crystallize history, society, or politics into completely rational constructs. It is precisely the "effectual truth of things" that demands that we account for human *fantasia* and give the literary imagination its due. From this perspective, the writing of history is not the opposite of poetic imagination, but integral, or at least complementary, to it. It may have been to some such insight that Machiavelli was alluding when he signed himself "historian, comedian, and tragedian" in his letter to Francesco Guicciardini of October 21, 1525.[14]

The *Asino* configures itself as the scene of a similarly composite mode of writing. Circe's handmaiden, serving now as a Cacciaguida stand-in, prophetically envisions the composition of the poem in which she speaks: "Let this voyage of yours, this your travail, / be sung [*cantato*] by historian or poet [*istorico o poeta*]" (4.17–18). Pairing "historian" with "poet" is not an either/or, as the use of the verb *cantare* (to sing) to designate both types of writing underscores. Indeed, the *Asino* is clearly sung by both the historian *and* the poet, for it presents us with a vision of the literary, not as dependent upon history for whatever truth value it may possess, but rather as the expression of the power of the imagination, which both shapes history (seen as the sum of the infinite, obsessive *fantasie* of humankind) and makes political reflection possible.

NOTES

This essay was composed collaboratively throughout. However, the section on the *Asino* derives primarily from dissertation research of Angela Matilde Capodivacca. Translations from *The Prince* and the letter to Vettori of December 10, 1513, are taken from *The Essential Writings of Machiavelli*, trans. Peter Constantine (New York: Modern Library, 2007). All other translations are our own.

1. Machiavelli, *Tutte le opere*, ed. Mario Martelli (Florence: Sansoni, 1971), p. 1248; *Machiavelli and His Friends: Their Personal Correspondence*, trans. James B. Atkinson and David Sices (Dekalb, Ill.: Northern Illinois University Press, 1996), p. 413.

2. *Opere*, pp. 1194–5; our translation; cf. *Correspondence*, p. 318.

3. *Opere*, pp. 940–50; *Machiavelli: The Chief Works and Others*, trans. Allan Gilbert, 3 vols. (Durham, N.C.: Duke University Press, 1989), 3:1444–57.

4. *Opere*, pp. 976–87; *Works*, 2:735–49.

5. *Opere*, p. 983.

6. *Opere*, p. 984.

7. *Opere*, pp. 998–1003; *Works*, 2:1016–21.

8. *Opere*, pp. 954–76; *Works*, 2:750–72.

9. "Lettera [of Giovanbattista Busini] a Benedetto Varchi" in *Opere di Benedetto Varchi ora per la prima volta raccolte ... aggiuntevi delle lettere di Gio. Battista Busini sopra l'assedio di Firenze* (Trieste: Lloyd Austriaco, 1858), p. 512.

10. Gian Mario Anselmi and Paolo Fazion, *Machiavelli, l'Asino e le bestie* (Bologna: CLUEB, 1984), pp. 90–3, note that there is an echo of Ariosto's verses in book 7 of the *Asino*.

11. *Opere*, p. 1003 (lines 1–4); *Works*, 2:1013.

12. Letter to Giovanbattista Soderini, *Opere*, p. 1083; *Correspondence*, p. 135.

13. *Opere*, p. 1191; *Correspondence*, p. 312.

14. *Opere*, p. 1224; *Correspondence*, p. 371.

FURTHER READING

Ascoli, Albert Russell, and Victoria Kahn, eds. *Machiavelli and the Discourse of Literature*. Ithaca, N.Y., Cornell University Press, 1993.

Bárberi Squarotti, Giorgio. *Machiavelli o la scelta della letteratura*. Rome, Bulzoni, 1987.

Cabrini, Anna Maria. "Intorno al primo Decennale," *Rinascimento*, 2nd series, 33 (1993): 69–89.

Dionisotti, Carlo. *Machiavellerie. Storia e fortuna di Machiavelli*. Turin, Einaudi, 1980.

Grayson, Cecil. "Machiavelli and Dante," in *Renaissance Studies in Honor of Hans Baron*, ed. Anthony Molho and John A. Tedeschi. Florence, Sansoni, 1971, pp. 363–84.

Najemy, John M. *Between Friends: Discourses of Power and Desire in the Machiavelli–Vettori Letters of 1513–1515*. Princeton University Press, 1993.

Patapan, Haig. "'I Capitoli': Machiavelli's New Theogony," *The Review of Politics* 65 (2003): 185–207.

Raimondi, Ezio. *Politica e commedia*. Bologna, Il Mulino, 1972.

Sullivan, Vickie B., ed. *The Comedy and Tragedy of Machiavelli: Essays on the Literary Works*. New Haven, Conn., Yale University Press, 2000.

Tusiani, Joseph, trans. and ed. *Lust and Liberty: The Poems of Machiavelli*. New York, Ivan Obolensky, 1963.

Von Vacano, Diego A. *The Art of Power: Machiavelli, Nietzsche, and the Making of Aesthetic Political Theory*. Lanham, Md., Lexington Books, 2007.

13

RONALD L. MARTINEZ

Comedian, tragedian: Machiavelli and traditions of Renaissance theater

Machiavelli best combined his talent with success when writing for the theater. His signature, "historico, comico et tragico," to a letter to Francesco Guicciardini of October 1525, sounding so much like an epitaph, suggests he knew as much.[1] But as the first element of that series indicates, his theatrical vocation was never independent of the study of antiquity and the coordinated observation of contemporary politics. Drama gave Machiavelli opportunities not only for mirroring the civil society of his day (one of the traditional definitions of the function of theater), but also for fashioning on the stage an image of the statecraft that he above all others was competent to dissect. Lodovico Ariosto's omission of Machiavelli from the canon of Italian poets in the 1516 edition of the *Orlando furioso* may have helped truncate Machiavelli's career as a narrative poet (the *Asino* and second *Decennale* remained unfinished), but Machiavelli, along with Ariosto and Bernardo Bibbiena, was a chief dramatic voice of the generation that witnessed "the ruin of Italy."

Readers and playgoers agreed: written around 1518, *Mandragola* enjoyed prestigious early performances (Rome 1520, Venice 1522, and Florence 1526) and was anthologized both early (1525) and later (1554) in the century; it was performed by the Accademia Olimpica in Vicenza in 1564, as was *Clizia* in 1569.[2] Machiavelli's plays influenced the work of dozens of authors, including the Paduan dialect author known as Ruzzante, the "divine" if salacious Pietro Aretino (author of six comedies), the ardently Medicean and prolific Giovan Maria Cecchi (over twenty comedies), and the Roman Francesco Belo, author of *Il pedante* (*The Pedant*, 1529), a remote source of Shakespeare's *Cymbeline*, while with broader strokes "machiavellism" became the countenance of cold-blooded *realpolitik* from the Ferrarese tragedies of Giraldi Cinzio to Cristopher Marlowe and Pierre Corneille. When Paolo Giovio included Machiavelli in his *Elogia* of 1545, he followed Machiavelli's valedictory order of topics, mentioning first the historical and political works, then the success of *Mandragola*, to conclude with the "tragedy" of political exile. Though treating Machiavelli coldly as an enemy of religion, Giovio praised the play's "salty Tuscan wit [*ethruscos sales*]."[3]

Machiavelli mulled over dramatic forms and techniques throughout his life. Like his rival Ariosto, he both schooled himself on the classics and closely observed contemporary theater. The inclusion among his papers of a stanza he copied from a s*acra rappresentazione* (religious drama) reveals his interest in late Quattrocento religious spectacle.[4] Parody of religious drama animates important scenes in *Mandragola*: Friar Timoteo refers to the adulterous embrace of Callimaco and Lucrezia as a *misterio* (a term for sacred plays), and echoes of the Florentine Purification of the Virgin play have been noted in the comedy, which explicitly invokes the popular feast in its final scenes.[5]

A decisive moment in Machiavelli's training in classical theater was his early and somewhat rough translation of Terence's *Andria*, possibly in the 1490s (followed by a second, corrected version in 1517–20).[6] The hastiness of the first translation suggests a commissioned project, but translating Terence's and Plautus' plays was a well-established tradition, and given *Andria*'s status as a humanist monument Machiavelli's translation was quite likely a formative encounter. Terence's play was already circulating, well supported by commentaries, especially that of Guido Juvenalis, which Machiavelli consulted; it had also been the object of a study by Poliziano, which gave a theoretical account of comedy that included the recommendation of the unities of action and time and the characterization of comedy as a mirror of social life.

Florentine literary gossip held that Gelli's *La Sporta* (The Purse) (1540s) exploited a lost translation by Machiavelli of Plautus' *Aulularia* (Pot of Gold). Indeed, there is plenty of other evidence of assiduous copying of both ancient and contemporary drama. Before entering the chancery, Machiavelli himself transcribed Terence's *Eunuchus* alongside Lucretius' *De rerum natura*.[7] He also copied his friend Lorenzo Strozzi's *Commedia in versi* and signed it "ego Barlachia recensui [I, Barlachia, have examined and corrected this]," taking the name of the Florentine herald and jokester Barlachia while aping the formula found at the end of ancient copies of Terence ("Calliopus recensui"), long thought to be a reference to the producer of Terence's plays. Giuliano de' Ricci, Machiavelli's grandson and custodian of his papers, claimed that Machiavelli adapted or imitated Aristophanes in a lost sketch entitled *Maschere*, which may have echoed *The Clouds*.[8]

That Machiavelli's satirical manner was inspired by the political immediacy and licentious satire of Aristophanic comedy was canonized for Machiavelli criticism by Giovio's *Dialogue* (1528) and *Elogia*. The collaboration with Strozzi, and possibly the Aristophanic inspirations, may have emerged from Machiavelli's visits to the Orti Oricellari, the gardens of the Rucellai family, which, in addition to providing a forum for political discussions (leading to the 1522 anti-Medici conspiracy), must often have witnessed discussion of drama; participants Jacopo Nardi, Lorenzo Strozzi, and Luigi Alamanni were play-wrights, and several were dedicatees of works by Machiavelli. Along with the stimulus offered by Ariosto's plays and Bibbiena's brilliant *Calandra* (1512), the Orti meetings plausibly furnished the workshop where Machiavelli refined his concepts of ancient and modern drama.

Machiavelli's theatrical imagination was not limited to his plays. Nearly all his works include episodes intrinsically dramatic, or, as one can say in Italian, *teatrabili* (realizable as theater). Debate over the authorship of the *Discorso o dialogo intorno alla nostra lingua* rages on; but with its explicit theatrical criticism, praising the plot but critiquing the language of a play that is clearly Ariosto's *Suppositi* (1509), and engaging in lively dialogue with a dramatized character of Dante, the *Dialogo* manifests its author's practical and theoretical involvement with drama. The *capitoli* in *terza rima* (poems on Fortune, Opportunity, Ambition, and Ingratitude) digest forces that, in Machiavelli's view of history, both animate and check human striving; these same forces drove the mechanism of Latin imitations of Greek new comedy (and of course of tragedy as well) that Machiavelli assiduously studied. Imprisoned in 1513 for suspected complicity in the anti-Medici Boscoli conspiracy, Machiavelli begged the mercy of Giuliano de' Medici in a sonnet that incorporates Machiavelli's identity as a playwright: he dreams that the Muse reproaches him for "motley dramas," having mistaken him for the poetaster Andrea Dazzi, "il Dazzo."[9]

Even some of Machiavelli's dispatches from diplomatic missions have recently been read not only as furnishing material that is *teatrabile*, but also as presenting it as such.[10] His keen interest in the fortunes of Cesare Borgia, to whom he was twice sent as Florentine envoy, generated several versions of Borgia's rise and fall: direct observation in the dispatches; allegorical satire in the first *Decennale*, where Borgia is a deadly "basilisk" (lines 394–9) luring his enemies to their death;[11] and political theory in *The Prince*, where he exemplifies *virtù* in state building. More three-dimensionally dramatic is Machiavelli's account of Borgia's vengeance against his faithless former allies, where the material is shaped, with foreshadowing and dramatic irony, both to illustrate the duke's sangfroid and to represent the tragedy of his disloyal lieutenants.[12] For parsing Borgia's career in dramatic guises, Machiavelli had precedents in the theatrical traditions of Urbino, where Borgia's conquest had been the subject of a lost "comedy" in 1504 (which concluded, like a medieval tragedy of fortune, with the deaths of Cesare and his father, Pope Alexander VI), and where Niccolò Grasso's *Eutychia*, which shared the boards with Bibbiena's *Calandra* during the Urbino carnival of February 1513, unfolds its comic plot against the background of dislocations inflicted by Borgia's capture of Urbino.[13]

The Prince itself has been read as having "tragic form"[14] and as furnishing, *mutatis mutandis*, the plot of *Mandragola* insofar as the play represents a program of political renewal compassed by a Medici prince. In addition to its tales of ambition checked by fortune, *The Prince* also dramatizes the spectacle (Machiavelli's word is "spettacolo") of power cruelly exercised: in an example (*Prince* 7) of opportunity (*occasione*) prudently seized, Borgia has his own severe magistrate, Ramiro de Lorqua, murdered and laid out, cut in two, in the piazza of Cesena. This was done, Machiavelli remarks, to stupefy the citizens and defuse ("purgare") their resentment of Borgia rule. With its suggestion of sacrifice (the bloody knife and wooden butcher's wedge for splitting carcasses were left alongside the body parts), the scene seems the climax to a political *sacra rappresentazione* with a purgative effect that recalls the catharsis prescribed for tragedy in Aristotle's *Poetics*.

Machiavelli's *Favola*, the actual title of the novella often called *Belfagor arcidiavolo*, also evokes the theater. The generic affiliation of the novella with *Mandragola* is signaled by the fact that *favola* is also used in the prologue to describe the play ("La favola *Mandragola* si chiama"), after the conventional Latin term for a play (*fabula*). In the novella, the governing council of Hell decides to investigate why so many of Hell's male denizens blame their wives for their fate. The council orders the devil Belfagor to assume human form, call himself Roderigo, go live in Florence, and take a wife. Quickly plunged into bankruptcy by debts incurred to support the extravagances of his haughty wife, Monna Onesta, Roderigo flees to the countryside, where he finds shelter with the peasant Gianmatteo. Roderigo agrees to compensate his rescuer by demonically possessing the daughters of wealthy men so that Gianmatteo can get rich performing exorcisms. When Gianmatteo is summoned to Paris by the king of France to rid his daughter of an evil spirit, the peasant instructs the king to build a large stage ("un palco grande") around an altar and hire twenty musicians for the exorcism he expects to carry out, with Roderigo's help, before the court, nobility, and clergy. But Roderigo, who has by now really possessed the king's daughter, announces that he is fed up with the agreement and refuses to do his part. Looking at the theater-like setting, he accuses Gianmatteo of trying to frighten him with its pomp and asks, using the word for stage sets: "What do you think you're doing with these *apparati* of yours?" Only Gianmatteo's suggestion that Monna Onesta's arrival is imminent terrifies the demon into fleeing the scene and releasing his grip on the girl.[15]

Machiavelli's letters abound with material that would fill out a *novella* or a comedy. His letter of August 26, 1513, to Francesco Vettori lists the crowned heads of Europe and gives to each a special attribute, as if recording the *dramatis personae* of a play. In a letter of June 20, 1513, also to Vettori, Machiavelli "plays" the pope by "putting himself in the person" of Leo ("mi sono messo nella persona del papa"). Writing to Guicciardini on May 17, 1521, he describes the trick he was playing on the Franciscan friars at Carpi, to whose meeting he had been sent as an observer. Pretending that a letter he received from Guicciardini was full of grave news concerning the European powers, and to which he was composing an equally important reply, he acted the part of one intimately involved in international negotiations by pausing and breathing deeply, as if in sober reflection. More notorious is the letter of December 8, 1509, in which Machiavelli writes to Luigi Guicciardini from Verona with an account of a lubricious encounter he claims to have had that is a low parody of the bed-trick scenes in his plays. Lured in the dark by one woman into a tryst with an ugly prostitute whose "mouth resembled that of Lorenzo de' Medici," he reacts with disgust when, after completing the act, he shines a light on her and sees with whom he has had sexual commerce. Perhaps invented, or embellished, as a literary experiment based on stories from Boccaccio, the letter makes use of theatrical devices of darkness and mistaken identity followed by light and recognition.

Even more elaborately theatrical are Machiavelli's contributions to an exchange of letters with Vettori concerning a widowed Roman matron and her children. In a letter of January 18, 1514, Vettori recounts how he has accepted the suggestion of two Florentine friends that he invite to dinner the agreeable widow next door (Vettori calls her a "buona compagna," a good-time gal, the same phrase Machiavelli will apply to Lucrezia's compliant mother, Sostrata, in *Mandragola*), along with her beautiful daughter Costanza and her son. At the dinner, Vettori's friends attempt to seduce both the daughter and the son; Vettori then reveals that he himself has become infatuated with Costanza. Replying a few weeks later, Machiavelli vividly recreates both the silly words and gestures of the friends and Vettori's besotted state, concluding with a mock-heroic exclamation borrowed from a scene in Terence's *Adelphoe* (The Brothers) in which a father discovers his sons (off-stage) with their paramours (790: "O heaven, O earth, O seas of Neptune"), and suggesting that Vettori, if he wants to have Costanza, would benefit from Jove's power of transforming himself, *inter alia*, into gold, as he did in the seduction of Danaë. That particular Jovian metamorphosis was iconic for theatrical tradition (and antitheatrical preaching) because it is used in Terence's *Eunuchus* (585–610) to motivate a young man to rape the girl he desires.[16]

The metamorphoses fostered by the theater inform Machiavelli's famous letter to Vettori of December 10, 1513,[17] where he describes his daily routine after his disgrace, a text echoed in his play *Clizia* a dozen years later. The expression with which he says he would appear in Rome if ever he could entertain more hopeful expectations of useful employment by the Medici ("Eccomi [Here I am]") echoes a formula of Latin comedy (*cf*. Plautus' *Miles gloriosus* 4.2: "Adsum; impera, si quid vis [Here I am, if you wish for anything, give me your commands]"). Machiavelli's willingness to serve the family "even if they should begin by having me roll a stone [*voltolare un sasso*]" alludes to the myth of Sisyphus that he knew from several sources, including Terence's *Eunuchus* and Lucretius' *De rerum natura*. In the same letter Machiavelli subtly deploys allusions to a fifteenth-century vernacular narrative poem, *Geta e Birria*, which rewrites Plautus' *Amphitruo*, in order to articulate aspects of his problematic relationship with Vettori.[18] The theatrical history invoked by Machiavelli's use of *Geta e Birria* not only valorizes the names of stock characters in Roman drama (the slaves Geta and Birria appear, respectively, in Terence's *Phormio* and *Andria*), but also brings into focus the special significance of *Amphitruo*. Sole tragicomedy in the Plautine corpus, *Amphitruo* is further exceptional in having Jove and Mercury appear disguised as, or rather transformed into, mortals: "eccum Iuppiter; in Amphitruonis vortit sese imaginem [here is Jove; he has turned himself into the shape of Amphitryon]" (*Amphitruo* 120–3).

The metamorphic deities of *Amphitruo* underwrite further transformations in the letter of December 10, 1513. The climax of Machiavelli's day comes when he doffs his everyday clothes, dons the humanist's cloak and enters his study, where he is received by the ancient authors and declares: "I transfuse myself entirely into them [*tucto mi transferisco in loro*]." For this sacred rite of humanist metempsychosis Machiavelli adopts a term of art harking back to Terence's prologues (*Andria*, 14; *Eunuchus*, 32) and their references to compositional *contaminatio* (admixture), Terence's stock-in-trade as a playwright, by which a plurality of Greek models were transposed (Terence's verb is *transfero*) into a new Latin play. The term, slightly modified, had already appeared as "transunto" in the prologue of Ariosto's vernacular comedy *I suppositi*, where he says he has "transumed part of his plot from the *Eunuch* of Terence and the *Captives* of Plautus." Such transumptions dot the continuum that connects translation and compilation with the other metamorphic processes of the stage, from the fungible stage sets, one day Rome and the next day Pisa (*Mandragola*, prologue 9–11), to the mercurial actors themselves, who with a change of garb can assume new identities. Machiavelli also understood theatrical metamorphoses as metaphors for the adjustments required in transposing material from ancient to modern contexts: perhaps especially Machiavelli, who frequently reiterated the view, drawn from Polybius, that human action was fated to be replayed (and retold) generation after generation.

Elements of language, plot devices, and underlying themes connect Machiavelli's translation of *Andria* with both *Mandragola* and *Clizia*. In Terence's *Andria*, the death of the courtesan Chrysis has bereaved her supposed sister, Glycerium, who is beloved of Pamphilus and carries his child. Pamphilus' father, Simo, plans to marry him to the daughter of the wealthy Chremes, and the play's action revolves around the disclosure, abetted by Pamphilus' clever servant Davos, of Glycerium's pregnancy in order to dissuade Chremes from accepting Pamphilus as a son-in-law. The discovery that Glycerium is really Chremes' daughter opens the way for Pamphilus to marry her.

Machiavelli's *Andria* begins with Simo and Sosia (a protatic or nonrecurring character that facilitates the inclusion of background) discussing the character of Pamphilo; similarly, at the beginning of *Mandragola* Callimaco bends Siro's ear with the account of his past life, just as Cleandro does with Palamede in *Clizia*. Other passages from the translation also anticipate vivid moments in *Clizia* and *Mandragola*. One of them is Ligurio's memorable calculation of the beneficial results that will come from aborting the fictional nun (*Mandragola* 3.4: "If you do this, look at how many good things come from it [*guardate, nel far questo, quanti beni ne resulta*]: you preserve the honor of the convent, the girl, the family; you give back a daughter to her father; you satisfy my lord here, and so many of his relatives, you offer so much in alms"). This parallels Simo's attempt to dissuade Chremete from breaking off his daughter's engagement to Pamphilo (*Andria* 3.3: "see how many good things ensue [*che ne può risultare ... guarda quanti beni*]: first, you restore a son to one of your friends, you'll have a steady son-in-law and your daughter a husband").[19] The words spoken by the dying Cryside in *Andria* 1.5 in entrusting Glicerio to Pamphilo ("I give you to her as husband, friend, teacher, and father") are echoed in Lucrezia's acceptance of Callimaco in *Mandragola* (5.4: "I take you for my lord, protector, and guide ... I want you to be my father, my defender, my every good"). Each speech echoes its playworld: Pamphilo's fidelity to Glicerio sums up the high-minded *Andria*, and the adulterous final arrangements of Lucrezia seal the deceptions in *Mandragola*.

The date of the composition of *Mandragola*, Machiavelli's theatrical masterpiece, is debated: an extant first edition of 1519, apparently published under Medici auspices in Siena, suggests that it was a product of the period of Machiavelli's visits to the Rucellai gardens around 1517, and thus roughly coeval with the *Discourses*, although verbal parallels to the play in letters from 1513 and 1514 might indicate those years as the period of the play's gestation. The earliest editions carried the title *Commedia di Callimaco e Lucrezia*, and Machiavelli and his correspondents referred to it as *Nicia*

(Lucrezia's foolish husband). The title *Mandragola*, as found in the prologue, only appears in print with the Calvo anthology published in Rome in 1525.[20] Its greater durability may be due in part to the fact that it names not a character, but the device used to weave the web of deception that animates the plot.

In *Mandragola*, the lawyer Nicia Calfucci's desire for an heir drives him to entertain cures proposed by Callimaco Guadagni, an exiled Florentine newly arrived from Paris, who disguises himself as a doctor in order to attempt the seduction of Nicia's wife, Lucrezia. In the scheme devised and managed by the parasite and matchmaker Ligurio and abetted by the corruptible friar Timoteo, doctor Callimaco will prepare a potion of mandrake root – reputed as an aid to conception in the Bible (Genesis 30.14–17), folklore, and Renaissance medical texts – and prescribe it as a cure for Lucrezia's presumed sterility. Since folk belief cautioned that the mandrake was poisonous if harvested at the wrong time, the apparent danger to the first inseminating male – presumed, of course, to be Lucrezia's husband, Nicia – presents an awkward complication to the plan. But Ligurio, relying on the same folklore, counters that the problem can be managed by substituting, on the first night, an expendable "garzonaccio" (scallywag) who will absorb the toxin: in reality, this will be Callimaco in disguise.[21] The stratagem is executed and delivers universal satisfaction, with Nicia remaining, to be sure, in the dark, and the play ends with a triumphal procession in which Lucrezia, rejuvenated by Callimaco's embrace, is brought to church in a parody of the Purification of the Virgin.

Machiavelli followed Bibbiena's (and Jacopo Nardi's) lead in drawing on Boccaccio's *Decameron* for plot material. Callimaco's departure from Paris, his disguise and his achievement of a permanent place in Nicia's household echo the tale of Beatrice and Lodovico in *Decameron* 7.7: after leaving Paris for Bologna to see the famously beautiful Beatrice de' Galluzzi, Lodovico disguises himself as a servant, Anichino, and succeeds through ingenuity in becoming the most trusted servant in the household, with full access to Beatrice. Another example: the doctor Callimaco's rejected suggestion of therapeutic public baths for Lucrezia echoes Boccaccio's story of Ricciardo Minutolo's deception of Catella Sighinolfi. Having been deceived into thinking she is taking the place of her husband's supposed lover at an assignation in a darkened *bagnio*, Catella is bed-tricked by Ricciardo; the switch once discovered, she is persuaded "how much tastier are the kisses of a lover" than those of a husband (*Decameron* 3.6.50), just as Callimaco persuades Lucrezia of the same thing once the "sacrificial" coupling is accomplished (5.4). Machiavelli yields only to Bibbiena in the extent of his plundering of the *Decameron*; between them, they make adaptation of material from the *Decameron* standard practice for Italian comedy – a vernacular equivalent of the *contaminatio* of Greek plays that Terence had defended to his critics.

But *Mandragola*'s resonance as a play about Florentine politics derives in larger part from its use of Livy's account of Roman Lucretia, from which Machiavelli borrowed key details,[22] and of which a series of adapted versions, often with moralizing commentary, descended from Augustine to Dante, Boccaccio, Coluccio Salutati, and the frequently reprinted late fifteenth-century vernacular *Historia di Lucretia Romana* in rhymed octaves.[23] In Livy, Collatinus' boasting of Lucretia's virtue inflames the lust of Sextus Tarquinius, the king's son. Callimaco's imitative desire is similarly roused when he hears reports in Paris of Lucrezia's incomparable beauty (1.1). Timoteo, in his travesty of pastoral care, tells Lucrezia that it is the will that sins, not the body, and that her adulterous embrace with the "garzonaccio" will therefore not be a sin since she will be doing her husband's and God's wish (3.11). The friar's arguments parody the attempts of Roman Lucretia's relations to dissuade her from suicide on the grounds that her will has remained chaste although her body has been violated. Finally, in preparing the bed-trick, Ligurio suggests to Callimaco that he blackmail Lucrezia by hinting that, if she refuses to accept him as her lover, he could bring about her disgrace (4.2), thus echoing Tarquin's threat to defame Lucretia if she refuses him. Callimaco's report of his night with Lucrezia omits this harsh detail and echoes instead, with its promise of marriage (5.4), the reconciliation the Romans effected with the Sabine women.[24] More broadly reminiscent of Lucretia's tragedy is the play's implicit political message: just as Brutus' clever manipulation of the shock of Lucretia's rape and suicide restores *virtù* to the men of Rome and precipitates the refoundation of Rome as a republic free of Tarquin tyranny, so the embrace of Lucrezia with the potent and youthful Callimaco produces her almost miraculous rejuvenation, and (so go many readings) suggests the salutary renewal of the Florentine civic body.

Whereas in Boccaccio and Livy seductions are compassed by individuals, in *Mandragola* the victory over Lucrezia's chastity requires a committee and thus a conspiracy. Callimaco's lust and Nicia's desire for an heir spark an effort that requires the nimble scheming of Ligurio and the corruption of Timoteo and Sostrata, as well as Callimaco's virtuoso sexual performance. At the critical moment, this array of forces surrounding Lucrezia sways her will and justifies the presentation of the action with the otherwise conventional Plautine comic language of stratagems and sieges; this becomes literally dramatic action during the nocturnal expedition to "trap" the disguised Callimaco for the bedroom sacrifice, to which Nicia even goes armed with a little sword, and in a battle formation based on a passage in Terence's *Eunuchus* (4.7.775).[25]

The collaborative nature of the assault on Lucrezia reflects a satire of Church and society aimed not just at individuals, but at institutions. Timoteo, for example, shrewdly maneuvered into dubious dealings by Ligurio, represents the corruption of the moral and spiritual mission of the Church by its appetite for power and wealth. Indeed, that the final scene is performed as the protagonists head toward church under Timoteo's guidance, and that he is, among the secondary characters, the one remembered in Machiavelli's *Clizia*, suggests how central he is to the satire, reflecting Machiavelli's conviction that the Church bore a heavy burden of responsibility for Italy's ruin.[26] Nicia, the chief butt of the play's humor, recalls Boccaccio's gullible Calandrino (and thus Bibbiena's Calandro), but his name also echoes that of the unsuccessful Athenian general Nikias; although he is a lawyer and conversant in simple Latin, his idiomatically provincial Florentine speech and outlook satirize Florence's recalcitrant political class, whose pursuit of narrow self-interest had, in Machiavelli's analysis, pushed the republic toward failure.[27]

Most complex of all is Lucrezia. Her final "rejuvenation," her sudden acquisition of decisiveness and authority, has been given widely divergent interpretations. Long ago, Russo and then Dionisotti rejected what they considered the Crocean "tragic and moralistic" view of the play as exposing the corruption, through Lucrezia, of the entire civic body.[28] Instead they saw in the play a triumphant and revolutionary proposal for the renewal of citizenry and state at the expense of conventional morality. This view has been supported, but also complicated, by claims that the play parallels *The Prince* in its implicit suggestion that the younger Lorenzo de' Medici (Callimaco) should take Florence (Lucrezia) in hand and give her, so to speak, the government she needs.[29] The corollary, that this allegorical subplot was coordinated with the play's initial performance at, or following, Lorenzo's marriage to Madeleine de la Tour d'Auvergne in 1518, has lost appeal because it is unsupported by documentation. Bausi nevertheless observes that political allegories were typical of early learned comedy: Strozzi's plays, from as early as 1502, contain pro-Medici programs, and Nardi's were addressed to the republican Florence of Soderini.[30] In the case of *Mandragola*, a character named Lucrezia could hardly escape comparison with Roman Lucretia, whose tragedy adorned many a Florentine bridal *cassone*, scaring its owners into jealously preserving their virtue, but also resonating with an entrenched anti-tyrannical iconography available for political uses.[31]

Mandragola's satirical intentions are announced early. Drawing on Terence's defensive prologues, which deploy "speaking ill" (*maledicere*) to retaliate against denigrators, Machiavelli insists in his prologue on his own competence in "speaking ill [*sa dir male anch'egli*]." Indeed, the play ridicules not merely stock or literary types, but real Florentines. The Calfucci, Nicia's family, were long gone, although in using their name Machiavelli hitches his satire to the lament of Dante's Cacciaguida in *Paradiso* 16 over the decay of Florentine noble houses, including the Calfucci. The virulence of the prologue prompted Francesco Guicciardini, who was planning to stage *Mandragola* in Faenza in early 1526, to suggest that Machiavelli write another prologue that would "portray the spectators more than yourself."[32] Giovio remarked, too, that Machiavelli's fellow citizens appeared to tolerate his sharply satirical representation of them on stage. Indeed, although in the fiction of the play the mandrake-lore is bogus, the pharmacological discourse suggests how in the real world of history the play might function as a violent emetic, a *pharmakos*, designed to diagnose and treat the diseased Florentine polity. Republics, Machiavelli writes in *Discourses* 3.1, must periodically be brought back to their origins, even through violence, the more so when diseased. It is in this light that Giorgio Padoan argues that *Mandragola* may be taken as the most authentic *tragedy* of the Cinquecento.[33] Indeed Livy himself comments on the resemblance of the story of Lucretia to the tragedy of a Greek royal house and offers his history as a remedy, or medicine, for Rome's moral decline.[34] In *Mandragola*, the "tragedy" springs from the fact that Lucrezia does *not* commit suicide, but yields and so permits the corruption of the state, a conclusion that would reinforce that vision of the play – held in such scorn by Dionisotti and Russo – as an anatomy of civic corruption. Yet the two views of the play, as tragic in implication and as "comic" rejuvenation, are from a Machiavellian perspective probably compatible. Machiavelli had certainly not forgotten how in Plautus' *Amphitruo* (54–5) Mercury offers to reverse a play's genus on his say-so alone: "I'll make a tragedy into a comedy without changing a word."

Machiavelli's last play, *Clizia*, sets both youth and social virtue against distempered old age.[35] Conceived for a production at the suburban villa of Jacopo Falconetti in 1525, and provided with a stage set by the much sought after Bastiano da Sangallo, *Clizia* adapts Plautus' *Casina*, a play that relies on the conventions of Latin new comedy: the foundling whose ultimately discovered noble birth makes her marriageable, and the senescent lover, the *senex amans*.

In *Clizia*, the seventy-year-old Nicomaco lusts after his foster daughter, Clizia, taken as a child by a gentleman soldier of the French army during its attack on Naples in 1494; she is subsequently entrusted to Nicomaco and his wife, Sofronia, after the Frenchman and the rest of the French army depart to fight the battle of the Taro in 1495, where the Frenchman perishes. To cloak his designs, Nicomaco schemes to marry Clizia to his servant Pirro and give him a house next door in order to facilitate his own access to the girl. Sofronia suspects her husband's motives (she literally smells them out as Nicomaco affects perfumes suitable to lovers but ridiculous at his age) and proposes Eustachio, the family's farmstead steward, as an alternative husband for Clizia. Cleandro, Sofronia's and Nicomaco's son, also loves Clizia, and the action thus turns on a group of rival males, all of whom, as Sofronia says, "have laid siege to her [*ognuno l'ha posto il campo intorno*]" (2.3). A lottery is decided to settle the question of whom the girl will marry. Pirro wins and Nicomaco insists that the wedding be celebrated immediately, intending of course to be the one who will greet Clizia in the bridal bed. But Sofronia arranges for Clizia to be substituted by the disguised servant Siro, who prods at the old man from behind with "something hard and stiff" (5.2) and then gives him a drubbing. A humiliated and chastened Nicomaco is forgiven by Sofronia, and when Clizia's gentle birth is revealed by the timely arrival of her Neapolitan father, Ramondo, all agree to the marriage of Cleandro and Clizia.

Mandragola and *Clizia* are linked in a number of ways. In *Clizia*, set in 1506, two years after the fictional date of *Mandragola*, Nicomaco tells Sofronia (2.3) that the prayers of their family confessor, Frate Timoteo, brought about the "miraculous" pregnancy of Mona Lucrezia, wife of Nicia Calfucci. Both plays refer to the French invasion of 1494 as the origin of their plots' predicaments. Both rely on Ariostean *supposizioni* (disguised substitutions) for their bed-tricks. Both exploit scandalous sexual images: Nicia's homoerotic response to the disguised Callimaco, whose flesh he delightedly palps (*Mandragola* 5.2); the ardent widow confessed by Frate Timoteo who is fearful of, and fascinated by, the "impaling" practiced by the Turks and nostalgic for her husband's reprehensibly oriented attentions (*Mandragola* 3.3); Nicomaco's near-sodomization by Siro (*Clizia* 5.2); and so on. Both deploy vivid, fantastic pharmacopoeia: the mandrake potion faked up for Lucrezia, the aphrodisiacs and sexual training meal Nicomaco orders to spark his performance (*Clizia* 4.2). Both plots aim at a rejuvenation with wider implications, successful in Lucrezia's case, abortive in Nicomaco's. Both turn on the consequentiality of the treatment of women, in *Mandragola* with allusion to the etiology of republican Rome, in *Clizia* because Nicomaco's disordered lechery enrages the norm-affirming Sofronia.

There are important differences as well. *Mandragola*, both in its political allegory and its prologue, addresses and chastises the Florentine body politic. *Clizia* treats, as comedy traditionally did, middle-class domestic matters; although political implications are there to be drawn, the entire drama unfolds within a family. Machiavelli wrote *Mandragola* as a discarded secretary searching for meaningful occupation and finding it in the puncturing of Florentine political lethargy. In *Clizia*, Nicomaco, the butt of the play, can be identified with the author himself, who was then engaged in an affair with the much younger singer and actress Barbera Salutati. Indeed, it is likely that, in the remark of Palamede, Cleandro's friend, about avoiding the company of tedious "singers, old men and those in love" (1.1), Machiavelli was mocking himself, and students of the play have seen in Sofronia's account of Nicomaco's virtuous routine before his infatuation (2.4) echoes of Machiavelli's December 1513 letter to Vettori about his daily existence after his removal from office.[36]

As *Mandragola*'s parody of virtuous political rejuvenation has suggested to some readers a tragic implication, so the harsh treatment of Nicomaco in *Clizia* appears incipiently tragic, especially in the light of formal elements of tragedy retained in the play, such as Clizia's reported (but invented) mad scene, which reiterates the original parody of classical tragedy in Plautus' *Casina*. Like a textbook return of the repressed, Siro's "stabbing" of Nicomaco's flanks (5.2) evokes in the old man's imagination the dagger Clizia was reported to have seized with murderous intent toward Nicomaco and Pirro (4.7). If *Mandragola* suggests how male potency and *virtù* might procreate a new state, *Clizia* sketches a gender war where feminine agency holds the advantage because it is associated with the cycles of time itself. Flush with his proxy victory in the lottery (3.7), Nicomaco orders immediate nuptials, riding roughshod over Sofronia's attempts at delay. She counters that Clizia may be indisposed for the marriage bed because she is menstruating and has the *ordinario* of women – the regular, as it were, constitutional cycles that mark women's time ("Dubito che la non abbia l'ordinario delle donne"). Nicomaco assumes that Clizia *lacks* something that should be remedied with "lo straordinario degli uomini," by which he means male sexual force. Just a few lines earlier, Sofronia had described Nicomaco's urgency to carry out the lottery as "furia ... estraordinaria."

The association of aggressive male sexuality with the political *straordinario*, which Machiavelli had identified in his political works as capable of bringing about either the ruin or renewal of political bodies, opposes the violence of "extra-ordinary" and hence "extra-constitutional" masculine *virtù* to the feminine *ordinario* of natural cycles, like the virtuous routine that Sofronia, whose name signifies the classical prudence and temperance that typically restrain aggressive action, praises in the Nicomaco she knew before his descent into disordered desire. This allegorical polemic permeates the play and culminates in Nicomaco's defeat in the "masculine wedding" with Siro, where, with poetic justice reminiscent of Dante's *contrappasso* (counterpunishment), the aged lover nearly suffers the penetrating treatment he was readying for Clizia. The joke is still on Nicomaco when, in the play's last, ambiguous words, Sofronia declares that the marriage that will unite Clizia and Cleandro is to be "female" and not "masculine" ("le nuove nozze, le quali fieno femmine, e non maschie," 5.6). Having restored the *ordinario* of a well-ordered household, in the end it is Sofronia who rules.

Given the onomastic mirroring of *Nicco-lò Machia-*velli in the name Nicomaco, the loss of vigor and authority afflicting Nicomaco might be thought Machiavelli's as well, were it not for the ways in which *Clizia*'s prologue is informed by its counterpart in Plautus' *Casina*. The prologue of the Latin play was rewritten after its author's death to honor him with a posthumous performance. By including Plautus among those who, "although dead and gone, have benefited living humankind [*tamen absentes prosunt pro praesentibus*]," it transforms him into a classical author, a resource for the ages. *Clizia*'s prologue does not translate *Casina*'s, but it enshrines its classical values by reiterating traditional norms for comedy (to mirror private life and to offer edifying and discouraging examples) and by affirming the notion that, human nature being constant, similar events recur cyclically over time: Machiavelli's Florentine story renews events that transpired in an Athens long gone. In this light, Machiavelli's vulnerabilities as an aging lover, hinted at in *Clizia*, will be amortized by his identification, as an author, with more ample cycles of existence and with classical exemplarity and permanence. Machiavelli the author has, in short, assimilated the lesson imparted by the allegorical Sofronia. Whereas aggressive political actors (like Cesare Borgia in *The Prince*) succumb to fickle Fortune, Nature, and time, Machiavelli stakes his claim to fame on the benefit he confers with his literary work: in this sense *Clizia* is Machiavelli's testament, through which he takes his place among writers who will live on in their books: "mi transferisco in loro."

NOTES

1. Niccolò Machiavelli, *Tutte le opere*, ed. Mario Martelli (Florence: Sansoni, 1971), p. 1224; *Machiavelli and His Friends: Their Personal Correspondence*, trans. James B. Atkinson and David Sices (DeKalb, Ill.: Northern Illinois University Press, 1996), pp. 369–71.
2. Giorgio Padoan, *L'avventura della commedia rinascimentale* (Padua: Piccin Nuova Libraria, 1996), pp. 32, 156 for dates of productions and editions.
3. Paolo Giovio, *Gli elogi degli uomini illustri: letterati, artisti, uomini d'arme*, ed. R. Meregazzi (Rome: Istituto Poligrafico dello Stato, 1972), pp. 111–12.
4. Filippo Grazzini, "Teatralità indiretta di Machiavelli: le *Lettere* e la novella di *Belfagor*," in Gennaro Barbarisi and Anna Maria Cabrini, eds., *Il teatro di Machiavelli* (Milan: Cisalpino, Istituto Editoriale Universitario, 2005), pp. 67–98 (67, note 1).

5. Anna Maria Cabrini, "Fra' Timoteo," in *Teatro di Machiavelli*, pp. 291–307 (305–7); Nerida Newbigin, ed., *Nuovo corpus di Sacre Rappresentazioni fiorentine del Quattrocento* (Bologna: Commissione per i Testi di Lingua, 1983), pp. 83–4.

6. Pasquale Stoppelli, *La Mandragola: storia e filologia (con l'edizione critica del testo secondo il Laurenziano Redi 129)* (Rome: Bulzoni, 2005), pp. 25–41.

7. Sergio Bertelli and Franco Gaeta, "Noterelle machiavelliane: un codice di Lucrezio e di Terenzio," *Rivista storica italiana* 73 (1961): 544–53.

8. Francesco Bausi, "Machiavelli e la commedia fiorentina del primo Cinquecento," in *Teatro di Machiavelli*, pp. 1–20, (4–7); Ezio Raimondi, *Politica e commedia: il centauro disarmato* (Bologna: Il Mulino, 1998), pp. 82–4, 111.

9. *Opere*, pp. 1003–4.

10. Jean-Jacques Marchand, "Teatralità nel primo Machiavelli. Il dispaccio ai Dieci di Balìa del 28 agosto 1506," in *Teatro di Machiavelli*, pp. 45–65.

11. *Opere*, p. 947.

12. "Descrizione del modo tenuto dal duca Valentino nello ammazzare Vitellozzo Vitelli, Oliverotto da Fermo ..." in *Opere*, pp. 8–11.

13. Luigina Stefani, "Coordinate orizzontali nel teatro comico del primo Cinquecento," *Belfagor* 36 (1981): 275–97.

14. Giorgio Bárberi Squarotti, *La forma tragica del "Principe" e altri saggi sul Machiavelli* (Florence: Olschki, 1966), pp. 103–280.

15. *Opere*, pp. 919–23.

16. Letters in *Opere*, pp. 1155, 1140, 1203–4, 1112, 1165–8; *Correspondence*, pp. 257–60, 236–8, 336–7, 190–1, 274–8.

17. *Opere*, pp. 1158–60; *Correspondence*, pp. 262–5.

18. John M. Najemy, "Machiavelli and Geta: Men of Letters," in *Machiavelli and the Discourse of Literature*, ed. Albert Russell Ascoli and Victoria Kahn (Ithaca, N.Y.: Cornell University Press, 1993), pp. 53–79.

19. *Cf.* Timoteo's similar enumeration to Lucrezia; *Mandragola* 3.11.

20. On the early editions: Stoppelli, *Mandragola: storia e filologia*, pp. 145–65.

21. See Giovanni Aquilecchia, "La favola *Mandragola* si chiama," in Aquilecchia, *Schede di italianistica* (Turin: Einaudi, 1976), pp. 97–126.

22. Ronald L. Martinez, "The Pharmacy of Machiavelli: Roman Lucretia in *Mandragola*," *Renaissance Drama* 14 (1983): 1–43; Hanna F. Pitkin, *Fortune is a Woman: Gender and Politics in the Thought of Niccolò Machiavelli* (Berkeley: University of California Press, 1984), pp. 115–31.

23. On the *Historia*, see Carlo Dionisotti, "Appunti sulla *Mandragola*," *Belfagor* 39 (1984): 621–44 (626). On Augustine: Gennaro Sasso, "Sul nome 'Lucrezia'," in *Machiavelli e gli antichi e altri saggi*, 4 vols. (Milan and Naples: Ricciardi, 1987–1997), 3:140–50.

24. Jane Tylus, "Theater's Social Uses: Machiavelli's *Mandragola* and the Spectacle of Infamy," *Renaissance Quarterly* 53 (2000): 656–86.

25. On military imagery: Martinez, "Pharmacy," pp. 12–13; for the passage in Terence: Stoppelli, *Mandragola: storia e filologia*, p. 76.

26. Anna Maria Cabrini, "Fra' Timoteo," in *Teatro di Machiavelli*, pp. 291–307; Daria Perocco, "Il rito finale della *Mandragola*," *Lettere italiane* 25 (1973): 531–7.

27. On Nicia: Raimondi, *Politica e commedia*, pp. 74–7; Claudio Vela, "La doppia malizia della *Mandragola*," in *Teatro di Machiavelli*, pp. 269–90 (275–6).

28. Dionisotti, "Appunti," discusses Russo's study of 1939.
29. Theodore A. Sumberg, "*Mandragola*: An Interpretation," in *Journal of Politics* 23 (1961): 320–40; Alessandro Parronchi, "La prima rappresentazione della *Mandragola*. Il modello per l'apparato – l'allegoria," *La bibliofilia* 66 (1962): 37–86; updated in Giorgio Inglese, "Contributo al testo critico della *Mandragola*," in *Annali dell'Istituto Italiano di Studi Storici* 6 (1979–80, but actually 1983): 129–73, esp. 131–2; and by Antonio Sorella, *Magia, lingua e commedia nel Machiavelli* (Florence: Olschki, 1990), pp. 9–99.
30. Bausi, "Machiavelli e la commedia fiorentina del primo Cinquecento," in *Teatro di Machiavelli*, pp. 1–20.
31. Martinez, "Pharmacy," pp. 7–9; on the *cassoni*: Cristelle Baskins, *Cassone Painting, Humanism, and Gender in Early Modern Italy* (Cambridge University Press, 1998), pp. 128–59.
32. *Opere*, p. 1225; *Correspondence*, pp. 372–3. The performance never took place.
33. Padoan, *L'Avventura*, pp. 33–9, one of the best discussions of the play.
34. Livy, *Ab urbe condita*, preface and 1.57–9; Martinez, "Pharmacy," pp. 10–12.
35. Readings of *Clizia*: Luigi Vanossi, *Lingue e strutture del teatro italiano del Rinascimento* (Padua: Liviana, 1970), pp. 57–108; Raimondi, *Politica e commedia*, pp. 84–97; Giulio Ferroni, '*Mutazione*' e '*Riscontro*' nel teatro di Machiavelli e altri saggi sulla commedia del Cinquecento (Rome: Il Bulzoni, 1972), pp. 19–137 (120–37); Giorgio Padoan, "Il tramonto di Machiavelli," *Lettere italiane* 33 (1981): 457–81; Ronald L. Martinez, "Benefit of Absence: Machiavellian Valediction in *Clizia*," in Ascoli and Kahn, eds., *Machiavelli and the Discourse of Literature*, pp. 117–44.
36. Dionisotti, "Appunti," pp. 635–6; for the association with the letter, see Raimondi, *Politica e commedia*, pp. 88–9, and Ferroni, '*Mutazione*,' pp. 110–11.

FURTHER READING

Andrews, Richard. *Scripts and Scenarios: The Performance of Comedy in Renaissance Italy*. Cambridge University Press, 1993.
Bernard, John. "Writing and the Paradox of the Self: Machiavelli's Literary Vocation," *Renaissance Quarterly* 59 (2006): 59–89.
Bottoni, Luciano. *La messinscena del Rinascimento*, vol. 2,: *Il segreto del diavolo e la Mandragola*. Milan, FrancoAngeli, 2006.
Brand, Peter. "Machiavelli and Florence," in *A History of Italian Theatre*, ed. Joseph Farrell and Paolo Puppa. Cambridge University Press, 2006, pp. 51–7.
Clubb, Louise George. *Italian Drama in Shakespeare's Time*. New Haven, Conn., Yale University Press, 1989.
   "Italian Renaissance Theater," in *The Oxford Illustrated History of Theatre*, ed. John Russell Brown. Oxford University Press, 1995, pp. 107–41.
Cope, Jackson. *Secret Sharers in Italian Comedy: from Machiavelli to Goldoni*. Durham, N.C., Duke University Press, 1996.
Faulkner, Robert. "*Clizia* and the Enlightenment of Private Life," in Sullivan, ed., *Comedy and Tragedy*, pp. 30–56.
Finucci, Valeria. *The Manly Masquerade: Masculinity, Paternity, and Castration in the Italian Renaissance*. Durham, N.C., Duke University Press, 2003.

Günsberg, Maggie. *Gender and the Italian Stage: From the Renaissance to the Present Day*. Cambridge University Press, 1997.

Mansfield, Harvey C. "The Cuckold in Machiavelli's *Mandragola*," in Sullivan, ed., *Comedy and Tragedy*, pp. 1–29.

Povoledo, Elena. "Origins and Aspects of Italian Scenography," in Nino Pirrotta and Elena Povoledo, *Music and Theatre from Poliziano to Monteverdi*, trans. Karen Eales. Cambridge University Press, 1981, pp. 281–373.

Ruggiero, Guido. "Machiavelli in Love: the Self-Presentation of an Aging Lover," in Ruggiero, *Machiavelli in Love: Sex, Self, and Society in the Italian Renaissance*. Baltimore, Johns Hopkins University Press, 2007, pp. 108–62.

Sullivan, Vickie B., ed. *The Comedy and Tragedy of Machiavelli*. New Haven, Conn., Yale University Press, 2000.

14

BARBARA SPACKMAN

Machiavelli and gender

When Gabriele D'Annunzio fantasized a new king of Rome in his 1894 novel, *The Virgins of the Rocks*, he supplied him with a Machiavellian motto, taken not from *The Prince*, as might be expected, but from the lesser known *Life of Castruccio Castracani of Lucca*: "I have taken her, not she me [*Io ho preso lei, non ella me*]." This pithy saying, in rhetorical terms a chiasmus, appears among the concluding list of witticisms purportedly drawn from the life of the exemplary Castruccio, who "in all fortunes acted the prince":

> Once there was a young woman with whom Castruccio associated intimately. For this, being reproached by a friend of his who said especially that it was bad for him to let himself be taken by a woman, "You are wrong," said Castruccio; "I have taken her, not she me."[1]

As the rhetorical figure that is a crossing of four terms which, through their crossing, are set up as belonging to two categories, the chiasmus is the figure par excellence of reversal and inversion. In Castruccio's case, the wittiness of his reply depends precisely upon such a reversal. The episode might encapsulate the relation of gendered subjects and their objects in Machiavelli's work as a whole and in the tradition of political thought that he inaugurated and to which D'Annunzio was heir. Male and masculine subjects of action are not to be themselves subjected by female or feminine actors, even as the very reversibility built into the rhetorical form of the chiasmus represents precisely this possibility. It is not by chance that the episode makes explicit the sexual nature of such subjection; virility in all its senses – gendered, generational, sexual, and as a set of character traits that includes boldness and self-discipline – is constituted and confirmed by displaying the ability to subject sexually a force figured as female. This force is not associated with the traditionally feminine quality of passivity, a trait reserved for "effeminacy" in Machiavelli's lexicon and associated, especially in the *Discourses*, with states that lack boldness, often as a result of the "idleness [*ozio*]" born of peacetime. Instead, this female force is frequently identified with *fortuna* and thus draws upon an already established tradition of gendered personification. As Hanna Pitkin and Wendy Brown have shown, Machiavelli adopts and adapts that tradition to his own purposes, demystifying it even as he deploys it. Indeed, Brown has claimed that it is precisely Machiavelli's "sharply gendered view of human beings and politics" that leads him "to subvert some of his own understandings about the political world."[2]

We begin, then, with a survey of Machiavelli's representations of fortune. In his deployment of fortune, he is perhaps at his most traditional in the tercets on "Fortune," at his most demystifying in the *Discourses*, and at his most rhetorically strategic in *The Prince*. In the tercets (of unknown date, but probably before 1512, given their dedication to Giovanbattista Soderini), Fortune is a two-faced, cruel, and violent goddess who inflicts harsh blows upon men, and whose palace contains as many turning wheels "as there are varied ways of climbing to those things which every living man strives to attain" (lines 61–3).[3] Allegorical characters abound: Laziness and Necessity turn her wheels, Luck and Chance sit above the gates of her palace, Opportunity frisks about, and Audacity and Youth make out best. This is not a goddess who can be conquered; if men were able to leap from wheel to wheel, they might always have good fortune, Machiavelli writes, but Fortune herself is the occult force that renders this impossible by endowing men with fixed characters. Even with this last glimpse of the possibility, held out only to be denied, of human intervention, this is a very medieval Fortune, whose power and unfathomable nature seem inextricably linked to her allegorical and gendered personification.

In the *Discourses*, Machiavelli reflects on the role of fortune stripped of allegorical dress and gendered only grammatically. Here there are no palaces and no turning wheels; bad fortune appears as the result of men's short-sightedness, their enthrallment to their own ambitions, their inability to fit their actions to the times. Good fortune, instead, can be made. For example, in discussing Numa Pompilius' success in introducing laws to ancient Rome (1.11), Machiavelli praises religion as instrumental in facilitating the establishment of laws: "Because religion caused good laws; good laws make good fortune; and from good fortune came the happy results of the city's endeavors." This is Machiavelli at his most demystifying and secular; Numa, after all, is not portrayed as a believer, but rather as a shrewd leader who "pretended he was intimate with a nymph who advised him," out of fear "that his own authority would not be enough." Such instrumentalization is not limited to Roman gods, in whom Machiavelli's readers can be supposed not to believe, but is extended to the Christian God as well. Machiavelli notes that the Florentines themselves had been persuaded that Savonarola spoke with God, although he remains agnostic on the question of "whether it was true or not, because so great a man ought to be spoken of with reverence."[4] Here it seems that gods are fictions that can be manipulated to men's ends, not divine beings who dictate human affairs. And the same is true of the goddess Fortune, downgraded to a common noun and shown to be the result of good laws instituted by shrewd leaders. Similarly, Machiavelli's comparison of the fates of Hannibal and Scipio in *Discourses* 3.21 suggests that fortune is of one's own making, indeed that *virtù* is the only actor on the stage of political life. Machiavelli's *virtù* is a densely weighted term that departs from Christian virtue to encompass a range of qualities from boldness and decisiveness to shrewdness and foresight. Hannibal and Scipio adopted opposite methods, the former employing cruelty and violence, the latter kindness and compassion, yet they produced the same effects, Scipio in Spain and Hannibal in Italy. "It therefore matters little which of these two roads a general travels, if only he is an able man [*uomo virtuoso*] and his ability [*virtù*] gives him renown among the people."[5] Fortune makes no appearance in this example, and *virtù* need not tangle with her in order to achieve its goals.

In Machiavelli's 1506 letter to Giovanbattista Soderini, in which he had anticipated the comparison of Scipio and Hannibal in the *Discourses*, he offers what one might call a Nietzschean genealogy of the allegorical figure of Fortune as little more than the reification of man's inadequate grasp of his historical circumstances:

> And truly, anyone wise enough to adapt to and understand the times and the pattern of events would always have good fortune or would always keep himself from bad fortune; and it would come to be true that the wise man could control [*comandassi*] the stars and the Fates. But such wise men do not exist: in the first place, men are shortsighted; in the second place, they are unable to master [*comandare*] their own natures; thus it follows that Fortune is fickle, controlling [*comanda*] men and keeping them under her yoke.[6]

It is a lack in men that causes Fortune to appear as an autonomous, commanding force personified as a goddess; the English translation enacts this transformation by promoting a lower case "fortune" in the first sentence to a capitalized "Fortune" in the second. Command or be commanded; the binary logic of the argument is not, in the first instance, modeled on a gendered binary. Rather, in an economy that Freud will be the first to explicate, male lack, here a lack of foresight and adaptability in response to events, is replaced and concealed by the invocation of an overwhelming female force and plenitude.

In chapter 25 of *The Prince*, as in the tercets on "Fortune," Fortune appears in personified form as an autonomous force that can hold men in her power. Machiavelli here deploys the very figuration of Fortune that he will demystify in the *Discourses* and introduces the most infamous of all Machiavellian metaphors: "Fortune is a woman" to be beaten, a friend to young men. This, the second of two metaphors for fortune in chapter 25, allows Machiavelli to answer the question of whether it is better for a prince to be "impetuous" or "cautious," with Pope Julius II offered as the example of a successful prince who "proceeded impetuously in all his affairs."

The first metaphor is that of raging, angry ("s'adirano") rivers that threaten to flood any terrain where precautions have not been taken, and especially Italy, figured as "a plain without dykes or embankments." Here too, however, foresight is possible:

> Yet though such it is, we need not therefore conclude that when the weather is quiet, men cannot take precautions with both embankments and dykes, so that when the waters rise, either they go off by a canal or their fury is neither so wild nor so damaging [*l'impeto loro non sarebbe né sì licenzioso né sì dannoso*]. The same things happen about Fortune.[7]

Ruinous rivers are here personified without being explicitly gendered (although grammatically "river" is masculine and overruns an Italy gendered as feminine); they are capable of anger and are endowed with violent force: "l'impeto," here translated as "fury," might, more in keeping with Machiavelli's use of the term elsewhere in the text, be rendered as "violence." Fortune-as-river thus shares a property with Pope Julius: the violent force of the former is the adversary of the violent force of the latter. Moreover, the violence of fortune-as-river is characterized as both "dannoso" and, literally, "licentious [*licenzioso*]": unruly, exceeding bounds or norms, but also, already in sixteenth-century Italian, exceeding the norms of modesty in sexual matters. The latter meaning would lie dormant, as it seems to elsewhere in Machiavelli's work (in the *Discourses*, for example, the people are twice described as "licenzioso" when given over to uprisings, hence exceeding the proper bounds of their freedoms), were it not for the second metaphor of fortune-as-woman, which appears when Machiavelli advises the prince on whether it is better to be cautious or impetuous:

> As for me, I believe this: it is better to be impetuous [*impetuoso*] than cautious [*respettivo*], because Fortune is a woman and it is necessary, in order to keep her under, to cuff and maul her. She more often lets herself be overcome by men using such methods than by those who proceed coldly; therefore always, like a woman, she is the friend of young men, because they are less cautious, more spirited, and with more boldness master her [*la comandano*].[8]

This is the moment in *The Prince* when the Latin *vir*, man, behind the Italian *virtù* steps forth most virulently, and the relation between men and their

circumstances is most starkly gendered and sexualized. Repeatedly characterized by his readers as a rape, and by Machiavelli as a beating in which the
victim is not unwilling, the scene counts as one of the most dramatic in *The
Prince*, and not surprisingly has commanded the attention of scholars.

Hanna Pitkin has claimed that Machiavelli was the first to use the personification of fortune as female "as a way of suggesting the sexual conquest of
fortune" and that he thereby introduced "into the realm of politics and
history concerns about manliness, effeminacy, and sexual prowess." Such a
personification has consequences for the way men's relations to their times
and circumstances are understood. No longer a goddess to whom they might
relate through prayer or supplication, fortune must now be dealt with
through "courtship, manipulation, and bold challenge," not to mention a
good beating. Pitkin's analysis also suggests an interpretation of the strategic
deployment, particularly in *The Prince*, of fortune's personification as woman
as a challenge to the masculinity of its readers, perhaps specifically Lorenzo
de' Medici; Fortune "is there for the taking – if you're man enough."[9] If
personifying fortune as a woman "redeems the possibility of action by relocating it in an interpersonal context," as Victoria Kahn has written,[10] the
sexualization of the figure enacts a homosocial dare, a taunt calling for a
proof of masculinity among heterosexual men and creating a necessity out of
what Pitkin argues is a fundamental ambivalence about masculinity in
Machiavelli's work, in particular about the degree to which masculinity
must prove itself independent of the feminine. For Pitkin, this ambivalence
pervades Machiavelli's *oeuvre* and is inextricable from a concern with autonomy: of states, of armies, of men as solitary founders, of men as manly.

John Freccero sees the specific nature of this challenge differently, arguing
that the image of the rape of Fortune challenges not so much relations of
gender as those of class. For Freccero, the point of the metaphor would be that
Fortune is said to be a *donna*, a courtly lady, not merely a *femmina*, female of
the species, and that the assault on her is consequently a figure for an assault
on class structure and the "prerogatives of the males to whom she belongs."[11]
From lady to be worshipped from afar, she is transformed into an object to be
possessed through physical violence. To this image of fortune Freccero juxta-
poses the figure of Caterina Sforza in *Discourses* 3.6, a Medusan and hence
threatening figure of autonomous sexuality and generativity (about whom
more below).

What links Pitkin's and Freccero's readings, despite this difference of view,
then, is the importance of autonomy, and in the relation between the two
metaphors of chapter 25 we might locate another instance of the concern with
autonomy. Why, after all, should Machiavelli offer two such different metaphors in close proximity? Anthony Parel has argued that the river metaphor

refers to the universal, to the relation of a state or polity to fortune, whereas the metaphor of fortune-as-woman applies to individuals.[12] But what does their relation tell us about either of them singly? The replacement of the river metaphor by that of fortune-as-woman not only redeems the possibility of action in the moment (a rushing river, after all, cannot be grabbed and beaten); it not only explicitly genders and sexualizes the nature of that action (requiring a display of heterosexual manliness not evident in the building of dykes); it also activates an undercurrent in the river metaphor in order to effect, rhetorically, an exchange of properties along the lines of the reversibility of a chiasmus: if the river is unruly and, in overflowing its limits, licentious, here it is the impetuosity of men that is unruly and oversteps the bounds of modesty, licentious in a fully sexualized sense. The river possesses a certain autonomy, and the substitution of the rape for the river in effect wrests that autonomy from fortune and attributes it to the man who would conquer. If fortune-as-river had threatened to overtake him, he now overtakes her. The underlying logic is that of the episode of Castruccio Castracani, in which the possibility of a woman taking a man is reversed in the context of a homosocial exchange. In the *Life of Castruccio*, the exchange is constituted by gossip about sex between two men; in *The Prince*, we might venture that the scene of the rape of fortune constitutes an equivalent exchange between Machiavelli and his intended addressee, providing both with an opportunity for masculine display.

As for why Pope Julius is offered as the example of the impetuous leader, given that he was already an old man at the time, this could be yet another element in the taunting dare, as if to say not only "take her if you're man enough," but also "look, even an old man can take her!" Insofar as Machiavelli understands fortune to be the consequence of men's inability to change their characters with the times, we can describe this dare as a strategic deployment of an understanding he elsewhere demystifies, just as his invocation of God at the end of *The Prince* is a strategy to incite to action. Yet, at the same time, to the extent that Machiavelli's own masculinity is implicated in this exchange, we cannot suppose him to be fully immune to its appeal. Indeed, given that *virtù* is locked into dialectical relation to fortune – *virtù* being inseparable from manliness and its supposed qualities, and manliness thus relying for its very definition on an opposition to women and their supposed qualities – we might say that Machiavelli has no ideological choice but to redeploy the very image of fortune he knows to be a myth.

The question of gendered display and its relation to mythmaking is, in fact, the thread we may follow through Machiavelli's other works, turning first to Caterina Sforza, one of the few historical women to appear in his political writings. The anecdote is recounted in *Discourses* 3.6 and again in the

Florentine Histories 8.34, and it has generated a rich intertextual history of its own. Antonio Gramsci, for example, interpreted Caterina Sforza as the emblem of the irruption of the proletariat into history, and D'Annunzio adopted her as a figure for political virility during his 1919–20 occupation of Fiume.[13] In the *Discourses*, the episode is offered as an example of the danger a conspirator may face after the deed is done if someone is left to avenge the death of a prince:

> In Forlì [in 1488] conspirators killed Count Girolamo [Riario] their ruler and captured his wife and small children. These conspirators knew they were not secure if they were not masters of the fortress, but the castellan was unwilling to surrender it. Then Madonna Caterina (for so the Countess was called) promised that if the conspirators would let her enter the fortress, she would have it surrendered to them; they might keep her children as hostages. With that promise, they let her enter. As soon as she was inside, she reproached them from the wall with the death of her husband, threatening them with every kind of revenge. And to show that she did not care about her children, she uncovered to them her genital members [*le membra genitali*], saying she still had means for reproducing more children.[14]

Machiavelli's version is one of several retellings, but, as Julia Hairston has shown in her comparative analysis of a number of contemporary vernacular accounts, he adds to the story the important gesture of Caterina's lifting of her skirts, drawing upon the topos of *anasyrmos*, the lifting of garments by women to reveal the lower half of the body. In Greek authors, including Plutarch and Herodotus, the gesture appears in stories of war, made by women to reproach men for leaving the battlefield. Whatever the specific meaning (for example, that men are to be shamed for not observing proper gender roles), it was understood to be terrifying in its effect, an apotropaic act meant to avert evil. Freccero argues that Caterina's action evokes the mythical Medusa and thus provides an explanation for the linguistic oddity of Machiavelli's use of "genital members" to refer to a woman: "The equivalent Latin phrase usually describes only the male sex. In written Italian before Machiavelli, there seems to have been only one recorded usage that applied to females."[15] According to Hairston, Machiavelli's version is the only one to suggest that the gesture's meaning was to demonstrate that she did not care about her children.[16]

Taken together, these details re-gender Caterina Sforza as masculine and represent her as a virago. As a masculine display, it might also be said to conquer the feminine; her enemies, after all, think they have conquered her because she is a mother and they hold her children hostage, but her reply suggests that she has conquered maternal love and exceeded the gendered and ultimately Aristotelian opposition between virile courage and maternal love. (Yet other versions specify that Caterina boldly claimed to have the "mold," the "form," or, in D'Annunzio's retelling, the "mint" with which to reproduce, thus endowing her with the "form" that, according to Aristotle, the male supplies in reproduction while the female supplies the matter, or matrix. It thus further underscores the extent to which the episode serves as a site for re-gendering several sets of traditional paradigms.) Hairston argues that, in omitting the apparent historical fact that Caterina, according to other accounts, announced that she was pregnant and hence carried within her a male heir who could be an avenger, Machiavelli "takes a perspicacious political move on Sforza's part and turns it into an empty, histrionic gesture."[17] Yet if we read it as political virility in which a masculine display, even by a female actor, gains currency through the subjugation of a female force, in this case maternal love, it can then appear to be another example of the gendered theatricality of Machiavelli's politics. From this vantage point, Caterina displays a political virility that would befit a Machiavellian prince: audacity, boldness, and a rendering public of what should remain private. As Gramsci suggested and Freccero has also noted, Machiavelli has here forged a political myth, one that, we would add, relies upon a paradoxically female virility.

Such audacious female virility is unique to Caterina Sforza in Machiavelli's work, as a glance at what might be considered a countertext will confirm. The text in question is drawn from Machiavelli's letters, where, as Guido Ruggiero has recently argued, Machiavelli puts on a "public performance of self" in which the pursuit of sexual pleasure plays a not inconsiderable role.[18] In analyzing Machiavelli's correspondence with Francesco Vettori in 1513–15, precisely when the unemployed Machiavelli composed *The Prince*, Ruggiero sees Machiavelli presenting himself not as the young man conjured as the commander of fortune, but as the aging lover and passive servant of love. But the letter that interests us here is the famous 1509 letter to Luigi Guicciardini, in which Machiavelli recounts his visit to a laundress whose merchandise includes a "shirt" she invites him to try on for size. The shirt turns out to be another woman, and, after satisfying his lust with her, Machiavelli wants to see the "merchandise." Holding a lamp to her face, he finds her so ugly, her breath so stinking, that he vomits on her, and in this way "repaid her in kind." The passage is worth citing in its entirety:

> Ugh! I nearly dropped dead on the spot, that woman was so ugly. The first thing I noticed about her was a tuft of hair, part white, part black – in other words, sort of whitish; although the crown of her head was bald (thanks to the baldness one could make out a few lice promenading about), still a few, thin wisps of hair

came down to her brow with their ends. In the center of her tiny, wrinkled head she had a fiery scar that made her seem as if she had been branded at the marketplace; at the end of each eyebrow toward her eyes there was a nosegay of nits; one eye looked up, the other down – and one was larger than the other; her tear ducts were full of rheum and she had no eyelashes. She had a turned-up nose stuck low down on her head and one of her nostrils was sliced open and full of snot. Her mouth resembled Lorenzo de' Medici's, but it was twisted to one side, and from that side drool was oozing, because, since she was toothless, she could not hold back her saliva. Her upper lip sported a longish but skimpy moustache. She had a long, pointy chin that twisted upward a bit; a slightly hairy dewlap dangled down to her Adam's apple. As I stood there absolutely bewildered and stupefied staring at this monster, she became aware of it and tried to say, "What's the matter, sir?" but she could not get it out because she stuttered. As soon as she opened her mouth, she exuded such a stench on her breath that my eyes and nose – twin portals to the most delicate of the senses – felt assaulted by this stench and my stomach became so indignant that it was unable to tolerate this outrage; it started to rebel, then it did rebel – so that I threw up all over her. Having thus repaid her in kind, I departed.[19]

Virilization is here part of uglification: the old woman has whiskers, a long moustache, an apparently prominent Adam's apple, and a mouth like Lorenzo de' Medici's; she is, in Juliana Schiesari's words, a "degraded phantasm of phallic femininity."[20] As Schiesari notes, critics have for the most part been either embarrassed by, or dismissive of, this vulgar display, loath to see in it connections to Machiavelli's *oeuvre* more generally, and quick to reduce it to a tall tale spun from his own frequenting of prostitutes.

Yet on display here is not only vulgarity, but literary virtuosity. Machiavelli's description is an especially elaborate version of the topos of the enchantress-turned-hag, the commonplace in which a beautiful young woman is revealed to be an ugly, toothless old hag. Frequently found in early modern literary texts, from Dante to Shakespeare, Ariosto to Tasso, the topos variously serves as a figure for the relation between appearance and essence, between rhetoric and plain speech, between falsehood and truth. Dante had already provided the Italian literary tradition with the "femmina balba" of *Purgatorio* 19.1–33; the pilgrim dreams of a stuttering woman with eyes asquint who is, in a second moment, transformed into a sweet siren, only to have her belly revealed, whence issues a stench so powerful it awakens the dreamer. The stuttering and stinking breath in Machiavelli's description cannot but recall the Dantean "femmina balba," and indeed they awaken him from his lustful state. At stake, then, is a literary competition, and the excessiveness of Machiavelli's description might be understood as a kind of literary one-upmanship.

Moreover, as Schiesari has shown, there is yet another competition at play; the episode is framed not only as a competitive exchange between men, but as an illustration of the workings of fortune:

> Hell's bells, Luigi, see how Fortune hands out to mankind different results under similar circumstances. Why, you had hardly finished fucking [*fottuto*] her before you wanted another fuck [*fotterla*], and you want to take another turn at it [*ne volete un'altra presa*]. But, as for me, why, I had been here three days, going blind for lack of the marriage bed, when I came upon an old woman who launders my shirts.[21]

Like a mock inversion of the comparison of Hannibal and Scipio, Guicciardini and Machiavelli come to different ends through the same means; if Luigi managed to screw Fortune, and even take her a second time, Niccolò ends up being taken in. Schiesari has argued that this highly constructed narrative condenses anxieties about both sexual and political economies. Indeed, at least part of the truth unveiled in Machiavelli's description is, she argues, that the hag is a figure for fortune: her baldness recalls the tradition, also noted by Pitkin, of representing the associated figure of Opportunity (*Occasione*) with a bald spot on the back of her head, the logic being that you cannot grab her after she has passed you by. The sexual encounter would thus be a grotesque parody of the rape of Fortune by *virtù*. (That the truth revealed is also that the hag is, in some figural sense, Lorenzo de' Medici, makes her proleptically – for the modern reader – a figure for Machiavelli's later political misfortune at the hands of the Medici, although the Lorenzo referred to in the letter is the elder Lorenzo, the "Magnificent," not the Lorenzo to whom Machiavelli dedicated *The Prince*.)

The doubling of the female figures – laundress and "shirt," procuress and prostitute – complicates the picture by introducing an economy in which women are both subjects and objects of exchange. The letter ends with the announcement that Machiavelli plans to do some "business" of his own ("fare qualche trafficuzo") upon his return to Florence. Although he has lost all sexual desire as a result of his encounter, he still has some small change left over to invest. Somewhat enigmatically, he writes of a desire to set up a chicken business ("fare un pollaiolo") and find himself a "go-between" ("uno maruffino") to oversee it. Given the context of the letter, this is clearly a substitution of a male-governed economy for a female-governed one, a reversal of fortunes in more senses than one. One may speculate as to what kind of henhouse might need a go-between to oversee it.

Interpreted by some as a figure for Machiavelli himself, Ligurio, a former go-between, oversees the plot of Machiavelli's 1518 comedy, *Mandragola*, which evokes yet another gendered political myth. Set in Florence in 1504,

Mandragola is an original play that draws upon classical precedents even as it subjects recognizably Machiavellian themes to carnivalesque inversions. Competing for access to, and control over, the body of virtuous Lucrezia are a young man, Callimaco, and a foolish old man, her husband, Nicia. Ligurio hatches a plot that involves a cast of corrupt characters in a conspiracy to overcome the chaste Lucrezia, and ultimately to satisfy both Callimaco's sexual desire and Nicia's reproductive desire. The character Lucrezia evokes Roman Lucretia, whose rape was mythologized by ancient Roman writers and Florentine humanists alike as the origin of the Roman republic. For our purposes, it is important to note that, like Caterina Sforza, Roman Lucretia belonged to a lineage of "virile" women; while her chastity made her an exemplar of womanly and wifely virtue, her suicide was a manifestation of "virile" courage. Machiavelli's Lucrezia is of course no suicide; she cedes instead to the corrupt community's machinations and appears "altered [*alterata*]" (5.5) after a night with the victorious Callimaco. For some readers, this alteration amounts to a redefinition of Lucrezia by male desire, a failure of ancient *virtù* as personified by Roman Lucretia. But for others Lucrezia is an embodiment of Machiavellian *virtù* because she adapts herself when circumstances demand it and demonstrates an ability to change her nature.[22] The "virility" of the self-sacrificing Roman Lucretia is thus transformed and replaced by the Machiavellian *virtù* of Florentine Lucrezia.

Machiavelli's last work, the comedy *Clizia*, first performed in 1525, offers itself as a final meditation on the conflict between the gendered forces of *virtù* and *fortuna*. If Caterina Sforza's *anasyrmos* acquired its meaning on the stage of politics as a dramatization of the realm of appearances, in *Clizia* Machiavelli turns to the literal stage to put on display a senescent virility. Based on Plautus' *Casina*, the plot of *Clizia* features an old man, Nicomaco, in love with his adopted daughter, Clizia, who is also desired by his son, Cleandro. Nicomaco plots to marry Clizia to his servant, Pirro, with the aim of substituting himself for his proxy in the marriage bed; in a counterplot meant to foil the old man, his wife, Sofronia, schemes to marry Clizia to another servant, Eustachio. Meanwhile, Cleandro encourages his mother's plotting, if only as a way to save Clizia from his father. When Pirro wins a drawing of lots, Nicomaco triumphs over the son and prepares himself for the wedding night. He has won the oedipal rivalry, it would seem, and Cleandro laments (*Clizia* 4.1), "Oh Fortune, since you are a woman, you usually are the mistress of young men: but this time you were the old man's mistress!"[23] The echo of *The Prince* is surely ironic, for neither aged father nor feckless son can be said to embody Machiavellian *virtù*.

In fact, the father–son rivalry is not the main focus of the play; it is upstaged and displaced by the conflict between Nicomaco and his wife, Sofronia.

"Nicomaco" plays on Niccolò Machiavelli's name, and critics have seen in the play autobiographical references to his own amorous passion late in life. Less noted is the fact that Nicomaco also shares features with the prostitute-hag and with Caterina Sforza; like the hag, he is "drooling, bleary-eyed, and toothless [*bavoso, cisposo, e sanza denti*]" (4.4) and has a "foul-smelling mouth [*fetida bocca*]"; his "stinking members [*puzzolente membra*]" (4.1) condense the stench of the hag and Caterina's "genital members." Senescent virility is parodied as degraded femininity and conquered by Sofronia who, knowing that her husband is plotting to seduce Clizia by first marrying her off to his servant, and then substituting himself for his proxy, has a plot of her own. Rather than substitute male for male, master for servant, she substitutes male for female in the marriage bed. Nicomaco spends the night not with Clizia, but with a male servant disguised as a woman; his humiliation is complete, and Sofronia emerges as she who governs: "he wants me to run [*ch'io governi*] everything my way [*a mio senno*] from now on" (5.4).

Clizia offers a new figure, original to Machiavelli, for this gendered conflict between husband and wife, between licentious male desire and an order, instituted by an older female character, that blocks that desire. When Nicomaco orders his wife to arrange the wedding and produce the ever-absent Clizia, Sofronia attempts to stall him by suggesting that Clizia might have her menstrual period: "I'm afraid she may have her female monthlies [*Io dubito che la non abbia l'ordinario delle donne*]," to which Nicomaco replies: "Let her adopt the extraordinary measures of men! [*Adoperi lo straordinario delli uomini!*]" (3.7). "Ordinario" and "straordinario" are paired terms no less important than *virtù* and *fortuna* in Machiavelli's political language. He commonly uses *ordini* and *ordinario* to refer to the lawful institutions of states; *straordinario*, literally "outside the *ordini*," refers instead to extreme measures, often violent ones, whose relation to the *ordini* is generally more pernicious than salutary. In the *Florentine Histories*, "straordinario" characterizes the methods adopted by Cosimo de' Medici to seize power in Florence. Although "extraordinary methods" are sometimes necessary to found or restore a republic and thus not always censurable (as in *Discourses* 1.9), apart from such exceptional situations they corrupt or destroy republics. As Machiavelli says in *Discourses* 1.7, when excessively powerful citizens are opposed "ordinariamente," or "per l'ordinario," only they suffer harm; when it is done "per lo straordinario," the result harms many others as well.

In *Clizia* the "straordinario delli uomini," embodied in the aged, stinking, toothless Nicomaco, is a corruption of the proper order of generation and gender. Placed within the broader context of Machiavelli's thought, Nicomaco also represents a corruption of political order. Indeed, Ronald

Martinez argues that the female order allegorized by Sofronia etymologically recalls the temperance and self-restraint of the Greek virtue of *sophrosyne* and thematically, through reference to women's menstrual cycle ("l'ordinario"), evokes the topos of *anakyklosis*, the cyclicality of time and nature. In this reading, the "straordinario" of Nicomaco is the target of the play's critique of aggressive male *virtù*. Machiavelli the author aligns himself with Sofronia in a "tempering" of his own "literary ethos and project."[24] Just as Sofronia substitutes male for female in the marriage bed, so Machiavelli substitutes female for male as governor and institutor of order. The fact that Sofronia addresses the audience directly in her final words, as Albert Ascoli has noted, also suggests that she has assumed the male authorial voice of the prologue.[25] The gender binary that had dominated Machiavelli's writing is skewed in this final work, the oppositional structure that it figured no longer firmly in place.

An additional example comes from the final act (5.2) when Nicomaco recounts to Damone his battle in bed with the servant Siro and reports that after the initial bout he thought it best to wait until morning, when Clizia might be more receptive. Damone agrees: "That is what you ought to have done from the start. If she didn't want you, you shouldn't have wanted her [*chi non voleva te, non voler lui*]!"[26] The translation gives us a perfectly symmetrical chiasmus that recalls and reverses the chiasmus with which we began ("I have taken her, not she me"), with the signal difference that in the translation "she" is the subject whose desire sets the figure in motion. Such a radical rewriting, however, is not supported by the original Italian ("Whoever didn't want you, don't want him"), which contains a linguistic trick that mimics the bed-trick, for no feminine pronoun appears in the phrase. The desiring male subject remains in place, but he no longer imposes his desires upon the world, upon a set of contingent circumstances gendered female.

It is all the more striking, then, that Sofronia's final words (5.6) oppose male to female nuptials in a teasingly ambiguous quip: "Let us go! And you, dear audience, can go on back home, because we shall not leave the house again until we have arranged this new wedding. And this time they will be female, and not male, nuptials, like those of Nicomaco [*si ordineranno le nuove nozze, le quali fieno femmine, e non maschie, come quelle di Nicomaco*]!"[27] It is clear what Sofronia means by "male nuptials" – Nicomaco's night with the servant Siro, orchestrated and "ordered" by her – but what is meant by "female nuptials" is more troublesome. To read it as a symmetrical reversal would imply a marriage between two women, a queer reading for which there is but a slight hint of textual support in Sofronia's earlier joking reference to the "miracle" of a nun impregnating another woman (2.3). Standard interpretations consequently take it to be an asymmetrical reversal signifying a marriage between a man and a woman. With this adjustment, it may allude to the unexpected arrival of Clizia's Neapolitan father, Ramondo, thanks to which, as Damone and Ramondo announce, Clizia acquires the class status necessary for Cleandro to marry her. But this obligatory reestablishment of the patriarchal order is accomplished through a deus ex machina whose artificiality is matched by Cleandro's invocation of Fortune (5.5); both come off as hackneyed at best. By contrast, in her last intervention (5.4) as a fully diegetic character, Sofronia had insisted that none of the men involved, including her son Cleandro, would have Clizia: "Neither you nor Pirro is going to have her. Nor you, Cleandro, because I want her to stay as she is [*io voglio che la stia così*]." Sofronia's last expressed desire contains yet another ambiguity, for "la" might refer to the state of things as much as to Clizia herself. Both would remain as they are, invulnerable to assault by male desire. At this point in the play, as at its conclusion, Clizia is safely sheltered in a convent; one wonders, then, whether Sofronia might still have her way, and whether the nuptials she plans might be the spiritual nuptials of a novice, marking entrance into a rather different womanly order, with different orders to take. However we interpret these ambiguities, it is telling that the play concludes by calling our attention to the interpretation of gendered references. The replacement of the relation of *virtù* and *fortuna*, once so central to Machiavelli's thought, by a new problematic embodied by Sofronia exposes the rigidity of the gendered binary itself.

In sum, throughout his life, and throughout the various genres of his work, Machiavelli saw relations of power and autonomy through often dramatically gendered lenses. In this respect, he belongs to a long tradition of Western thought for which gender is a primary means of representing relations of power and subordination. Machiavelli's innovation in this tradition may lie in the sexualization of men's relation to their circumstances, often embodied in the figure of Fortune, and in the importance given in particular to gendered and sexualized displays in the realm of politics. Displays of virility and manliness in relation to the subordination of a force represented as female or feminine are a defining feature of the gendered theatricality of Machiavelli's politics. As display, gender is understood to be an appearance produced through action, a doing rather more than a being. Machiavelli's conception of gender at its most radical might thus be said to be in keeping with the importance of appearance on the stage of politics in *The Prince*, and even to resonate with current understandings of gender as performance. At the same time, however, virile display often depends upon a reification of the gendered binary itself, and hence relies upon the reinforcement of traditional gendered roles. Only late in Machiavelli's life and thought does he begin to open the possibility of a new terrain in which those roles might be not only inverted, but displaced by a new order, intimated yet not defined in *Clizia*.

NOTES

1. Niccolò Machiavelli, *Tutte le opere*, ed. Mario Martelli (Florence: Sansoni, 1971), pp. 615–28 (627–8); trans. Allan Gilbert, *Machiavelli: The Chief Works and Others*, 3 vols. (Durham, N.C.: Duke University Press, 1965), 2:533–59 (556). Unless otherwise noted, English translations are Gilbert's.
2. Wendy Brown, "Renaissance Italy: Machiavelli," in *Feminist Interpretations of Niccolò Machiavelli*, ed. Maria J. Falco (University Park, Penn: Pennsylvania State University Press, 2004), pp. 117–71 (118).
3. *Opere*, p. 977; *Works*, 2:746.
4. *Works*, 1:225–6.
5. *Works*, 1:478.
6. *Machiavelli and His Friends: Their Personal Correspondence*, ed. and trans. James B. Atkinson and David Sices (DeKalb, Ill.: Northern Illinois University Press, 1996), p. 135; *Opere di Niccolò Machiavelli*, vol. 3, *Lettere*, ed. Franco Gaeta (Turin: UTET, 1984), p. 244.
7. *Works*, 1:90.
8. *Works*, 1:92.
9. Hanna Fenichel Pitkin, *Fortune Is a Woman: Gender and Politics in the Thought of Niccolò Machiavelli* (Berkeley: University of California Press, 1984), pp. 144, 292–3.
10. Victoria Kahn, *Machiavellian Rhetoric: From the Counter-Reformation to Milton* (Princeton University Press, 1994), p. 41.
11. John Freccero, "Medusa and the Madonna of Forlì: Political Sexuality in Machiavelli," in *Machiavelli and the Discourse of Literature*, eds. Albert Russell Ascoli and Victoria Kahn (Ithaca, N.Y.: Cornell University Press, 1993), p. 164.
12. Anthony J. Parel, *The Machiavellian Cosmos* (New Haven, Conn.: Yale University Press, 1992), pp. 68–70.
13. Barbara Spackman, *Fascist Virilities: Rhetoric, Ideology and Social Fantasy in Italy* (Minneapolis: University of Minnesota Press, 1996), pp. 19–24.
14. *Works*, 1:444.
15. Freccero, "Medusa and the Madonna of Forlì," pp. 175–6.
16. Julia L. Hairston, "Skirting the Issue: Machiavelli's Caterina Sforza," *Renaissance Quarterly* 53 (2000): 687–712.
17. *Ibid.*, p. 709.
18. Guido Ruggiero, *Machiavelli in Love: Sex, Self, and Society in the Italian Renaissance* (Baltimore: Johns Hopkins University Press, 2007), pp. 108–41 (108).
19. *Correspondence*, pp. 190–1; *Lettere*, pp. 321–3.
20. Juliana Schiesari, "Libidinal Economies: Machiavelli and Fortune's Rape," in *Desire in the Renaissance: Psychoanalysis and Literature*, ed. Valeria Finucci and Regina Schwartz (Princeton University Press, 1994), p. 177.
21. I have modified the translation by Atkinson and Sices.
22. Giulio Ferroni, "'Transformation' and 'Adaptation' in Machiavelli's *Mandragola*," in Ascoli and Kahn, eds., *Machiavelli and the Discourse of*

Literature, pp. 81–116; Melissa M. Matthes, *The Rape of Lucretia and the Founding of Republics* (University Park, Penn.: Pennsylvania State University Press, 2000), pp. 77–97.

23. Here and below, translations of passages from *Clizia*, slightly modified, are from *The Comedies of Machiavelli*, ed. and trans. David Sices and James B. Atkinson (Hanover, N.H.: University Press of New England, 1985).

24. Ronald L. Martinez, "Benefit of Absence: Machiavellian Valediction in *Clizia*," in Ascoli and Kahn, eds., *Machiavelli and the Discourse of Literature*, pp. 117–44 (120–1, 133–40).

25. Albert Russell Ascoli, "Pyrrhus' Rules: Playing with Power from Boccaccio to Machiavelli," *Modern Language Notes* 114 (1999): 54.

26. *Comedies of Machiavelli*, trans. Sices and Atkinson, pp. 380–1.

27. *Ibid.*, pp. 394–5 (translation of last sentence modified).

FURTHER READING

Carroll, Linda L. "Machiavelli's Veronese Prostitute: *Venetia Figurata?*" in *Gender Rhetorics: Postures of Dominance and Submission in History*, ed. Richard Trexler. Binghamton, Center for Medieval and Early Renaissance Studies, 1991, pp. 93–106.

Martinez, Ronald L. "The Pharmacy of Machiavelli: Roman Lucretia in *Mandragola*," *Renaissance Drama* 14 (1983): 1–43.

O'Brien, Mary. "The Root of the Mandrake: Machiavelli and Manliness," in *Feminist Interpretations of Niccolò Machiavelli*, ed. Maria J. Falco. University Park, Penn., Pennsylvania State University Press, 2004, pp. 173–95.

Pitkin, Hanna Fenichel. *Fortune Is a Woman: Gender and Politics in the Thought of Niccolò Machiavelli*. Berkeley, University of California Press, 1984.

Saxonhouse, Arlene W. "Comedy, Machiavelli's Letters, and His Imaginary Republics," in *The Comedy and Tragedy of Machiavelli: Essays on the Literary Works*, ed. Vickie B. Sullivan. New Haven, Conn., Yale University Press, 2000, pp. 57–77.

"Niccolò Machiavelli: Women as Men, Men as Women, and the Ambiguity of Sex," in Falco, *Feminist Interpretations*, pp. 93–116.

Tylus, Jane. "Theater and Its Social Uses: Machiavelli's *Mandragola* and the Spectacle of Infamy," *Renaissance Quarterly* 53 (2000): 656–86.

15

VICTORIA KAHN

Machiavelli's afterlife and reputation to the eighteenth century

In book 2, chapter 5, of the *Discourses*, Machiavelli argues that Christianity was unable to eradicate the glorious deeds of pagan antiquity because it continued to use the Latin language. If, instead, Christian writers "had been able to write in a new language, the other persecutions they carried on indicate that we should have no record of things past."[1] With this sardonic observation, Machiavelli signals his awareness that revolutions in political thought are first and foremost revolutions in language: transformations in the way we speak about politics can themselves produce a new understanding of political action. Machiavelli was not of course the first to write about politics in the vernacular. His innovation was instead to inaugurate an entirely new "discourse" about politics, one that eviscerated the reigning humanist pieties and recommended force and fraud to tyrants and republics alike.

Machiavelli boldly announces this innovation in both his major political works. In *The Prince*, he says he is the first to analyze the "verità effettuale" of politics; in the *Discourses* (book 1, preface) he claims to "enter upon a path not yet trodden by anyone" and to discover new "modes and orders." Although his bid for fame was not heard in his lifetime, it was remarkably prophetic of his afterlife and reputation. In Machiavelli's time, Aristotle was the most famous political thinker in the West; in our time, Machiavelli is.

Rhetoric and reception history

This chapter is an essay in what we moderns call reception history or the history of reading, an account not only of the formal aspects of a text but also of the material circumstances, including publishing history, that shape its reception. In Machiavelli's time, reception history was part of the discipline of rhetoric, which codified the forms of argument and devices of style available to writer and reader alike. To write was to employ these forms (often in new ways) and to read was to decode, imitate, and recycle them. As a discipline centered on the notion of decorum – the idea that the speaker should suit his words to the occasion – Renaissance rhetoric was implicitly historicist, attentive to the changing circumstances of speaker and audience. Implicit in the rhetorical tradition is the idea that reading has a history. At the same time, the humanist notion that writers should use their art to persuade to the good imposed, at least ideally, a constraint on such historical relativism.

As Renaissance readers already recognized, this tension between the ethics and history of reading is explicit in Machiavelli's political works. In *The Prince*, he famously recommended that the prince change his behavior to suit changing circumstances, but this endorsement of decorum included such immoral practices as breaking one's promises if keeping them would be detrimental. In the *Discourses*, Machiavelli showed the Roman republic making use of the same flexible practices, including the resort to force and fraud, in the interests of conquest and expansion. In both works, Machiavelli pressed the classical notions of decorum and imitation to their logical conclusion, in the process subverting the moralizing interpretation of rhetoric from within. In both works, he recommended the use of religion for purposes of persuasion and deception, to instill fear and obedience, thereby aggravating the conflict between antiquity and Christianity in the eyes of his readers. Thus, although it is often said that we need to distinguish between a writer's intentions and the reception of his work, such a distinction may be impossible in the case of Machiavelli. To the extent that Machiavelli self-consciously engages and reflects on the humanist rhetorical tradition, to the extent that he invites us to see that techniques of persuasion can be used for good or ill, republics or principalities, he could be said to anticipate his own reception, his own bifurcated place in the history of reading.

In one common account of this history, Machiavelli was read and misunderstood as the evil "Machiavel" in the sixteenth century, and only correctly understood as a defender of republicanism in the seventeenth century. Religious belief, so the argument runs, led to a simple-minded condemnation of Machiavelli as a rhetorician, atheist, and defender of tyranny, while the crisis of sovereignty in seventeenth-century England produced a new appreciation of Machiavelli's "republican" *Discourses*. In fact, however, this dual reception of Machiavelli is evident from the very beginning and applies equally to *The Prince* and the *Discourses*. Sixteenth-century readers were capable of reading *The Prince* as a defense of tyranny or an ironic critique of it, just as they could see the *Discourses* either as subverting religion or as offering pragmatic advice for preserving the state. For some, Machiavelli simply described the way princes acted, while for others he boldly uncovered the *arcana imperii* (secrets of state). Contrary to the view of some modern scholars, religious belief was less an obstacle than a precondition for understanding Machiavelli's new, secular approach to political power; in a similar way, the rhetorical training of many Renaissance readers allowed them to see that his arguments could be read (and used) for and against tyranny or republicanism, depending on the historical situation and the needs of the moment.

Manuscripts, editions, and translations

We know little about the initial reception. Machiavelli discussed with his friend Francesco Vettori whether he should give a presentation copy of *The Prince* to the Medici, but we have no evidence that he did so. To judge from their correspondence, Vettori was highly skeptical of the arguments of *The Prince*, especially the advice about mastering the contingencies of fortune. Francesco Guicciardini, in his *Ricordi* and *Considerations on the* Discourses *of Machiavelli*, similarly criticized Machiavelli's love of ancient examples to the detriment of a clear-sighted analysis of present realities. Remarkably, the first editions of *The Prince* and the *Discourses* were published in Rome with the papal imprimatur. These early responses suggest that Machiavelli was initially seen not as the "Machiavel" but as a political thinker with a typically humanist love of ancient Rome, colored by a penchant for hyperbole and a flair for the provocative. But even in these early years there were exceptions to the benign reading. Machiavelli's friend Biagio Buonaccorsi sent a manuscript copy of *The Prince* to Pandolfo Bellacci with a letter urging Bellacci to defend the work against those who were certain to criticize it out of "malignità o invidia" (spite or envy).[2] In 1523 Agostino Nifo plagiarized much of *The Prince* in the first four books of his *De regnandi peritia*, ostensibly only to offer, in the fifth and last book, a "cure" for Machiavelli's poisonous teachings.[3] The preface to the 1532 Giunta printed edition of *The Prince* takes this line of argument one step further: Machiavelli teaches about the poisons of political life only in order to warn against them, and any art or science can, like medicine, be used for good or evil purposes.

The Giunta edition suggests that, at its initial publication, the four basic elements of the later reception of *The Prince* were already in place: (1) the view of Machiavelli as a teacher of tyrants; (2) the view of Machiavelli as a secret critic of tyranny; (3) the view that Machiavelli was merely describing the world of politics, not recommending a particular course of behavior; or (4) that he was peddling a particular art or skill, a technique of political power, that could be used well or badly. All these arguments appear in later Renaissance editions and translations of *The Prince* in Basle, France, and England. These editions make clear what is perhaps always the case, although not always so evident: that the textual apparatus of any edition frames the reception of the work, and that reading Machiavelli was inseparable from reading about his reception. Over two hundred printed editions of his works appeared in the sixteenth century, another hundred in the seventeenth century, and more than one hundred seventy in the eighteenth.[4]

The complicated reception of Machiavelli is well illustrated by the editions of the Protestant printer Pietro Perna of Basle. In 1560 he published Sylvester Telius's Latin translation of *The Prince*; in 1580 he reprinted it and bound it with the Huguenot treatise *Vindiciae contra tyrannos* and Theodore Beza's *De iure magistratuum* – controversial Protestant works advocating resistance to tyrants – and with orations pro and contra monarchy from the Roman/Greek historian Dio Cassius. In one of the edition's dedicatory letters, the Catholic Nicolaus Stupanus wrote that the binding together of contradictory texts was intended as a rhetorical exercise in deliberation: "so that the clever reader, by weighing arguments on either side, might more easily judge this controversy concerning the absolute power of princes and magistrates over their subjects." In another issue of this edition, Perna both defended Machiavelli against the charge of teaching tyranny ("as if the doctor were the cause of death") and argued that the non-Machiavelli texts provided the reader with an "antidote" to *The Prince*. A later edition of the Telius translation (Ursellis, 1600) included a discussion by the Counter Reformation writer Antonio Possevino, who represented Machiavelli as a Protestant subversive *avant la lettre*.[5]

French editions of Machiavelli display a similar range of interpretations. In his 1553 translation of *The Prince* Guillaume Cappel praised Machiavelli's knowledge of politics and compared him to a doctor who must recommend strong medicine to cure a diseased body. Gaspard d'Auvergne, in his translation of the same year, agreed with Machiavelli that the prince who wants to hold onto power will need to use "vice" in dealing with his powerful neighbors and rebellious subjects and that God himself approves such tactics for dealing with fallen and corrupt humanity.[6] In the changed political circumstances of the seventeenth century, however, Machiavellian realism was used as a weapon against French absolutism. In his annotated 1683 translation of *The Prince*, Abraham-Nicolas Amelot de la Houssaye began by defending Machiavelli as an empirical analyst of reason of state who correctly understood the civil uses of religion, but then turned him into a Tacitean critic of princely power who was recognized in his lifetime as a defender of the Florentine republic.[7]

As these examples suggest, editors and translators of Machiavelli often shifted the responsibility for the meaning of Machiavelli's work from author to reader. Some suggested that Machiavelli was only describing how princes act in reality; others argued that he deliberately designed his texts as a test of the reader's interpretive skills. In his 1584 edition of *The Prince* and the

Discourses, the English publisher John Wolfe described his own readerly conversion to Machiavelli:

> The more I read [these works], the more they pleased me, and to speak truly, every hour I discovered new doctrine in them, new sharpness of wit, and new methods of learning the true way of drawing some utility from the profitable reading of histories, and, in brief, I realized that I had learned more from these works in one day about the government of the world, than I had in all my past life, from all the histories I had read. I learned exactly what difference there was between a prince and a tyrant, between government by many good men and government by a few bad ones, and between a well-regulated commonwealth and a confused and licentious multitude.[8]

For Wolfe, Machiavelli offered a new method of reading history, more profitable than the usual humanist moralizing, and he defended Machiavelli against the charge of immorality by insinuating that he was not really teaching tyranny so much as asking the reader to discriminate between a good prince and a tyrant.

Edward Dacres, the seventeenth-century English translator of Machiavelli's *Prince* and *Discourses*, also argued that these works could teach prudent discrimination, though he appears to have been less confident that this was Machiavelli's intention, at least in *The Prince*. Dacres condemned Machiavelli's praise of Cesare Borgia in chapter 7 and his separation of politics and ethics in chapter 15. Yet, in the prefatory letter to the reader, Dacres emphasized the reader's responsibility for taking up the text "without hurt"; and in his dedication of the translation to James, duke of Lennox, Dacres appealed to Machiavelli's "ambidexterity" to defend *The Prince*: "This book carryes its poyson and malice in it; yet mee thinks the judicious peruser may honestly make use of it in the actions of his life, with advantage."[9] In Dacres's view, *The Prince* cannot infect anyone not already infected, but it can teach the well-intentioned reader how to recognize snares and tricks. Dacres thus implied that Machiavelli's description of evil actions was not prescription but something closer to ironic indirection or criticism. Alberico Gentili, professor of law at Oxford, developed this argument further by asserting that Machiavelli's irony or rhetorical indirection was in the service of republicanism. Adapting an argument associated with Tacitus, and used by Wolfe, Gentili claimed that "It was not [Machiavelli's] purpose to instruct the tyrant, but by revealing his secret counsels to strip him bare, and expose him to the suffering nations."[10] Like Wolfe, Dacres and Gentili appreciated Machiavelli not only for his ironic indirection but also for his new method of reading history. Dacres praised Machiavelli for his "discovery of the first foundations, and analyzing of the very grounds upon which the *Roman* Common-wealth was built" and underscored the relevance of Machiavelli's instructions for the present "turbulent times."[11] Gentili also praised the Machiavelli of the *Discourses* as an exemplary reader of history, as did Jean Bodin in his *Method for the Easy Comprehension of History* (1566).[12]

The notion that Machiavelli was simply an empirical analyst of princes and tyrants was reinforced by the perception that at least some of his observations could be found in Aristotle. In his 1549 commentary on Aristotle's *Politics*, the Florentine historian Bernardo Segni observed that *The Prince* echoed Aristotle's recommendations about how to acquire power. A year later, commenting on Aristotle's *Ethics*, Segni noted similarities between Aristotle's and Machiavelli's discussions of liberality and parsimony. Other Renaissance readers drew a connection between *The Prince* and book 5 of the *Politics*, where Aristotle advises the tyrant to feign virtue if he wants to preserve his power. In his 1568 commentary on the *Politics*, Louis Le Roy claimed that "Machiavelli, writing his *Prince*, drew from this passage the principal foundations of his teaching."[13] Although some commentators condemned Machiavelli for recommending what Aristotle only described, others saw Aristotle and Machiavelli alike as dispassionate analysts of political reality, much like Tacitus in his *Annals* and *Histories*. Tacitus, in fact, quickly became a code word for Machiavelli, and those who felt uncomfortable praising the author of *The Prince* could instead write commentaries on Tacitus. But not everyone was fooled by this strategy: some critics, like Giovanni Botero, explicitly linked Tacitus to Machiavelli and condemned both as proponents of a secular, amoral approach to politics.[14] Others attempted to distinguish between Tacitus and Machiavelli on the grounds that Machiavelli recommended the tyrannical behavior and courtly intrigue that Tacitus, like Aristotle, only recorded.

The "Machiavel"

The first representation of Machiavelli as the evil "Machiavel" came from the English Catholic prelate and cardinal Reginald Pole, who wrote in his *Apologia ad Carolum Quintum* (1539) that *The Prince* was written "by Satan's hand." He condemned Machiavelli's divorce of ethics from politics and his merely instrumental use of the virtues as immoral cunning.[15] Denunciations of Machiavelli soon became commonplace in Counter Reformation polemics, where Machiavelli's subversiveness was associated with Luther and Calvin. The Dominican Ambrogio Catarino criticized Machiavelli and Luther as enemies of the Church.[16] In 1559 Machiavelli appeared on the papal Index of Prohibited Books. In his *Atheismus triumphatus* (written 1605, published 1631), Tommaso Campanella described

Machiavelli and Calvin as "heretics" and "pseudo-politicians." The Jesuits Antonio Possevino and Pedro de Ribadeneyra drew similar connections between Machiavelli and the Reformers.[17]

In the imagination of their contemporaries, Machiavelli and Luther contributed equally to the new secular discourse of politics. Although Machiavelli famously wrote that he loved his country more than his soul, and Luther valued individual salvation over the salvation of the state, Counter Reformation writers correctly intuited that Machiavelli and Luther were mirror images of each other. Luther's separation of the private realm of conscience from the public role of the prince opened up a space for secular political power that was perceived as compatible with Machiavelli's secular analysis of politics. According to Campanella and Possevino, the same was true of Calvin. It was not only that the Reformers, in criticizing the Church, gave aid and comfort to the state; Protestants such as Beza also authorized resistance to tyranny in ways that contemporaries associated with Machiavelli.

But the "Machiavel" was not the exclusive property of the Counter Reformation. In his 1576 *Discours sur les moyens de bien gouverner, et maintenir en bonne paix un Royaume ou autre principauté ... que doit tenir un Prince: Contre Nicolas Machiavel, Florentin*, the Huguenot Innocent Gentillet blamed the Saint Bartholomew's Day massacre of French Protestants on the "Machiavellian" court of Catherine de' Medici. In the dedicatory letter to the anonymous 1577 Latin translation of the *Discourses*, Machiavelli is presented as a teacher of atheism and vice, and Machiavellism as Satan's response to the Reformation. But Gentillet's representation of Machiavelli as the "Machiavel" did not preclude a genuine, if critical, understanding of Machiavelli's rhetorical method. Gentillet's *Discours* was quickly translated into Latin in 1577 and into English by Simon Patericke in 1602.

By the late sixteenth century, it was not necessary actually to read Machiavelli to know what he said or, perhaps more accurately, what he meant for his contemporaries. Just as we modern Westerners "know" Freud and Marx from the air we breathe, so Renaissance men and women "knew" the author of *The Prince*. Machiavelli, we could say, had become an "ideologeme," a cultural discourse regarding the use of force and fraud, including the feigning of religion, in the realm of politics. Although Possevino attacked Machiavelli in his 1592 *Iudicium*, he appears not to have read him and simply borrowed his attack from Gentillet. Even Cardinal Pole seems to have read Machiavelli only after damning him in the *Apologia*. Like Gentillet's *Contre-Machiavel*, Possevino's and Pole's attacks may have been one-sided, but they were not completely wrong. All three correctly understood the challenge Machiavelli's method posed to the Christian humanist synthesis of morality, religion, and politics.

The "Machiavel," the amoral teacher of force and fraud, cunning, and deception, immediately captured the popular imagination and became a stock figure in pamphlets, broadsheets, and, not least, on the Renaissance stage. In Shakespeare's *Henry VI, Part III*, he appears as the personification of acting itself in the figure of Richard III, who declaims:

> I can add colours to the chameleon;
> Change shapes with Proteus for advantages;
> And set the murdrous Machiavel to school.
> Can I do this and cannot get a crown?   (3.2.191–4)

Although the stage "Machiavel" is a caricature of Machiavelli's prince, he captures an important insight about the theatrical dimension of Machiavelli's politics. The Machiavellian Prince was first and foremost an actor, capable of adopting new roles according to changing circumstances. And just as the new prince used his theatrical skills against the forces of custom and tradition, including the traditional notion of virtue, so the "Machiavel," a protean figure of near demonic energy, employed the skills of self-fashioning and self-presentation against the intrinsic authority of hierarchy and status. In his preoccupation with the baser passions and interests, the stage "Machiavel" also captured something of Machiavelli's anthropology, his voluntarism, and his perception that politics is, first and foremost, a relation of forces. And he did so not only as a courtier, social climber and parvenu, but also as a conspirator and usurper. If the "Machiavel" crystallized contemporary fears about the destabilizing role of rhetoric and theatricality in the new urban and courtly cultures of the period, he also represented the threatening realities of de facto political power, the tricks of casuistry, and the new doctrine of reason of state. Then, as now, the dramatization of such illicit practices proved to be powerfully seductive. Like contemporary fans of horror films, early modern men and women flocked to hear theatrical Machiavels advertising their corruption from the stage.

Historians of political thought wrongly condescend to the Machiavel, arguing that it is based on a misreading of *The Prince* and an utter neglect of the *Discourses*. Machiavelli assumes the same view of human nature and recommends the same techniques in both works. Both present a rhetorical and theatrical understanding of politics, including a clear-sighted recognition of the uses of force and fraud and an instrumental view of religion, and celebrate *virtù* and the glory of military conquest. Whether the emphasis is on fraud or conquest, the important point is that Machiavelli severs the tie between politics and ethics as traditionally conceived and represents politics as a relation of forces underpinned by a secular "anthropology of desire,"[18] which assumes that *virtù* can master fortune half the time: another way of saying that "Nature has made men able to crave everything but unable to attain everything" (*Discourses* 1.37). Although *virtù* is capable of great achievements, human desire and ambition are ultimately overmastered by the forces of time and nature. The "Machiavel" stands for this perception of Machiavelli as rhetorician, disillusioned anthropologist, and secular analyst of political power.

Casuistry and reason of state

Two discourses in particular quickly became associated with Machiavelli: casuistry and reason of state. Casuistry was the art of adjudicating difficult moral cases, and between 1550 and 1650 there was a huge outpouring of treatises and manuals designed to deal with the new ethical conflicts generated by competing religious and political allegiances. Reason of state referred to the idea that any behavior, however apparently immoral, was justified if its goal was to preserve the state. In practice, this idea was as old as politics itself, but it received new life, and a new name, in the Renaissance with the consolidation of nation states. Casuistry and reason of state became mirror images of each other: the former dealt with issues of private conscience; the latter extended such considerations to the public sphere of the state. Both were concerned with prudential deliberation and weighing claims of expediency against those of morality. Both had close ties to the classical rhetorical tradition, with its analysis of the *honestum* and the *utile*. Although critics stigmatized casuistry and reason of state by linking them to Machiavelli, some statists and casuists drew on Machiavelli in elaborating their own flexible account of virtue. They differed from him, however, in their concern with the problem of "dirty hands." Whereas Machiavelli showed no interest in assuaging the individual conscience, they aimed to justify the means by the ends or by arguing for legitimate exceptions to moral law. The term "ragione di stato" – used by Guicciardini,[19] but not by Machiavelli – indicates the desire to clothe politically expedient action in the guise of rationality, albeit a rationality intrinsic to politics itself.

While condemning the casuist as a "Machiavel," some sixteenth-century writers also secretly appreciated Machiavelli's political casuistry and assimilated his insights to the new discourse of reason of state. An early example is the Portuguese bishop Jeronimo Osorio, whose *De nobilitate christiana* [On Christian Nobility] (second edition, 1552) shows familiarity with Machiavelli and takes offense at his view that the Church undermined *virtù*, insisting that Christianity encouraged military success. This focus on the practical benefits of faith was characteristic of reason of state literature. According to the first treatise by this title, Giovanni Botero's *Ragion di stato* (1589), reason of state is the "knowledge of the means appropriate to founding, preserving, and extending the state" (1.1). Like Machiavelli, Botero insisted on the impossibility of exact rules in the realm of practical politics and advanced a rhetorical view of politics, according to which circumstances dictate the best course of action. Unlike Machiavelli, however, Botero wanted to prove that a politics informed by Christianity is the most effective kind of reason of state. Botero went so far as to argue that, since all power comes from God, faith is the ultimate pragmatism: it is in the "interest" of the prince not only to profess religion but to be religious because having God on your side will help you succeed (2.15). Here the distinction between bad reason of state (statecraft for the sake of mere domination or personal self-aggrandizement) and good reason of state (Christian statecraft in the interests of morality, religion, and the welfare of all) tends to collapse, for once right intention has been guaranteed the political agent can be as calculating as necessary. The irony is that, in attempting to answer Machiavelli on his own terms, critics such as Botero ended up adopting his criterion of practical success. As "Machiavel" notes in the prologue to Marlowe's *Jew of Malta*, "Admired I am of those that hate me most." Reason of state, it turns out, was acceptable to both Catholics and Protestants if it was pursued for reasons of faith, that is, governed by a godly intention. Botero's treatise was quickly translated into Spanish, French, Latin, and later into German, with enormous influence on subsequent treatises on reason of state.

Reason of state did not always require the sanction of religion. In his *Politicorum libri sex* [Six Books of Politics] (1589), the Flemish scholar Justus Lipsius advocated a Machiavellian "mixed prudence," that is, prudence tempered with considerations of expedience, on the grounds of political necessity. Lipsius drew an explicit connection between prudence and rhetorical decorum: echoing Cicero's definition of decorum in *De oratore*, he observed, "Now, if the things themselves are uncertaine, *Prudence* itselfe likewise must of necessitie be so, and so much the rather, because it is not onely tied to the things themselves, but to their dependents, having regard unto the times, the places, and to men and for their least change, she changeth her selfe."[20] Part of Lipsius's own prudence was to disguise his Machiavellianism with hundreds of quotations and maxims from Tacitus. Like Botero, Gentillet, and others, Lipsius understood that the maxim, with its pithy form and flexible use, was the rhetorical equivalent of political *virtù*. Accordingly, the *Politics* reads as a Machiavellian storehouse of quotations, arguments, and examples to be adapted as needed.

In England, Gabriel Harvey, Walter Raleigh, and Francis Bacon read Machiavelli in much the same way, noting the relevance of Machiavelli's rhetorical method to his practical politics. In a marginal note in his text of

Livy, Harvey wrote: "Machiavelli certainly outdid Aristotle in observation of this [history] above all, though he had a weaker foundation in technical rules and philosophical principles. Hence I generally prefer Aristotle's rules, Machiavelli's examples." Bacon also singled out Machiavelli's method of writing in *The Advancement of Learning*:

> And therefore the form of writing which of all others is fittest for this variable argument of negotiation and occasions is that which Machiavel chose wisely and aptly for government; namely, discourses upon histories or examples. For knowledge drawn freshly, and in our view, out of particulars, knoweth the best way to particulars again; and it hath much greater life for practice when the discourse attendeth upon the example, than when the example attendeth upon the discourse.[21]

In his commonplace book, *The Cabinet-Council*, Raleigh illustrated this way of reading Machiavelli by digesting his teaching into a series of pithy maxims and examples. For Harvey, Lipsius, and Bacon, Machiavelli's rhetorical attention to circumstances produced a new language of politics, one that explicitly departed from the classical and scholastic idioms of law and morality to focus on empirical observation. Here the reception of Machiavelli was perceived to be compatible with both an emerging secular historiography and Baconian science.

Empirical observation was often equated with the analysis of "interest," sometimes used as a synonym for individual passions or desires, but eventually connoting a clear-sighted and dispassionate analysis of the political terrain, unconstrained by moral considerations. For example, Trajano Boccalini, an admirer of the Venetian Republic and the Dutch revolt against Spain, criticized Machiavellian reason of state while defending a Machiavellian analysis of the people's interest. Boccalini, author of a commentary on Tacitus, explicitly discussed the princely recourse to reason of state in his satirical *Ragguagli di Parnaso* [News from Parnassus] of 1612–13. But like other Tacitean readers of Machiavelli, Boccalini also suggested that the depiction of princely rule could be a weapon against it. In a brilliant rhetorical move, Boccalini has "Machiavelli" himself explain as much in the *Ragguagli*. Brought before the court of Apollo and charged with teaching the princes of Europe "rules of state [*regole di stato*]," "Machiavelli" protests that he has only copied the behavior of princes, not invented anything new. His accuser charges him with teaching the art of imitation, here linked to the pursuit of self-interest: Machiavelli "was found by night amongst a flock of sheep, whom he taught to put … dogs teeth in their mouthes."[22] By having "Machiavelli" teach the meek sheep – the people – to defend themselves by imitating their watchdogs and adopting their weapons, Boccalini transforms

Machiavelli's revelation of the secrets of princely rule into a subversive critique of tyrants.

The republican Machiavelli

Some sixteenth-century readers saw Machiavelli as a defender of the Florentine Republic or of republicanism more generally, but the republican dimension of Machiavelli's thought had its greatest influence in seventeenth-century England and Holland and eighteenth-century France. During the Protectorate, English readers turned to Machiavelli to justify the de facto political rule of Cromwell and the oath of engagement to the new government, but they also drew on the *Discourses* to elaborate a specifically republican discourse.[23] This republican Machiavelli was not necessarily perceived as incompatible with religious belief. Although some adopted a purely secular idiom of political analysis, others, like John Milton, drew on Deuteronomy 17 and 1 Samuel 8 to argue that God preferred a free state. Hobbes might have been thinking of Machiavelli as well as of Milton when he complained that reading the ancients was a source of political "tumults."[24] In 1650 Marchamont Nedham wrote a defense of a free commonwealth (*The Case of the Commonwealth of England, Stated*) in which he cited Machiavelli with approval, although he later tarred Cromwell with the Machiavellian brush. In *Oceana* (1656), James Harrington singled out Machiavelli's "modern" prudence as the closest thing to the prudence of the ancients and defended the Machiavellian armed citizen as a model for England, while adding the possession of property as a requirement of civic virtue. Other "commonwealthmen," such as John Milton, Algernon Sidney, and Henry Neville, adapted Machiavelli's notions of civic virtue, participation, the salutary effects of conflict, and the corrupting effects of idleness to contemporary republican theory. Neville edited and translated Machiavelli's works for publication in 1675 and again in 1680, together with a fictional letter – "Nicholas Machiavel's Letter to Zanobius Buondelmontius in Vindication of Himself and His Writings" – in which "Machiavelli" addresses the friends who met for conversation in the Rucellai gardens and defends his "affection to the Democratical Government" while excusing *The Prince* as "both a Satyr against [tyrants], and a true Character of them."[25]

Dutch republicans of the seventeenth century were also interested in Machiavelli. Johan and Pieter de la Court drew on Machiavelli's *Discourses* to defend the balance of interests in a republic. Their republicanism in turn influenced Spinoza's republican *Tractatus theologico-politicus* (1670). In the introduction to the later *Tractatus politicus* Spinoza defended a realist account of politics, obviously influenced by chapter 15 of *The Prince*. He nonetheless asserted that Machiavelli was "favorable to liberty" and that *The Prince* could be read as an implicit defense of republicanism: "perhaps he wished to show how cautious a free multitude should be of entrusting its welfare absolutely to one man."[26] This interpretation remained controversial among Machiavelli's European readers. In 1740, Amelot de la Houssaye's edition appeared with a commentary by Frederick II of Prussia and a preface by Voltaire, who explicitly rejected Amelot's Tacitean defense of Machiavelli as a critic of tyranny, noting that "it is very cowardly and awful to hate it while teaching it." Frederick compared Machiavelli to Spinoza:

> Machiavelli's *The Prince* is for Morals what the work of Spinoza is for matters of Faith. Spinoza weakened the basis of Faith, and tried nothing less than to overthrow the edifice of Religion; Machiavelli corrupts Politics, and undertakes to destroy the precepts of healthy Morals.[27]

Voltaire's contemporary, Montesquieu, offered a more nuanced appreciation of Machiavelli. In his *Considérations sur les causes de la grandeur des Romains et de leur décadence* [Considerations on the Greatness and the Decline of the Romans] (1734), and *De l'esprit des lois* [Spirit of the Laws] (1748), Montesquieu adopted a Machiavellian vision of the centrality of passion and interest in human affairs and a Machiavellian skepticism about the classical idiom of virtue and the good. Like Machiavelli, Montesquieu declared that political virtues were not identical with moral virtues and that Christian idealism was at odds with political pragmatism. Montesquieu then used Machiavelli's own pragmatic mode of reasoning to argue that the expansionist foreign policy of the ancient Roman Empire, like that of the modern French state, undermined itself. Machiavelli had similarly analyzed the long-term failure of Roman expansion in *Discourses* 3.24, but Montesquieu turns this failure into an argument against Machiavelli that recuperates a normative conception of justice and constitutional democracy. As he says in the *Considérations* (chapter 5), "Nature has given states certain limits to mortify the ambitions of men."

In *The Social Contract* Rousseau represented Machiavelli as a covert republican who "under the pretence of instructing kings taught important lessons to the people." He paraphrased Machiavelli's remarks, in the preface to the *Florentine Histories*, to the effect that disturbances in the state "give vigor to the soul": in ancient Greece "the civil virtue of the citizens, their morals, and their independence, served more effectively to strengthen it than all their dissensions may have done to weaken it."[28] Robespierre boldly declared that "the plan of the French Revolution was written large in the books ... of Machiavelli."[29] The lineaments of the republican Machiavelli are also traceable in the founders of the American republic, who recast

Machiavelli's insight concerning the beneficial effects of internal conflict or "disunione" (*Discourses* 1.4) in terms of the checks and balances of the branches of government and the salutary effects of faction and interest. In *The Federalist Papers* James Madison argued: "Extend the sphere [of a republic] and you take in a greater variety of parties and interests; you make it less probable that a majority of the whole will have a common motive to invade the rights and interests of others."[30]

Conclusion

In his survey of Machiavellism and reason of state, Friedrich Meinecke wrote that Machiavelli plunged a sword into the body politic of the West. In *The Civilization of the Renaissance in Italy*, Jacob Burckhardt famously argued that the Renaissance, especially Machiavelli, conceived of the state as a work of art.[31] These two observations capture the destructive and creative dimensions of Machiavelli's thought. Machiavelli was shocking to his contemporaries because he forced them to confront the unresolved tensions between antiquity and Christianity, and thus the real message of their beloved classics. These included not only the lessons concerning necessity and the role of force in politics, but also the celebration of empire, expansion, glory, and "grandezza." Yet, in true Machiavellian fashion, by returning Renaissance culture to its origins (the "ridurre ai principii" of *Discourses* 3.1), Machiavelli also founded a new discourse about politics – a new republic of discourse – and in this way came to stand for the distinctively modern. In this discourse, human relations are relations of power and the state is a human artifact, a bulwark erected against the tide of fortune. Laws, too, are things made, rather than natural principles, and are imposed by will upon the recalcitrant matter of human needs and desires. Implicit in this analysis, as Meinecke recognized, is a kind of historicism, according to which necessity in the form of historical circumstance, rather than a transhistorical moral code, dictates norms of behavior. But this historicism is balanced in Machiavelli by an ahistorical conviction that human nature is essentially the same in all ages: "He who considers present affairs and ancient ones readily understands that all cities and all peoples have the same desires and the same traits and that they always have had them" (*Discourses* 1.39; see also 3.43).[32] Against these forces of entropy – historical necessity and unchanging human nature – Machiavelli asserts what Meinecke called the "idealism" of *virtù*, which embraces the conviction, not only that human beings can respond creatively to fortune, but also that the "virtuous" course of action will emerge from a practical analysis of the situation at hand: the man of *virtù* will see that republics are in the long run better than principalities. Ultimately, Machiavelli stands for this dialectic of pragmatism and idealism, which helps explain his varied reception and lasting influence on the history of political thought.

NOTES

1. Machiavelli, *The Chief Works and Others*, trans. Allan Gilbert, 3 vols. (Durham, N.C.: Duke University Press, 1989), 1:340.
2. Quoted in L. Arthur Burd, ed., *Il Principe* (1891; Oxford University Press, 1968), p. 34. Translated in *The Prince by Niccolò Machiavelli with Related Documents*, ed. William J. Connell (Boston: Bedford/St. Martin's, 2005), pp. 145–6.
3. Brian Richardson, "*The Prince* and Its Early Italian Readers," in *Niccolò Machiavelli's "The Prince": New Interdisciplinary Essays*, ed. Martin Coyle (Manchester University Press, 1995), pp. 18–39 (29–33).
4. Sergio Bertelli and Piero Innocenti, *Bibliografia machiavelliana* (Verona: Edizioni Valdonega, 1979).
5. Adolf Gerber, *Niccolò Machiavelli: Die Handschriften, Ausgaben und Übersetzungen seiner Werke im 16. und 17. Jahrhundert* (1912–13; reprinted Turin: Bottega d'Erasmo, 1962), part 3, pp. 60–75 (67, 69, 74); *Bibliografia*, pp. 47, 62, 83.
6. Guillaume Cappel, trans., *Le Prince de Nicolas Machiavelle secretaire et citoyen de Florence* (Paris, 1553), preface; Gaspard d'Auvergne, trans., *Le Prince de Nicolas Macchiavelli secretaire et citoien de Florence* (Poitiers, 1553), preface; *Bibliografia* p. 38.
7. A.-N. Amelot de la Houssaye, *Le Prince de Nicolas Machiavel* (Amsterdam, 1683), preface; *Bibliografia*, p. 118.
8. "Lo stampatore al benigno lettore," in John Wolfe, *I Discorsi di Nicolo Machiavelli, sopra la prima deca di Tito Livio*, fol. 2, bound with *Il Prencipe di Nicolo Machiavelli ... con alcune altre operette* (Palermo [actually London], 1584); *Bibliografia*, pp. 64–5; translation, slightly modified, by Peter S. Donaldson, *Machiavelli and Mystery of State* (Cambridge University Press, 1988), p. 93.
9. E.D. [Edward Dacres], trans., *Nicholas Machiavel's Prince* (London, 1640); *Bibliografia*, pp. 100–1.
10. Alberico Gentili, *De legationibus libri tres*, trans. Gordon J. Laing, 2 vols. (New York: Oxford University Press, 1924), 2:156.
11. Edward Dacres, trans., *The Discourses* (London: 1636), dedicatory letter to James, duke of Lennox; *Bibliografia*, p. 99.
12. Jean Bodin, *Method for the Easy Comprehension of History*, trans. Beatrice Reynolds (New York: W. W. Norton, 1945), e.g., chap. 4, pp. 54, 57.
13. Louis Le Roy, *Les Politiques d'Aristote* (Paris: 1568), pp. 788–9.
14. Giovanni Botero, *The Reason of State*, ed. P. J. and D. P. Waley (New Haven, Conn.: Yale University Press, 1956), dedicatory letter, p. xiii.
15. *Epistolarum Reginaldi Poli, Pars I* (Brescia, 1744).
16. Ambrogio Catarino [Lancelotto Politi], *De libris a Christiano detestandis et a Christianismo penitus eliminandis* [Books to Be Hated by a Christian and Completely Eliminated from Christendom] (Lisbon, 1552).
17. Tommaso Campanella, *Atheismus Triumphatus* [Atheism Conquered] (Rome, 1631), preface; Antonio Possevino, *Iudicium de Nouae militis Galli, Joannis*

Bodini, Philippi Mornaei, et Nicolai Machiavelli quibusdam scriptis [Judgment of Various Writings of the French Soldier La Noue, Jean Bodin, Philippe de Mornay, and Niccolò Machiavelli] (Venice, 1592); Pedro de Ribadeneyra, *Tratado de la religión y virtudes que deve tener el Principe Christiano, para governar y conservar sus Estados, contro lo que Nicolas Machiavelo y los Politicos deste tiempo enseñan* [Treatise on the Religion and Virtues Which a Christian Prince Ought to Have to Govern and Conserve His States against That Which Niccolò Machiavelli and the Politicians of This Time Teach] (Madrid, 1595).

18. The phrase is from Joseph Anthony Mazzeo, *Renaissance and Revolution: The Remaking of European Thought* (London: Secker & Warburg, 1967), p. 75.

19. Francesco Guicciardini, *Dialogo del Reggimento di Firenze*, in *Opere*, ed. Emanuella Lugnani Scarano, 3 vols. (Turin: UTET, 1970), 1:465; trans. Alison Brown, *Dialogue on the Government of Florence* (Cambridge University Press, 1994), p. 159.

20. Trans. William Jones, *Six Bookes of Politickes* (London, 1594), p. 60.

21. Harvey quoted from Lisa Jardine and Anthony Grafton, "'Studied for Action': How Gabriel Harvey Read His Livy," *Past and Present* 129 (1990): 61; Francis Bacon, *The Advancement of Learning*, ed. G. W. Kitchin (London: J. M. Dent, 1973), p. 186.

22. Trajano Boccalini, *I ragguagli di Parnasso, or Advertisements from Parnassus*, trans. Henry Carey (London, 1656), book 1, chap. 89, pp. 175–6; also translated in Robert M. Adams, *The Prince* (New York: W. W. Norton, 1977), pp. 262–4.

23. E.g., the anonymous *Anti-Machiavell, or Honesty against Policy* (London, 1647); Anthony Ascham, *A Discourse, wherein is examined, what is particularly lawfull during the Confusions and Revolutions of Government* (London, 1648). The first refers to Machiavelli critically, the second more positively.

24. Thomas Hobbes, *Leviathan* (1652), ed. Richard Tuck (Cambridge University Press, 1991), chap. 21, p. 150.

25. *The Works of the Famous Nicholas Machiavel, Citizen and Secretary of Florence* (London: John Starkey, 1680), no pagination; *Bibliografia*, pp. 114–15, 117–18, 136–7.

26. Benedict de Spinoza, *A Theologico-Political Treatise and A Political Treatise*, trans. R. H. M. Elwes (New York: Dover, 1951), p. 315 (chap. 5, sec. 7).

27. Quoted in Jacob Soll, *Publishing the Prince: History, Reading, and the Birth of Political Criticism* (Ann Arbor: University of Michigan Press, 2005), pp. 115, 117.

28. Jean-Jacques Rousseau, *The Social Contract*, trans. Maurice Cranston (Harmondsworth: Penguin, 1968), book 3, chap. 6, p. 118; book 3, chap. 9, p. 131n.

29. Quoted by Hannah Arendt, *On Revolution* (New York: Viking, 1963), p. 30.

30. *The Federalist Papers*, ed. Clinton Rossiter (New York: New American Library, 1961), no. 10, p. 83.

31. Friedrich Meinecke, *Machiavellism: The Doctrine of Raison d'État and Its Place in Modern History*, trans. Douglas Scott (New Haven, Conn.: Yale University Press, 1957), p. 49; Jacob Burckhardt, *The Civilization of the Renaissance in Italy*, trans. S. G. C. Middlemore (London: Phaidon Press, 1945), part 1, pp. 53–6.

32. *Works*, 1:278, 1:521.

FURTHER READING

Anglo, Sydney. *Machiavelli – The First Century: Studies in Enthusiasm, Hostility, and Irrelevance.* Oxford University Press, 2005.

Bireley, Robert. *The Counter-Reformation Prince: Anti-Machiavellianism or Catholic Statecraft in Early Modern Europe.* Chapel Hill, N.C., University of North Carolina Press, 1990.

De Mattei, Rodolfo. *Il problema della ragion di Stato nell'età della Controriforma.* Milan and Naples, Ricciardi, 1979.

Fink, Zera S. *The Classical Republicans: An Essay in the Recovery of a Pattern of Thought in Seventeenth-Century England.* Evanston, Ill., Northwestern University Press, 1945.

Haitsma Mulier, Eco. "The Language of Seventeenth-Century Republicanism in the United Provinces: Dutch or European?" in *The Languages of Political Theory in Early-Modern Europe,* ed. Anthony Pagden. Cambridge University Press, 1987, pp. 179–95.

Kahn, Victoria. *Machiavellian Rhetoric from the Counter-Reformation to Milton.* Princeton University Press, 1994.

Lefort, Claude. *Le travail de l'oeuvre Machiavel.* Paris, Gallimard, 1972.

Pocock, J. G. A. *The Machiavellian Moment: Florentine Political Thought and the Atlantic Republican Tradition.* Princeton University Press, 1975.

Procacci, Giuliano. *Studi sulla fortuna del Machiavelli.* Rome, Istituto Storico Italiano, 1965.

Raab, Felix. *The English Face of Machiavelli: A Changing Interpretation, 1500–1700.* London, Routledge & Kegan Paul, 1964.

Rahe, Paul A., ed. *Machiavelli's Liberal Republican Legacy.* Cambridge University Press, 2006.

Robbins, Caroline. *The Eighteenth-Century Commonwealthman: Studies in the Transmission, Development and Circumstance of English Liberal Thought from the Restoration of Charles II until the War with the Thirteen Colonies.* Cambridge, Mass., Harvard University Press, 1959.

Senellart, Michel. *Machiavélisme et raison d'État.* Paris, Presses Universitaires de France, 1989.

JÉRÉMIE BARTHAS

Machiavelli in political thought from the age of revolutions to the present

Machiavelli's work in progress

When he wrote *The Prince* and the *Discourses*, which were published only after he died, Machiavelli was a defeated and suspect man. Reading the prefaces and dedication of the *Discourses on Livy*, one feels that the author had lost all hope that more auspicious times might come for Florence and himself and that he was placing his hopes elsewhere: with his restless and immanent wisdom he was trying to reach peoples in other places and times, hoping his books could teach them to decipher and demystify their own history. Because of Machiavelli's denial of divine providence and his assertion that humans make their own history, his work invites them to take control of their own fate by seizing the first appropriate opportunity. Although he offers a political analysis devoid of moral prejudice, his writings are not without a certain use of dissimulation. "Machiavelli," wrote Leo Strauss, "does not go to the end of the road; the last part of the road must be travelled by the reader who understands what is omitted by the writer."[1] This is why, in more than one sense, Machiavelli considered his *Discourses* a work in progress.

As Machiavelli himself emphasized, history is most often written for the benefit of the winners; by contrast, his work is like a thorn in their flesh. He invites us to mistrust authority, including that represented by tradition and constituted power. However, he does not deny that some such power may be necessary to defend freedom against its enemies. The history of the interpretation and instrumentalization of Machiavelli's thought has much to do with this very dialectic. As illustrated by the fact that defenders as well as opponents of the powers that be have often brandished his name, this dialectic is not reducible to the twentieth century's great political dichotomy between Left and Right. Authors from antagonistic camps easily agree when it comes to using the oldest stereotypes of anti-Machiavellism against

Machiavelli. Fascists, conservatives, Catholics, liberals, and socialists, for instance, have at times sung together the old tune according to which Machiavelli conceived the people as matter to be modeled by a duce, party, or political elite with absolute power. Thus, in most cases, the dialectic inherent in Machiavelli's thought is resolved by way of an abstraction: that is, by seeing nothing in Machiavelli except a cynical, immoral view of power and human relations. But general agreement is not a demonstration of truth. The resistance offered by Machiavelli's texts leaves room for dissent, and one can always find independent-minded readers. Hegel, for instance, from his Jena lectures on *The Philosophy of the Spirit* (1805) to his Berlin lectures on *The Philosophy of History* (1822–30), defended Machiavelli against the accusations of moralizers, insisting on the necessity of approaching his thought historically, while also warning against any purely historical treatment whose effect would be to transform ideas into dead opinions.

This chapter offers a synthetic interpretation of Machiavelli's presence in the work of major political thinkers since the age of revolutions, focusing on the problems that revolutionary change posed for the perception and comprehension of Machiavelli. One may, schematically, distinguish between two phases separated by the threshold of Antonio Gramsci's notes on Machiavelli (1931–4) in his *Prison Notebooks*. These phases may have overlapped during the interwar period, but they separated again with the trauma of totalitarianism. In the first phase, the main issue is Machiavelli's theoretical role in the revolutionary project of materializing the very concept of the state, understood, as Hegel put it, as the politically organized people "united for the common defence of the totality of its property."[2] The second phase involves the attempted elimination of the revolutionary tradition and of the place given to Machiavelli in that undertaking.

The criterion for selecting the authors discussed in this chapter is their fame as political theorists (which is easy to establish for the "classical" authors of the nineteenth century), although not all wrote directly on Machiavelli. Some "minor" political thinkers deserve inclusion because they played an important cultural role in promoting a certain representation of Machiavelli. Although the exegesis of his writings and their critical history, which requires philological methods, time, patience, and caution, is not always accompanied by original political thought, they do sometimes intersect. Nevertheless, Machiavelli's durably demonic image has led authors to develop a variety of approaches to his texts, from silence to outraged denunciation, and the next two sections consider some of the strategies adopted and the significance of his negative reputation.

Strategies of approach

From the French Revolution to the interwar period

Immanuel Kant did not explicitly mention Machiavelli. However, in his *Conjectures on the Beginning of Human History* (1786), a critical reflection on the philosophy of history of Johan Gottfried Herder (himself an admirer of Machiavelli), Kant addressed the relationship between the march of the poor toward liberty and the necessity for them to take part in the military defense of the community. This sounds like an echo of Machiavelli. Similarly, in *On Perpetual Peace* (1795), Kant's critique of standing armies and public debt as a means of financing war, inspired by the recent experience of the French people in arms during the Revolution, also testifies to the resilience of Machiavelli's legacy. Hegel and Tocqueville, as we shall see, produced perspicacious writings, which remained unpublished during their lifetimes, on the historical problem, faced by Machiavelli, concerning the organization of the Florentine territorial state.

In a letter to the Italian historian Pasquale Villari in 1872, John Stuart Mill expressed his hope that scholarship on Machiavelli and his times would bring important benefits to European thought and "help to train the thinkers of the time to come."[3] Yet the hopes Mill placed in Villari's *Life and Times of Machiavelli* (1877–82) were belied by Villari's moralizing interpretation. More challenging, if less historically documented, was Francesco De Sanctis's *History of Italian Literature* (1870–1), which, in promoting a cultural policy aimed at sustaining the national unification of Italy, established Machiavelli as the founder of modernity. In 1857, however, Mill had refused to take part in supporting an edition of Machiavelli's unpublished manuscripts. Although he probably read Machiavelli in Italian, in his published works the leading British philosopher of the nineteenth century evidently preferred not to mention him, perhaps because the Florentine's reputation rendered suspect all those who invoked him. Nevertheless, in his lecture on *The British Constitution* (1826),[4] not published in his lifetime, the young Mill boldly relied on Machiavelli to develop a position, of rare radicalism in the history of political thought, about the negative aspects of Britain's constitutional system and of any form of aristocratic or "elitist" government. Offering a different evaluation of the French Revolution from the then prevailing view of Edmund Burke, Mill quoted *Discourses* 1.58: "The opinion against the people arises from this cause, that of the people every one may speak without danger, even where the people reign." This chapter of the *Discourses*, presented in French translation in the July 12, 1791, issue of the *Gazette nationale ou moniteur universel*, thereby became the locus of an official encounter between Machiavelli and the Revolution.

Friedrich Nietzsche was foreign to the spirit of the Revolution and remained silent about the political implications of Machiavelli's work. Nonetheless, he could claim, as in *Beyond Good and Evil* (1886), whose title may have been inspired by a passage in Villari's book, which Nietzsche read and praised, to be following Machiavelli's irreligious spirit and bold style. In an 1888 note, later published in *The Will to Power* (1901), Nietzsche provocatively hailed an aesthetics of pure Machiavellism as appropriate for the *Übermensch*: "no philosopher will be in any doubt as to the type of perfection in politics; that is Machiavellianism. But Machiavellianism, pure, without admixture, crude, fresh, with all its force, with all its pungency, is superhuman, divine, transcendental, it will never be achieved by man, at most approximated."[5] Similarly, Benedetto Croce, one of the most influential Italian philosophers of the twentieth century, made scattered references to Machiavelli throughout his work, ranging from early critical comments on Villari's moralism to the late assertion that one finds in Machiavelli a superior form of morality that deprives moral hypocrisy of its own means.[6] But one does not find in Croce, a political conservative, any extended analysis of the content of Machiavelli's political thought.

In Max Weber's famous lecture, *Politics as a Vocation* (1919), one senses the author's deep attraction to Machiavelli as well as the influence of Johan Gottlieb Fichte's popular tract *Ueber Machiavell als Schriftsteller* (1807), which was republished three times around 1918. However, the only aspect of Machiavelli's theory on which Weber wrote explicitly is his patriotism, which was for a long time the only way to mount an admissible defense of the author of *The Prince*. In 1807, Fichte had used this strategy to denounce censorship and criticize the offensive war waged by the army of Napoleon. Patriotism, widely discussed throughout the nineteenth century, still established the narrow limits within which Weber deemed it acceptable to write about Machiavelli's political thought. Attempting to amend the definition of the state as mere force, violence, and power (a definition promoted by Heinrich von Treitschke, a nineteenth-century German political theorist and proponent of power politics), Weber was careful not to associate this view with Machiavelli. Weber referred to Machiavelli a limited number of times and invited his readers to compare *The Prince* to the *Arthasastra* of the Indian philosopher Kautilya (*c.* 300 BCE), republished in 1915: the violence of the alleged Machiavellism of the *Arthasastra* could attenuate the scandal represented by *The Prince*.

From the Second World War to the present

Leo Strauss was a strong opponent of Weber's epistemology and its fact–value distinction, which he blamed for leading to relativism and nihilism.

Strauss, who placed Machiavelli at the root of this tendency and produced an extensive exegesis of his major works, was indebted to Fichte for the emphasis on the unity of *The Prince* and the *Discourses* and for his sense of Machiavelli's irreligion, but also for the thesis of evil human "nature," which was largely foreign to Machiavelli. He also shared with Nietzsche a fascination with Machiavellism understood as the privilege of an aristocracy. Strauss remained sensitive to the scandal and the rupture represented by Machiavelli's thought. Although he was aware of his republicanism and his importance as a source for seventeenth-century English classical republicans, the starting point of Strauss's reflections was nonetheless Ernst Cassirer's *Myth of the State* (1946), in which Machiavelli was associated with National Socialism. Strauss began his *Thoughts on Machiavelli* (1958) with a violent diatribe against Machiavelli, the "teacher of evil," combined with a hyperbolic eulogy of America. Yet these pages become immediately unreliable in view of the importance that Strauss – a Jewish philosopher from Germany who emigrated to the United States – gave to the art of writing, suggesting that he himself practiced it precisely when Senator Joseph McCarthy's regime of persecution imposed a limitation on civic rights and freedom of expression in the name of objectives of national security.

In opposition to Strauss, Hans Baron, Isaiah Berlin, J. G. A. Pocock, and Quentin Skinner have emphasized more consensual and less offensive aspects of Machiavelli. They succeeded in reintroducing Machiavelli into the current political debate, but at the cost of neutralizing the scandalous elements of his thought. In 1971, Berlin, renowned for his 1958 Oxford lecture on *Two Concepts of Liberty*, published an important essay on "The Originality of Machiavelli" in which he sought to abolish the putatively insoluble conflict between politics and morality that, according to Croce, Machiavelli had detected, discovering instead a pluralism of values in Machiavelli that he considered consonant with the spirit of political liberalism. Baron, Pocock, and Skinner have similarly attempted to redefine a republican tradition in which Machiavelli plays a cardinal role, but where *The Prince* stands out as an embarrassing work. They either ignored this conflict or reduced *The Prince* to the provocations of an author playing the fool in order to be noticed and to find employment.[7]

In *Le travail de l'œuvre Machiavel* (1972), a thick, encyclopedic treatise for Machiavelli scholarship, Claude Lefort offered a systematic reading, chapter by chapter, of *The Prince* and the *Discourses*. Paying attention to the dialectical movement of Machiavelli's argument, Lefort combined Strauss's reflections on the art of writing with a historical approach, mainly based on the now classic studies of the historian Felix Gilbert. Lefort challenged a large number of commonplaces about Machiavelli: for instance, his presumed fascination with the Romans, the utilitarian view of religion as a necessary cement for society, and the view of *The Prince* as a tool for Medici rulers. Surveying Machiavelli's fortune across the centuries (before selecting eight representative interpretations, including those of De Sanctis, Gramsci, Cassirer, and Strauss), Lefort showed how any approach to Machiavelli is already embedded in a critical tradition.[8]

Machiavelli's negative reputation

Strategies used to approach his texts may therefore be considered products of the history of censorship practiced against Machiavelli, of its efficacy, and of the ways of escaping it. Machiavelli's repulsive force also explains the attraction he exerts, even though the latter sometimes borders on superficiality or conformism.

The image of Machiavelli and the German catastrophe

In fact, Machiavelli's image is easier to handle than his texts are to interpret. The French political scientist Raymond Aron, for instance, confessed in his *Memoirs* (1983) that he wrote about Machiavelli before undertaking a patient study of his work. In writings from 1938–40, which Aron refrained from publishing, Machiavelli was presented as the precursor of totalitarianism and power politics, insofar as he had degraded the political into mere technique (as the old Catholic accusation goes).[9] Aron later found in Machiavelli an ally against Marxism.

Reading Machiavelli without close analysis of either the texts or historical context is sometimes transformed into a methodological principle. *The Prince* is consequently reduced to a description of political techniques that a sovereign can use for the conquest and preservation of power, a view based on the literal reading of a few separate propositions and an oversimplified understanding of Machiavelli's reception. Conflicts of interpretation are thereby abolished, and the only thing reputed historically relevant is a certain appropriation of Machiavelli, reduced to a proponent of Machiavellism, reason of state, power politics, and totalitarianism. Michel Foucault, for example, in his lecture on governmentality (1978),[10] fell prey to the sirens of the classic work of the German historian Friedrich Meinecke, *Machiavellism: The Doctrine of Raison d'État and Its Place in Modern History* (1924).

In the aftermath of the First World War, Meinecke constructed and rejected a kind of evil trinity of Machiavellism, Hegelianism, and the "abstract" ideas of the French Revolution that Hegel had defended. Meinecke endorsed the view of continuity between Machiavelli and the First World War (and, as he later added, the Second World War). If Treitschke was not without reservations concerning Machiavelli's political thought, his admiration for the Florentine's ability to consider the state in an immoral way revealed, for Meinecke, the whole truth about Machiavelli's work. In *The German Catastrophe* (1946), Meinecke took up the old charge against Machiavelli and adapted it to his own time: by lifting the veil of secrecy and mystery that had long shrouded the rules of Machiavellism and reason of state, Machiavelli had spread a poison, and in liberating this esoteric knowledge, more properly reserved to an aristocracy, he made possible a mass Machiavellism, whose potential the German Third Reich turned into reality in the most horrible way.

Politics and ethics in a Machiavellian moment: is the question over?

As suggested by Croce's oft-repeated but sibylline dictum of 1924 that Machiavelli had discovered "the necessity and autonomy of politics," a central question about Machiavelli's thought is the relationship between politics and morality.[11] Perhaps this question should be asked anew, but this time separately from the problem of reason of state to which Meinecke connected it. In the appendices to his *Perpetual Peace*, Kant sided with Robespierre (in the name of the Committee of Public Safety) in his philosophical response to the British prime minister William Pitt's attacks on the revolutionary French people, whom Pitt accused of Machiavellism, rebellion, immorality, and irreligion.[12] For Kant, the *Declaration of the Rights of Man and of the Citizen* and the Republican Constitution demonstrated that "true politics cannot progress without paying homage to morality."[13] Kant's position was later echoed in Hegel's *Philosophy of Right* (1821), paragraph 337:

> There was at one time a great deal of talk about the opposition between morality and politics and the demand that the latter should conform to the former ... The allegation that, within this alleged opposition, politics is always wrong is in fact based on superficial notions of morality, the nature of the state, and the state's relation to the moral point of view.[14]

It is noteworthy that Kant and Hegel developed these reflections within the framework of a positive approach to Machiavelli, a questioning of the discourses of Machiavellism, and a consideration of the philosophical meaning of the French Revolution. Without this framework, these reflections are to a large extent misunderstood as belonging to endless and excessively vague arguments concerning *ethos* and *kratos*. During the twentieth century, the complacent repetition of Croce's words concerning Machiavelli's discovery deadened thought and marginalized such reflections. Gramsci, however, reminded us of their essentially revolutionary meaning, a meaning already in Machiavelli's thought. This, Gramsci felt, was one of the principal causes of the persistence of anti-Machiavellism.[15]

Machiavelli and the age of revolutions: state, economics and society, religion

The age of revolutions included the economic revolution in England, the political revolutions in America and France, as well as the philosophical revolution in Germany. The founding texts here are Adam Smith's *Inquiry into the Nature and Causes of the Wealth of Nations* (1776), Kant's *Critique of Pure Reason* (1781), and the *Declaration of the Rights of Man and of the Citizen* (1789). As it happens, this threefold revolution coincided with a revolution in the study of Machiavelli's historical role. Impatiently expected since the important French translation of *The Prince* by Abraham-Nicolas Amelot de la Houssaye (1683) and Pierre Bayle's article on Machiavelli in his *Historical and Critical Dictionary* (1697), both of which furnished an apparatus for the reading of Machiavelli by the Encyclopedists, Robespierre, and Hegel, the publication in 1760 of Machiavelli's *Discourse on Florentine Affairs after the Death of the Younger Lorenzo* of 1520 was a major event in Machiavelli scholarship – its equivalent of the storming of the Bastille. And the publication in 1782 of the *Opere di Machiavelli* by the Florentine bookseller Gaetano Cambiagi confirmed, with more evidence, that Machiavelli was a republican at a moment when republicanism was still subversive.

State-building and citizen-soldiers

In the *Discourse*, the former secretary of the Florentine Republic urged the reopening of the Great Council, the symbol, foundation, and chief organ of the popular government of 1494–1512. By proposing to the Medici Pope Leo X a constitutional reorganization (one contemporary called it "eccentric [*stravagante*]")[16] in which the dissolution of the Medici regime would be followed by the reconstruction of a popular state, Machiavelli remained faithful to his anti-aristocratic convictions. The history of Florence, however, decided otherwise.

In 1836, Alexis de Tocqueville commented in a notebook (published in 1865, six years after his death) on the lack of historical knowledge that he considered a major difficulty in understanding Machiavelli, who wrote for people well informed about the laws of their country. Readers lacking such knowledge could have only a confused view of Florence's political and social constitution. Nonetheless, reading Machiavelli's *Florentine Histories*, Tocqueville managed to identify some central issues concerning the Florentine state of Machiavelli's time: the people had a large part in government, but only in Florence itself, while the inhabitants of its territory were subjects living under a confusing mix of obligations and privileges; and executive, legislative, judicial, financial, and military powers overlapped in confusing ways. The author of *Democracy in America* seems not to have realized, however, that these features of a republic characterized by such contradictions constituted the underlying problem that Machiavelli confronted in his theoretical work. In his correspondence, Tocqueville agreed with the reproach against Machiavelli that he was indifferent to distinctions between just and unjust.[17]

Hegel had already taken the problem of the internal contradictions of the Florentine territorial state as characteristic of Italy as a whole and as an opportunity to view from a different angle the supposedly detestable means that Machiavelli advocated. In his *German Constitution* (written around 1800, published only in 1893), he suggested a striking parallel between Machiavelli's Italy and the still disunited Germany of his time and wrote: "Italy was supposed to become a state ... Machiavelli starts from this general premise; this is his demand and the principle which he opposes to the misery of his country."[18] In view of Machiavelli's reflections on the necessity of organizing states, Hegel rejected the interpretation of those who, in order to save *The Prince* from its critics, read it as an ironic text and subtle mockery.

The light that this revolutionary context sheds on Machiavelli enables us to perceive more clearly *The Prince*'s inherent contradiction, which was transmitted, unresolved, to the reading of Machiavelli in the twentieth century by the Italian historian Federico Chabod: how to reconcile the tyrant and the nation in arms? This question had already been asked by Giuseppe Ferrari, the Italian theorist of a European federation whose spearhead was to be revolutionary France, and the author of pioneering works on the history of political thought. His *Machiavel, juge des révolutions de notre temps* (1849) argued that the ideas of *The Prince* were shaped by the contradictions of Machiavelli's Italy, which, given that Machiavelli wanted to arm the people without having first defined their rights, he was incapable of overcoming. Ferrari asserted that Machiavelli still deserved to be considered the prophet of future revolutions, even though the Revolution made it possible to assess the inadequacies of Machiavelli's proposals for his own times. Yet the institution of a public armed force had been the practical condition in the Revolution for the birth of the constitution. After 1790, the soldiers demanded and obtained their rights by force, and the victory at Valmy led to the proclamation of the republic. Consequently, Gramsci could see in the French Revolution a particularly significant moment in the realization of Machiavelli's concept of the "people in arms":

> Any formation of a national-popular collective will is impossible, unless the great mass of peasant farmers bursts *simultaneously* into political life. That was Machiavelli's intention through the reform of the militia, and it was achieved by the Jacobins in the French Revolution. That Machiavelli understood it reveals a precocious Jacobinism that is the (more or less fertile) germ of his conception of national revolution.[19]

Machiavelli, who defended the idea of extending some elements of citizenship to the subject populations, may have had rather broad ambitions with his concept of the "people in arms," broader indeed than he could say explicitly. Thus, to evaluate the contradiction of *The Prince* as defined by Ferrari, one must take seriously the hypothesis of simulation and dissimulation, especially for an author who lived under the shadow of the Medici. Around 1925, however, Chabod's aim in insisting on the limitations of *The Prince* was to weaken Fascism's ritual appeal to Machiavelli as a forerunner. For instance, Vilfredo Pareto, one of the founders of twentieth-century political sociology, praised in his political testament of 1923 the measures taken by the Fascist regime and declared them to be inspired by a "model" found in *The Prince*: the institution of a national militia and the concentration of power in the hands of an elite for the purpose of subduing the masses.[20] Subsequently, the militarization of society in totalitarian regimes, followed by the professionalization of armies after the Vietnam War, excluded from contemporary political thought the Machiavellian concept of the "people in arms," now viewed as promoting an ideology of war.

Economics and society

In emphasizing the contradictions of Machiavelli's thought, Ferrari maintained that it lacked economic and social analysis. With Adam Smith, the advent of political economy, and the study of the capitalist mode of production, a new field emerged which seemed to render obsolete earlier methods of social analysis. It became common to consider Machiavelli a founder of modernity because of his "realist" and demystifying political analysis, and yet at the same time a superseded thinker of the past, given what some saw as the insufficiencies of his economic and social analysis, which, so it was thought, stopped at the city walls of Florence. For this reason, some considered Pareto or Gaetano Mosca Machiavellians superior to Machiavelli. But Mosca, the influential author of *The Ruling Class* [*Elementi di scienza politica*] (1896; second edition, 1923) who viewed his own theory as an antidote to the democratic fiction of popular sovereignty, expressed his agreement with anti-Machiavellians in assessing the limits of Machiavelli's "political science."

One should avoid retrospective judgments that evaluate Machiavelli from the standpoint of socioeconomic categories and methods of analysis that emerged only at the end of the nineteenth century and focus instead on those aspects of economy and society relevant to Machiavelli. The long disintegration of "liberality," a concept central to the socioeconomic culture of the ancien régime, whose erosion, already in evidence in the article on "liberality" in Diderot's *Encyclopedia* of 1765, was achieved in part by the abolition of the feudal system in 1789, began with Machiavelli. Machiavelli's critique of liberality, which cannot be reduced to a mere provocative attack against the humanist and Christian catalog of virtues, led political thinkers of the ancien régime to examine power from a financial and fiscal perspective.[21] But political thinkers of our time have generally overlooked this important element of Machiavelli's theory and confused the critique of liberality in *The Prince* with a sarcastic attitude toward ideas of equality and social justice, comparable to those of disillusioned liberals like Pareto.

Although Machiavelli obviously did not furnish an analysis of the capitalist mode of production born with the industrial revolution, Karl Marx nonetheless emphasized the maturity of his concept of society as divided into classes. Already a reader of Machiavelli's *Discourses* while he was drafting the *Communist Manifesto* (1848), Marx insisted in 1857 on the interest of the *Florentine Histories* (which he called a "masterpiece") as well as the importance of studying the development of the Italian military system in the fifteenth century – another of Machiavelli's central themes – to understand better the "connection between productive forces and social relations."[22] Marx was thereby indicating a context within which the Machiavellian project of arming the people as a condition for the redefinition of social relations could make sense. No later than 1897, Croce saw Marx as "the most notable successor" of Machiavelli and expressed his surprise that no one had ever thought of calling Marx the "Machiavelli of the labour movement."[23] Croce did not specify Machiavelli's class sympathies, and Gramsci hesitated between the Florentine bourgeoisie and the subaltern classes, chiefly the Tuscan peasantry, whom Machiavelli enrolled in his militia. In his *Defense of the Constitutions of Government of the United States* (1787), John Adams praised Machiavelli's 1520 *Discourse* for its theory of the separate representation of class interests, which he saw as consonant with his own, even as he rejected Machiavelli's notion of the necessity of protecting the majority against the wealthy minority. Adams considered Machiavelli the author "most favorable to a popular government," but also the founder of a "plebeian philosophy" whose "illiberal exclamations against illustrious families as the curse of Heaven" (referring to Machiavelli's *Florentine Histories* 3.5) Adams called "shallow" and "execrable."[24] And a critical observer of the French Revolution, Benjamin Constant, who identified in the struggle against the system of hereditary privilege the question of the century, cast Machiavelli as the founding father of those who "have written in favor of equality, and acted or spoken on behalf of the descendants of the oppressed and against the descendants of the oppressors."[25]

Religion

According to the German poet Heinrich Heine, who attended Hegel's lectures on the philosophy of history in the 1820s, the blows Kant struck against divinity and divine providence in his *Critique of Pure Reason* made him more radical in philosophy than Robespierre was in politics. Robespierre represented the death of the king as an act of national providence before rejecting atheism and prostrating himself before the Supreme Being.[26] In the ancien régime, the irreligious revolution attributed to Kant was constantly associated with the name of Machiavelli, the "prince of atheists" who denied divine providence and theorized the political imposture of religions and their historical relativity. Tocqueville, who read Machiavelli when he was also reading the seventeenth-century religious writer Bossuet, a proponent of a providentialist conception of history, perceived, and was troubled by, the absence of divine providence in Machiavelli's thought. Without divine providence, authority cannot come from God, and no motivation to submit to authority can come from fear of God. This demystification of authority, which is consistent with Machiavelli's agonistic and dynamic conception of society and history, contributed to the decline of a central tenet of the political thought of the ancien régime. By contrast, in *Roman Catholicism and Political Form* (1923), the German jurist Carl Schmitt defended the political virtues of Catholicism against Machiavelli, who had denounced Christianity as a religion of slaves that weakened the peoples that came under its sway. Schmitt repeatedly criticized the Machiavellian approach to politics for its tendency to separate the question of power and authority from the dimension of mystery and transcendence – a dimension that the tradition of reason of state, with its medieval roots, had been able to preserve. On this point, Pareto's analysis of religion, in *The Mind and Society* (1916), seems closer to Machiavelli's, to whom it indeed acknowledges its debt. Yet, despite the discovery in 1961 of a manuscript entirely in Machiavelli's handwriting of Lucretius' book-length antireligious poem, *De rerum natura*, some scholars still claim that Machiavelli was a friend of religion because he presented it as politically useful and as a force ensuring moral and social cohesion.[27] During his lifetime and through the ancien régime, however, Machiavelli's attitude toward religion was considered subversive and even heretical.

The return to Machiavelli and the rejection of the revolutionary tradition

The developments outlined thus far point to the growing neglect and disappearance of elements once seen as integral to Machiavelli's subversive stance. But Machiavelli has nonetheless remained a major figure of moral, religious, social, and political subversion, from the inclusion of his works on the Index in the mid-sixteenth century (reconfirmed in 1897) to our day. Leo Strauss went so far as to turn Machiavelli into a symbol of the first wave of modernity from which, via the egalitarian "illusions" of the republicans of 1793 and nineteenth-century communists, contemporary nihilism emerged: we are condemned today, Strauss wrote, to choose between "irresponsible indifference to politics and irresponsible political options."[28] For some, only the ghost of Marx evokes the same revulsion. For others Robespierre is the only historical figure to inspire a similar hatred, due primarily to the reputation he acquired from his devotion to the plebs. In *On Revolution* (1963), Hannah Arendt blamed Machiavelli for being "the spiritual father of [the] revolution" continued by Robespierre and Lenin: they made the dangerous mistake, she argued, of posing the "social question," that is, of introducing the theme of equality in political life, thereby causing the masses to make their irruption into politics.[29] These views had a crucial influence on two political thinkers in whose work Machiavelli occupies a central place: J. G. A. Pocock and Claude Lefort.

Historical revisionism and Machiavelli

Pocock's *Machiavellian Moment* (1975) seems indeed to take up Arendt's exhortation to rethink the ideological origins of the American Revolution in order to unearth the "lost treasure" of a revolution whose merit lies in its supposed avoidance of the "social question."[30] Pocock's book severs the link between Machiavelli and Jacobinism: not only does it leave out the French Revolution, it also plays down Machiavelli's extraordinary and highly original theory of the positive consequences of social conflicts, and thus seems the history of an aristocratic concept of the republic rather than a popular one. Yet, although he stops with the American Revolution, Pocock's recovery of the value of a Machiavellian republican tradition in political theory, which he opposes to the liberal tradition, led him to identify in certain seventeenth-century English "Machiavellians" a mode of analysis we later find in Marx and characterized by an awareness that social and economic change has an impact on values as well as on the perception of social reality.

Lefort, by contrast, turned the concept of social division and conflict at the heart of Machiavelli's work into a principle of his own political thought. In the intellectual aftermath of 1968, the abandonment of Marxist theory gave birth to a dialogue with psychoanalytic concepts, particularly those of Jacques Lacan as influenced by Alexandre Kojève's teaching in Paris between 1933 and 1939 on the "dialectic of desire and recognition" in Hegel. In describing the centrality of the analysis of civil conflict in Machiavelli, Lefort spoke of his "economy of desire," emphasizing that "desiderio" is indeed one of the terms Machiavelli used to reflect on the differences between the *popolo* and the *grandi*.[31]

This return to Machiavelli is widely believed to have set in motion a kind of rediscovery of the political, organized around the names of Strauss, Aron, and Arendt, whose goal was to respond to the reductive rationalism of Ricardian "economism," which had become dominant in Marxist analysis as well as in political science. In fact, Lefort's rediscovery of the political could be seen as a way of reactivating Hegel's notion of a struggle for recognition, although tacitly bypassing Hegel. Obviously, Marx did not deny the importance of politics and Hegel did not ignore questions of the distribution of wealth and property. It is noteworthy, however, that Hegel was studying Machiavelli and reflecting on Robespierre when giving his 1805 Jena lectures on the *Philosophy of Spirit* (printed posthumously), which come close to proposing an initial theorization of the struggle for recognition. In the *Phenomenology of Spirit*, published in 1807, this theorization, proposed within the context of a commentary on the revolutionary motto "freedom or death," appears complete. As in 1805, the problem of the revolutionary Terror and of the ways of resolving it remains central, but the reference to Machiavelli is now absent.

The historical problem that motivated Lefort to return to the theme of conflict and desire was totalitarianism. Machiavelli seemed to him to have formulated a theory of society in which social divisions could not be resolved, and which was therefore in opposition to Marxist prophecy (already denounced by Aron) as well as to any ideology of a harmonious society in which social relations are transparent. Lefort's project was to formulate, starting from Machiavelli, a theory of democracy that places conflict at the core of political thought, while rejecting and remaining radically distinct from an undifferentiated revolutionary tradition running from Jacobinism to Bolshevism. In this sense, Lefort and Pocock both partake in a movement that some historians of philosophy have recently called "historical revisionism": celebration of the American Revolution on the one hand, and rejection of the French Revolution, seen as the first step in a devastating process leading to the October Revolution, on the other.[32] Machiavelli, now associated with Tocqueville, has become the shroud covering the specters of Robespierre and Marx.

An alienated Machiavelli

This brings us to the following paradox. Although Machiavelli remains the main representative of the subversion of the Catholic anthropology of the ancien régime that prepared the French Revolution, and although our historical knowledge of him, his times, and his reception has progressed measurably, the transformations that accompanied the age of revolutions seem to have made Machiavelli's thought foreign to itself and its subversive role. To reflect on our contemporary world, critics today generally find it more satisfactory to start from Adam Smith and Kant, or even from Tocqueville, than from Machiavelli.

The two political thinkers around whom most theoretical discussions in the Western academic world revolved at the end of the twentieth century, Jürgen Habermas and John Rawls, have kept Machiavelli at bay in their work. The early Habermas, in *Theory and Practice* (1963), wrote a few pages on Machiavelli, more as a concession to anti-Machiavellism than as an effort to read and interpret Machiavelli. John Rawls, in *A Theory of Justice* (1971), ignored Machiavelli and seems not to have had a real knowledge of him; in his later work he expressed doubts about the legitimacy of including the author of the *Discourses* in the tradition of classical republicanism, which Rawls considers better represented by Tocqueville than by Machiavelli.[33] In a brief "Note on Machiavelli" (1949), Maurice Merleau-Ponty wrote that Machiavelli was preparing the conditions for a serious humanism grounded in a radical critique of bourgeois humanism.[34] Although the humanist and democratic intentions of Rawls and Habermas cannot be denied, their work still awaits a response of the kind formulated by Machiavelli against Florentine civic humanism. It is perhaps precisely the ideal of transparency, in its current form in political thought as communicative ethics or as ahistorical rationality, that has made so many of our contemporaries insensitive to the strategies of expression used by thinkers, beginning with Machiavelli, who advocated a certain necessity of dissimulation in both political action and the art of writing and contributed to the subversion of the anthropology of the ancien régime.[35] To ignore this is certainly not without consequences for contemporary political thought, insofar as it prevents one from understanding what was at stake in the struggles of the past and, consequently, what is still at stake now.

Machiavelli thus remains to this day a symbolic figure, much the same as the one burned in effigy by the Jesuits in Ingolstadt in 1559. Whenever brute force, shameless lying, absence of scruples, authoritarian executive powers, general control of citizens, and denial of the enemy's humanity, with or without the pretext of a divine mission, become the norms of the policy of any state, it is customary to blame the teaching of Machiavelli or his commentators. One could say, with the seventeenth-century libertines, that these practices of government were already described in the Bible, by the fathers of the Church, or by historians. And one could also respond, as Pierre Bayle suggested in 1687, by noting that many factors other than Machiavelli's ideas determine the actions of princes: "Let one burn his books, another refute them, another translate them, that one comments on them, [Machiavelli] will, in spite of it, be no more and no less influential in relation to government."[36] To understand the excesses of any hegemonic power, rather than accusing Machiavelli's influence it would be far more challenging and fruitful, for example, to begin with the worries that Dwight Eisenhower expressed in 1961 when he warned of the dangers represented by the military, industrial, and financial complex. Machiavelli's political thought was animated by an analogous concern to prevent the seizure of power by an aristocracy or to take back power it had already seized. To the recurring question, "What is still living in the philosophy of Machiavelli?" one may still respond, as Francis Bacon did in 1623, that above all Machiavelli proposed a new intellectual instrument or weapon well adapted to its object: the *res politica*, politics.[37]

NOTES

This chapter was translated from French by Jean Terrier.

1. Leo Strauss, *Thoughts on Machiavelli* (University of Chicago Press, 1958), pp. 34–5.
2. G. W. F. Hegel, *The German Constitution*, in Hegel, *Political writings*, ed. Laurence Dickey and H. B. Nisbet, trans. H. B. Nisbet (Cambridge University Press, 1999), pp. 6–101 (15).
3. John Stuart Mill, *Collected Works*, ed. J. Robson *et al.* (Toronto University Press, 1963–), 17:1873.
4. *Ibid.*, 26:358–71 (369).
5. Friedrich Nietzsche, *The Will to Power*, ed. Walter Kaufmann, trans. Walter Kaufmann and R. J. Hollingdale (New York: Vintage Books, 1968), p. 170.
6. Benedetto Croce, *Historical Materialism and the Economics of Marx*, ed. A. D. Lindsay, trans. C. M. Meredith (London: Allen & Unwin, 1914; reprinted New Brunswick, N.J.: Transaction Books, 1981), p. 110, note 1; also his 1949 essay, "La questione del Machiavelli," in Croce, *Indagini su Hegel e schiarimenti filosofici*, ed. A. Savorelli (Naples: Bibliopolis, 1998), pp. 175–86.

7. Hans Baron, "Machiavelli the Republican Citizen and Author of *The Prince*," *English Historical Review* 76 (1961): 217–53; J. G. A. Pocock, *The Machiavellian Moment: Florentine Political Thought and the Atlantic Republican Tradition* (Princeton University Press, 1975); Quentin Skinner, *The Foundations of Modern Political Thought*, 2 vols. (Cambridge University Press, 1978).

8. See Lefort's synthesis of his work, "Machiavelli and the *veritá effetuale*," in Claude Lefort, *Writing: The Political Test*, trans. David Ames Curtis (Durham, N.C.: Duke University Press, 2000), pp. 109–41.

9. Raymond Aron, *Machiavel et les tyrannies modernes* (Paris: DeFallois, 1993).

10. *The Essential Foucault*, ed. Paul Rabinow and Nikolas Rose (New York: New Press, 2003), pp. 229–45.

11. Benedetto Croce, "Machiavelli and Vico," in Croce, *Politics and Morals*, trans. Salvatore J. Castiglione (New York: Philosophical Library, 1945), pp. 58–67 (59).

12. Maximilien Robespierre, "Response of the National Convention to the Manifestos of the Kings Allied against the Republic" (December 1793), "On the Principles of Political Morality" (February 1794), in Robespierre, *Virtue and Terror*, ed. Jean Ducange, trans. John Howe, intro. Slavoj Žižek (New York: Verso, 2007), pp. 91–7 and pp. 108–25.

13. Immanuel Kant, *To Perpetual Peace: A Philosophical Sketch*, trans. Ted Humphrey (Indianapolis: Hackett Publishing, 2003), p. 36.

14. G. W. F. Hegel, *Elements of the Philosophy of Right*, ed. Allen W. Wood, trans. H. B. Nisbet (Cambridge University Press, 1991), p. 370.

15. Antonio Gramsci, *Selections from the Prison Notebooks*, ed. and trans. Quintin Hoare and Geoffrey Nowell Smith (London: Lawrence & Wishart, 1971), p. 136.

16. Alessandro de' Pazzi, "Discorso al Cardinale Giulio de' Medici" (1522), *Archivio storico italiano* 1 (1842): 420–32 (429).

17. "Note sur Machiavel," in Alexis de Tocqueville, *Œuvres complètes*, ed. Jean-Pierre Mayer (Paris: Gallimard, 1951–2003), 16:541–50; "Lettre à Royer-Collard, 25 août 1836," ibid., 11:18–21.

18. Hegel, *German Constitution*, in *Political Writings*, ed. Dickey, p. 81.

19. Gramsci, *Prison Notebooks*, p. 132.

20. Vilfredo Pareto, *Scritti politici*, vol. 2, *Reazione, libertà, fascismo (1896–1923)*, ed. Giovanni Busino (Turin: UTET, 1974), pp. 795–800.

21. Alain Guery, "Le roi dépensier: le don, la contrainte et l'origine du système financier de la monarchie française d'Ancien Régime," *Annales* 39 (1984): 1241–69.

22. Karl Marx and Friedrich Engels, *Collected Works*, trans. Richard Dixon et al. (New York: International Publishers, 1975–2004), 40:186 (letter to Engels, September 25, 1857).

23. Croce, *Historical Materialism*, p. 118.

24. John Adams, *Works*, ed. Charles Francis Adams, 10 vols. (Boston: Little, Brown, 1850–56), 5:183; 5:11; 6:396.

25. Benjamin Constant, *Principles of Politics Applicable to All Governments*, ed. Etienne Hofmann, trans. Dennis O'Keeffe, intro. Nicholas Capaldi (Indianapolis: Liberty Fund, 2003), p. 188.

26. Heinrich Heine, *On the History of Religion and Philosophy in Germany*, ed. Terry Pinkard, trans. Howard Pollack-Milgate (Cambridge University Press, 2007), pp. 77–9.

27. Maurizio Viroli, *Il Dio di Machiavelli e il problema morale dell'Italia* (Rome: Laterza, 2005).
28. Leo Strauss, *What Is Political Philosophy? and Other Studies* (Glencoe, Ill.: Free Press, 1959), p. 55.
29. Hannah Arendt, *On Revolution* (New York: Viking, 1963), pp. 30, 53–110: "The Social Question."
30. *Ibid.*, pp. 217–34 (223–4).
31. Claude Lefort, "Machiavel: la dimension économique du politique," in Lefort, *Les formes de l'histoire* (Paris: Gallimard, 1978), pp. 127–40; 2nd edition (2000), pp. 215–37 (231).
32. Domenico Losurdo, *Il revisionismo storico: problemi e miti* (Bari: Laterza, 1996), p. 17.
33. John Rawls, *Political Liberalism* (New York: Columbia University Press, 1993), p. 205, note 37.
34. Maurice Merleau-Ponty, *Signs*, trans. Richard C. McLeary (Evanston, Ill.: Northwestern University Press, 1964), pp. 211–23.
35. See Jean-Pierre Cavaillé, *Dis/simulations. Religion, morale et politique au XVIIe siècle* (Paris: Honoré Champion, 2002), pp. 371–84.
36. Trans. Jacob Soll, *Publishing the Prince: History, Reading, and the Birth of Political Criticism* (Ann Arbor: University of Michigan Press, 2005), p. 111.
37. Francis Bacon, *De augmentis scientiarum*, 8.34, in Bacon, *Works*, ed. James Spedding *et al.* (London: Longmans, 1857–74), 1:769; 5:56.

FURTHER READING

Audier, Serge. *Machiavel, conflit et liberté*. Paris, Vrin/EHESS, 2005.

Berlin, Isaiah. "The Originality of Machiavelli," in *Studies on Machiavelli*, ed. Myron P. Gilmore. Florence, Sansoni, 1972, pp. 149–206; also in Berlin, *Against the Current: Essays in the History of Ideas*, ed. Henry Hardy, intro. Roger Hausheer. Princeton University Press, 2001, pp. 25–79.

Carta, Paolo, and Xavier Tabet. *Machiavelli nel XIX e XX secolo*. Padua, CEDAM, 2007.

Gilbert, Felix. *History: Choice and Commitment*. Cambridge, Mass., Harvard University Press, 1977.

Hulliung, Mark. *Citizen Machiavelli*. Princeton University Press, 1983.

Losurdo, Domenico. *Hegel and the Freedom of Moderns*, trans. Marella and Jon Morris. Durham, N.C., Duke University Press, 2004.

Macek, Josef. *Machiavelli e il machiavellismo*. Florence, Nuova Italia, 1980.

Meinecke, Friedrich. *Machiavellism: The Doctrine of Raison d'État and Its Place in Modern History*, trans. Douglas Scott. New Brunswick, N.J., Transaction Publishers, 1998.

Procacci, Giuliano. *Machiavelli nella cultura europea dell'età moderna*. Bari, Laterza, 1995.

Vatter, Miguel E. *Between Form and Event: Machiavelli's Theory of Political Freedom*. Boston, Kluwer Academic Publishers, 2000.

INDEX

(Machiavelli's writings are listed individually under their titles as translated into English)

Cambridge Companions to . . .

AUTHORS

TOPICS